# YOUTH CRIME & JUSTICE

## 2ND EDITION

EDITED BY

# BARRY GOLDSON
# JOHN MUNCIE

SAGE

Los Angeles | London | New Delhi
Singapore | Washington DC

Los Angeles | London | New Delhi
Singapore | Washington DC

SAGE Publications Ltd
1 Oliver's Yard
55 City Road
London EC1Y 1SP

SAGE Publications Inc.
2455 Teller Road
Thousand Oaks, California 91320

SAGE Publications India Pvt Ltd
B 1/I 1 Mohan Cooperative Industrial Area
Mathura Road
New Delhi 110 044

SAGE Publications Asia-Pacific Pte Ltd
3 Church Street
#10-04 Samsung Hub
Singapore 049483

Editor: Natalie Aguilera
Editorial assistant: James Piper
Production editor: Sarah Cooke
Copyeditor: Solveig Gardner Servian
Proofreader: Thea Watson
Indexer: Silvia Benvenuto
Marketing manager: Sally Ransom
Cover design: Wendy Scott
Typeset by: C&M Digitals (P) Ltd, Chennai, India
Printed and bound by CPI Group (UK) Ltd,
Croydon, CR0 4YY

**Library of Congress Control Number: 2014948709**

**British Library Cataloguing in Publication data**

A catalogue record for this book is available from
the British Library

ISBN 978-1-44621-082-6
ISBN 978-1-44621-083-3 (pbk)

# YOUTH CRIME & JUSTICE

**SAGE** was founded in 1965 by Sara Miller McCune to support the dissemination of usable knowledge by publishing innovative and high-quality research and teaching content. Today, we publish more than 750 journals, including those of more than 300 learned societies, more than 800 new books per year, and a growing range of library products including archives, data, case studies, reports, conference highlights, and video. SAGE remains majority-owned by our founder, and after Sara's lifetime will become owned by a charitable trust that secures our continued independence.

Los Angeles | London | Washington DC | New Delhi | Singapore

# CONTENTS

# LIST OF CONTRIBUTORS

**Tim Bateman** is Reader in Youth Justice at the University of Bedfordshire, England.

**Stephen Case** is Associate Professor of Criminology at Swansea University, Wales.

**Brendan Coyle** is a Doctoral Research Student at Queen's University Belfast, Northern Ireland.

**Chris Cunneen** is Professor of Criminology at the University of NSW, Sydney, Australia.

**Adam Edwards** is Senior Lecturer in Criminology at Cardiff University, Wales.

**Loraine Gelsthorpe** is Professor of Criminology and Criminal Justice at the University of Cambridge, England.

**Barry Goldson** holds the Charles Booth Chair of Social Science at the University of Liverpool, England.

**Kevin Haines** is Professor of Criminology and Youth Justice at Swansea University, Wales.

**Harry Hendrick** is Associate Fellow in History at the University of Warwick, England.

**Gordon Hughes** is Professor of Criminology at Cardiff University, Wales.

**Rob MacDonald** is Professor of Sociology at Teesside University, England.

**Brendan Marsh** is a Doctoral Research Student and a Research Associate at Queen's University Belfast, Northern Ireland.

**Shadd Maruna** is Professor of Criminology and Dean of the School of Criminal Justice at Rutgers University-Newark, USA.

**Lesley McAra** is Professor of Penology at the University of Edinburgh, Scotland.

Susan McVie is Professor of Quantitative Criminology at the University of Edinburgh, Scotland.

John Muncie is Professor Emeritus of Criminology at the Open University, England.

Gilly Sharpe is Lecturer in Criminology at the University of Sheffield, England.

David Smith is Professor Emeritus of Criminology at Lancaster University, England.

Rachel Swann is Lecturer in Criminology at Cardiff University, Wales.

Colin Webster is Professor of Criminology at Leeds Metropolitan University, England.

Rob White is Professor of Criminology at the University of Tasmania, Australia.

# EDITORS' INTRODUCTION

In the time that has passed since the publication of the first edition of this title in 2006, much has changed in national and international youth justice. In many respects, both the scale and the nature of such change have been counter-intuitive. In writing the introduction to the first edition, for example, we reflected upon the 'heavily interventionist' and 'ultimately punitive interventions' that had increasingly come to characterise the youth justice system in England and Wales (Goldson and Muncie, 2006: ix). Indeed, at the 'shallow end' of the system the interventionist thrust was clearly apparent and, in 2006–07, the rate of children and young people aged 10–17 receiving their first reprimand, warning or conviction ('first time entrants') peaked at 2,040 per 100,000 of the 10–17 year old population (Ministry of Justice, 2010: 1). In other words, in a single year 118,164 children were formally criminalised and entered the youth justice system for the first time (ibid.: 6). Similarly, at the 'deep end' of the system punitivity was manifest and in 2006–07 the average daily child prisoner population stood at 2,914 (Ministry of Justice, 2014a). Since that time, however, both interventionist zeal and punitive intent have diminished significantly. On the one hand, the rate of first-time entrants to the youth justice system per 100,000 of the 10–17 year old population fell to 1,160 in 2009–10 (Ministry of Justice, 2010: 1), or 64,761 children in total (ibid.: 6). On the other hand, by 2013–14 the average daily child prisoner population had plummeted to 1,233 and, by May 2014, the number of child prisoners had fallen further still to 1,091 (Ministry of Justice, 2014a). To express such trends differently, when the first edition of this title was published less than 10 years ago, the youth justice system in England and Wales was approximately twice as interventionist (criminalising) and almost three times more punitive (inclined to incarcerate) than it is today. This raises pressing questions.

What is more curious is that the same trends – when they are located within an international/comparative context – look to be out of sync with developments elsewhere. Whilst the youth justice system appears to have 'softened' in England and Wales, it seems to have 'hardened', over precisely the same period of time, in other parts of Europe where Bailleau et al. have observed:

> Social intolerance in various States is rising against a backdrop of a drift to hard-line law-and-order policies and practices. The deviant youth is perceived first and foremost as a social problem ... to the detriment of a vision that saw the 'child in danger' as someone whom society also had to protect ... There has also been a shift in the State's orientations and strategies in the public management of youth deviance ... The main consequence of this new orientation is ... the extension of criminalisation. (2010: 8–9)

Similarly, Snacken and Dumortier (2012: 2–3) detect 'a decline in rehabilitative ideals, harsher prison conditions, more emotional and expressive forms of punishment emphasising shaming and degradation' across much of Europe. At face value, therefore, developments in Europe appear to be moving in a diametrically opposite direction to those in England and Wales. Indeed, if the conventional claim that youth justice in most European countries is shaped in accordance with a paternalistic welfare model (Bailleau and Cartuyvels, 2002) is beginning to look tenuous, our earlier characterisation of England and Wales as 'probably the most punitive system in Europe' (Goldson and Muncie, 2006: ix) also no longer appears to hold true.

Other apparent developments in international youth justice are equally puzzling, counter-intuitive and even contradictory. For many years the USA has attracted the critical attention of the international community for its excessively punitive responses to children in conflict with the law. However, the Annie E. Casey Foundation – reporting the results of its Juvenile Detention Alternatives Initiative (JDAI) that extends across 300 local jurisdictions and 39 states – explains:

> The broadest indicator of detention utilization is the average daily population (ADP), because it reflects both the number of youth admitted to detention and the length of time that those youth stay. By this indicator, JDAI sites had reduced their use of detention by 44 per cent in the aggregate. Collectively, sites detained almost 3,600 fewer youth per day in 2013 than they did prior to JDAI. This translates into more than 1.3 million fewer detention days used per year. (2014: 9)

At the same time that child imprisonment is falling in the USA, however, Defence for Children International (n.d.) has appealed to the United Nations General Assembly to launch a 'global study on children deprived of liberty', in recognition of the excessive use of penal detention within youth justice systems in many parts of the world, and the exposure of child prisoners to 'abuse, violence and acute discrimination' (ibid.: 1).

Finally, for present purposes at least, in attempting to comprehend such temporally and spatially incoherent motions it is crucial to remain mindful of their contingent, volatile and even fragile nature. The directions that such developments follow are neither set nor fixed; youth justice reform is ever susceptible to radical and unexpected departure and, at one and the same time, may even accommodate seemingly contradictory impulses. By way of illustration, whilst diversion and decarceration might appear to signal the direction that youth justice is currently following in England and Wales, it has not dampened the Coalition government's appetite for further – and highly controversial – penal experimentation. Indeed, the government has announced plans to build three new penal institutions – euphemistically badged 'Secure Colleges' – to be managed by the private sector and each with the capacity to detain up to 320 boys and girls at any given time (Ministry of Justice, 2013, 2014b). If the initial plan to build a 'pathfinder Secure College' is followed through and implemented – 'it is envisaged that construction ... will commence in early 2015, with the establishment opening in spring 2017 (Ministry of Justice, 2014b: 7) – the 'pathfinder Secure College' will comprise the largest penal establishment for children and young people in Europe, or, as the Conservative Peer, Lord Cormack, put it during a Parliamentary debate in the House of Lords: an 'institution which would be – I hate to think of this – a sort of national for-profit institution' (Hansard, 23 July 2014: Column 1177).

Youth justice policy developments, the complex contexts from which they emerge and within which they are sustained – or abandoned – and their contested sources of legitimacy, demand rigorous analysis and critical scrutiny. This volume explores such phenomena. It examines the intrinsic tensions – even contradictions – between knowledge and 'evidence' (drawn from both international academic research and practice experience) and policy formation, and it engages with some of the most pressing debates in the ever-changing terrain of contemporary youth justice. In order to present an integrated and coherent text, the book is organised in three inter-related parts. Moreover, whilst adopting some different analytical positions, each of the authors' engage with comparable conceptual themes and concerns including: a critical assessment of the key sources of 'evidence' in respect of their particular subject-matter; an analysis of what the 'evidence' actually tells us and how it might be understood (historically, theoretically and/or empirically); a consideration of the extent to which 'evidence' is informing contemporary youth justice law, policy and practice in the UK and elsewhere; and a reflective account of how any discordance between 'evidence' and policy formation might be explained and understood.

Part One situates youth crime and youth justice within historical and social-structural contexts. In Chapter 1, Harry Hendrick historicises youth crime and youth justice by tracing key policy developments and the rationales that drove them, from the early nineteenth century to the late 1980s. By profiling change, order, professional/administrative and class agendas, political priorities and inter-generational relations, Hendrick's analysis contextualises the conditions that served to re-popularise and re-politicise youth crime and justice. In Chapter 2, Rob White and Chris Cunneen explore the relations between social class, structural marginalisation and criminalisation. They argue that a critical understanding of such relations 'has rarely been more relevant to social analysis and to any consideration of juvenile justice in particular'. In Chapter 3, Colin Webster builds upon and develops some of the key themes introduced by Hendrick, White and Cunneen, and shapes his discussion around the intersections of social class and 'race' for identifiable groups of children and young people – the 'usual suspects' – who are 'repeatedly drawn into cycles of contact with the youth justice system and for whom such contact has damaging consequences'. In Chapter 4, Gilly Sharpe and Loraine Gelsthorpe engage with the question of gender and, more specifically, with girls and young women within the youth justice system. Despite some notable exceptions, such analyses continue to be neglected within 'malestream' criminology and Sharpe and Gelsthorpe redress some of the imbalance by drawing our attention to 'the deficiencies in state (non)intervention which so frequently fail to protect girls from harm, leaving them without support and vulnerable to increased punishment'.

Taken together, the four chapters in Part One of the book re-establish both the importance of historical memory for understanding the present, and the primary significance of structural relations and social divisions for conceptualising the adverse socio-economic and cultural contexts within which identifiable groups of children and young people are growing up in 'advanced' industrial societies, and the means by which particularly disadvantaged young people are disproportionately regulated, controlled, criminalised and punished by youth justice agencies. In short, the historical reflections demolish the myth that the nature and scope of youth crime is an aberration of 'late modernity', whereas the class, 'race' and gender-based analyses shift the conceptual emphases from individualised constructions of criminogenic pathology and responsibilisation, to the complex social-structural formations that give rise to social harm, adversity and the injustices of the 'justice' process.

Part Two engages explicitly with contemporary trends in the incidence and nature of youth crime and the direction that youth justice policy and practice is taking. It follows that, taken together, Chapters 5–13 subject both the evidence and its relation to policy and practice to rigorous analytical scrutiny. In Chapter 5, Tim Bateman discusses 'problems of interpretation' when reading and examining statistical evidence and the associated complexities of determining 'fact' and 'truth'. He presents a persuasive account of 'alternative interpretations of the data' and the 'importance of critical engagement with official statistics' in order to offset their 'potential to mislead', and to avoid the prospect of forming 'unwarranted assumptions'. By applying a sharp analytical lens, Bateman presents an informed account of the 'seemingly more progressive shift in youth justice policy' but warns that it is being driven by 'pragmatic rather than principled' imperatives. In Chapter 6, David Smith reflects upon 'the nature of knowledge in the social sciences, what counts as evidence, and how it might be used'. Smith, like Bateman, considers both the possibilities and the complexities of applying research, knowledge and evidence to youth justice policy formation but he warns that 'crude versions of positivism' are unhelpful, not least because the 'social world can never be made entirely predictable'. Smith concludes by suggesting that whilst it is 'unrealistic' to expect that knowledge and evidence – derived from research – will ever singularly determine the direction of youth justice policy, it 'ought to be realistic to expect that [policy] will be informed and influenced by it'.

From analyses of the wider bodies of knowledge and 'evidence' to more sharply focused reflections, the next five chapters are directed towards specific modes of youth justice intervention. In Chapter 7, Stephen Case and Kevin Haines critically examine the preoccupation with 'risk management' and 'early intervention' within contemporary youth justice policy and practice. In Chapter 8, Lesley McAra and Susan McVie subject the very concept of 'intervention' to searing critique and make a compelling and empirically grounded case for 'diversion and minimum necessary intervention'. In Chapter 9, Chris Cunneen and Barry Goldson engage with a detailed critical analysis of 'restorative justice' and argue that, despite its global appeal, there are strong grounds for being 'profoundly sceptical' about the manner in which 'restorative' approaches are typically applied in the youth justice sphere. In Chapter 10, Shadd Maruna, Brendan Coyle and Brendan Marsh address the social and individual 'factors' that shape the capacities of children and young people to 'desist from crime' as they are growing up and passing into adulthood. In echoing the work of McAra and McVie in Chapter 8, Maruna and his colleagues argue that whilst there is 'nothing magical' about transitioning into adulthood 'that instantly transforms individuals away from lives of crime', it remains the case that 'maturation is more powerful than any "programme" designed by the police, youth justice agencies, the prison service or other correctional bodies to reduce crime'. In Chapter 11, Barry Goldson traces the 'circular motions of penal politics' that create ebbs and flows in the extent to which child imprisonment is applied within youth justice systems, alongside a critical analysis of the 'pervasive irrationalities' and corrosive harms that typify penal custody.

The final two chapters within Part Two of the book serve to extend the analytical gaze beyond the strictures of conventional youth justice inquiry. In Chapter 12, Adam Edwards, Gordon Hughes and Rachel Swann present an analytical account of the 'policing' of young people (in a broad sense) and the impact of austerity measures on the state's (central and local) capacity to 'govern safety'. Edwards and his colleagues draw on pan-European research, alongside more sharply focused localised case studies, to unravel the complexities of community safety and to 'question what policy agendas exist for public safety and social justice for young people, and how the variegated governing arrangements indicated by partnerships of state and non-state actors in local political economies, enable or frustrate these agendas'. In Chapter 13, Rob MacDonald returns to the question of transitions that Maruna and his colleagues introduced in Chapter 10. By drawing on his extensive experience of longitudinal qualitative youth research, MacDonald provides both detailed and nuanced insights into the connections between structurally disfigured 'youth transitions' and 'criminal careers'. Throughout the discussion, he remains attentive to the catastrophic consequences of economic restructuring for identifiable groups of children and young people and, in this sense MacDonald not only builds upon and extends some of the key themes that were introduced in earlier chapters within Part Two of the book, but he also loops back to Part One by restating the significances of history, class, 'race' and gender for comprehending the structural conditions that shape the biographies of children and young people.

Part Three comprises an extended concluding chapter in which we return to our longstanding research interests in comparative/international analyses, the human rights provisions of international law, standards, treaties, rules, guidelines and conventions and their applications in the youth justice sphere. We consider both the wider international and the UK evidence-bases in presenting a critical analysis of the practical limitations of international human rights instruments and the means by which they are systematically compromised through processes of partial and selective implementation at best, and gross violation at worse. Notwithstanding this, we conclude the chapter – and the book – by arguing that comparative youth justice research 'clearly suggests possibilities for progressive reform'. By drawing upon the international human rights framework, exemplars of progressive policy and practice that can be found from comparative research and the key messages that the knowledge- and evidence-bases articulate, therefore, we end positively by mapping the contours of a 'youth justice with integrity'.

Barry Goldson and John Muncie

August 2014

# REFERENCES

Annie E. Casey Foundation (2014) *Juvenile Detention Alternatives Initiative: 2013 Annual Results Report Inter-site Conference Summary.* Baltimore: Annie. E. Casey Foundation.

Bailleau, F. and Cartuyvels, Y. (eds) (2002) 'La justice pénale des mineurs en Europe' (Criminal juvenile justice in Europe), *Déviance et Société* (Deviance and society), 26 (3): 283–96.

Bailleau, F., Cartuyvels, Y. and de Fraene, D. (2010) 'The criminalisation of youth and current trends: the sentencing game', in Bailleau, F. and Cartuyvels, Y. (eds), *The Criminalisation of Youth: Juvenile Justice in Europe, Turkey and Canada.* Brussels: VUBPress (Brussels University Press).

Defence for Children International (n.d.) *Call for a Global Study of Children Deprived of the Liberty.* Geneva: Defence for Children International. Available at: www.childrendeprivedofliberty.info/wordpress/wp-content/themes/forestly/images/GSCDL_Brochure.pdf (accessed 8.8.14).

Goldson, B. and Muncie, J. (2006) 'Editors' Introduction', in Goldson, B. and Muncie, J. (eds), *Youth Crime and Justice.* London: Sage.

Ministry of Justice (2010) *Youth Crime: Young people aged 10–17 receiving their first reprimand, warning or conviction, 2000–01 to 2009–10,* Ministry of Justice Statistics Bulletin. London: Ministry of Justice.

Ministry of Justice (2013) *Transforming Youth Custody: Government Response to the Consultation.* London: Ministry of Justice.

Ministry of Justice (2014a) *Youth Custody Data.* London: Ministry of Justice. Available at: www.gov.uk/government/publications/youth-custody-data (accessed 8.8.14).

Ministry of Justice (2014b) *Transforming Youth Custody: Government Response to the Consultation.* London: Ministry of Justice.

Snacken, S. and Dumortier, E. (2012) 'Resisting Punitiveness in Europe? An Introduction', in Snacken, S. and Dumortier, E. (eds), *Resisting Punitiveness in Europe? Welfare, Human Rights and Democracy.* London: Routledge.

# PART ONE

# HISTORICAL AND SOCIAL-STRUCTURAL CONTEXTS

# 1 HISTORIES OF YOUTH CRIME AND YOUTH JUSTICE

## HARRY HENDRICK

Nostalgia (upon which authoritarianism feeds) is a powerful cultural force, and nowhere is it more on display than in the public (adult) condemnation of the behaviour of young people. Whether it be the consequences of 'permissiveness', the influence of celebrity culture, impudence towards authority, the 'decline' in parental discipline, too much pocket money, or the so-called 'crisis' of childhood, children and adolescents today, it is claimed, pose more of a threat to the social order than at any time in the past. Governments, in conjunction with the media, continually devise 'new' policies to deal with this 'new' malaise in an effort to return to 'the old days' when, apparently, civil society was just that: civil, peaceable, respectful and cohesive (Muncie, 2004; Pearson, 1994). In exposing these cruelly deceptive myths, this chapter illustrates the variability of concepts such as 'juvenile delinquency', 'anti-social behaviour' and 'youth justice'. Through brief discussions of a chronological selection of debates and policy developments, from c.1800 to the end of the 1980s, the chapter summarises the overwhelming conclusion of historical and sociological research, namely that 'juvenile delinquency', in common with 'crime', can only be understood if the meaning of the terms is considered within a broad socio-political context (Bailey, 1987; Gattrell, 1990; Gelsthorpe and Morris, 1994; Muncie, 2004; Pearson, 1983). In other words, the argument here, albeit schematically presented, is that youth crime and youth justice (an integral feature of which has, until recently, been the welfare-justice binary), should be approached historically in relation to matters that at first sight may appear to be marginal to the topic, notably i) 'change' (particularly social, political, economic and personal); ii) 'order' (cultural, social and political); iii) the influence of professional and administrative class agendas; iv) party political programmes for the content and management of governance; and, last but by no means least, v) age and generational relations. As will become evident, these contexts are not presented hierarchically; rather they are integrated within and across the narrative.

# THE EARLY NINETEENTH CENTURY: 'THE CHILD' AS DELINQUENT

With respect to the early nineteenth century, current scholarship speaks of a 'reconception' rather than an 'invention' of 'juvenile delinquency', and argues that it was not until then 'that a specific definition of the criminal child, particular in legal discourse, really started to emerge' (King, 1998: 199; Shore, 1999: 148). Three main developments have been noted: an increase in *recorded* juvenile crime, a widespread and influential public debate, and the evolution of penal and legal strategies to cope with the growing problem (Shore, 1999: 15). Why should this have been so? First, the period c.1780s–1820s, which witnessed the early stages of the 'industrial revolution', was one of seminal historical *change*, including the social and political upheaval caused by the Napoleonic Wars (1793–1815), the growth in population, rapid developments in urbanisation, and an increase in levels of poverty owing to the effects of industrialisation on rural and urban labour markets (Royle, 1987; Thompson, 1963). Such trends and events affected a range of politically explosive issues, particularly the overriding problem of social stability, of which 'crime' is always a feature bearing in mind its variable significance in different historical epochs (Gattrell, 1990).

The second reason lies in the 'birth' of modern 'childhood', which heralded an innovative stage in *age relations*. The process is usually ascribed to four sources: the influence of Rousseau through his elevation of the 'natural' child; the place of the 'child figure' in Romantic literature (notably Blake and Wordsworth); the very different kind of place of the child in the teachings of the Evangelical Revival; and the role of the child in the 'domestic ideal' as a cultural norm. Rousseau's claim that 'Nature wants children to be children before they are men' and the Romantic's belief in 'original innocence' collided with and in many respects was subdued by the puritanical Evangelical view that children 'are sinful polluted creatures', but each opinion was played out in *the family* within the bourgeois 'home' (cited in Hendrick, 1997: 36–9). As 'the child' emerged in the new post-enlightenment industrialising society, so 'its' identification as both 'victim' and 'threat' became central to a number of socio-political and literary debates, notably those involving child labour, the adjustment of 'the self' to 'the social', and juvenile delinquency (Andrews, 1994; Berry, 1999; Coveney, 1967; Hendrick, 1997, 2003: 7–11).

Given the contemporary political environment, however, it was not children per se, but the 'children of the poor' who were said to present the greatest threat to the precarious social order (Cunningham, 1991). No wonder, then, that among the numerous causes of delinquency identified, the most important were 'the improper conduct of parents; the want of education; the want of suitable employment; and the violation of the Sabbath and the habits of gambling in the public streets' (cited in Shore, 1999: 20). Thereafter various legislative Acts, themselves in part the results of governmental and philanthropic inquiries and responses to 'public' concern, broadened the notions of 'crime' and 'criminality' to include many behaviours that had previously been regarded as 'nuisances', including public gambling and stealing apples from orchards and gardens (May, 1973), and also encouraged the apprehension of 'all loose, idle and disorderly persons not giving good account of themselves' (quoted in Muncie, 2004: 58–9). This was a significant widening of the net for the legislation reflected a growing unwillingness to overlook the 'crimes' of children and, therefore, expressed a policy of consciously drawing 'children into the criminal justice system' (Shore, 1999: 150).

The reconception of juvenile delinquency can be explained if the inclusion of children into the increasingly complex and heterogeneous justice system is seen in terms of a 'search for order', as the old 'moral economy' was declining under the impact of an evolving and completely new urban industrial capitalism: for example, the years of political 'crisis and repression' (1815–21); the pros and cons of working-class education; arguments for and against child labour; agitation and riots preceding the Great Reform Act (1832); and the intensely controversial New Poor Law Act (1834) (Thompson, 1963; Royle, 1987). Young people could no longer be left outside of what was known as 'the social': they were perceived as a conspicuous 'threat' to the urban equilibrium, not least owing to their growing numbers (Royle, 1987). Clearly, with respect to 'juvenile delinquency' (which was a feature of generational tension), 'crime' was becoming 'a vehicle for articulating mounting anxieties about issues which really had nothing to do with crime at all: social change and the stability of social hierarchy. These issues invested crime with new meanings, justified vastly accelerated action against it, and have determined attitudes to it ever since' (Gattrell, 1990: 249). The importance of this observation can hardly be exaggerated.

## THE EARLY TO MID-VICTORIAN YEARS: CREATING 'WILLING OBEDIENCE' THROUGH THE JUSTICE/WELFARE IMPERATIVE

The social unrest of the early nineteenth century, which appeared to have been successfully quelled by the 1830s, made a new and dramatic appearance through Chartism – the first mass working-class movement, especially the 'uprising' of 1842 and the subsequent show trial of 59 leaders (Royle, 1987). In response, Lord Ashley, England's 'greatest' social reformer, called for the compulsory education of the children of the 'dangerous classes', and warned of the 'fearful multitude of untutored savages' (a recurring image, along with 'children of the streets'), which represented a problem 'so prodigiously vast, and so unspeakably important' (cited in Pearson, 1983: 159; Cunningham, 1991: 97–134). Reformers were fearful that '[the delinquent] ... is a little stunted man already – he knows much and a great deal too much of what is called life ... he has to be turned again into a child' (cited in May, 1973: 7). Here was one of the first unambiguous expressions of a hierarchical age relationship. That 'age' mattered in a number of ways, as we have seen, had been known since the end of the eighteenth century. However, from the 1830s onwards there was a growing need to theorise social-penal issues in relation to the specificity of 'childhood' and 'youth' (in certain respects following the example set by the 1833 Factory Act) in order to better understand the nature of issues and to create policy. Although in 1838 Parkhurst was opened as the first juvenile penal institution, the exact nature of the appropriate response within what would become a 'penal-welfare complex' (Garland, 1985) was still undecided. Central to the question was how to conceptualise the child: as a *victim* or as a *threat* (Hendrick, 2003: 7–10)?

Besides Lord Ashley, the other influential Evangelical reformer was Mary Carpenter, who did so much to define the issue in terms of the 'dangerous' and the 'perishing' classes, and who, in common with other commentators, attributed the plight of outcast children to a moral deficit on the part of parents, rather than to poverty (Pearson, 1983: 175; Radzinowicz and Hood, 1986: 161–78). This moralistic conception of 'need' was significant since it framed the solution in terms of moral reclamation. According to Carpenter, existing methods of dealing with delinquents (and neglected children) did nothing to rehabilitate them – they were merely punished. Prisons, she said, had failed to reform because they could not obtain a *'willing* obedience' since there was no 'softening power of love' to subdue the delinquent: 'It is utterly vain to look for any real reformation where the heart is not touched' (cited in Pearson, 1983: 180). While the concept of 'welfare' was implicit rather than explicit, the notion of a 'willing' obedience was critical for the mid-Victorian debate on social stability and working-class compliance, as it expressed a growing political view that respectable working men should be brought within the Constitution through enfranchisement, to which they would then give their consent. In other words, the debate on juvenile delinquency more than mirrored political anxieties regarding the governance of a society known as 'the workshop of the world'.

In response, for the first time Parliament legislatively recognised juvenile delinquency 'as a distinct social phenomenon' in passing the Youthful Offenders Act, 1854 (which established Reformatories for convicted delinquents – *threats*) and the Industrial Schools Act, 1857 (which provided schools for 'neglected' children – *victims*) (Goldson, 2004: 87–92 ; May, 1973: 7–29). The legislation (and subsequent Acts in the 1860s) consolidated the importance of 'age' as a distinguishing feature of penal policy. In this way imprisonment, whipping and transportation slowly began to yield to a structure of institutional surveillance and control, with a combined inmate population (in Industrial Schools and Reformatories) of more than 30,000 young persons by the end of the century (Radzinowicz and Hood, 1986: 181).

# THE LATE VICTORIAN AND EDWARDIAN YEARS: 'CHILD SAVING' IN THE 'MODERN' SOCIAL SERVICES STATE

In place of the child 'savage', the period c.1880–1914 had a new spectre: 'hooliganism', a term used to describe the 'loutish' behaviour of working-class youth, and portrayed by the press as a particularly virulent form of urban unrest (Pearson, 1983: 74–5). Statistically, apprehension about the perceived rise in delinquency had some validity. For while rates of recorded adult crime were declining, there was a decided upward trend in recorded juvenile crime (Gillis, 1975: 99). But the apparent 'increase' in 'crime' begged at least two important questions: why and how. First, the 'crimes' were largely of the non-indictable variety such as drunkenness, malicious mischief, loitering, begging and dangerous play. Second, the conviction rate owed more to the aggressive attitude of the police and courts in prosecuting 'traditional' working-class youthful leisure activities than either to a greater propensity among juveniles to commit crime or to new forms of delinquent behaviour (Gillis, 1975; Springhall, 1986). This is a clear example of juvenile delinquency being *created* through structural and administrative procedures which, as is shown below, were reactions to social and political change.

During this period there were important developments in both class and age relations that help to explain middle-class sensitivity towards 'youth culture'. Although the matter of participatory democracy for adult men had more or less been settled by the end of the century, the female franchise remained a contentious subject. Where class antagonism was concerned, there were serious issues surrounding the 'rediscovery' of poverty, the 'new' trades unionism, industrial unrest, socialism and the spectre of physical degeneration. Furthermore, imperialism presented a number of economic, political and military anxieties, while the muddle of the Boer war (1899–1902) unleashed an elitist movement calling for 'national efficiency', not least to counter the relative decline in the strength of the economy. This is not to say that everything was doom and woe but, as the new century opened, Britain's position in the world and the social and physical health of its society was by no means secure (Freeden, 1978; Harris, 1993). Historical understanding of adult attitudes and policies towards juvenile delinquency requires consideration of these larger political contexts for it is they that determine how 'social constructions' of young people (and 'crime') are 'put together' (Hendrick, 1997: 34–5).

The early 1900s are famous for the Liberal Reform Programme (1906–11), which created a 'social services state' (Fraser, 1973). The overriding objective of the government was to increase the stability of institutions by giving the male working class an interest in maintaining them (an example of 'willing obedience') (Harris, 1993). In addition to the innovative pensions and national insurance schemes, the Programme included a number of 'child saving' measures: infant welfare, protection against cruelty, school meals, school medical inspection and treatment, and the care and education of the physically and mentally disabled (Hendrick, 1994, 2003). Aside from the Youthful Offenders Act 1901 and the Probation Act 1907, both of which extended the use of alternatives to prison, the major policy response to juvenile delinquency and neglected children was the Children Act 1908. This Act was notable for its attempt to reconcile welfare and justice imperatives through the establishment of 'juvenile courts' with both civil jurisdiction over the 'needy' child and criminal jurisdiction over the offending child. In effect, the Act promoted the principle of *rehabilitation*, articulated through positivist psycho-medicine with its emphasis on *treatment* (Garland, 1985: 231–63; Muncie, 2004: 77). However, as the court was to be an agency 'for the rescue *as well as* the punishment of juveniles', so 'conflict and ambivalence were embedded' in the very concept of its existence (Gelsthorpe and Morris, 1994: 951).

With reference to the significance of age relations, there were three important developments peculiar to these years. First, the evolving science of psychology promoted the emergence of 'adolescence' (primarily related to boys) as a psychological and social 'fact' – a stage of life with, it was claimed, precise and potentially threatening characteristics if not made subject to good guidance, discipline and physical exercise. Second, there was a 'panic' of sorts by social and economic commentators with regard to the juvenile labour market – 'the boy labour problem' – which, although a complex matter involving the nature of skill and differential labour demands, was often portrayed as a situation whereby boys were lured into 'blind alley' employment with relatively high wages. Third, there occurred a rapid growth of youth clubs and uniformed youth organisations, which in turn was part of the wider 'child saving' movement (Hendrick, 1990, 1994; Springhall, 1986). Considered together, the new concept of adolescence, the problem of 'boy labour' and the middle-class attempt to provide 'rational recreation' may be seen as indices of social change.

It is sometimes claimed that 'a stage of life, adolescence, had replaced station in life, class, as the perceived cause of misbehaviour' (Gillis, 1975: 97). The psychology of adolescence was certainly influential, but it combined with, rather than replaced, social class as the principal concern of penal reformers and youth workers (Hendrick, 1990: 101–6, 120). Where 'juvenile delinquency' is concerned, 'social class' has never been far from the thoughts of governments. And the reason is simple: 'the poor' in particular, as opposed to the children of the 'respectable' working class, are always regarded as liable to disrupt social stability, if only through low-level anti-social behaviour. Thus delinquents (embodied in a fused image of both class and age) are a convenient 'Other', who are presented to us as a constant reminder of how precarious and fragile *our* apparently civilised values are and, therefore, of the need for constant surveillance, discipline and punishment (Garland, 1985: 231–63).

# THE INTER-WAR YEARS: RATIONALISING THE WELFARE-JUSTICE MODEL

The foregrounding of 'welfare' as a legitimate feature of juvenile justice continued in the inter-war period through a growing acceptance of 'the social conception of delinquency', which understood offending as 'merely a symptom of a delinquent's social and personal condition' and saw juvenile crime as 'but one inseparable portion of the larger enterprise of child welfare' (Bailey, 1987: 62; Burt, 1927: 610; Davis, 1990: 72–3; Hendrick, 2003, 113–24). This view was associated with a broader psycho-social movement represented by newly established child guidance clinics, 'progressive' elementary education, and the propagation of liberal child-rearing methods via psychodynamic principles (Hendrick, 1994, 2003; Wooldridge, 1995). The impact of the subtle interplay between this movement and the theory and practice of juvenile justice was historically significant for it not only sought to delineate new understandings of 'welfare' and 'justice', but also implicitly to establish the contours for more nuanced age relations in general. Its role (together with that of Home Office officials who were under its influence) is evident in the Children and Young Persons Act 1933, which provided for juvenile courts to act *in loco parentis* as a closer link was forged between delinquent and neglected children in the belief that 'there is little or no difference in character and needs between the delinquent and the neglected child' (cited in Hendrick, 1994: 182) The Act expressed the prevailing 'hegemony of child welfare', with the wider use of probation, approved schools and boarding out (Bailey, 1987: Part 2), as well as a wider use of varieties of 'knowledge' (from parents, teachers, doctors and others) about the young person before the court (Garland, 1985; Rose, 1985). The approach, however, remained controversial with the police and magistrates, particularly as the welfare measures resulted in an increased rate of recorded delinquencies (Bailey, 1987: 165).

# JUVENILE JUSTICE IN THE WELFARE STATE: 1948–70s

In order to understand conceptions of juvenile delinquency and resulting legislation in the decades prior to 'Thatcherism' (that consolidated in UK politics in the 1980s), we have to appreciate the political significance of the post-1945 Welfare State, governed through a broad political consensus, informed by Keynesian economic theory, and providing full employment and a significant rise in the average standard of living. It is within this context that the period is often described in terms of 'the cult of youth', 'the youth spectacle', 'the teenage revolution' and similar phrases (Davis, 1990; Osgerby, 1998; Pearson, 1983).

Certainly a major characteristic of those years was the promotion of a 'succession of spectacular fringe delinquent working-class youth subcultures': Teddy Boys (1950s), Mods (early 1960s), Skinheads (1960s–70s), together with a number of middle-class youth movements associated with the expansion of higher education and political protest (Davis, 1990: 142). In general, the post-war period up to the 1970s was unquestionably that of 'youth' (not so much of children) and this cultural 'moment', with all its unforeseen tensions, together with the consensual, if limited, acceptance of 'welfare' as a political principle, profoundly influenced all manner of attitudes and policies. Not for the first time, the 'youth question' served to provide a means of discussing the multiplicity of social, economic, political and cultural issues that arise at a time of fundamental social change. Put another way, the 'state of the nation' was viewed through the perceived condition of its youth (Davis, 1990; Gelsthorpe and Morris, 1994; Osgerby, 1998).

From the late 1940s, the subject of juvenile delinquency began to feature in various academic and professional discourses, largely within the welfarist framework of the 1948 Children Act, which established a local authority child care service (Gelsthorpe and Morris, 1994: 953–7; Hendrick, 2003: 133–40). Throughout the 1950s there was much talk about the effects of the war on young people and of the impact of 'Americanisation', which was thought to be threatening the 'British way of life' (Pearson, 1983: 20). By the early 1960s the dominant mood was one of introspection as to why the 'welfare state' was failing to eradicate crime altogether, combined with a growing realisation that 'youth' was representative of 'new' (and worrying) cultural forces (Davis, 1990; Osgerby, 1998: 5–49; Springhall 1998: 190–2). Delinquent youth, argued the liberal intelligentsia, was the product of 'deeper structural conflicts within British society', brought about by the consequences of affluence, the dissolution of the Empire, the erosion of economic and political supremacy, the advance of science and technology, and new sexual and familial (and gendered) patterns of behaviour, many of which weakened 'the family' and undermined 'traditional' moral values (Davis, 1990: 148–9, 151–57; Marwick, 1990; Springhall, 1986: 192–99). Despite these anxieties, however, the fact that 'youth' was also viewed sympathetically reflected a continuing belief in the future. Alongside this, however, there remained major concerns with wider issues relating to generational conflict and the governance of an affluent mass democracy.

When it came to policies, the culminating legislation of the 1960s, the product of a decade of debate, was the Children and Young Persons Act 1969 (Bottoms, 2002: 216–27). The decade opened, however, with the Ingleby Report (1960) with its critical identification of a major weakness in the juvenile court system, namely the confusion between the expectation of 'just deserts' raised by 'the forms of a *criminal* trial' and the direction that when considering treatment the court had a duty to have regard 'for the welfare of the child or young person' (cited in Bottoms, 2002: 218). This highlighted one of the central problems in conceptualising juvenile delinquency within a 'criminal' jurisdiction: in the early stages of apprehension, the 'delinquent' tends to be treated as a rational being by the police and the court, but in the later stages there is more of an emphasis on pathology, psychic disturbance or 'welfare' (Bottoms, 2002: 218–19; Hendrick, 2003: 142–4). Much of the 1960s debate was about how this contradiction should be resolved.

The subsequent Children and Young Persons Act 1963 raised the age of criminal responsibility to 10, and gave local authorities powers to do preventive social work, thereby confirming the view that 'it is the situation and the relationships within the family which seem to be responsible for many children being in trouble, whether the trouble is called delinquency or anything else' (cited in Hendrick, 2003: 143). In effect, the 1963 Act maintained the perception of young people as a 'threat' while simultaneously attempting to reconcile this with a notion of 'neglect' (victim). Using the framework of the local authority child care service it sought to do this through a broadening of the therapeutic complex involving social workers, teachers, psychologists, doctors and probation officers (Hendrick, 2003, 140–7; Rose, 1990). However, despite the apparent rise in the number of juvenile offenders (Hendrick, 2003: 147), the debate continued to be shaped by largely welfarist sentiments.

These sentiments were most radically expressed in the controversial Children and Young Persons Act 1969, which sought to raise the age of criminal responsibility from 10 to 14, to substitute non-criminal care proceedings in place of criminal procedures for the 10–14 age group, to encourage a more liberal use of non-criminalised care proceedings for those aged 14–17, and to involve parents with social workers in deciding on a course of 'treatment' in order to avoid a court appearance. The Act, which was the result largely of a conjunction of social work and civil servant interests and Labour Party ideology (Bottoms, 2002: 225–6), represented 'the high point of therapeutic familialism as a strategy for government through the family' since the court was to become 'a place of last resort' (Hendrick, 2003: 149–53; Rose, 1990: 175). The weight of authority and discretion moved from the police, magistrates and the prison department towards local authorities and the Department of Health and Social Security: it seemed that 'the hour of the "child-savers" had finally arrived' (Thorpe et al., 1980: 6). The newly elected Conservative government (1970), however, which was sympathetic to different professional interests (the police and magistracy who opposed the 'welfare' orientation of the Act), ensured that it was never fully implemented. On reflection, the significance of the decade's debate is that it was 'a political metaphor' for a legislative programme 'geared to the development of ... a more just society' and, therefore, in certain respects the Act was the last gasp of post-war Labour party liberalism in criminal affairs (Gelsthorpe and Morris, 1994, 958; Muncie, 2004: 253).

The failure of Liberalism to protect welfarism in juvenile penal policy was caused by a complex set of factors, perhaps the immediate one being the technical and inherent difficulty in trying to match the punishment and welfare approaches into a single piece of legislation that would reassure all political interests. But there was another influential factor: the issue of governance among an electorate that was increasingly disillusioned with the promise and the vision of the post-war welfare state. The new mood was aptly captured in the Conservative general election manifesto, which referred to law and order 'peculiar to the age of demonstration and disruption'. This link between law-breaking and defiance of authority would prove to be significant in the future, not least because it was the beginning of the effective Conservative reaction to the 'permissiveness' of the 1960s, a decade when Britain had become the most liberal nation in Europe (Downes and Morgan, 1994: 183–4, 187–8; Pugh, 1999: 297–310). In the subsequent 'retreat from welfare' that proceeded throughout the 1970s, a key feature was a 'widespread shift in the techniques for governing the family and its troublesome offspring' (Gelsthorpe and Morris, 1994: 963–71; Rose, 1990: 29). This was due mainly to the break-up of the alliance of progressives within politics, social work and medicine which, in underlining the important role of professional interests, since the 1950s had projected the family as a 'therapeutic agent' in a programme of rehabilitative interventionism. The social changes of the 1960s, in particular feminism, anti-psychiatry, 'radical' social work, mounting critiques of the 'failures' of the welfare state and, perhaps most importantly, economic difficulties, all led to a loss of direction by the Liberal Left, and enthused the New Right with confidence to advance neo-liberalism with its free markets and economic libertarianism.

# THE 1980s: NEO-LIBERAL REACTION AND CONTRADICTION

By the mid-1970s, the image of Britain was of a society in 'national decline' with: economic problems, 'racial' tensions, discontent with the health and social services, violent political struggles between Left and far-Right demonstrators, trade union militancy, the emergence of a so-called 'underclass', criminality and juvenile 'delinquency', all of which culminated in the 'winter of discontent' of 1978–9. The media deemed Britain to be 'ungovernable', and Labour lost the general election (Downes and Morgan, 1994: 189–90). Soon 'crime' was being associated with 1960s permissiveness, which was said to have undermined traditional values, encouraged the spread of pornography and glamourised violence, especially political violence. The Conservatives, with a significant and innovatory agenda regarding governance, argued that this 'decline' in public morality was not simply a matter for the police, but should be the concern of parents, teachers and the community, and in so doing introduced a new emphasis on the role of 'active citizenship' and 'community' action (Downes and Morgan, 1994: 191–2, 225; Gelsthorpe and Morris, 1994: 971). Thus juvenile justice was yet again incorporated into a larger debate about the nature of social and political 'order'.

Despite the tough-talking of the Conservative government, policy responses were relatively liberal, for while it was politically secure at the polls, the decade from 1982 through to 1992 presents an intricate picture, having been described as a 'time of optimism', albeit limited optimism, in youth justice. The use of custody declined; there was a fall in recorded juvenile delinquency; and the 'youth justice system' itself seemed to be in decline (Gelsthorpe and Morris, 1994, 971–80; Newburn, 1996: 74). In fact there emerged a somewhat paradoxical coalescence between a number of disparate factors including academic research, social work with juvenile offenders, certain policy objectives of Thatcherism, and the interests of the police and the courts to reduce all forms of delinquency (Goldson, 1997: 124). Consequently, a 'fragile consensus' developed, hinging as it did on three principles: 'diversion, decriminalisation and decarceration', which produced a remarkably progressive period in the treatment of juvenile delinquents (Goldson, 1999: 4). In terms of policy responses, these principles were 'minimum necessary intervention, systems management, effective monitoring, intra-agency strategies, systematic diversionary approaches, community supervision and alternatives to custody' (Goldson, 1999: 4). Not only did the Conservatives echo academic researchers in proclaiming that juveniles 'grow out of crime' (quoted in Newburn, 1996: 67), but the courts were also reminded that they had to have regard for the welfare of those young persons brought before them. Of course, the 1980s did not witness an ideological conversion to welfarism. The efficiency of the police and the courts in reducing 'criminal' activity was being questioned and keeping young people out of penal custody was one means of meeting a key objective of Thatcherism, namely reducing overall expenditure. Given the onset of neo-liberal styles of governing, increasing attention was being given to 'unofficial' forms of discipline and control (Gelsthorpe and Morris, 1994: 980; Muncie and Hughes, 2002: 1–16).

All in all, the nature and the existence of the 'consensus' illustrates the contradictions of juvenile justice in contemporary society. The post-war 'moment' of political and cultural optimism finally collapsed with the failure of 'liberalism' to provide solutions to a problematic economy, muddled moral codes, labour market restructuring and uncertain class relations. After the killing of the toddler Jamie Bulger by two 10 year old boys in 1993, a media-induced 'crisis in childhood' consolidated (Scraton, 1997). This offered government and adult authority the opportunity to self-righteously express their anger and disappointment while seeming to be 'doing something', thereby relieving their sense of frustration and impotence. Thus it was ultimately disillusionment that gave way to 'authoritarian populism' (Newburn, 1996: 98) which, in accelerating the 'adulteration' of juvenile justice, has severely undermined the historical principle of child and youth 'welfare' in favour of 'self responsibility and obligation' (Muncie and Hughes, 2002: 4–5).

# CONCLUSION

This historical overview has been concerned with *change*, *order*, *party political agendas*, *professional* and *administrative influence*, and *age relations*. It has sought to show that there is nothing 'new' about debates concerning young people's behaviour. Nor until the end of the 1980s was there much in the way of policy innovation for, as we have seen, from the early nineteenth century the central theme in policy discourse was how, within the context of the evolving relationships between individual and society and family and state, to reconcile 'welfare' with 'justice' in a variety of circumstances. The reconciliation took different forms during the period, but essentially it always dealt with the control, rehabilitation and punishment of young people who found themselves somewhere along the spectrum of victim/threat/neglected/delinquent. Only since the end of the 1980s has the welfare-justice model been significantly restructured in line with a form of neo-liberalism.

In seeking to grasp the essence of debates (past and present) on juvenile delinquency and juvenile justice, two themes are worth reiterating. First, 'juvenile justice' is not simply a response to variations in apparent crime rates since it fundamentally reflects strategies for coping with social and political change and the related search for stability. This was obviously so throughout the nineteenth century in relation at least to the demands of a developing democracy, industrial relations, population growth and urban discipline, as it has been in the war-torn twentieth century in relation to Britain's much disputed world economic and political position, the development of a liberal democracy, the emergence of the affluent society and the rise of neo-liberalism. In other words, how society *creates* and reacts to juvenile misbehaviour 'ultimately tells us more about social order, the state and political decision-making than it does about the nature of young offending and the most effective ways to respond to it' (Muncie, 2004: 303).

Second, it should now be clear that 'juvenile delinquency' in all its forms and ambiguities is fundamentally a matter of *both* class *and* age relations, which are usually intertwined in subtle and complex notions of troubled and troubling young people (victims and threats). This matter of 'age', which is culturally embedded, often goes unquestioned as 'natural', and therefore is downplayed in preference either to 'class' or 'the state'. But, as has been shown, the nineteenth century reformers had no doubt as to the importance of age vis-à-vis what is known as 'the child figure' in political and fictional writing. From Rousseau onwards, 'age' became a critical conceptual tool in understanding both the 'self' and the 'social', and without it a notion of juvenile delinquency could hardly have evolved. In the late Victorian–Edwardian period, the 'invention' of adolescence added a critical psycho-biological dimension to what had hitherto been simply a class perspective of delinquency, and throughout the 1920s and 1930s the 'new psychology' (Child Guidance clinics) gained increasing significance in explaining 'maladjustment' as a sociological function of varieties of modernity. In the post-war period up to the 1970s, age relations took on an importance hitherto unknown, as 'youth' was positioned in classic figurative form: between past, present and future; a visible expression of cultural evolution, with all the ambivalence and ambiguity such a status entails. So, as has been shown here, 'age', like 'social change', is a permanent feature of all histories of youth crime and justice.

# REFERENCES

Andrews, M. (1994) *Dickens and the Grown-up Child*. Basingstoke: Macmillan.

Bailey, V. (1987) *Delinquency and Citizenship: Reclaiming the Young Offender, 1914–1948*. Oxford: Clarendon.

Berry, L.C. (1999) *The Child, the State and the Novel*. Charlottesville, PA: University of Pennsylvania Press.

Bottoms, A. (2002) 'On the decriminalisation of English juvenile courts', in Muncie, J., Hughes, G. and McLaughlin, E. (eds), *Youth Justice: Critical Readings*. London: Sage. pp. 216–27.

Burt, C. (1927) *The Young Delinquent*. London: University of London Press.

Coveney, P. (1967) *The Child Figure in Literature*. Harmondsworth: Pelican.

Cunningham, H. (1991) *Children of the Poor*. Oxford: Blackwell.

Davis, J. (1990) *Youth and the Condition of Britain*. London: Athlone.

Downes, D. and Morgan, R. (1994) '"Hostages to fortune?": the politics of law and order in post-war Britain', in Maguire, M., Morgan, R. and Reiner, R. (eds), *The Oxford Handbook of Criminology*. Oxford: Clarendon.

Fraser, D. (1973) *The Evolution of the British Welfare State*. Basingstoke: Macmillan.

Freeden, M. (1978) *The New Liberalism*. Oxford: Clarendon.

Garland, D. (1985) *Punishment and Welfare*. Aldershot: Gower.

Gattrell, V. (1990) 'Crime, authority and the policeman-state', in Thompson, F.M.L. (ed.), *Cambridge Social History of Britain 1750–1950*, Vol. 3. Cambridge: Cambridge University Press.

Gelsthorpe, L. and Morris, A. (1994) 'Juvenile justice, 1945–1992', in Maguire, M., Morgan, R. and Reiner, R. (eds), *The Oxford Handbook of Criminology*. Oxford: Oxford University Press.

Gillis, J.R. (1975) 'The evolution of juvenile delinquency in England 1890–1914', *Past and Present*, 67: 96–126.

Goldson, B. (1997) 'Children in trouble: state responses to juvenile crime', in Scraton, P. (ed.), *'Childhood' in 'Crisis'?* London: UCL Press.

Goldson, B. (1999) 'Youth (in)justice: contemporary developments in policy and practice', in Goldson. B. (ed.), *Youth Justice: Contemporary Policy and Practice*. Aldershot: Ashgate.

Goldson, B. (2004) 'Victims or threats? Children, care and control', in Fink, J. (ed.), *Care: Personal Lives and Social Policy*. Bristol: The Policy Press in association with The Open University.

Harris, J. (1993) *Private Lives, Public Spirit: Britain, 1870–1914*. London: Penguin.

Hendrick, H. (1990) *Images of Youth: Age, Class and the Making of the Male Youth Problem, 1880–1920*. Oxford: Clarendon.

Hendrick, H. (1994) *Child Welfare: England 1872–1989*. London: Routledge.

Hendrick, H. (1997) 'Constructions and reconstructions of British childhood: an interpretative survey, 1800 to the present', in James, A. and Prout, A. (eds), *Constructing and Reconstructing Childhood*, 2nd edn. Basingstoke: Falmer.

Hendrick, H. (2003) *Child Welfare: Historical Dimensions, Contemporary Debate*. Bristol: The Policy Press.

King, P. (1998) 'The rise of juvenile delinquency in England 1780–1840: changing patterns of perception and prosecution', *Past and Present*, 160: 116–66.

Marwick, A. (1990) *British Society Since 1945*. London: Penguin.

May, M. (1973) 'Innocence and experience: the evolution of the concept of juvenile delinquency in the mid nineteenth-century', *Victorian Studies*, 17 (1): 7–29.

Muncie, J. (2004) *Youth and Crime*, 2nd edn. London: Sage.

Muncie, J. and Hughes, G. (2002) 'Modes of youth governance: political rationalities, criminalization and resistance', in Muncie, J., Hughes, G. and McLaughlin, E. (eds), *Youth Justice: Critical Readings*. London: Sage.

Newburn, T. (1996) 'Back to the future? Youth crime, youth justice and the rediscovery of "authoritarian populism"', in Pilcher, J. and Waggs, S. (eds), *Thatcher's Children*. London: Falmer.

Osgerby, B. (1998) *Youth in Britain Since 1945*. Oxford: Blackwell.

Pearson, G. (1983) *Hooligan: A History of Respectable Fears*. London: Macmillan.

Pearson, G. (1994) 'Youth, crime and society', in Maguire, M., Morgan, R. and Reiner, R. (eds), *The Oxford Handbook of Criminology*. Oxford: Oxford University Press.

Pugh, M. (1999) *State and Society, 1870–1997*. London: Arnold.

Radzinowicz, L. and Hood, A. (1986) *A History of English Criminal Law*, Vol. 5. London: Stevens and Sons.

Rose, N. (1985) *The Psychological Complex: Psychology, Politics and Society in England, 1869–1939*. London: RKP.

Rose, N. (1990) *Governing the Soul: The Shaping of the Private Self*. London: Routledge.

Royle, E. (1987) *Modern Britain: A Social History, 1750–1985*. London: Arnold.

Scraton, P. (ed.) (1997) *'Childhood' in 'Crisis'?* London: UCL Press.

Shore, H. (1999) *Artful Dodgers: Youth and Crime in Early Nineteenth Century*. London: Boydell.

Springhall, J. (1986) *Coming of Age: Adolescence in Britain 1860–1960*. London: Gill and Macmillan.

Springhall, J. (1998) *Youth, Popular Culture and Moral Panics*. Basingstoke: Macmillan.

Thompson, E.P. (1963) *The Making of the English Working Class*. London: Gollancz.

Thorpe, D., Smith, D., Green, C. and Paley, J. (1980) *Out of Care*. London: Allen and Unwin.

Wooldridge, A. (1995) *Measuring the Mind*. Cambridge: Cambridge University Press.

# 2 SOCIAL CLASS, YOUTH CRIME AND YOUTH JUSTICE

## ROB WHITE AND CHRIS CUNNEEN

This chapter discusses the central place of class in understanding the reasons for the marginalisation and criminalisation of substantial sections of the youth population in the 'advanced' industrialised countries. Given the prevalence of neo-liberal ideologies, the huge changes taking place in basic class relationships due to globalisation, and the impoverishment of growing numbers of young people associated with these changes, it is important to understand the structural impacts of social inequality. A substantial part of the chapter, therefore, considers the making of an 'underclass', its key features and the response of the state to the growth in such 'surplus populations'. Youth justice systems have a major role to play in these social processes.

## CLASS, CRIMINALISATION AND CRIME

Class has rarely been more relevant to social analysis and to any consideration of juvenile justice in particular. Class, as defined here, is basically a *social relation*. It is directly associated with economic, social and political power, and is evident in how laws are framed, institutions are organised and societal resources are distributed (White, 2008). Class is also a lived experience. People act in the world in accordance to their relationship with other people around them, and as shaped by the communal resources available to them (see e.g. Chatterton and Hollands, 2003; White and Wyn, 2013). Such resources are both material and cultural in nature. The class situation of young people is, therefore, contingent – it very much depends upon family and community resources and it changes over time. Typically, young people's class situation is defined and distinguished on the basis of: the type and geographical location of their housing; the capacity of their parent/s to provide material support; the nature of their education (state school or private school); the age at which their formal education terminates; their age at entry into the labour market and the nature of their employment (if any); and the type of leisure activities that they pursue (Jamrozik, 2001; White and Wyn, 2013). Community resources are distributed via the market, the state, and informal community and family networks. For young people, what happens in each of these spheres has a huge bearing on their class situation. The phenomenon of unemployment is the biggest single factor in the transformation of young people, their families and their communities. In a wage-based economy, subsistence is largely contingent upon securing paid employment. If this is not available, then a number of social problems are often invoked, including and especially crime (Wacquant, 2008).

The context within which concern about juvenile offending is occurring, and is perceived to be a growing problem, is defined by the reconfiguration of economic and political relations, one consequence of which is the increasing polarisation of rich and poor, both between countries and within countries. Wealth and power are increasingly concentrated into fewer and fewer hands. Simultaneously, there is the impoverishment of many communities, neighbourhoods and families around the globe, and the escalation of unemployment (and under-employment) worldwide (Standing, 2011; Wacquant, 2008). The global financial crisis of 2008 further exacerbated the unemployment problem. The jobless rate among the 34 countries of the Organisation for Economic Co-operation and Development (OECD), for example, was predicted to be around 8 per cent at the end of 2014, leaving some 48 million people out of work (OECD, 2013).

We also know that those states that have the greatest levels of inequality also tend to be the most punitive in their criminal justice responses (Wilkinson and Pickett, 2009). Those states that have most fully embraced the neo-liberal agenda like the USA, Australia, New Zealand and the UK have simultaneously adopted more punitive penal policies, particularly compared to some European jurisdictions that have sustained more social democratic and corporatist forms of government and more moderate criminal justice policies (Lacey, 2008; Muncie, 2013).

For young people in particular, the collapse of the full-time labour market has been devastating. The decline in manufacturing employment, use of new labour-saving technology, the movement and flight of capital away from inner-cities and regional centres, changing workplace organisation based on casualised labour, massive retrenchments by private and public sector employing bodies, and competition from older (especially female) workers have all served to severely diminish the employment opportunities and conditions of young people in Western countries (White and Wyn, 2013). Young people continue to face record unemployment levels in many countries, with rates in 2013 exceeding 60 per cent in Greece, 52 per cent in South Africa, 55 per cent in Spain and around 40 per cent in Italy and Portugal (Goldson, 2014; OECD, 2013). This is the context within which youth crime routinely occurs.

Why is it that the social profiles of 'young offenders' tend to look basically the same throughout youth justice systems in 'advanced' industrialised countries? Predominantly young men with an over-representation of youth drawn from minority ethnic groups, with low income, low educational achievement, poorly paid and/or casualised employment (if any) and strained familial relations, are the standard defining characteristics of children and young people most frequently found in juvenile detention centres and custodial institutions, whether this be in Australia (Cunneen and White, 2011), England and Wales (Goldson, 2009; Muncie, 2013), Canada (Schissel, 2002) or the USA (Krisberg, 2005). The processes whereby identifiable groups of young people are criminalised tend to follow a distinctive social pattern. In effect, the youth justice system has a series of filters which screen young people on the basis of both offence categories (serious/non-serious; first time/repeat offending) and social characteristics (gender, ethnic status, cultural background, family circumstances, education, employment, income). It is the most disadvantaged and structurally vulnerable young people who tend to receive the most attention from youth justice officials at all points of the system.

The propensity for some young people to engage in criminal activity is mirrored in, and an outcome of, the prevalent divisions and social inequalities characteristic of wider social and economic forms. It is also very much influenced by the processes of criminalisation in themselves. Entrenched economic adversity has been accompanied by state attempts to intervene in the lives of marginalised groups, usually by coercive measures, which is itself a reflection of a broader shift in the role of the state, from concerns with 'social welfare' to renewed emphasis on the 'repressive' (Goldson, 2005; Wacquant, 2008; White, 1996). The intrusiveness of the state is, in turn, biased toward some groups of young people more than others. This is indicated, for example, in the extreme over-representation of indigenous young people in the youth justice systems in Australia (AIHW, 2013), New Zealand (Ministry of Justice and the Ministry of Social Development, 2002) and Canada (Munch, 2012). It is also demonstrated in the massive over-representation of African Americans in gaol, prison or on probation or parole in the USA (Krisberg, 2005), and the ways in which black young people are disproportionately negatively treated in England and Wales (Goldson, 2011; Webster, this volume). The history and dynamics of state intervention in particular communities varies considerably. There can be no doubt, however, that institutionalised racism, including that which is evident in the ways in which societal resources are allocated to different communities, has been, and will continue to be, extremely damaging to these groups.

The reputation of some communities, and some groups, as being 'no hopers', an 'underclass', as 'dangerous', as 'criminal', feeds back into the very problems of marginalisation and unemployment that lie at the heart of much youthful criminality (see Hagedorn, 2008; Inniss and Feagin, 1989; Schissel, 2002; White, 2013). That is, the structural transformations in global political economy are refracted socially in ways that reinforce negative images of, and the repressive law enforcement practices directed at, the most vulnerable sections of the community. These processes serve to entrench further the unemployability, alienation and social outsider status of members of such communities. The core picture of neo-liberal ideology and practice includes permanent structural unemployment and underemployment, privatisation of state services and withdrawal of income support, a shrinking of capital's contribution to the tax base as well as reducing overall state revenue as a proportion of gross domestic product, and the internationalisation of the economy. The social impact of capitalist restructuring is manifest in the immiseration of large numbers of people and the polarisation of income. One aspect of this is the expansion of the truly disadvantaged, invariably youthful in appearance and social construction.

Many young people in 'modern' and 'advanced' industrialised societies are not simply marginal to the labour market, they are literally excluded from it – by virtue of family history, structural restrictions on education and job choices, geographical location, racial and ethnic segregation, stigmatised individual and community reputation and so on (Goldson, 2014). Put simply, economic restructuring on a global plane has sharpened the disjuncture between viable reserve labour and non-viable reserve labour, and it is the long-term unemployed who are slipping into the most marginalised situation as skills and knowledge become redundant. In addition to absolute unemployment, marginality is also constituted through permanent part-time work; through seasonal or irregular employment combined with unemployment; through minimum or sub-standard conditions at, near or even below the poverty line; through short-term contract employment; and through accelerated reductions in the social wage (e.g. education and health) through the privatisation of services and the introduction of 'user-pays' services. This comprises a condition of existence for a substantial proportion of working-class young people. The class situation of young people is ultimately defined by the contours of unemployment and the general status of wage-labour in the economy.

# THE SOCIAL ECOLOGY OF POVERTY AND UNEMPLOYMENT

Analyses of the social ecology of poverty and unemployment are crucial to understanding the precise nature and extent of juvenile offending in any particular locale. While in many respects school exclusion and/or youth unemployment is the principal foundation underpinning offending (witness the social background of most juveniles in detention), it is within conditions of multiple and intersecting modes of social adversity that it has its most profound impact. In other words, examining the extent of inequality in specific community resources, of which unemployment is but one indicator, is essential in order to begin to account for youthful offending.

More particularly, to understand existing patterns of juvenile offending, we must appreciate the prime influence of local community conditions on youth behaviour and life experiences. The concentration of large numbers of unemployed young people in particular geographical locations increases the difficulties of gaining work for specific individuals (Hagedorn, 2008; Wacquant, 2008, 2012; Wilson, 1996). This is further compounded by limited educational opportunities. A recent Australian study found that 42 per cent of young people aged 17 to 24 from the lowest socio-economic backgrounds were neither in full-time employment or education (COAG Reform Council 2013: 65), and similar phenomena have been reported across Europe (Goldson, 2014). Such demographic concentration simultaneously fosters the shared identification and physical congregation of unemployed young people with each other. It thus can act both to preclude young people from attaining jobs and to make them more visible in the public domain as an 'outsider' group. In essence, the young poor are being locked into areas characterised by concentrations of poverty, scarce educational and employment prospects and overall declining economic fortunes. Poverty is being entrenched at a spatial level and this has major ramifications in terms of local community infrastructure. Poor people often live in areas with deteriorating housing, they suffer more profoundly any cutbacks in public amenities, and they are more likely to experience declining quality in their health, educational and welfare services. In addition, the neighbourhoods become heavily stigmatised as 'crime prone', thus giving rise to a policy of containment and attracting the more repressive interventions from state agencies.

The most structurally vulnerable, the most dispossessed, the poorest and the most deprived people are funnelled into ghettoised neighbourhoods. As indicated in British research, unemployment, disability and sole parenthood are particularly prevalent in certain geographically defined residential locations. The composition of these areas and housing estates (e.g. disproportionately high numbers of those suffering from mental illness) is such that 'nuisance neighbours' are more commonplace than might otherwise be the case in more socially heterogeneous neighbourhoods (see Burney, 2000, 2005). The recent history of public housing has, in essence, been witness to consolidating forms of residualisation. As also demonstrated in British research, it is the most vulnerable of the vulnerable who are forced into the least attractive accommodation (Goodchild and Cole, 2001). Such trends have obvious implications for the employment and educational opportunities of young people, and how they perceive themselves and their future prospects.

The social status and crime rate of specific neighbourhoods impact upon the likelihood of young people becoming involved in offending behaviour independent of their specific socio-economic status (Reiss, 1986). For example, a young person from a low income background living in a high crime rate area is far more likely to engage in offending behaviour than the same person living in a low crime neighbourhood. Community context is, therefore, an integral part of why some unemployed young people have a greater propensity to commit crime, and to be criminalised, than other young people in a similar social position (Weatherburn and Lind, 2001). The level and extent of welfare provision and services at a local level also have a major impact on youth lifestyle and life chances, as indicated in Canadian research on 'street-present' young people (Hagan and McCarthy, 1997).

# BLAMING THE VICTIMS: INDIVIDUALISATION, RESPONSIBILISATION AND COERCION

Where large numbers of young working-class people congregate in particular areas, they constitute visible evidence of failing social and economic conditions within which poverty and inequality are rife, and the threats to social order posed by such structural failure. Such analyses are increasingly peripheralised within dominant discourses that tend to privilege individual agency, underpinned by notions of marginalised young people constituting a particular type of *moral category*. In this way, members of the so-called 'underclass' are perceived and portrayed as morally corrupt and as a group needing to be disciplined and reformed (see especially Herrnstein and Murray, 1994; Murray, 1990). As well, and particularly in the light of recent urban riots, youth behaviour is framed in terms of 'gang talk' that reduces complicated social issues to incidences of individual and group pathology (Goldson, 2011; Hallsworth, 2013; Hallsworth and Young, 2008; White, 2013). The dominant political offensive in periods of high unemployment and low levels of collective labour mobilisation is to place even greater pressure on 'losers' to either 'cope' with their situation or to face the coercive penalties of state intervention.

One way in which the social expense of inequality and disadvantage is neutralised within state ideology is through 'official' constructions that serve to reinforce the individualised nature of complex social problems. A related response is through state coercive action, generally involving some form of criminalisation of the poor, and containment of social and economic difference via geographical segregation.

In effect, welfare and law enforcement policies serve to reinforce the distinction between 'the virtuous poor' (who are thought to exhibit positive attitudes toward self-improvement, healthy lifestyle and ready submission to state criteria for welfare assistance) and the 'vicious poor' (who are conceptualised as lacking industry and the work ethic, and who are seen as idle, wanderers and generally unrespectable). It is the 'deserving' poor who are the object of state welfare, while the 'undeserving' poor are subject to unrelenting intervention by the more repressive and coercive arms of the state, including criminal/youth justice systems (Goldson, 2002). The new 'dangerous classes' are framed within discourses of contempt and fear – a social attitude that pervades the popular media and political elites.

The ideological representation of the poor and deprived as an irresponsible, feral 'underclass' is built into the policy apparatus of the state in relation to both welfare and criminal justice. Unemployment is reduced to 'bad attitudes' and 'bad families'. The response, therefore, is to impose varying forms of mutual obligation on the poor – below poverty line benefits and inadequate services in return for work search obligations and imposition of training and employment programmes. For those who do not 'play the game', there is exclusion from state support. For those who 'ignore the game' and make a living through alternative means, there is state coercion in the form of increased policing, harsher sentencing and greater use of imprisonment.

The dilemma facing the most marginalised has been expressed as:

> [T]he hypercasualization of the labour market, and fall in opportunities and incentives for formal employment of less skilled workers, has led to an increase in informal activities of many kinds, including crime. It has also generated informal clubs of various sorts, based on the acquisition, consumption and exchange of semi-legal or illegally acquired goods, the sharing of information about informal activities, and the pooling of risks associated with illegality. In this way, poor and excluded people have sought to compensate themselves for the inequities of market-based outcomes, to 'tax' the better-off of the unjustified gains they have made, and to gain revenge on the various authorities that oppress them, as well as on the mainstream population who despise and exclude them. (Jordan, 1996: 218)

The response in many places to this phenomenon has been to introduce expanded law enforcement measures (including a wide range of legislation intended to deal with 'anti-social behaviour', including youth curfews) and more intensive and extensive regulation of welfare provision (including 'workfare'-type rules). The crux of state intervention is how best to manage the problem of disadvantaged groups (their presence and activities), rather than to eradicate disadvantage, poverty, inequality and consolidating modes of social and economic polarisation (Wacquant, 2009).

# SOCIAL EXCLUSION, PUBLIC SPACE AND SOCIAL IDENTITY

The systematic marginalisation of young people (and their communities) is marked by the disintegration of connections with mainstream social institutions (such as school and work), and a tenuous search for meaning in an uncaring and unforgiving world. The quality and quantity of youth crime are heavily overlaid by geographical location in that local economic resources, social networks and the spatial organisation of (un)employment shape the options and opportunities available to young people. Making ends meet, therefore, is contingent upon local contacts and local alternative economic structures.

For those without adequate economic resources to buy consumer goods, there are strong pressures to engage in alternative consumptive activity, and to compensate for the lack of consumer purchasing power by taking the possessions of others (Adamson, 2000). Exclusion from the legitimate spheres of production (paid employment) and thus exclusion from other forms of legitimate identity formation (as workers) also force attention to alternative sites where social identity can be forged. In particular, if social identity and social belonging have been made problematic due to institutional exclusion from paid work and commodity consumption, then the appeal of 'street culture' and the 'street scene' becomes more appealing.

The phenomenon of groups of young people 'hanging out' in the public domains of the streets, shopping centres and malls is one manifestation of the search for social connection. The precise character and composition of these groups varies enormously depending upon national and local context (see Goldson, 2011; Hagedorn, 2008; White, 2013). There is a diversity of youth subcultural forms, as well as youth gangs, although youth formations of this type have long been a source of consternation among sections of the adult population (Cohen, 1973; Davies, 2011; Pearson, 1983; Pearson, 2011). The social status of young people in groups today has also been influenced by broader changes in the nature of public space itself. This is evident in research that has examined the rise of consumerism, the mass privatisation of public space and intensified regulation of this space (Davis, 1990). The use of public space by low income, marginal groups of young people has been accompanied by concerted efforts to make them invisible in the urban landscape. The response of state police and private security companies to their presence in the 'commercial' spaces of shopping centres, for example, has been to move them on, to exclude them from community life and participation (see White and Alder, 1994). Thus the very use of space itself is increasingly constructed around the notion of space as a commodity – those with the resources have access; those without are denied. This process of imposed social exclusion and criminalisation is not class neutral. It is primarily directed at the most marginalised sections of the youth population. Ultimately, what is at issue is the containment of the most dispossessed and structurally vulnerable sections of the working class (often compounded by processes of racialisation) living in the more disadvantaged areas of towns and cities (Collins et al., 2000; Goldson, 2011; Hagedorn, 2008).

# HOLLOWED-OUT COMMUNITIES AND SOCIAL CONTROL

The concentration of poor people in poor areas carries with it a range of implications for social policy and state intervention. In the Australian context, for instance, the reality for many such neighbourhoods is that even when job growth and economic fortunes are generally on the rise, these areas tend not to benefit. Poverty is thus spatially entrenched, and this entrenchment persists over time. In describing these kinds of social processes in the USA, Wilson makes the point that:

> The consequences of high neighborhood joblessness are more devastating than those of high neighborhood poverty. A neighborhood in which people are poor but employed is different from a neighborhood in which people are poor and jobless. Many of today's

problems in the inner-city ghetto neighborhoods – crime, family dissolution, welfare, low levels of social organization, and so on – are fundamentally a consequence of the disappearance of work. (1996: xiii)

As economic formations 'modernise' and global economic restructuring leads to diminishing employment opportunities (particularly in manufacturing industries) in many Western countries, whole communities are negatively affected. Significantly, however, when these jobs are lost, it is particular ethnic minority migrant groups who are most affected. As the number of jobs in particular geographical areas decline, so too do amenities within the neighbourhood. In other words, economic transformations (involving the demise of manufacturing) and economic recession (characterised by high levels of unemployment) compound the physical deterioration of particular locales and hasten the social and economic homogenisation – characterised by impoverishment – of specific neighbourhoods. The flight of capital, including small businesses, from these areas, combined with the inability of residents to afford to either travel or live outside the area, cements such processes. The net result is ghettoisation, as middle-class people retreat to different suburbs, governments disinvest in public infrastructure (such as schools and hospitals) and neighbourhoods become marked with negative reputations and known as 'no-go' zones.

For young people in these circumstances life is hard, and legitimate opportunities for social advancement are seriously circumscribed. Doing it 'tough' can translate into the creation of alternative social and economic structures at the local level. For example, if no paid work is available in the formal waged sectors of the economy, the alternative economy may comprise the only viable option. Here we may see the emergence of what could be called 'lumpen capitalists and outlaw proletarians': people who subsist through illegal market activity. Davis (1990) illustrated this when discussing how cocaine, once the preserve of the rich, was transformed into a 'fast-food' drug known as 'crack cocaine', thereby opening up both extensive new markets, and entrepreneurial activity at the street level (MacDonald, this volume). The emergence of 'gangs' is likewise linked to both economic necessity (if activity is centred around illegal means of accessing money and goods) and social imperative (a method of acquiring a sense of meaning, purpose and belonging).

New social structures at the local neighbourhood level, based upon networks of friends, families and peers, can serve to collectively reconstitute the 'social' at a time when the welfare state is in retreat. The 'Family' or the 'Gang' may represent a turn to subterranean sources of income, emotional support, and sharing and distribution of goods and services when formal market mechanisms and state supports are of negligible assistance. Furthermore, communal networks of this kind can consolidate around shared social markers, such as geography, ethnicity and local history. Coming from a certain area may thus be transposed as a badge of communal membership and internal territorial identity, to counter the external stigma pertaining to the area due to its low economic status and negative reputation (Goldson, 2011). In other cases, identity can be constructed within the crucible of conflict. For instance, there may over time be continuous cultural and physical resistance to aggressive (racist) policing, and this may be manifest in the language of the streets, in its music and dance, and in police–citizen confrontations including, at the extremes, uprisings and urban riots.

The response of the state to social disadvantage and alternative cultural formations can take several different forms, typically comprising the criminalisation of specific 'types' of young people and activities via anti-social behaviour legislation, imposition of curfews, electronic monitoring and surveillance technologies, aggressive prosecution of family members and the application of sanctions on parents. Alternatively, the petty bourgeois layers of particular populations may be called upon to play a mollifying and pacifying role (see Davis, 1990; Headley, 1989). More specifically, there is an instrumental role for 'community leaders' (often with regard to ethnic minorities) in assisting with the implementation of containment strategies vis-à-vis the most marginalised sections of the young working class. In return for public kudos within the symbolic politics of 'community', and the possibility of investment and financial gain, 'community leaders' pledge to 'clean up the streets' as vociferously as the most repressive state agencies.

The intersection of class and 'race' is illuminated by Wilson's analysis of the over-representation of African Americans within the unemployed in the USA. A crucial factor is the location of many black Americans in segregated ghettos, a process exacerbated by specific government policies and programmes (Wacquant, 2009; Wilson, 1996). Similar concentrations of ethnic minority groups in heavily disadvantaged areas is apparent in Sydney, Australia (see Collins et al., 2000). So, too, in Germany, segregation based upon class and 'race' is a major problem:

> First, market expansion is being encouraged to promote individual competitiveness and allegedly make German society more dynamic. This approach ignores that resulting inequities when mapped on persisting spatial segregation will further expand disadvantages of the weaker social groups, including large shares of youth. Campaigns for a new morality, as a second policy thrust, promote normative compliance regardless of the social conditions and the status pressures youth confront on a daily basis. Preference for new measures of repression accompanied by stronger control and surveillance in urban space constitute a third policy approach to manage social change and growing uncertainty. (Heitmeyer, 2002: 106)

Resurgent interest in street gangs, youth and violence in North America (Hagedorn, 2008), Europe (Goldson, 2011; Hallsworth, 2013) and Australasia (White, 2013) provides increasingly important insights into the consequences of such complex social phenomena.

From a class perspective, mention also has to be made of the particular and peculiar role of local elites and civic/community 'leaders' in the regulation of specific populations. As described earlier, such people may be recruited or implicated in 'community' attempts to 'clamp down' on undesirable behaviour. This specific political role of local elites, however, is bolstered by the general vulnerabilities experienced by local small businesses that lend support, particularly on matters of law and order:

[T]heir deep and pervasive perception – supported somewhat by practical experience – is that their businesses, personal property, and physical integrity are front-line targets for street crime (e.g., armed robbery, breaking and entering, shoplifting, mugging, etc.). For them, the visibility of working-class street culture, particularly that of various underclass strata, is a source of anxiety for their own persons, their property, their customers, and trade. (White and van der Velden, 1995: 69)

This anxiety translates into perpetual 'moral panics' over 'street-present' working-class young people in particular (Pearson, 2011). Congregations of young people, especially if they are not spending money as consumers, may constitute both symbolic and material barriers to commerce – conceptualised as representing disorder and decline. Young people often congregate and 'hang out' in and around *commercial spaces* and their very visibility, perceived lack of financial power and behaviour (hanging around in groups, making noise) can render them an unwelcome presence, regardless of whether or not they actually transgress the law or actively engage in offensive activity.

# CONCLUSION

The principal aim of this chapter has been to briefly survey changes in the class situation of young people (especially in relation to the most marginalised sections of the working class) and the responses of the state to the existence and activities of the disadvantaged (primarily through mobilisation of the forces of law and order). Fundamentally, the dearth of paid employment in 'advanced' industrial economies is the key reason for heightened social dislocation and disorganisation. When accompanied by neo-liberal policies that place great emphasis on moral agency and individual responsibility within a material context defined by the retreat of state welfare support, this becomes a recipe for compounded structural disadvantage.

The consequence of class inequality and transformations in the class structure that deepen this inequality is a sharpening of social tension and antagonism. A big issue for young people is that they are increasingly made to feel as if they are 'outsiders'. This is confirmed daily in the form of exclusionary policies and coercive security and policing measures which are designed precisely to remove them from the public domain. For young people, this is often seen as unfair and unwarranted. It can certainly breed resentment and various forms of social resistance (see e.g., Ferrell et al., 2008; White and Wyn, 2013).

In responding to youth crime and the images of youth deviance, many countries employ a combination of coercive measures (such as youth curfews, aggressive street policing, anti-gang interventions) and developmental measures (such as sports programmes, parent classes, educational retention programmes). While the specific approach to youth justice varies considerably from jurisdiction to jurisdiction (see Muncie, 2013; Muncie and Goldson, 2006), a common element is the essential construction of the problem and those young people who are held to be responsible. Most justice systems deal predominantly with offenders from working-class backgrounds (including indigenous and ethnic minority people), and thereby reflect the class biases in definitions of social harm and crime, as well as basing responses on these biases. In so doing, they reinforce the ideological role of law and order discourse in forging a conservative cross-class consensus about the nature of social problems. The reinforcement of this discourse also unwittingly enhances the legitimacy of coercive state intervention in the lives of working-class young people, even if under the rationale of 'repairing harm' as in the case of restorative justice (Cunneen and Goldson, this volume). At a social structural level, such processes confirm the role of 'crime' as the central problem (rather than poverty, unemployment, racism), neglecting or avoiding entirely the roles of class division and social inequality.

# REFERENCES

Adamson, C. (2000) 'Defensive localism in white and black: a comparative history of European-American and African-American youth gangs', *Ethnic and Racial Studies*, 23 (2): 272–98.

Australian Institute of Health and Welfare (AIHW) (2013) *Youth Detention Population in Australia*. Canberra: AIHW.

Burney, E. (2000) 'Ruling out trouble: anti-social behaviour and housing management', *Journal of Forensic Psychiatry*, 11 (2): 268–73.

Burney, E. (2005) *Making People Behave: Anti-Social Behaviour, Politics and Policy*. Devon: Willan Press.

Chatterton, P. and Hollands, R. (2003) *Urban Nightscapes: Youth Cultures, Pleasure Spaces and Corporate Power*. London: Routledge.

COAG Reform Council (2013) *Education in Australia 2012: Five Years of Performance*. Sydney: COAG Reform Council.

Cohen, S. (1973) *Folk Devils and Moral Panics*. London: Paladin.

Collins, J., Noble, G., Poynting, S. and Tabar, P. (2000) *Kebabs, Kids, Cops and Crime: Youth, Ethnicity and Crime*. Sydney: Pluto Press.

Cunneen, C. and White, R. (2011) *Juvenile Justice: Youth and Crime in Australia*, 4th edn. South Melbourne: Oxford University Press.

Davies, A. (2011) 'Youth gangs and late Victorian society', in Goldson, B. (ed.), *Youth in Crisis? 'Gangs', Territoriality and Violence*. London: Routledge.

Davis, M. (1990) *City of Quartz: Excavating the Future in Los Angeles*. London: Vintage.

Ferrell, J., Hayward, K. and Young, J. (2008) *Cultural Criminology: An Invitation*. Los Angeles, CA: Sage.

Goldson, B. (2002) 'New Labour, social justice and children: political calculation and the deserving-undeserving schism', *The British Journal of Social Work*, 32 (6): 3–695.

Goldson, B. (2005) 'Taking liberties: policy and the punitive turn', in Hendrick, H. (ed.), *Child Welfare and Social Policy*. Bristol: Policy Press.

Goldson, B. (2009) 'Child incarceration: institutional abuse, the violent state and the politics of impunity', in Scraton, P. and McCulloch, J. (eds), *The Violence of Incarceration*. London: Routledge.

Goldson, B. (ed.) (2011) *Youth in Crisis? 'Gangs', Territoriality and Violence*. London: Routledge.

Goldson, B. (2014) 'Youth justice in a changing Europe: crisis conditions and alternative visions', in European Commission and the Council of Europe, *Perspectives on Youth: 2020 What Do You See?* Strasbourg: Council of Europe Publishing. Available at: http://youth-partnership-eu.coe.int/youth-partnership/publications/Perspectives/PoY1 (accessed 20.9.14).

Goodchild, B. and Cole, I. (2001) 'Social balance and mixed neighbourhoods in Britain since 1979: a review of discourse and practice in social housing', *Environment and Planning D: Society and Space*, 19: 103–21.

Hagan, J. and McCarthy, B. (1997) *Mean Streets: Youth Crime and Homelessness*. Cambridge: Cambridge University Press.

Hagedorn, J. (2008) *A World of Gangs: Armed Young Men and Gangsta Culture*. Minneapolis, MN: University of Minnesota Press.

Hallsworth, S. (2013) *The Gang and Beyond: Interpreting Violent Street Worlds*. Basingstoke: Palgrave Macmillan.

Hallsworth, S. and Young, T. (2008) 'Gang talk and gang talkers: a critique', *Crime Media Culture*, 4 (2): 175–95.

Headley, B. (1989) 'Killings that became "tragedy": a different view of what happened in Atlanta, Georgia', *Social Justice*, 16 (4): 55–74.

Heitmeyer, W. (2002) 'Have cities ceased to function as "integration machines" for young people?', in Tienda, M. and Wilson, W.J. (eds), *Youth in Cities: A Cross-National Perspective*. Cambridge: Cambridge University Press.

Herrnstein, R. and Murray, C. (1994) *The Bell Curve*. New York: Basic Books.

Inniss, L. and Feagin, J. (1989) 'The black "underclass" ideology in race relations analysis', *Social Justice*, 16 (4): 13–34.

Jamrozik, A. (2001) *Social Policy in the Post-Welfare State: Australians on the Threshold of the 21st Century*. Frenchs Forest, NSW: Pearson Education Australia.

Jordan, B. (1996) *A Theory of Poverty and Social Exclusion*. Cambridge: Polity Press.

Krisberg, B. (2005) *Juvenile Justice: Redeeming Our Children*. Thousand Oaks, CA: Sage.

Lacey, N. (2008) *The Prisoners' Dilemma: Political Economy and Punishment in Contemporary Democracies*. The Hamlyn Lectures. Cambridge: Cambridge University Press.

Ministry of Justice and the Ministry of Social Development (2002) *Te Haonga Youth Offending Strategy: Preventing and Reducing Offending and Re-Offending by Children and Young People*. Available at: http://www.justice.govt.nz/publications/publications-archived/2002/youth-offending-strategy/documents/youth-strategy.pdf/view (accessed 7.3.05).

Munch, C. (2012) *Youth Correctional Statistics in Canada*. Ottawa: Statistics Canada. Available at: http://www.statcan.gc.ca/pub/85-002-x/2012001/article/11716-eng.htm (accessed 13.10.14).

Muncie, J. (2013) 'International juvenile (in)justice: penal severity and rights compliance', *International Journal for Crime, Justice and Social Democracy*, 2 (2): 43–62.

Muncie, J. and Goldson, B. (eds) (2006) *Comparative Youth Justice*. London: Sage.

Murray, C. (1990) *The Emerging Underclass*. London: Institute of Economic Affairs.

Organisation for Economic Co-operation and Development (OECD) (2013) *OECD Employment Outlook 2013*. Paris: OECD Publishing.

Pearson, G. (1983) *Hooligan: A History of Respectable Fears*. London: Macmillan Education.

Pearson, G. (2011) 'Perpetual novelty: youth, modernity and historical amnesia', in Goldson, B. (ed.), *Youth in Crisis? 'Gangs', Territoriality and Violence*. London: Routledge.

Reiss, A. (1986) 'Why are communities important in understanding crime?', in Reiss, A. and Tonry, M. (eds), *Communities and Crime*. Chicago, IL: University of Chicago Press.

Schissel, B. (2002) 'Youth crime, youth justice, and the politics of marginalization', in Schissel, B. and Brooks, C. (eds), *Marginality and Condemnation: An Introduction to Critical Criminology*. Halifax: Fernwood.

Standing, G. (2011) *The Precariat: The New Dangerous Class*. London: Bloomsbury Academic.

Wacquant, L. (2008) *Urban Outcasts: A Comparative Sociology of Advanced Marginality*. Cambridge: Polity Press.

Wacquant, L. (2009) *Prisons of Poverty*. Minneapolis, MN: University of Minnesota Press.

Wacquant, L. (2012) 'A janus-faced institution of ethnoracial closure: a sociological specification of the ghetto', in Hutchinson, R. and Haynes, B. (eds), *The Ghetto: Contemporary Global Issues and Controversies*. Boulder, CO: Westview Press.

Weatherburn, D. and Lind, B. (2001) *Delinquent-Prone Communities*. Cambridge: Cambridge University Press.

White, R. (1996) 'The poverty of the welfare state: managing an underclass', in James, P. (ed.), *The State in Question: Transformations of the Australian State*. Sydney: Allen and Unwin.

White, R. (2008) 'Class analysis and the crime problem', in Anthony, T. and Cunneen, C. (eds), *The Critical Criminology Companion*. Sydney: Federation Press.

White, R. (2013) *Youth Gangs, Violence and Social Respect: Exploring the Nature of Provocations and Punch-ups*. Basingstoke: Palgrave Macmillan.

White, R. and Alder, C. (eds) (1994) *The Police and Young People in Australia*. Melbourne: Cambridge University Press.

White, R. and van der Velden, J. (1995) 'Class and criminality', *Social Justice*, 22 (1): 51–74.

White, R. and Wyn, J. (2013) *Youth and Society: Exploring the Social Dynamics of Youth Experience*, 3rd edn. South Melbourne: Oxford University Press.

Wilkinson, R. and Pickett, K. (2009) *The Spirit Level*. New York: Bloomsbury.

Wilson, W.J. (1996) *When Work Disappears*. New York: Knopf.

# 3 'RACE', YOUTH CRIME AND YOUTH JUSTICE

## COLIN WEBSTER

Black and minority children and young people are again facing a crisis – again not of their making – despite apparent progress in the ridding of racism from British society. Progress since Hall et al.'s (1978) seminal *Policing the Crisis*, which captured the mood and the means by which a post-colonial Britain criminalised many of its young black citizens, seems elusive today. *Policing the Crisis* described and analysed a period of visceral street conflict between a new generation of British black youth and the police during the 1970s and 1980s. Later, Hall recalled that this generation, the first to be born and to have grown up in Britain, would have 'committed a kind of collective social suicide' without the birth of a new black British identity, rooted in defiance of racism and marginality at school, in employment and in the ways black young people were policed (Phillips and Phillips, 1998). If Hall's imagery evoked the felt isolation and precariousness of being black at that time in British society, this chapter asks what has happened to black young people's social conditions, their experiences of crime, and their treatment at the hands of the police and criminal justice system since. These seem particularly timely questions given the publication of the 35th anniversary edition of *Policing the Crisis*. For, as the authors argue in the Afterword to this edition:

> Over the last forty years, all the relevant indices implicating criminalisation and crime have worsened for those on the wrong side of the tracks: coercive state powers; socio-economic conditions; media-fanned public fears; and the crime figures themselves (robbery up 905 per cent, 1970–97, after which the counting rules change) ... the contemporary 'folk devil', commensurate with this worsening scenario, is no longer only black, but has widened to include all disaffected youth ... Structural inequalities and worklessness, social exclusion and racism, criminalisation and brutalisation remain toxic symptoms of the present conjuncture, as they were of the one we explored in *PTC*. The crisis may be different, but it is still being vigorously policed. (Hall et al., 2013: 392)

Drawing on these terms and claims, this chapter focuses on change and continuity in the experiences of successive generations of black and minority ethnic children and young people, and the implications of these historical and social processes for understanding 'race', youth crime and justice in the present.

The main aim of the chapter is to explain the reasons why so little progress has been made in reducing ethnic and racial disparity and disproportion in youth crime, the ways in which young people are policed and, therefore, the profile of the 'suspect youth population' entering the youth justice system. Despite reforms to the police and the youth justice system carried out over many years, most notably since the Stephen Lawrence Inquiry in 1999 (Macpherson, 1999), and evidence of a strong decline in racist thinking (or at least in racist attitudes) among younger people and some younger police officers, policing and youth justice seem little touched by these reforms and changed attitudes.

# BLACK AND MINORITY ETHNIC PROGRESS AND YOUTH TRANSITIONS?

Any progress made over time in black and minority ethnic young people's involvement in crime and their treatment by the police and the youth justice system depends on whether intergenerational replacement has shifted a sufficient proportion of a people's attitudes in a particular direction. Whether this shift has been away from racism and towards a more ethnically and racially diverse and tolerant 'post-racial' society, as some claim, ought to influence attitudes and practices in the policing of young people and their treatment by the youth justice system. We shall return to this in the conclusion after considering the evidence. British Attitudes Surveys from 1983 to 2010 have shown that racist attitudes have been in long-term decline. As younger generations have succeeded older generations, racist attitudes appear to have virtually disappeared among younger people (Ford, 2008; Phillips and Webster, 2014). It appears though that treatment of black and Asian children and young people by the police and youth justice has been immune to these shifts in attitudes (FitzGerald, 2013).

Further evidence of a lack of progress is found in the question of whether young people themselves believe they have a future. A YouGov poll for the Prince's Trust found that one in three long-term unemployed young people (unemployed over a year) had seriously thought about suicide; one in four said they had self-harmed; they were also more than twice as likely to be prescribed antidepressants compared with their peers (25 per cent compared with 11 per cent) (Patterson, 2014). Clearly, their judgements about close adults and knowledge of local prospects and opportunities for training and jobs, the sorts of work offered and its availability, become important influences on their trajectories into adult life (MacDonald, this volume). The same YouGov poll found that nearly 60 per cent of the young people polled said they didn't have a parent they could call 'a role model'. Nearly one-fifth said they didn't even have a role model, often living in a house where no one works (Prince's Trust 2010, 2013). As young people grow up they too become parents and influence successive generations, positively or negatively (Webster, 2012c).

Early support or lack of support when experiences are problematic in childhood and teenage years have been shown to have an important influence on whether someone is likely to offend and whether offending is serious and persists (McAra and McVie, 2012a). This is as true for minority as it is for majority youth transitions, although support may differ and be mediated by culture and structure (Calverley, 2014; Gunter, 2010; Wright et al., 2010). The prolonging, complication and individualisation of youth biographies in most advanced western societies increases the risk that transitions go awry (MacDonald, this volume; Roberts, 2009). As Thompson (2013) has shown, the youth to adult unemployment ratio began to rise again from the turn of the millennium, even when economic prospects were much more positive.

# CHANGE AND CONTINUITY IN THE LIVES OF BLACK AND ASIAN YOUNG PEOPLE

Often marginalised and disadvantaged, black and Asian young people faced a series of cumulative crises and disruptions in their transitions to adulthood as they adopted new identities and adapted to economic and social change (see Webster, 2012a). If the recent history of youth transitions in Britain is marked by increased precariousness and vulnerability visited on marginalized young people by social and economic crisis, this section plots developments and progress since the publication of *Policing the Crisis* 35 years ago. The evidence shows few signs of a diminution of what was then a worsening and intensifying conflict between the British state and marginalised black (and white, and now Asian) working-class young people.

## Social, education and welfare policy

If the 1970s were the years of crisis, the 1980s brought the 'solutions' to this crisis – a series of cumulatively repressive policy measures against working-class young people in general and black young people in particular. Social and economic restructuring in the 1980s and 1990s worsened the social conditions of working-class young people. Incomes, benefit entitlements, training opportunities, job availability and security previously enjoyed were taken away, first from 16–17 year olds, later from 18–25 year olds. As a consequence transitions became increasingly extended, precarious and sometimes chaotic over decades that increasingly disadvantaged white, black and Asian young people (Furlong and Cartmel, 2007; Mason, 2003; Webster, 2009; White and Cunneen, this volume).

Young people who found themselves disconnected from or 'not in education, employment or training' (NEET), and those who had lived in the state public care system (in care), were particularly vulnerable (Bentley and Gurumurthy, 1999; Britton et al., 2002; Social Exclusion Unit, 1998). In particular, as is well known, offender populations are disproportionately drawn from young people who are NEET. Estimates suggest that up to 20 per cent of 16 and 17 year olds are NEET at any one time and 10 per cent of the NEET population appears to be from minority ethnic groups. Young people who are NEET are concentrated in poor areas and African Caribbean, Bangladeshi and Pakistani young people are especially at risk of NEET (Britton et al., 2002; Social Exclusion Unit, 1999; Stone et al., 2000; Williamson, 1997). Young people and children most likely to become NEET (and offend) are those who truant and are excluded from school early on, and previous data has shown this to be disproportionately the case among young African Caribbean boys and children in care (Social Exclusion Unit, 1998). Britton et al.'s (2002) qualitative study of white, black, Bangladeshi and Pakistani 16–17 year olds' intermittent routes into NEET found that disaffection and boredom at school were linked to troubles and traumas outside of school, so that early school disaffection, truancy, troubled early and later lives and negative experiences of being in care were linked. For minority ethnic young people the disadvantages of care interact with their experience of racism in care.

Although the increased precariousness of youth transitions and disengagement from education, employment and training disproportionately affects some minority ethnic young people, for other groups this has not been the case. Growing diversity, or even polarisation within different minority ethnic groups in terms of education and occupational status, complicates processes of social exclusion and disadvantage in respect of these groups (Heath, 2014). There is evidence of both upward and downward inter-generational and intra-generational educational and occupational mobility (Pilkington, 2003). Although for most ethnic minority groups, the second and third generation have made significant educational progress – especially some groups and women. Caribbean, Pakistani and Bangladeshi boys have made least progress. When social class background is taken into account, Caribbean boys in particular continue to do less well than their white counterparts. There has, nevertheless, been improvement particularly in the educational performance of previously disadvantaged minority groups. This is improvement from a low base whereby previously there was a long tail of poorly performing, educationally disadvantaged groups such as African Caribbean, Pakistani and Bangladeshi. Today the distribution of educational performance among black and minority groups is better likened to a more polarised situation between the educationally successful and unsuccessful within and between ethnic groups. In other words, educational stratification among second or third generation young people across a wide range of black and minority groups has in a sense 'normalised'; that is, become more similar to educational stratification in the white population. This has not though, so far, delivered the expected corresponding occupational success (Webster, 2012c).

It is also important to note that educational inequality on the basis of class is, after a short improvement, growing again (Demos, 2014). Large differences in unemployment persist in the second and third generation between ethnic minorities and whites. The absence of any convergence in the second generation with white British rates of unemployment is particularly striking and concerning, and suggests that there may be continuing patterns of racial discrimination and exclusion in British society (Heath, 2014). Here, vital class processes interpenetrate with ethnicity to produce enduring structures of disadvantage, but they do not necessarily override the influence of ethnic inequality.

Although minority children do better at school than they did, when school failure occurs as both cause and symptom of negative educational experiences, it is not difficult to see why some working-class boys – particularly Muslim, black and white – come under the spell of peer-based resistance to teachers and scholasticism (Gillborn and Youdell, 2000; Sewell, 1997). An 'exaggerated masculinity' grows by way of compensation against humiliation and anticipated school 'failure' (an expectation reinforced by teachers and school structures), the outcome of which is permanent school exclusion or self-exclusion, especially among black boys (Parsons et al., 2004). The sources of this disaffection include the ways in which racist assumptions are coded through the discourse of 'ability', and black and working-class white boys are considerably more likely to be judged as lacking in ability in the context of increasing school competition in the A-to-C economy, which pressures schools and pupils to meet attainment targets of GCSE grades A to C. (Gillborn and Youdell, 2000: 212).

Longer-term changes in social, education and welfare policy detrimental to children and young people, which began in the 1970s, consolidated in the 1980s and 1990s continue today. In schooling and youth training, the Education Maintenance Allowance (EMA) Scheme, which paid up to £30 a week to children from poorer families who remained in post-16 education, was withdrawn in 2011. This was despite the EMA significantly increasing participation rates in post-16 education among young adults (see Chowdry and Emmerson, 2010). In eligibility for, and entitlement to, welfare benefits, the progressive withdrawal of state welfare from young people aged 16–25 between 1980 and 1993 was accompanied by the removal of young people's protection from unacceptably low wages by Wages Councils, which were abolished (Roberts, 1995). Today, the deregulation of policies that previously aimed to protect young people continues apace. In a speech to the Conservative Party Conference in 2013 the Prime Minister promised that under-25s would lose their automatic right to housing benefit and jobseeker's allowance if they refused to take up offers of work, training or education (see BBC News, 2013). Just as governments have done in the past, the Coalition government has withdrawn support and worsened the conditions by which young people make their transitions to adulthood, precisely at a time when they are at the most vulnerable stage of the life-span, compounded because of their vulnerability to changes in youth labour markets and drug markets, and changes to young people's neighbourhoods (Furlong, 2012; MacDonald, this volume; Webster, 2009; White and Cunneen, this volume).

Youth unemployment has been a particular fault-line running through youth transitions since the 1970s, and this remains so today. Describing youth employment trends, Crisp et al. (2012: i) argue that since the economic downturn in 2008 youth unemployment has emerged as one of the most pressing issues for successive governments and has 'returned as a central feature of the social, political and policy landscape' (MacDonald, 2011). Underlying structural unemployment among young people has been rising since the relative boom period of the mid-2000s and is likely to persist even when the economy picks up again. This is in part because since the onset of recession in 2008, youth unemployment has risen at a much greater rate than general unemployment because of falling labour demand, yet is slower to pick up when labour demand once again rises. Youth worklessness is geographically concentrated in the older industrial areas and within pockets of deprivation in the better performing regions of the South and East. It is this persistent and pervasive social-structural aspect of specifically youth unemployment that still does not appear to be understood among policy-makers. Although significant numbers of young people are economically inactive and in receipt of out-of-work benefits, a wider definition of worklessness greatly increases the scale of the problem of labour market access for young people. Young people are significantly over-represented within the benefits system: 30 per cent of all jobseekers allowance claimants are aged under 25; under 25s also account for 30 per cent of all recipients of income support for lone parents (Crisp et al., 2012).

A young person in the UK is now nearly four times more likely to be unemployed than someone over the age of 25 (Office for National Statistics, 2013). Unemployment among young people (16–26 year olds) is back to the level it was in the 1992 recession, and has risen sharply since May 2010, with all the now well-known consequences long-term unemployment has on the future prospects of those affected. The 18–24 unemployment rate is up over the same period from 17.8 per cent to 18.6 per cent, as is the rate for 16 and 17 year olds, up from 33.5 per cent to 35.5 per cent since the Coalition government took office (Branchflower, 2014). This is despite the UK having one of the lightest regulated labour markets in Europe that should, theoretically, favour youth employment as the economy improves. Again, however, the evidence suggests that youth unemployment is not just a recessionary but also a structural issue. Even when young people are lucky enough to have a job that pays the minimum wage (those aged 18 to 21 receive £5.03 compared to £6.31 for adults, at the time of writing), the worsening and collapse of previously more favourable social and economic conditions for working-class young people greatly increases the negative effects on their aspirations, thus making involvement in criminality more likely (Roberts, 1995). None of this is to deny that particular 'problem groups' such as young offenders had difficulties gaining employment in periods of very low youth unemployment to the mid-1970s in any case, only that the choices and pathways are greatly diminished for the majority of young people who don't go to university.

Among black and minority ethnic young people the unemployment situation is much worse than it is on average for white young people. The unemployment rate for whites aged 16–24 was 19 per cent in September 2013. The rate was 46 per cent for young Bangladeshi and Pakistanis and 45 per cent for young black people. Ethnic minority unemployment is actually rising, while white majority unemployment has remained stable. Again the most recent figures show that Britain's most disadvantaged young ethnic minority groups have been particularly affected by unemployment. Sixteen to 24 year olds who are from ethnic minority backgrounds now have an unemployment rate of 37 per cent, up from 33 per cent in 2012. For the UK as a whole, unemployment in this age group is 21 per cent and has been constant for the past three years (Datablog, 2014).

Returning to those who are NEET, recent reliable figures show that the number of 16–24 year olds not in education, employment or training (NEET) was at a record high at the end of 2010. Some 938,000 young people in this age group were 'NEETs', and this is likely to rise over the next five years (Shepherd, 2011). As already mentioned, research has shown that it is from this group that offenders are most likely drawn and are most likely to be 'available' to be stopped and searched by the police. Their core are some of the most marginalised, socially excluded young people who lack trust in the police and accrue a surfeit of 'risk factors' associated with severe deprivation and sometimes criminality. Their members disproportionately belong to white, black and minority ethnic groups from lower socio-economic backgrounds (House of Commons Home Affairs Committee, 2007). The accruing of experiences more likely to lead to antisocial and delinquent behaviour has been intergenerational. We have been here before and policy-makers forget this at their peril as the long-term, intergenerational effects and costs on social cohesion and justice are well documented and very considerable indeed (Ferri et al., 2003).

# A LEGACY OF RACIALISATION AND CRIMINALISATION

At the beginning of the 1970s, black youth unemployment began to rise, but it was their experience of school that marked the new generation. ESN (educationally subnormal) Special Schools and approved schools contained disproportionate numbers of black children because of the influence of teachers' prejudice and low expectations of black children's abilities and performance (Cashmore and Troyna, 1982; Coard, 1971). Beginning in 1975, the police made a series of highly public statements claiming disproportionate black criminality. Collusion between the police and the media ran this story for the next decade. Whether the police consciously conspired to criminalise young black people by exaggerating them as a threat to law and order to enhance their own powers and resources, holding back a tide of alleged black criminality

(Cashmore and McLaughlin, 1991), or simply that black young people were over-policed because the police actually believed that disproportionate black crime existed (Lea and Young, 1993), the effect was to harass and criminalise very large numbers of young black men they deemed to be 'suspicious'. The police swamping of black areas gave rise to large-scale urban disorder in 1980, 1981 and 1985. At that time, black young people constituted over one-third of detention centre and borstal populations in the South of England. The numbers of 14–16 year old males (white and black) sent to custody more than doubled between 1971 and 1981.

The 1990s followed a similar pattern but took a different turn. Again, collusion between the police and media constructed 'Asian' ethnicity in the language of criminality, alleging the widespread involvement of Asian young men in street rebellion, gang violence, crime and drugs. Parlous deprivation, high levels of imposed residential segregation, school failure, increasing conflict with the police and local racism all conspired to racialise and criminalise young British Pakistanis and Bangladeshis. This complex of factors eventually resulted in widespread disorders in Bradford in 1985 and in Bradford, Burnley and Oldham in 2001 (Bujra and Pearce, 2011; Goodey, 2001; Kalra, 2003; Webster, 2009).

Although heightening group identity and resistance, the racialisation and criminalisation of black (and later, Asian) men funnelled them into unemployment or unproductive and uncreative work at the bottom of the labour market (Cashmore and Troyna, 1982; Hall et al., 1978). Then, like today, black youth unemployment was key to the crisis in young black people's transitions. In 1982, 60 per cent of 16–20 year old black young people available for work were without a job (Muncie, 2004). The 1970s and 1980s generation of black young people – the parents and grandparents of today's children – were marginalised by age, school experience, place and employment. Since these earlier times police powers to stop and search have widened and strengthened with predictably disproportionate consequences for minority young people (Dodd, 2012). Research by Ben Bradford of Oxford University (cited in Dodd, 2013) found that the rate of stop and searches of black and Asian people doubled in the decade after the publication of Macpherson's (1999) landmark inquiry, while the rate for white people rose only slightly. Ethnic minority Britons were subjected to nearly one-and-a-half million more stop and searches in the 10 years after the Macpherson report than if the police had treated them the same as white people. This was despite the report finding the biggest force, the Metropolitan police in London, to be 'institutionally racist' (Dodd, 2013).

What is striking is the continuation, over 30 years, of large-scale conflict between the police and black and working-class young people, including the August 2011 disorders in London and elsewhere (Newburn et al., 2011; Webster, 2013). There has been a growing punitiveness, seen in the inexorable rise in disproportionate black youth custody. By 2004/05, black people accounted for one-third of all arrests for notifiable offences in London; and in 2005, nearly half of black British male prisoners were incarcerated for robbery or drugs offences (Hall et al., 2013). In 2012, 11 per cent of British national prisoners were of black/black British origin, while this group comprised only 3 per cent of the general population and those of Asian/Asian British origin were proportionately represented (Ministry of Justice, 2013). Overall, black and Asian disproportionality rates for searches, arrests and the prison population (except for British Asians) were all getting worse. All these concerns, so viscerally described by the authors of *Policing the Crisis* over three decades ago (Hall et al., 1978), have not only persisted but worsened. In other words, from this point of view, little progress has been made in racial justice over the last three decades and more of reform.

## MINORITY CRIME, VICTIMISATION AND SOCIAL STRUCTURE

It has already been suggested that processes of racial discrimination play a key part in explaining disproportionality in the youth justice system, but it is evident from victim reports that elevated offending rates among some minority ethnic groups are part of the picture. For some numerically rare crimes, such as robbery and homicide (Clancy et al, 2001; Smith, 2003), black men are more likely to offend than other ethnic groups, and this may also apply to other volume crimes (Fitzgerald, 2013; Webster 2012a; Webster, 2012b). For example, black young people made up 27 per cent of robbery offences dealt with by the Youth Justice Service in 2004, but were only 3 per cent of the 10–17 year old population. This disproportion is unlikely to be *solely* predicated on discrimination by police officers or youth justice agencies. Approaching a third of all 'muggings' are committed by black offenders and only half by whites; a third of 'muggings' and 43 per cent of police recorded robberies were in London; and over half of those arrested for robbery in London were judged by officers to be black (Clancy et al., 2001; Smith, 2003).

The policing of working-class areas, however, can be disproportionate to local crime levels, particularly in relation to robbery offences, and particularly in London (Miller et al., 2000; Smith, 2003). The astonishing geographical concentration of robbery in London may in part be because it is one of the most unequal cities in western neo-liberal societies, offering opportunity and vulnerability in a place where consumer culture is often at the centre of young black lives (Hallsworth, 2005). These same factors, of course, turn out to explain rates of street crime in other areas also, where the majority of robbers are white (Murray, 2014). Regardless of ethnicity, the occurrence of street robbery is highly correlated with areas of concentrated deprivation (FitzGerald, 2013; FitzGerald et al., 2002, 2003).

Although rare – and popularly perceived as the most individualistic and emotional crime – homicide is strikingly disproportionate in its ethnic *and* social characteristics. Murder rates have noticeably increased among young men living in poor areas from the early 1980s recession, most recently reaching unprecedented levels for the youngest men (Dorling, 2005, 2008). Black young people are much more likely than white people to fall victim to violent and weapon-enabled crime, including homicide involving guns, but no more likely to fall victim to some other sorts of non-violent crime. In London, the largest numbers of homicides in the black group were of males aged 21 to 30, but the greatest disproportionality was at younger ages, where black males accounted for nearly two-thirds of all murders of 10–17 year olds (House of Commons Home Affairs Committee, 2007; Webster, 2012b). In London between 1999 and 2006, 64 per cent of all homicide victims were young black men aged 10–17 and 58 per cent aged 18–20, yet black men make up only 7 per cent of London's population. Nationally, between 2007 and 2010, 12 per cent of homicide victims were black, and British Asians too were overrepresented. Black victims were much more likely to be children and young people, and homicide by sharp instrument and shooting was much more likely within this group. Concentrated in London, the West Midlands and Manchester, black victims were usually killed by someone from the same ethnic group (Smith et al., 2010). The main explanation for this, the most individualistic of crimes, is social structural.

# POLICING BLACK AND MINORITY ETHNIC YOUNG PEOPLE

A young person's visible ethnicity, social status and age increase the risk of their becoming involved in the sorts of crime which may bring them to the attention of the police. The police in turn disproportionately target young males whose profile tends to be of lower class background, living in lone parent families, who have often been in care, who lack education and/or are unemployed, who live in urban areas of high crime and social deprivation, who have an active street life and who, consequently, are most likely to be intensively policed. Once having come to the attention of the police, young people are sucked into a spiral of amplified contact and conflict. All these risks and situations are more present among mixed 'race', black, Asian and marginalised white working-class groups of young people when compared with the general white British youth population (FitzGerald, 2013; McAra and McVie, 2005). McAra and McVie's (2005; this volume) longitudinal Edinburgh study of pathways in and out of the youth justice system offers insight into the impact of social structure on youth crime. The study found that the police continue to unfairly target categories of young people because of their 'form' and suspiciousness, and thus construct a population of permanent suspects among children and young people, to whom the police return again and again. It is not just the availability of youngsters on the street that publicly places them at greater risk of adversarial contact with the police. Instead distinctions appear to be made by police officers on the basis of social class – whether an individual is deemed socially respectable or unrespectable – in ways that do not always take account of serious and persistent offending, and which disciplines, labels and keeps under surveillance a group of permanent suspects. In other words, the police make distinctions and judgements about culpability and suspicion, who is accorded leniency and who is not, based as much on socio-economic status (and by extension, ethnicity in some places) as knowledge about serious and persistent offending, in their interactions with young people.

The provisions of the Crime and Disorder Act 1998 and the Anti-Social Behaviour Act 2003, which empowered the police to target anti-social behaviour, had a particularly negative impact on sections of the young working class (Squires, 2006). Contrary to expectations, the Coalition government that was elected in 2010 made matters worse for such young people. The Antisocial Behaviour, Crime and Policing Act 2014 permits injunctions against anyone aged 10 years or older who 'has engaged or threatens to engage in conduct capable of causing nuisance or annoyance to any person'. Monbiot (2014) argues that: 'these laws will be used to stamp out plurality and difference, to douse the exuberance of youth, to pursue children for the crime of being young and together in a public place.' Predictably, the new powers are much more likely to be used against Asian, African Caribbean and marginalised white working-class young people.

Returning to police powers of stop and search and their discriminatory and unlawful use – although it must be said that particular police forces use their stop and search powers differently (Equality and Human Rights Commission, 2010; Miller et al., 2000) – their increased use particularly criminalises and disaffects children and young people. For example, an Edinburgh University Study (Murray, 2014) found stop and search rates in Scotland at a record level, and the highest in the UK. The study discovered that children under 14 were searched 26,000 times in 2010 without statutory authority. That included 500 searches of children aged 10 or under, and 72 searches of children aged seven or younger. In the same year, the study reported that police made 145,600 stop-searches without legal cause against 15–20 year olds across Scotland. Most of those stopped were white. The use of stop and search powers, nevertheless, against minority and marginalised children and young people are a crucial aspect of a range of broader formal 'regulatory orders' (imposed by schools and the police on young people), including school exclusions and police warnings and charges which drive and worsen the development of offender identity. According to McAra and McVie, 'formal orders differentiate between categories of young people on the basis of class and suspiciousness' (2012b: 347), and such encounters propel rather than discourage repeated persistent offending (see also McAra and McVie, this volume). Similarly, Parmar's study of police labelling and stigmatising of young Muslims reveals the lasting and negative consequences of such processes because the 'indignity of being repeatedly labelled as something you are not, promotes an entrenched sense of resentment … injustice and humiliation' (2014: 133).

How to explain the nature of how young people are policed? Through direct observation of operational policing across two contrasting police force areas,

Loftus (2008) studied police culture through engagement with officers of different social backgrounds, gender and ethnicity, and found resistance and resentment towards reforms addressing 'race' and the policing of diversity, articulated principally by white, heterosexual, male officers. It is this nostalgic, 'imperious' white culture that seems to explain how some officers still perceive, and interact with, poor and (some) minority children and young people in public encounters. While pervasive, discrimination is difficult to pin down because of its often subtle, elusive, coded and covert presence. Loftus' study concludes that today, as in the past, police officers express a resentful, defensive posture towards reform and towards individuals and groups they perceive as of low status, including some minorities. More than anything else, Loftus' study reveals 'the stubborn and powerful significance of class as a determinant of police practice and object of officers' unchallenged scorn' (ibid.: viii).

Loftus' analysis of the ethnic and economic exclusion and division of young people by the police is *both* class-based:

> [T]he marginal underclass created in western societies are a new and extended guise of police property. Poor young men are prime inhabitants of this category and, because of their increasing unemployment, are propelled to live out more of their daily lives in public – and thus police – space. (2009: 40)

*and* based on 'race' and gender:

> [P]art of the police treatment of ethnic minorities and women is undoubtedly class-related. Although these groups are accorded prominence in diversity agendas, it is striking that economically impoverished minority ethnic groups and females invariably continue to experience the undesirable face of operational policing ... the occlusion of class within current debates is further problematic because economic deprivation often coexists with the adverse policing of cultural and gendered groups. (ibid.:198)

# BLACK AND MINORITY ETHNIC YOUNG PEOPLE IN THE YOUTH JUSTICE SYSTEM

Feilzer's and Hood's (2004) ground-breaking study of minority ethnic young people in the youth justice system found that at different stages of youth justice decision-making processes, different outcomes were consistent with discriminatory treatment of Asian and black males, and especially mixed-parentage males and females, in respect of: prosecution; remand; conviction; the use of more restrictive community penalties; and longer sentences of penal custody. A key finding was that large differences or discriminatory treatment of minority ethnic young people were found between Youth Offending Team areas, which were tantamount to youth justice by race and geography.

An important question is whether it is different treatment by the police that leads to young people entering the youth justice system in the first place. A study by May et al. (2010) presents evidence to help explain how young people are brought into the youth justice system and what happens to them as they pass through it; in particular, the processes by which the police bring young people into the youth justice system. May and her colleagues differentiate two main routes by which young people can enter the youth justice system: either because victims and witnesses report cases to the police (reactive policing), or because the police uncover offences in the course of their work (proactive policing). Police-initiated arrests account for a significant number of all arrests, leaving ample room for different treatment on grounds of class and ethnicity (particularly with regard to drug and road traffic offences). Again, there are large differences in policing methods between areas that impact upon the way in which young people are drawn into the youth justice system. In some areas policing methods are highly proactive and more adversarial, placing less priority on respectful and fair treatment and instead reflecting long histories of difficult relations between the police and the public and, in particular, the police and working-class and minority ethnic communities (May et al., 2010).

Furthermore, having entered the youth justice system May et al. (2010) found that the manner in which young people pass through it involved discrimination against ethnic minorities, given that the different outcomes between ethnic groups could not be accounted for by any specific features of the offences or criminal histories of the suspects or defendants.

# DISCUSSION AND CONCLUSION

Policing and schooling are key agencies in the production of a group of youngsters – the 'usual suspects' – who are repeatedly drawn into cycles of contact with the youth justice system and for whom such contact has damaging consequences. According to McAra and McVie (2010; this volume), young people's early adversarial contact with formal agencies of control (schooling, policing and youth justice) and their deep involvement with such agencies actually serves to *inhibit* desistance from crime by confirming and consolidating 'offender' identities.

Marginalisation occurs across different domains of transition – from family, schooling, care, policing, and youth justice to employment – for many white, black and Asian working-class young people growing up in Britain (MacDonald, this volume; White and Cunneen, this volume). Young black men in particular, disproportionately find themselves under the supervision of a continuum of regulatory agencies – including, it must be said, the informal ones of their own peer groups (see McAra and McVie, 2010, 2012b). For such groups, over three decades of de-industrialisation and economic restructuring have: worsened their social conditions; destabilised their families and neighbourhoods; subjected them to harassment and discrimination by the police, youth justice, care and schooling systems; and offered them – at best – a precarious future at the bottom of a low waged, insecure youth labour market (Mah, 2012).

The politicisation and racialisation of youth crime and justice has lent legitimacy to the measures of regulatory control that economic recession requires, whilst at the same time producing and reproducing deep racial divisions in society (Keith, 1993).

# REFERENCES

BBC News (2013) 'David Cameron suggests cutting benefits for under-25s', *BBC News*, 2 October. Available at: www.bbc.co.uk/news/uk-politics-24369514 (accessed 30.9.14).

Bentley, T. and Gurumurthy, R. (1999) *Destination Unknown: Engaging with the Problems of Marginalized Youth*. London: Demos.

Branchflower, D. (2014) 'The plight of the young and unemployed is truly scary – and this government seems to have no answers', *Independent*, 18 January.

Britton, L., Chatrik, B., Coles, B., Craig, G., Hylton, C. and Mumtaz, S. (2002) *Missing Connexions: The Career Dynamics and Welfare Needs of Black and Minority Ethnic Young People at the Margins*. Bristol: Policy Press.

Bujra, J. and Pearce, J. (2011) *Saturday Night and Sunday Morning*. Skipton: Vertical Editions.

Calverley, A. (2014) *Cultures of Desistance: Rehabilitation, Reintegration and Ethnic Minorities*. Abingdon: Routledge.

Cashmore, E. and McLaughlin, E. (1991) *Out of Order? Policing Black People*. London: Routledge.

Cashmore, E. and Troyna, B. (eds) (1982) *Black Youth in Crisis*. London: Allen and Unwin.

Chowdry, H. and Emmerson, C. (2010) *An Efficient Maintenance Allowance?* London: Institute for Fiscal Studies. Available at: www.ifs.org.uk/publications/5370 (accessed 30.9.14).

Clancy, A., Hough, M., Aust, R. and Kershaw, C. (2001) *Crime, Policing and Justice: The Experience of Ethnic Minorities: Findings from the 2000 British Crime Survey*, Home Office Research Study 223. London: Home Office.

Coard, B. (1971) *How the West Indian Child is Made Educationally Sub-normal in the British School System*. London: New Beacon.

Crisp, R., Gore, T. and Powell, R. (2012) *Scoping Study on Worklessness and Employability*. Sheffield: Centre for Regional Economic and Social Research, Sheffield Hallam University.

Datablog (2014) 'Rising unemployment for UK's ethnic minorities: who's affected?', *Guardian*, 8 January. Available at: www.theguardian.com/news/datablog/2014/jan/08/rising-unemployment-for-uk-ethnic-minorities-race-whos-affected (accessed 30.9.14).

Demos (2014) *A Tale of Two Classrooms*. Available at: www.demos.co.uk/press_releases/ataleoftwoclassroomslondonresultsskewnationalpictureaseducationalin equality-ontherise (accessed 20.9.14).

Dodd, V. (2012) 'Police up to 28 times more likely to stop and search black people – study', *Guardian*, 12 June.

Dodd, V. (2013) 'New research finds that stop and searches for black and Asian people doubled while rate for white people rose only slightly', *Guardian*, 22 April.

Dorling, D. (2005) 'Murder in Britain', *Prison Service Journal*, 166.

Dorling, D. (2008) 'Commentary', *Environment and Planning A*, 40: 255–7.

Equality and Human Rights Commission (2010) *Stop and Think: A Critical Review of the Use of Stop and Search Powers in England and Wales*. London: EHRC.

Feilzer, M. and Hood, R. (2004) *Differences or Discrimination? Minority Ethnic People in the Youth Justice System*. London: Youth Justice Board.

Ferri, E., Bynner, J. and Wadsworth, M. (eds) (2003) *Changing Britain, Changing Lives: Three Generations at The Turn of The Century*. London: Institute of Education.

FitzGerald, M. (2013) '"Race", ethnicity and crime', in Hale, C., Hayward, K., Wahidin, A. and Wincup, E. (eds), *Criminology*, 3rd edn. Oxford: Oxford University Press.

FitzGerald, M., Hough, M., Joseph I. and Qureshi, T. (2002) *Policing for London*. Cullompton: Willan.

FitzGerald, M., Stockdale, J. and Hale, C. (2003) *Young People and Street Crime*. London: Youth Justice Board.

Ford, R. (2008) 'Is racial prejudice declining in Britain?', *British Journal of Sociology*, 59 (4): 609–36.

Furlong, A. (2012) *Youth Studies: An Introduction*. London: Routledge.

Furlong, A. and Cartmel, F. (2007) *Young People and Social Change: Individualization and Risk in Late Modernity*. Maidenhead: Open University Press.

Gillborn, D. and Youdell, D. (2000) *Rationing Education*. Buckingham: Open University Press.

Goodey, J. (2001) 'The criminalization of British Asian youth', *Journal of Youth Studies*, 4 (4): 429–50.

Gunter, A. (2010) *Growing Up Bad: Black Youth, Road Culture and Badness in an East London Neighbourhood*. London: Tufnell.

Hall, S., Critcher, C., Jefferson, T., Clarke, J. and Roberts, B. (1978) *Policing the Crisis: Mugging, the State, and Law and Order*. London: Macmillan.

Hall, S., Critcher, C., Jefferson, T., Clarke, J. and Roberts, B. (2013) *Policing the Crisis: Mugging, the State, and Law and Order*, 35th anniversary edn. London: Macmillan.

Hallsworth, S. (2005) *Street Crime*. Cullompton: Willan.

Heath, A. (2014) 'Introduction: patterns of generational change: convergent, reactive or emergent?', *Ethnic and Racial Studies*, 37 (1): 1–9.

House of Commons Home Affairs Committee (2007) *Young Black People and the Criminal Justice System*. London: House of Commons.

Kalra, V.S. (2003) 'Police lore and community disorder: diversity in the criminal justice system', in Mason, D. (ed.), *Explaining Ethnic Differences: Changing Patterns of Disadvantage in Britain*. Bristol: Policy Press.

Keith, M. (1993) *Race, Riots and Policing: Lore and Disorder in a Multi-racist Society*. London: UCL Press.

Lea, J. and Young, J. (1993) *What is to be Done about Law and Order?* Revised edn. London: Pluto.

Loftus, B. (2008) 'Dominant culture interrupted: recognition, resentment and the politics of change in an English police force', *British Journal of Criminology*, 48 (6): 778–97.

Loftus, B. (2009) *Policing Culture in a Changing World*. Oxford: Oxford University Press.

MacDonald, R. (2011) 'Youth transitions, unemployment and underemployment: *plus ça change, plus c'est la même chose?*', *Journal of Sociology*, 47 (4): 427–44.

Macpherson of Cluny, Sir William (1999) *The Stephen Lawrence Inquiry: Report of an Inquiry by Sir William Macpherson of Cluny*, Cmnd 4262–1. London: The Stationery Office.

Mah, A. (2012) *Industrial Ruination, Community, and Place: Landscapes and Legacies of Urban Decline*. London: University of Toronto Press.

Mason, D. (ed.) (2003) *Explaining Ethnic Differences: Changing Patterns of Disadvantage in Britain*. Bristol: Policy Press.

May, T., Gyateng, T. and Hough, M. (2010) *Differential Treatment in the Youth Justice System*, EHRC Research Report 50. London: Equality and Human Rights Commission.

McAra, L. and McVie, S. (2005) 'The usual suspects? Street-life, young people and the police', *Criminal Justice*, 5 (1): 5–36.

McAra, L. and McVie, S. (2010) 'Youth crime and justice: key messages from the Edinburgh study of youth transitions and crime', *Criminology & Criminal Justice*, 10 (2): 179–209.

McAra, L. and McVie, S. (2012a) 'Critical debates in developmental and life-course criminology', in Maguire, M., Morgan, R. and Reiner, R. (eds), *The Oxford Handbook of Criminology*, 5th edn. Oxford: Oxford University Press.

McAra, L. and McVie, S. (2012b) 'Negotiated order: the groundwork for a theory of offending pathways', *Criminology and Criminal Justice*, 12 (4): 347–75.

Miller, J., Bland, N. and Quinton, P. (2000) *The Impact of Stops and Searches on Crime and the Community*, Police Research Series Paper 127. London: Home Office.

Ministry of Justice (2013) *Statistics on Race and the Criminal Justice System 2012*. London: Ministry of Justice.

Monbiot, G. (2014) 'At last, a law to stop almost anyone from doing almost anything', *Guardian*, 7 January.

Muncie, J. (2004) *Youth and Crime*, 2nd edn. London: Sage.

Murray, K. (2014) *Stop and Search in Scotland: An Evaluation of Police Practice*. University of Edinburgh: Scottish Centre for Crime & Justice Research.

Newburn, T., Lewis, P. and Metcalf, J. (2011) *A New Kind of Riot? From Brixton 1981 to Tottenham 2011*. Available at: http://www.theguardian.com/uk/2011/dec/09/riots-1981-2011-differences (accessed 13.10.14).

Office for National Statistics (2013) *Labour Market Statistics November 2013*. Available at: www.ons.gov.uk/ons/dcp171778_332467.pdf (accessed 9.12.13).

Parmar, A. (2014) 'Configuring ethnic identities: resistance as a response to counter-terrorist policy', in Phillips, C. and Webster, C. (eds), *New Direction in Race, Ethnicity and Crime*. Abingdon: Routledge.

Parsons, C., Godfrey, R., Annan, G., Cornwall, J., Dussart, M., Hepburn, S., Howlett, K. and Wennerstrom, V. (2004) *Minority Ethnic Exclusions and the Race Relations (Amendment) Act 2000*. London: Department for Education and Skills.

Patterson, C. (2014) 'Both left and right have failed the jobless young', *Guardian*, 4 January.

Phillips, C. and Webster, C. (eds) (2014) *New Directions in Race, Ethnicity and Justice*. London: Routledge.

Phillips, M. and Phillips, T. (1998) *Windrush: The Irresistible Rise of Multi-Racial Britain*. London: Harper Collins.

Pilkington, A. (2003) *Racial Disadvantage and Ethnic Diversity in Britain*. Basingstoke: Palgrave Macmillan.

Prince's Trust (2010) *The Prince's Trust YouGov Youth Index 2013*. London: Prince's Trust. Available at: www.princes-trust.org.uk/pdf/Youth_Index_2010.pdf (accessed 30.9.14).

Prince's Trust (2013) *The Prince's Trust Youth Index 2013*. London: Prince's Trust. Available at: www.princes-trust.org.uk/pdf/youth-index-2013.pdf (accessed 30.9.14).

Roberts, K. (1995) *Youth and Employment in Modern Britain*. Oxford: Oxford University Press.

Roberts, K. (2009) *Youth in Transition: Eastern Europe and the West*. Basingstoke: Palgrave.

Sewell, T. (1997) *Black Masculinities and Schooling: How Black Boys Survive Modern Schooling*. London: Trentham.

Shepherd, J. (2011) 'Record number of young people not in education, work or training', *Guardian*, 24 February.

Smith, J. (2003) *The Nature of Personal Robbery*, Home Office Research Study 254. London: Home Office.

Smith, K. (ed), Flatley, J. (ed.), Coleman, K., Osborne, S., Kaiza, P. and Roe, S. (2010) *Homicides, Firearm Offences and Intimate Violence 2008/09 Supplementary Volume 2 to Crime in England and Wales 2008/09*, Home Office Statistical Bulletin 01/10. London: Home Office.

Social Exclusion Unit (1998) *Truancy and Social Exclusion*, Cmnd 3947. London: SEU/Stationary Office.

Social Exclusion Unit (1999) *Bridging the Gap*, Cmnd 4405. London: SEU/Stationary Office.

Squires, P. (2006) 'New Labour and the politics of anti-social behaviour', *Critical Social Policy*, 26 (1): 144–68.

Stone, V., Cotton, D. and Thomas, A. (2000) *Mapping Troubled Lives: Young People Not in Education, Employment or Training*. London: Department for Education and Employment.

Thompson, S. (2013) *States of Uncertainty: Youth Unemployment in Europe*. London: IPPR.

Webster, C. (2009) 'Young people, race and ethnicity', in Furlong, A. (ed.), *International Handbook on Youth and Young Adulthood*. London: Routledge.

Webster, C. (2012a) 'Different forms of discrimination in the CJS', in Sveinsson, K. (ed.), *Criminal Justice v Racial Justice: Over-Representation in the Criminal Justice System*. London: Runnymede Trust.

Webster, C. (2012b) 'The discourse on "race" in criminological theory', in Hall, S. and Winlow, S. (eds), *New Directions in Criminological Theory*. London: Routledge.

Webster, C. (2012c) 'The construction of British Muslim criminality and disorder', in Wetherly, P., Farrar, M., Robinson, S. and Valli, Y. (eds), *'Islam' in 'the West': Key Issues in Multiculturalism*. Basingstoke: Palgrave.

Webster, C. (2013) 'Return of the repressed? A retrospective on policing and disorder in England, 1981 to 2011', in Winlow, S. and Atkinson, R. (eds), *New Directions in Crime and Deviancy*. London: Routledge.

Webster, C. (2014) 'Race, religion, victims and crime', in Davies, P., Francis, P. and Greer, C. (eds), *Victims, Crime and Society*. London: Sage.

Williamson, H. (1997) 'Status zero, youth and the "underclass"', in MacDonald, R. (ed.), *Youth, the 'Underclass' and Social Exclusion*. London: Routledge.

Wright, C., Standen, P.J. and Patel, T. (2010) *Black Youth Matter: Transitions from School to Success*. Abingdon: Routledge.

# 4 GIRLS, CRIME AND JUSTICE

## GILLY SHARPE AND LORAINE GELSTHORPE

During recent years there has been a burgeoning interest amongst criminologists – from both 'mainstream' and 'feminist' perspectives – in crime and violence perpetrated by girls and young women. However, the girl crime 'problem' has often been constructed in ways which are distant from girls' everyday experiences, with too great a focus on individual girls in explaining their pathways into crime, and too little attention given to the structural and political factors leading to their criminalisation. Representations of young women offenders continue to be embodied and rooted in social class and focused on their moral character to a far greater degree than is the case with young men. Part of the problem is that popular representations of young women in general depict them as either violent or vulnerable, as empowered or in crisis (Aapola et al., 2005), which is reflected in dualistic and paternalistic thinking about girls in trouble with the law.

Following an outline of the history of young women and youth justice, in this chapter we focus on recent trends in girls' lawbreaking and criminalisation as well as on the ways in which girls' 'risky vulnerabilities' frequently lead to their criminalisation and punishment. Concern about increases in the number of young women entering the youth justice system has prompted attempts to reconfigure criminal justice responses to them, through gender-specific programming. We question the extent to which such initiatives increase justice for young women in trouble with the law and conclude instead that there is a need, in research, policy and practice, to address the deficiencies in state (non)intervention which so frequently fail to protect girls from harm, leaving them without support and vulnerable to increased punishment.

## A BRIEF HISTORY OF YOUNG WOMEN AND YOUTH JUSTICE

The history of penal governance in respect of girls is a history of regulating 'inappropriate' female behaviour and reinforcing dominant expectations of white middle-class femininity. Although young women have traditionally been near-invisible within the formal youth justice apparatus, the voluntary sector and associated networks of welfare institutions have been prominent in attempts to reform wayward young women into respectable female citizens (Cox, 2003). Definitions and representations of delinquent or offending girls and young women are historically contingent and influenced by trends in youth justice policy and practice, criminological theorising, and often also by broader socio-political concerns. However, what seems to have changed little is that concern about 'bad' girls from the early twentieth century onwards has consistently reflected the belief that gender differences are reducing and that behavioural norms amongst girls and boys are converging (Jackson and Tinkler, 2007).

Historical conceptualisations of boys' and girls' offending as essentially different have underscored assumptions that girls' lawbreaking stems from individual or family pathology, as opposed to youthful immaturity or rebellion. While boys' delinquency has tended to be understood simply as bad behaviour, girls' transgressions have more often been seen as an indication of defective or immoral character (Gelsthorpe, 1989; Priestley et al., 1977). The majority of empirical studies of offending girls undertaken during the last century were based on institutional samples. Given the courts' practices of institutionalising girls due to precocious and unmarried sexual behaviour or on other moral welfare or 'protection' grounds, such studies have been criticised for being unrepresentative of actual lawbreakers, as well as for their uncritical acceptance of the sexual double standard that frequently led to girls' incarceration (Smart, 1976). A key theme in these depictions was 'that unhappiness, sexual promiscuity and familial rejection [were] all seen as features of the girls' problematic behaviour' (Gelsthorpe, 1989: 6). Representations of delinquent girls as lonely and socially isolated individuals, acting out their psychological disturbances, were commonplace. Psychologist T.C.N. Gibbens, for example, declared that girls' acquisitive offending, which he believed was superseded by sexual delinquency in mid-adolescence, resulted from unhappiness and a lack of love:

[M]any unhappy girls who before puberty play truant, and steal from home or from shops, turn at 15 to disobedience at home, staying out late, running away and making undesirable friendships with boys. Waywardness may replace delinquency in those for whom stealing represented a substitute for affection. (1959: 86)

In the twenty-first century, the popular spotlight has been increasingly directed at 'underclass' young women, whose assumed 'trashiness', and sometimes sexual orientation, are frequently highlighted by the popular press (Chesney-Lind and Eliason, 2006; Sharpe, 2012). Aided by new technologies, girls – and particularly their bodies – have become hyper-visible in popular discourse and the subject of recurrent moral panics, allegedly becoming increasingly 'mean', violent and 'wild' (Chesney-Lind and Irwin, 2008). Spurious claims have been made that a 'new breed' of female criminal has emerged, and even that girls' offending will eventually outstrip that of their male counterparts. In an ostensibly 'post-feminist' world, contemporary fears about young women's alcohol consumption and violent behaviour in public purview arguably reflect a desire to uphold or reinstate traditional gender roles and expectations.

# RECENT TRENDS IN GIRLS' LAWBREAKING AND CRIMINALISATION

Girls and women break the law significantly less than boys and men, and those who do offend commit less serious and less frequent offences. Girls account for fewer than one-fifth of offences committed by young people under 18, and around 5 per cent of imprisoned young people in England and Wales (Ministry of Justice, 2014a[1]), and are similarly under-represented in crime and justice statistics internationally. Self-report studies indicate a slightly more convergent pattern of lawbreaking between the sexes than these official statistics suggest: for example, 26 per cent of men and 17 per cent of women aged 10–25 report having broken the law at least once during the past year (Roe and Ashe, 2008). However, the gender disparity becomes substantially more marked where frequent and/or serious offending (including burglary, robbery, selling drugs and assault resulting in injury) is concerned (Roe and Ashe, 2008; Smith and McAra, 2004).

Lawbreaking by females is a particularly youthful pursuit. In England and Wales at present, for example, female offending peaks at 14–15 years (some 3–4 years younger than males), at which age the gender gap in offending is smallest and 26 per cent of girls (compared with 37 per cent of boys) report having committed at least one offence during the previous 12 months (Roe and Ashe, 2008).[2] Young women 'grow out of crime' (Rutherford, 1986) rather sooner than their male counterparts: two-fifths of boys under 18, compared with one-quarter of girls, are apprehended for re-offending within 12 months of being sentenced or receiving an out-of-court disposal, and the gender gap widens further with age (Ministry of Justice, 2014a).

The racialisation of youth punishment, although rarely discussed through the lens of gender, is also very significant. Minority girls, like their male counterparts, are over-policed, under protected (Miller, 2008; Webster, this volume) and disproportionately punished (Feilzer and Hood, 2004; May et al., 2010). One British survey of girls in custody found that 44 per cent of black and minority ethnic (BME) girls, compared with 14 per cent of white girls, reported

---

[1] In October 2013 there were 54 girls and 1,123 boys in custody in England and Wales (Ministry of Justice, 20141b).

[2] The peak age for male self-reported offending in England and Wales hovered around 18 for many years, although the latest Offending Crime and Justice Survey data put the peak for both males and females in the mid-teenage years (Roe and Ashe, 2008).

having been victimised by custodial staff (Worsley, 2006). The double punishments meted out to Asian girls in trouble with the law in England (Toor, 2009) and the excessive criminalisation of Gitana girls in Spain (Pozo Gordaliza, 2013) provide further evidence of racial disproportionality in the punishment of young women, albeit that both populations are invisible in their respective jurisdictions' official crime and punishment statistics. Relatively little is known about the penal governance of migrant or trafficked girls (although see O'Connell Davidson, 2011; Pearce et al., 2013), although recent studies highlighting the inappropriate criminalisation of sexually exploited young women (Phoenix, 2012) and adult migrant women (Hales and Gelsthorpe, 2012) suggest that it might be substantial.

Young women's historically low involvement in criminal offending has been challenged during the past twenty years by statistical 'evidence' indicating a dramatic rise in girls' lawbreaking, and particularly female violence, across Western jurisdictions, a trend which a proliferation of newspaper headlines have blamed on 'ladette culture' and female binge drinking (Sharpe, 2012) – the purportedly 'dark side' of female emancipation (Chesney-Lind and Irwin, 2008).[3] However, the increase in female youth crime evident in official statistics has been subjected to extensive critical examination and found to be unrelated to any significant change in young women's behaviour. Rather, the rise appears to be an artefact of 'zero tolerance' policing (Bateman, this volume; Steffensmeier et al., 2005), as well as the reclassification of welfare matters – including running away from home and arguments with family members – as either violent crimes or technical violations for 'failure to comply' (Sprott and Doob, 2009).

A brief analysis of recent trends in recorded female youth crime in England and Wales provides a striking illustration of the vicissitudinous nature of policy change in the construction of girl offenders. Offending by girls under 18, according to official sources, increased by 41 per cent between 2002/03 and 2006/07 alone, while violent crime rose by a massive 80 per cent during the same four-year period, generating considerable public and political anxiety.[4] Detailed empirical analysis revealed that the apparent crime wave was artefactual, and driven by changes in policing practices, most notably a national government target, introduced in 2002, to increase the number of 'offences brought to justice' (OBTJ). The target had the unintended effect of criminalising minor offences committed by unsophisticated and easy-to-catch offenders – namely children and young people, and particularly girls (Bateman, 2008; Bateman, this volume; Sharpe, 2012).

---

[3] This 'liberation hypothesis' is not new (see, for example, Adler, 1975). However, the contemporary twin focus on *young* women and *violent* crime represents a departure from earlier concerns about women's lawbreaking in general.

[4] Recorded offences amongst females under 18 increased from 41,833 in 2002/03 to 59,236 in 2006/07, and violent offences increased from 8,702 to 15,672 during this period (Youth Justice Board 2004, 2008).

Between 2006/07 and 2012/13 the upward trend swiftly – and rather unexpectedly – reversed, and recorded female youth offending dropped even more dramatically than it had risen in the preceding period, proving an exception to continuing international increases in young women's crime rates. During these years the number of recorded offences committed by girls fell by more than 70 per cent, while violent offences decreased by 64 per cent.[5] The most credible explanation for the crime drop is the modification, in 2007, of the earlier OBTJ target to focus only on serious offences, and its removal altogether in 2010 (Bateman, this volume; Morgan and Newburn, 2012). Additionally, in July 2008, the then government set a target to reduce the number of first-time entrants into the youth justice system, thereby encouraging informal responses to youthful misbehaviour amongst children with no previous police 'form' (ibid.). This policy had the exact opposite effect of the earlier OBTJ target and led to a sharp drop in female (and male) recorded youth crime – and thus in the number of criminalised young women. However, it seems that this fall was no less artefactual than the rise that preceded it.

## OUT OF PLACE: CRIMINALISED GIRLS' RISKY VULNERABILITIES

Biographical studies of girls in the youth justice system have repeatedly shown that their lives are characterised and constrained by poverty, victimisation, family disruption and violence, educational exclusion, state 'care' and (often related) substance misuse and mental ill health (Batchelor, 2005; Schaffner, 2006; Sharpe, 2012). Their substantial welfare needs, as well as concerns about their sexual behaviour, have, ironically, long been used as grounds for extensive penal (and often punitive) intervention. At the height of welfarism in youth justice during the 1970s, the moral policing of girls by the police and the courts reflected broader concerns about the dangers of female emancipation and attendant sexual freedoms, and girls were often sentenced as harshly, if not more so, for transgressing 'feminine' behavioural norms as they were for breaking the law (Carrington, 1993; Smart, 1976). Young women fared little better in the justice approach of the 1980s and subsequently; indeed, they were arguably 'responsibilised' and punished, in gender-neutral mode, on the spurious basis of 'equal opportunities' (Worrall, 2004), with little or no regard for the gendered and generational context of their lives or their crimes, a practice which Chesney-Lind (2006) has described as 'vengeful equity'.

---

[5] Recorded crimes fell from 59,236 in 2006/07 to 17,546 in 2012/13, and violent offences dropped from 15,672 to 5,691 (Ministry of Justice, 2014a; Youth Justice Board, 2008).

The ascendancy of risk in youth justice since the 1990s has also had particular implications for the penal control of girls. Hannah-Moffat's (2005) contention that risk and need have become increasingly hybridised reinvigorates long-standing concerns about the elastic and ambiguous nature of risk where women and girls are concerned (Hudson, 1989). Risk has arguably become the dominant paradigm in contemporary youth justice policy in England and Wales (and elsewhere), as reflected in the youth justice system's principal statutory aim of offending prevention[6] and the implementation, in 2010, of the 'Scaled Approach', a systematised actuarial framework for determining levels of intervention for young people subject to criminal court orders (Youth Justice Board, 2010; for a critical analysis, see Case and Haines, this volume). The basis of the Scaled Approach is this: a young person is assessed, using the standardised 'Asset risk/need' assessment tool; an individual risk score is calculated, and this score determines one of three recommended tiers or levels of intervention – standard, enhanced or intensive. The Scaled Approach is intended, inter alia, to assist youth justice practitioners in recommending the most appropriate sentence for a young person, leading one commentator to claim that it has 'institutionalis[ed] the risk minimisation imperative at the point of sentence' (Bateman, 2011: 173). The risk-led logic of the Scaled Approach demands an intervention (i.e. punishment) that is commensurate with the intensity of a young person's risks/needs or problems, rather than proportionate to the seriousness of her offending. Girls' substantial needs in relation to victimisation, mental health and other gendered 'vulnerabilities' may be translated into elevated risk scores warranting more intensive penal control. The very limited evidence that exists indicates that practitioners may 'over score' girls when completing risk/need assessments (Baker et al., 2005) – in other words, girls may be assessed as high risk on the basis that they have complex and considerable welfare needs, despite presenting little danger to society. All other things being equal, young women appearing in court are more likely than young men to receive restrictive community penalties (Feilzer and Hood, 2004), reflecting assumptions that they require moral tutelage or guidance. In addition, there is a long history of 'protective' incarceration where girls are concerned (Cox, 2003).

Of special pertinence to young women is the contemporary 'vulnerability zeitgeist' (Brown, 2014), wherein certain girls and women are positioned as having 'particular vulnerabilities' (Corston, 2007) which render them 'at risk' of offending. Despite the benevolent connotations of assignations of vulnerability, some critics have argued that the term is paternalistic (Brown, 2014). Moreover, it may serve to individualise problems or disadvantages which are social-structural in origin (Case and Haines, this volume). Along with the label 'at risk', evidence of girls' vulnerabilities – some of which may have arisen due to increased conditionality in youth welfare and leisure services, or indeed their reconfiguration as crime prevention programmes, as well as an absence of pastoral support at school – may serve to legitimate punishment in the name of

---

[6] Crime and Disorder Act 1998, section 37. Muncie (2006) reminds us that in practice, welfare, justice and risk imperatives co-exist, often with contradictory effects.

both protection and offending prevention. We might suggest that this is 'covert punishment'.

Conceptualising girls' delinquency as a mental health issue also risks individualising their problems. While we broadly support a psychosocial understanding of girls' offending (Ryder, 2013), at least in some circumstances, the social is often invisible in proposals as to how best to divert young women from offending. For example, a report by the Centre for Mental Health importantly highlights the extremely high prevalence of abuse, victimisation, family-related trauma and school-related problems in gang-associated girls' lives (Khan et al., 2013; see also Miller, 2001; Young, 2011).[7] However, some of the interventions proposed by the report's authors to reduce girls' involvement in gangs – including 'building robust neural architecture in [girl] infants' by 'providing [their] expectant mothers with support' in order to 'reduce the impact of … toxic stress' and 'jump-start electrical activity in the brain' (Khan et al., 2013: 22) – are problematic and potentially highly stigmatising.

# GENDER-SPECIFIC PROGRAMMING: DOING JUSTICE TO GIRLS?

The relatively low – although in many jurisdictions, growing – proportion of young women in the youth justice system has led a number of critics to contend that girls have been shoe-horned into inappropriate, and even damaging, services designed for young men (Bloom and Covington, 2001; Bloom et al., 2002, 2003). Young women in penal custody have suffered even greater structural and familial disadvantages than girls who are subject to community supervision (Douglas and Plugge, 2006; Jacobson et al., 2010), and their experiences of profound adversity interact with particular gendered and generational pains of imprisonment, including being held far from home and the use of solitary confinement as a form of behaviour management.[8] Recent data from England and Wales indicate that young women are apprehended for assaults

---

[7] We acknowledge that definitions of gangs and gang membership are fiercely contested (Aldridge et al., 2008) and that young women involved in gangs or 'on road' in British research – in so far as they are acknowledged at all – have generally been dichotomously presented as either highly masculinised or as hapless victims or sex objects (see Batchelor, 2011 and Young, 2011 for further discussion). The Centre for Mental Health report exemplifies the latter perspective (Khan et al., 2013).

[8] A case in point is the ongoing public inquiry into the management by Her Majesty's Prison Service of 'SP', a 16 year old girl who self-harmed in prison over a period of more than two years between 2003 and 2005, and was frequently held in solitary confinement as a response to her distressed behaviour. SP was hospitalised more than 20 times following the loss of large volumes of blood, before finally obtaining an injunction preventing her return to prison, leading to her eventual transfer to a psychiatric institution.

committed in prison at twice the rate of young men; similarly, they are restrained by prison staff twice as often as their male counterparts, which may well reflect differential behavioural expectations. Of greatest concern is the startling frequency of self-harm amongst incarcerated girls – around six times the already extremely high rate of young men (Ministry of Justice, 2014a: 44–6).

The number of girls sentenced to and remanded in custody has, in line with other groups, increased significantly in recent years (notwithstanding a recent overall drop in numbers of young people in custody in England and Wales) (Goldson, this volume). Observers of the massive increase in the use of custody for young women in the USA have argued that one of the reasons for the increase is a lack of community alternatives (Chesney-Lind et al., 2008). However, evidence from England and Wales indicates that the number of girls both in penal custody and subject to community penalties during the last decade have increased – and subsequently decreased – in tandem with one another (Sharpe, 2012). In fact, the size of the female (and male) youth custodial population in England and Wales appears to have been driven primarily by activity at the 'front end' of the youth justice system – namely the number of young people arrested and charged (Bateman, 2012; Bateman, this volume). Moreover, although the provision of gender-specific criminal justice services for adult women has undergone considerable expansion during the last decade, the number of women being imprisoned, most notably for short sentences or on remand, has continued to rise sharply, due to a failure to effect meaningful policy change (Hedderman, 2012), but also, importantly, due to an expansion of discourses legitimating women's imprisonment on the grounds that the prison, in addition to (or even instead of) its incapacitative purpose, is able to provide respite, therapy, protection or other forms of 'help' to vulnerable women (Carlen and Tombs, 2006).

The increase in the use of penal custody for girls has prompted calls for more gender-specific youth justice programmes and services, on the grounds that young women's developmental pathways, including their routes into offending, are different from those of boys, and the idea that relationships are of central importance in girls' identity construction (Bloom and Covington, 2001; Bloom et al., 2002; Greene et al., 1998). The now-frequent criticism that risk assessment tools, and the youth justice interventions and programmes based on them, are derived from samples of males has prompted scholarship examining gender differences in risk factors for offending (Belknap and Holsinger, 2006; Bloom et al., 2002). Drawing on the findings of 'feminist pathways' research – most notably, evidence that there is a substantial overlap between abuse victimisation and subsequent lawbreaking by young women – this body of work has also highlighted the prevalence of mental health problems, self-harm, substance misuse and low self-esteem amongst girls in conflict with the law.

However, the epistemological basis of gender-specific risk factors research is not unproblematic. Claims that risk factors for offending, and by implication young women's 'programming needs', are structured principally by gender tend to rely on research evidence from surveys of practitioners or samples of incarcerated young women. The subjective nature of practitioners' assessments and the potential for gender stereotyping, wherein judgements about the respectability and reformability of girls may be influenced by 'race' and class considerations, are rarely discussed. Moreover, there may be important differences between young women who break the law and those caught up in the youth justice system; the majority of young women's offences evade detection, and arrest, charge and sentencing patterns are subject to bias according to class and ethnicity (McAra and McVie, 2005; White and Cunneen, this volume; Webster, this volume), as well as gender (Feilzer and Hood, 2004; May et al., 2010). Like their older counterparts, white middle-class girls rarely find themselves within the purview of the courts, a fact that has received scarcely any criminological attention. And while some studies have emphasised that the experience of abuse, bereavement and other traumatic events over-determines boys' routes into offending, as well as those of girls (Belknap and Holsinger, 2006), the search for a list of gender-specific needs may have the effect of merely replacing one prescriptive menu of targets for correctional intervention with another, or a male norm with a female one (Hannah-Moffat, 2010), and fails to acknowledge contextual differences in how girls' experiences of oppression and injustice differ according to generation, class and ethnicity (Goodkind, 2005).

Whilst relatively slow to be established elsewhere, gender-specific programming (GSP) is now well-established in the USA, with its own funding streams and policy and practice documentation (Greene et al., 1998; Morgan and Patton, 2002), and is widely believed to be a positive development. The conceptual starting point of GSP is that girls and women are gendered subjects, with particular, gendered, social experiences, who therefore require a holistic, therapeutic approach to intervention in recognition of the social origins of their troubles. However, GSP as a response to lawbreaking is enacted within a risk reduction/offending prevention framework: it 'aims to help girls already in trouble, while preventing future delinquency among girls who are at risk' (see Greene et al., 1998: Summary). Consequently, the holistic intent of GSP, which, in theory, recognises the impact of the disadvantaged structural positioning of young women, is subordinated to a risk reduction rationality, with the result that the target for intervention becomes the individual, rather than society, and oppressive social experiences are translated into individual, predominantly psychological, risks/needs. Empirical research examining the practice of gender-specific therapeutic governance in penal – and especially carceral – settings in the USA and Canada has revealed that efforts to empower women and girls and improve their self-esteem have functioned as a mode of governmentality, targeting individual psychological needs rather than social circumstances (Goodkind, 2009; Haney, 2010; Pollack, 2007). As a consequence, instead of improving the social conditions experienced by *all women*, the focus becomes 'to promote the transformation of *individual women, one at a time*' (Goodkind, 2009: 400, italics added).

Addressing need in a (punitive) penal context inevitably surrenders to the logic of risk reduction and fails to challenge the legitimacy of penal responses to young women's behaviour. One of the most consistent findings of feminist research on girls' pathways into offending is that criminalised young women have a range of 'vulnerabilities', some of which relate to their experiences of victimisation at the hands of (usually male) family members, boyfriends and peers (see Chesney-Lind and Shelden, 2004: ch. 6 for an overview). Those who have harmed these young women are rarely brought to justice, and the state frequently fails to protect such girls from further victimisation. In view of this, for a young woman to be ordered, as a result of what may be a relatively minor infraction of the law, to undertake a community or custodial penalty aimed at addressing her past victimisation experiences, low self-esteem, 'risky' relationship choices and so on, in order to prevent further offending by her (and often in the absence of any therapeutic support having been offered prior to her arrest) has very questionable legitimacy.

A final but crucial consideration is whether GSP facilitates young women's desistance from offending. Given that any involvement in the formal youth justice system may be iatrogenic (McAra and McVie, 2007; McAra and McVie, this volume; Petrosino et al., 2010) and impede the natural maturational process of desistance which, as discussed above, tends to occur earlier and more quickly for girls than for boys, an important question is whether GSP reduces young women's (re)offending. There is scant evidence as to 'what works' with criminalised young women. Zahn et al.'s (2009) review of 16 programmes for girls in custody or under juvenile justice supervision in the USA[9] highlights the paucity of the evidence-base as well as substantial flaws in the small number of extant evaluations, including weak research designs, inadequate sample sizes, an absence of control groups, and differing outcome measures. It is important to note that the proliferation of gender-specific youth justice programmes in the USA in recent years has not led to a reduction in the number of criminalised girls; indeed, quite the reverse.

# JUSTICE WITHOUT WELFARE?

Notable in their absence from discussions about GSP – or indeed responses to young female lawbreakers more broadly – are the perspectives of girls subject to youth justice sanctions, and what little research there is paints a far from positive picture. Of particular concern are criminalised young women's frequent histories of 'welfare inaction' (Myers, 2013). Many of the girls interviewed by Sharpe (2011) were angry at their treatment by teachers and social workers and felt a sense of injustice at their abandonment by 'helping' professionals. A frequent refrain was that youth justice intervention had failed

---

[9] Of these 16 programmes nine targeted girls only, while six targeted both girls and boys.

to effect change in their everyday circumstances. What welfare and education professionals' (in)actions communicate to young women, in terms of the extent to which they are valued as people, have important intrapsychic consequences as well as setting the tone for subsequent interactions with criminal justice professionals. Failure to provide material and welfare assistance may over-determine young women's lawbreaking and also their entry into the formal justice system, as well as render desistance and rehabilitation meaningless. Crucially, welfare inaction serves to construct criminalised young women as 'self-reliant subjects … [who must] negotiate the dangerous outside world on their own' or, worse, with the aid of toxic substances and/or exploitative men (Myers, 2013: 229).

# CONCLUSION: DIRECTIONS FOR THE FUTURE

Recent attempts to further knowledge about risk factors for girls' offending, and to refine or reformulate criminal justice programmes for them, have ultimately done little to reconceptualise justice for young women. Moreover, the search to identify gender-specific needs has not nearly been matched by scholarship focusing on the institutional processes and practices which lead girls into the justice system. We suggest, therefore, that future research needs to transgress the narrow boundaries of crime and criminal justice and focus, as did earlier work (Cain, 1989), on how practitioners – including education and welfare professionals – recognise (or fail to recognise) and respond to (or ignore) girls' routine experiences of victimisation, neglect and other violations, and how young women's encounters with state agencies vary by age, ethnicity and class, as well as across different jurisdictions and practice cultures.

Turning to policy and practice, the best way to meet the needs of 'vulnerable' girls, criminalised or otherwise, is by addressing and ameliorating the structural, patriarchal and anti-youth systems that have failed to protect them from violence (and neglected to punish those who have used violence against them) and to educate them adequately, and the fiscal policies that constrain their capacity for independence, such as increased conditionality and tougher sanctions with regard to state assistance and a shift from welfare to workfare. To this end, a new justice strategy, and one well aligned with the aim of empowering young women, would be the development of critical education projects oriented towards social action, in order to help young women lawbreakers:

> [M]ake sense of their biographies by analysing the ways in which larger social forces have shaped their families, communities and individual life chances [such that] attempting to change social structure *becomes the intervention*. (Goddard and Myers, 2011: 662–3, italics added)

Such critical political engagement might also enable the anger that precipitates some girls' lawbreaking – most notably violence towards others, as well as towards themselves – to be channelled into less destructive ends, with transformative potential for individual girls themselves and also for other young women. Attempts should be made to bring young women together across agency boundaries, in recognition that criminalised young women have much in common with other 'risky' girls, such as teenage mothers, drug misusers and sex workers, whose different institutional labels are likely to conceal many common experiences.

# REFERENCES

Aapola, S., Gonick, M. and Harris, A. (eds) (2005) *Young Femininity: Girlhood, Power and Social Change*. Basingstoke: Palgrave Macmillan.

Adler, F. (1975) *Sisters in Crime*. New York: McGraw-Hill.

Aldridge, J., Medina, J. and Ralphs, R. (2008) 'Dangers and problems of doing "gang" research in the UK', in van Gemert, F., Peterson, D. and Lien, I.-L. (eds), *Street Gangs, Migration and Ethnicity*. Cullompton: Willan.

Baker, K., Jones, S., Merrington, S. and Roberts, C. (2005) *Further Development of Asset*. London: Youth Justice Board.

Batchelor, S. (2005) '"Prove me the bam!" Victimisation and agency in the lives of young women who commit violent offences', *Probation Journal*, 52 (4): 358–375.

Batchelor, S. (2011) 'Beyond dichotomy: towards an explanation of young women's involvement in violent street gangs', in Goldso, B. (ed.), *Youth in Crisis? 'Gangs', Territoriality and Violence*. Abingdon: Routledge.

Bateman, T. (2008) '"Target practice": sanction detection and the criminalisation of children', *Criminal Justice Matters*, 73 (1): 2–4.

Bateman, T. (2011) 'Punishing poverty: the "Scaled Approach" and youth justice practice', *Howard Journal of Criminal Justice*, 50: 171–83.

Bateman, T. (2012) 'Who pulled the plug? Towards an explanation of the fall in child imprisonment in England and Wales', *Youth Justice*, 12: 36–52.

Belknap, J. and Holsinger, K. (2006) 'The gendered nature of risk factors for delinquency', *Feminist Criminology*, 1: 48–71.

Bloom, B. and Covington, S. (2001) 'Effective gender-responsive interventions in juvenile justice: addressing the lives of delinquent girls'. Paper presented at the 2001 Annual Meeting of the American Society of Criminology. Atlanta, Georgia, 7–10 November.

Bloom, B., Owen, B., Deschenes, E.P. and Rosenbaum, J. (2002) 'Moving toward justice for female juvenile offenders in the new millennium: modelling gender-specific policies and programs', *Journal of Contemporary Criminal Justice*, 18: 37–56.

Bloom, B., Owen, B., Rosenbaum, J. and Deschenes, E.P. (2003) 'Focusing on girls and young women: a gendered perspective on female delinquency', *Women and Criminal Justice*, 14: 117–36.

Brown, K. (2014) 'Questioning the vulnerability zeitgeist: care and control practices with 'vulnerable' young people', *Social Policy and Society*, 13 (3): 1–17.

Cain, M. (ed.) (1989) *Growing Up Good: Policing the Behaviour of Girls in Europe*. London: Sage.

Carlen, P. and Tombs, J. (2006) 'Reconfigurations of penality: the ongoing case of the women's imprisonment and reintegration industries', *Theoretical Criminology*, 19: 337–60.

Carrington, K. (1993) *Offending Girls: Sex, Youth and Justice*. St. Leonards, NSW: Allen and Unwin.

Chesney-Lind, M. (2006) 'Patriarchy, crime, and justice: feminist criminology in an era of backlash', *Feminist Criminology*, 1 (1): 6–26.

Chesney-Lind, M. and Eliason, M. (2006) 'From invisible to incorrigible: the demonization of marginalized women and girls', *Crime, Media, Culture*, 2: 29–47.

Chesney-Lind, M. and Irwin, K. (2008) *Beyond Bad Girls: Gender, Violence and Hype*. New York: Routledge.

Chesney-Lind, M. and Shelden, R.G. (2004) *Girls, Delinquency and Juvenile Justice*, 3rd edn. Belmont, CA: Wadsworth.

Chesney-Lind, M., Morash, M. and Stevens, T. (2008) 'Girls' troubles, girls' delinquency, and gender responsive programming: a review', *Australian and New Zealand Journal of Criminology*, 41: 162–89.

Corston, J. (2007) *The Corston Report: A Review of Women with Particular Vulnerabilities in the Criminal Justice System*. London: Home Office.

Cox, P. (2003) *Gender, Justice and Welfare: Bad Girls in Britain, 1900–1950*. Basingstoke: Palgrave Macmillan.

Douglas, N. and Plugge, E. (2006) *Female Health Needs in Young Offender Institutions*. London: Youth Justice Board.

Feilzer, M. and Hood, R., in consultation with Fitzgerald, M. and Roddam, A. (2004) *Differences or Discrimination? Minority Ethnic Young People in the Youth Justice System*. London: Youth Justice Board.

Gelsthorpe, L. (1989) *Sexism and the Female Offender*. Aldershot: Gower.

Gibbens, T.C.N. (1959) 'Supervision and probation of adolescent girls', *British Journal of Delinquency*, 10: 84–103.

Goddard, T. and Myers, R. (2011) 'Democracy and demonstration in the gray area of neo-liberalism: a case study of Free LA High School', *British Journal of Criminology*, 51 (4): 652–70.

Goodkind, S. (2005) 'Gender-specific services in the juvenile justice system: a critical examination', *Affilia*, 20: 52–70.

Goodkind, S. (2009) '"You can be anything you want, but you have to believe it": commercialized feminism in gender-specific programs for girls', *Signs*, 34: 397–422.

Greene, Peters, & Associates (1998) *Guiding Principles for Promising Female Programming: An Inventory of Best Practices*. Washington, DC: Office of Juvenile Justice and Delinquency Prevention. 'Summary' available at: www.ojjdp.gov/pubs/principles/exesum.html (accessed 1.10.14).

Hales, L. and Gelsthorpe, L. (2012) *The Criminalisation of Migrant Women*. Cambridge: Institute of Criminology, University of Cambridge.

Haney, L. (2010) *Offending Women: Power, Punishment, and the Regulation of Desire*. Berkeley, CA: University of California Press.

Hannah-Moffat, K. (2005) 'Criminogenic needs and the transformative risk subject: hybridizations of risk/need in penality', *Punishment and Society*, 7 (1): 29–51.

Hannah-Moffat, K. (2010) 'Sacrosanct or flawed: risk, accountability and gender-responsive penal politics', *Current Issues in Criminal Justice*, 22: 193–215.

Hedderman, C. (2012) *Empty Cells or Empty Words? Government Policy on Reducing the Number of Women Going to Prison*. London: Criminal Justice Alliance.

Hudson, A. (1989) '"Troublesome girls": towards alternative definitions and policies', in Cain, M. (ed.), *Growing Up Good: Policing the Behaviour of Girls in Europe*. London: Sage.

Jackson, C. and Tinkler, P. (2007) '"Ladettes" and "Modern Girls": "troublesome" young femininities', *Sociological Review*, 55 (2): 251–72.

Jacobson, J., Bhardwa, B., Gyateng, T., Hunter, G. and Hough, M. (2010) *Punishing Disadvantage: A Profile of Children in Custody*. London: Prison Reform Trust.

Khan, L., Brice, H., Saunders, A. and Plumtree, A. (2013) *A Need to Belong: What Leads Girls to Join Gangs*. London: Centre for Mental Health.

May, T., Gyateng, T. and Hough, M. (2010) *Differential Treatment in the Youth Justice System*. London: Equalities and Human Rights Commission.

McAra, L. and McVie, S. (2005) 'The usual suspects? Street-life, young people and the police', *Criminal Justice*, 5: 5–36.

McAra, L. and McVie, S. (2007) 'Youth justice? The impact of agency contact on patterns of desistance from offending', *European Journal of Criminology*, 4 (3): 315–45.

Miller, J. (2001) *One of the Guys: Girls, Gangs and Gender*. New York: Oxford University Press.

Miller, J. (2008) *Getting Played: African American Girls, Urban Inequality, and Gendered Violence*. New York: New York University Press.

Ministry of Justice (2014a) *Youth Justice Statistics 2012/13*. London: Ministry of Justice.

Ministry of Justice (2014b) *Youth Custody Report*. London: Ministry of Justice. Available at: www.gov.uk/government/publications/youth-custody-data (accessed 30.9.14).

Morgan, M. and Patton, P. (2002) 'Gender-responsive programming in the justice system – Oregon's guidelines for effective programming for girls', *Federal Probation*, 66: 57–65.

Morgan, R. and Newburn, T. (2012) 'Youth crime and justice: rediscovering devolution, discretion, and diversion?', in Maguire, M., Morgan, R. and Reiner, R. (eds), *The Oxford Handbook of Criminology*, 5th edn. Oxford: Oxford University Press. pp. 490–530.

Muncie, J. (2006) 'Governing young people: coherence and contradiction in contemporary youth justice', *Critical Social Policy*, 26 (4): 770–93.

Myers, R. (2013) 'The biographical and psychic consequences of "welfare inaction" for young women in trouble with the law', *Youth Justice*, 13 (3): 218–33.

O'Connell Davidson, J. (2011) 'Moving children? Child trafficking, child migration, and child rights', *Critical Social Policy*, 31 (3): 454–77.

Pearce, J., Hynes, P. and Bovarnick, S. (2013) *Trafficked Young People: Breaking the Wall of Silence*. London: Routledge.

Petrosino, A., Turpin-Petrosino, C. and Guckenburg, S. (2010) *Formal System Processing on Juveniles: Effects on Delinquency*. Oslo: The Campbell Collaboration.

Phoenix, J. (2012) *Out of Place: The Policing and Criminalisation of Sexually Exploited Girls and Young Women*. London: The Howard League.

Pollack, S. (2007) '"I'm just not good in relationships": victimization discourses and the gendered regulation of criminalized women', *Feminist Criminology*, 2: 158–74.

Pozo Gordaliza, R. (2013) 'Young Gitana women and punishment in Andalusia', in Malloch, M. and McIvor, G. (eds), *Women, Punishment and Social Justice*. Abingdon: Routledge. pp. 178–93.

Priestley, P., Fears, D. and Fuller, R. (1977) *Justice for Juveniles: The 1969 Children and Young Persons Act: A Case for Reform*. London: Routledge and Kegan Paul.

Roe, S. and Ashe, J. (2008) *Young People and Crime: Findings from the 2006 Offending, Crime and Justice Survey*, Home Office Statistical Bulletin 09/08. London: Home Office.

Rutherford, A. (1986) *Growing Out of Crime: Society and Young People in Trouble*. Harmondsworth: Penguin.

Ryder, J. (2013) *Girls and Violence: Tracing the Roots of Criminal Behavior*. Boulder, CO: Lynne Rienner.

Schaffner, L. (2006) *Girls in Trouble with the Law*. New Brunswick, NJ: Rutgers University Press.

Sharpe, G. (2011) 'Beyond youth justice: working with girls and young women who offend', in Sheehan, R., McIvor, G. and Trotter, C. (eds), *Working with Women Offenders in the Community*. Cullompton: Willan. pp. 151–72.

Sharpe, G. (2012) *Offending Girls: Young Women and Youth Justice*. Abingdon: Routledge.

Smart, C. (1976) *Women, Crime and Criminology: A Feminist Critique*. London: Routledge and Kegan Paul.

Smith, D. and McAra, L. (2004) *Gender and Youth Offending*, Edinburgh Study of Youth Transitions and Crime Research Digest No. 2. Edinburgh: Centre for Law and Society, University of Edinburgh.

Sprott, J.B. and Doob, A.N. (2009) *Justice for Girls? Stability and Change in the Youth Justice Systems of the United States and Canada*. Chicago, IL: University of Chicago Press.

Steffensmeier, D., Schwartz, J., Zhong, H. and Ackerman, J. (2005) 'An assessment of recent trends in girls' violence using diverse longitudinal sources: is the gender gap closing?', *Criminology*, 43 (2): 355–406.

Toor, S. (2009) 'British Asian girls, crime and youth justice,' *Youth Justice*, 9 (3): 239–54.

Worrall, A. (2004) 'Twisted sisters, ladettes, and the new penology: the social construction of "violent girls"', in Alder, C. and Worrall, A. (eds), *Girls' Violence: Myths and Realities*. Albany, NT: State University of New York Press.

Worsley, R. (2006) *Young People in Custody 2004–2006: An Analysis of Children's Experiences of Prison*. London: Her Majesty's Inspectorate of Prisons/Youth Justice Board.

Young, T. (2011) 'In search of the "shemale" gangster', in Goldson, B. (ed.), *Youth in Crisis? 'Gangs', Territoriality and Violence*. Abingdon: Routledge.

Youth Justice Board (2004) *Youth Justice Annual Statistics 2002/03*. London: Youth Justice Board.

Youth Justice Board (2008) *Youth Justice Annual Workload Data 2006/07*. London: Youth Justice Board.

Youth Justice Board (2010) *Youth Justice: The Scaled Approach*. London: Youth Justice Board.

Zahn, M.A., Day, J.C., Mihalic, S.F. and Tichavsky, L. (2009) 'Determining what works for girls in the juvenile justice system', *Crime and Delinquency*, 55: 266–93.

# PART TWO

## TRENDS, EVIDENCE, POLICY AND PRACTICE

# 5 TRENDS IN DETECTED YOUTH CRIME AND CONTEMPORARY STATE RESPONSES

## TIM BATEMAN

It is one of the ironies of recent youth justice history in England and Wales that as youth crime became increasingly politicised, from the early 1990s onwards (Goldson, 1999; Pitts, 2000), politicians attempted to legitimise their respective prescriptions for dealing with children who contravened the law in apolitical terms as value-free manifestations of where the evidence led. New Labour, while in power (1997–2010), was insistent that 'what matters is what works' (Stephenson et al., 2011: 1), but the Conservative/Liberal Democrat Coalition government, elected in May 2010, was equally concerned to emphasise its commitment to '*effective*' punishment (Ministry of Justice, 2010). Frequently, statistical information is adduced in support of such claims as hard incontrovertible 'fact', implying thereby that any criticism of the trajectory of policy involves a wilful disregard of the evidence-base.

But it is not so obvious that statistical data point unambiguously to the conclusions drawn by successive administrations; nor is it clear that recent trends justify the assumptions around which policy has been shaped. Indeed, one might note that, on attaining power, new governments are keen to distance themselves from the youth justice agenda of their predecessors, even though the knowledge base remains largely unchanged. In 1997, New Labour sought 'to draw a line under the past ... [with] a new approach to tackling youth crime' (Home Office, 1997: 1). For its part, the Coalition government proclaimed 'a fundamental break with the failed and expensive policies of the past ... finding out what works' (Ministry of Justice, 2010: 2). Arguably, in both cases, while the swings in electoral fortune comprised shifts of some significance, the scale of discontinuity was exaggerated for political effect. Roger Smith (2007), for example, points out that few of New Labour's early reforms where incompatible with the law and order agenda of the previous Conservative administration. Conversely, the three targets for youth justice set by the Conservative/Liberal Democrat Coalition government – to effect reductions in first-time entrants to the system, reoffending and custody – had each concerned New Labour prior to the election. But, to the extent that change of government signalled policy change, the claims of both administrations to be evidence-led is testimony to the manner in which *different* policies and practices are legitimised by reference to the *same* underlying statistical 'evidence'.

# PROBLEMS OF INTERPRETATION

There is no shortage of crime data in England and Wales. Annual Criminal justice statistics report on offences that lead to a formal outcome and are disaggregated by age. Since 2002/03, the Youth Justice Board for England and Wales (YJB) has published yearly data pertaining specifically to youth crime. These are supplemented by police-recorded offences, large-scale victimisation surveys (particularly the Crime Survey for England and Wales (CSEW)[1]) and studies of self-reported offending. Any analysis of youth crime has, accordingly, a plenitude of statistical information from which to draw, but the various sources of data can be read in different ways (Maguire, 2012).

In January 2008, the *Daily Telegraph* reported a 21 per cent rise in youth crime between 2003 and 2006 while adult offending had increased by less than 1 per cent (Leapman, 2008). The article implied that the growth in the former was a consequence of leniency, since 'more than half of young offenders were let off with cautions, whereby they … were spared a court appearance and were not punished' (Leapman, 2008). A year later, relying on equivalent figures, the *Sunday Express* similarly contended that youth crime was both rising and becoming more serious (Jeory and Douglas, 2009) although the explanation proffered – that the 'worst' offences 'often mimic the most violent computer games and films so freely available in Britain today' – had a different interpretive gloss. The emphasis focused particularly on the behaviour of girls that was (mis) represented as 'an unprecedented crime wave among teenage girls' (cited in Sharpe, 2012:1). Such reporting leaned heavily on sources of official statistical data that showed the number of children receiving a youth justice disposal for an indictable offence[2] rising by 21 per cent in the four-year period from 2003, with the increase for girls more pronounced than for boys (35 compared to 16 per cent) (Bateman, 2013a). The data were presented without any explanatory analysis, however, implying that they simply reflected an underlying reality.

---

[1] Previously known as the British Crime Survey.

[2] Indictable offences are more serious incidents that can, in the case of an adult, be tried in the Crown Court.

# TARGETING CHILDREN

Alternative interpretations of the data are possible, however. By taking a longer-term perspective Nacro (2008a), for instance, demonstrated that youth crime had in fact fallen by 12 per cent between 1992 and 2007. Moreover, other measures of youth crime fail to evidence any such escalation in children's criminal activity. Rather than mirroring any significant increase in youth criminality, the apparent uplift in recorded youth crime might instead reveal changing responses to children in conflict with the law, not least harsher policing of young people prompted by a government-imposed target to narrow 'the justice gap' (Home Office, 2002).

In 2002, the New Labour government, intent on demonstrating its tough stance on law and order, introduced a target to increase the number of 'offences brought to justice' (OBTJ) from 1.025m in 2002 to 1.25m in 2007/08. The target was met early: figures for the year ending June 2007 showed a 43 per cent growth in 'sanction detections'[3] over the baseline year (Home Office, 2007). This 'success' was not, however, an indication of improved performance, since the 'clear-up rate' for offences recorded by the police showed no corresponding rise (Bateman, 2008). It was, instead, a function of formal disposals being imposed for behaviour that would not previously have attracted such an outcome; it represented a fundamental change in 'decision-making in relation to matters that already come to police attention' (2008: 2): a shift from informal action to 'sanction detection' (ibid.:3).

Children were disproportionately disadvantaged by this process. Analysis of the data shows that the rise in *detected* offending for *all* children was greater than that for young adults and the increase for children aged 10–14 outweighed that for 15–17 year olds. Furthermore, far from youth crime becoming more serious, as the media contended, the expansion in summary offences was considerably greater than that for indictable matters (39 against 19 per cent) (Bateman, 2008). As younger children, with no antecedent history, were formally drawn into the youth justice system for less serious offending, the proportion of cases resulting in a pre-court disposal, rather than prosecution, rose. The expansion in cautioning, therefore, rather than indicating a growth in youth crime, actually reflected an increased propensity to officially record and formally respond to minor youthful transgressions that had previously gone unrecorded and/or had not elicited any formal response.

The impact of the new police 'offences brought to justice' target on girls was particularly marked. As shown in Figure 5.1, the rise in detected youth crime was considerably higher for girls than for boys. The more limited, less serious, nature of female criminality dictated that, until the introduction of the performance measure, girls were more likely than boys to have benefited from

---

[3] The following outcomes constitute a sanction detection: reprimand, warning, caution, cannabis warning, penalty notice for disorder, charge or summons.

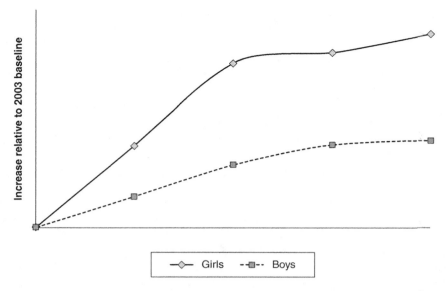

**Figure 5.1** *Changes in detected offending relative to a 2003 baseline by gender: 2003–2007 (indictable offences)* (Bateman, 2013a)

informal outcomes. They were accordingly at greater risk of 'net-widening' (Kelly, 2008) once the target took hold and, accordingly, the media-inspired moral panic about 'ladette thugs' was based on a fundamental misreading of official statistics (Sharpe, 2012: 1).

# THE POTENTIAL TO MISLEAD

The prospect of statistics being used to support divergent interpretations of the realities of youth crime raises questions as to how such data might most accurately be understood or, moreover, whether the data can illuminate our understanding of youth crime at all (Muncie, 2009). There are at least five distinct, but interrelated, difficulties.

First, what constitutes a crime varies over time and place. The age of criminal responsibility is key in this respect (Bateman, 2012a; Goldson, 2013). Whereas in Scandinavian countries anyone below the age of 15 years is deemed incapable of committing an offence, in England and Wales a child is criminally responsible from 10 years. Until 1998, it was presumed that a child under 14 years of age was incapable of distinguishing between right and wrong sufficiently to justify criminal proceedings unless the prosecution was able to adduce evidence to the contrary. The abolition of this presumption of *doli incapax* in that year ensured the criminalisation of thousands of younger children who would previously have benefited from that legal safeguard. There was an immediate impact which continued to be felt over the longer term: between 1997 and 2007, there was an 87 per cent rise in convictions for 10–12 year olds and a 55 per cent increase for those aged 13–15 years. The growth in respect of children aged 16–17 was, by comparison, just 8 per cent (Bateman, 2012a).

Second, police-recorded crime invariably only gives a partial account since, for a variety of reasons, fewer than four in ten criminal incidents are reported (Parfremont-Hopkins, 2011). Many are not brought to police attention because they are deemed insufficiently serious (Osborne, 2010). Conversely, any expansion in insurance cover can inflate the number of minor matters included in police statistics since making an insurance claim requires a 'crime number'. Conversely, crimes against those who lack the means to insure their property are under-represented.

Third, many offences have no direct victim (i.e. possession of cannabis), or alternatively escape the victim's attention. Such 'victimless' incidents are bypassed by both CSEW and police data: awareness of victimisation is central to what appears on the statistical radar. Crime figures thus understate white-collar and corporate offences, committed predominantly by professional adults, the wealthy and the powerful, rather than (predominantly poor, working-class) children (Whyte, 2008).

Fourth, unless an offender is apprehended, it is not possible to attribute responsibility for a particular act. In 2011/12, just 28.4 per cent of all crimes recorded by the police were detected (Taylor and Bond, 2012), rendering the question of how much of the remaining 71.6 per cent can reasonably be attributed to children as a matter of conjecture.

Fifth, as the OBTJ target confirms, fluctuations in youth crime figures may have little, if anything, to do with shifts in children's criminality but rather derive from changes in legislation, policy or practice. Finally (as discussed below), statistical data can be used to justify the introduction of favoured policy options that might, in turn, feed back into crime figures in unanticipated ways.

The importance of critical engagement with official statistics becomes clear, but doing so requires asking the right questions. Intrinsic limitations of the data preclude an accurate assessment of the *volume* of youth crime. Providing that judicious caution is exercised and proper account taken of contextual information, it may nonetheless be possible to draw reasonable conclusions about *trends* where different data sets point in a consistent direction or, alternatively, inconsistencies can be systematically explained. Any comprehensive account of what statistics reveal will, moreover, need to look beyond youth offending itself, to the nature of state interventions in the lives of children who transgress the law. Histories of youth justice can be usefully analysed in this light.

# FROM STATISTICAL ANALYSIS TO THE 'NEW YOUTH JUSTICE'

As intimated above, successive New Labour governments largely reinforced pre-existing policy trends rather than instigating a break with the immediate past. Nonetheless, the provisions of the Crime and Disorder Act 1998 (CDA) were sufficiently distinctive to usher in a 'new youth justice' (Goldson, 2000a), a concrete manifestation of the increasing politicisation of youth crime and a reduced tolerance for children who offend (Goldson, 2010). The Audit Commission's (1996) influential report *Misspent Youth* was credited with providing a blueprint for the reforms, and the report relied heavily on a particular reading of youth crime trend data. In particular, it argued that statistics that appeared to evidence a substantial reduction in youth crime since the early 1980s had been misinterpreted. That conclusion, complemented by a political stance that much youth crime was routinely minimised through a misguided adherence to a 'welfarist' paradigm (Fionda, 2008), was exploited by the New Labour administration that formed in 1997, to justify an approach characterised by *No More Excuses* (Home Office, 1997). Forthwith even a minor infraction of the law, if committed by a child, would elicit a formal criminal justice intervention.

As the logic of the interventionist impulse played out, the limits of the youth justice system became increasingly blurred. Low-level 'disorder' was conflated with 'crime', evidenced by a near obsession with 'anti-social behaviour' and the development of enforcement measures that targeted children disproportionately (Squires and Stephen, 2005). Children deemed 'at risk', who by dint of age or lack of adjudicated offending would previously have been regarded as beyond the purview of criminal justice responses, were now routinely criminalised and 'preventive work' became an area of rapid growth. This despite limited evidence to support such an approach (Armstrong, 2004; Goldson, 2000b) and in the face of well articulated concerns about the likely negative impact of early induction into the youth justice system 'on the self-perceptions, and subsequent conduct of the children identified' (Pitts, 2005: 9).

# UNWARRANTED ASSUMPTIONS

Given the role played by the Audit Commission's analysis in legitimising the above developments, it is important to subject its core claims to careful scrutiny. Figures showed a sustained reduction of detected youth crime over the decade and a half preceding the publication of *Misspent Youth* (in 1996). Between 1980 and 1990, the number of children aged 10–16 years cautioned or convicted of indictable offences fell from 175,700 to 110,800 (Rutherford, 1992). The Criminal Justice Act 1991 extended the jurisdiction of the youth court to include 17 year olds, making comparison with the earlier period problematic. Nonetheless, the apparent decline in youth crime continued unabated after 1992. By 1996, when the Audit Commission's report appeared, detected youth crime was 14 per cent lower than it had been just four years previously, a trend that continued for the remainder of the decade (Bateman, 2013a).

The Audit Commission was not convinced by such data, however, arguing that they did not necessarily demonstrate a reduction in youth crime. One disputed issue concerns the proportion of offences not reported to the police, or those recorded but not detected, that can be reasonably attributed to children. *Misspent Youth* assumed that if one in four *known* offenders was below the age of 18 years, it was legitimate to infer that children were responsible for one-quarter of *all* crime. Since both CSEW and police-recorded data suggested that the overall volume of crime was higher in 1996 than in 1981, it was inferred that youth crime must have risen. But Denis Jones (2001), in a perceptive critique, provides three reasons for rejecting this assumption. First, the attrition rate (from undetected to detected crime) is likely to be lower for children whose offending is 'less sophisticated, less pre-meditated and more liable to detection' (2001: 365). Second, children are less likely to commit offences such as fraudulent use of credit cards, theft from employer and a range of more serious crime involving firearms, blackmail and murder, and cannot reliably be considered responsible for one-quarter of such episodes. Third, children are over-represented in the figures for detected offending. Youth offending is frequently more visible because it tends to occur in public places, rather than in the home or in the office, thus generating higher arrest rates. At the same time, police stop-and-search powers are disproportionately directed at younger people, particularly those from minority backgrounds or residing in deprived neighbourhoods (Goldson and Chigwada-Bailey, 1999).

There are also positive reasons to take seriously the fall in youth crime shown in the figures for detected offending. During the 1990s, other measures are broadly consistent with such a trend. Police-recorded crime fell every year between 1992 and 1999, with a similar trend evident from 2003/04 to the year ending June 2013. The CSEW shows sharp reductions in victimisation from 1995 onwards and by 2013, estimates of total crime derived from this measure were the lowest since the survey began (Office for National Statistics, 2013). While not conducted with the same regularity, and acknowledging difficulties of comparison over time, self-report studies equally provide no evidence that youth crime rose during the relevant period (Budd et al., 2005).

But if analysis provides grounds for supposing that the fall in detected youth crime in the 1980s and 1990s was real, similar considerations suggest that the sharp rise in detected youth offending from 2003 to 2007 did not actually reflect changes in the underlying level of criminal activity. The CSEW and police-recorded crime both manifested a continued decline during this period. Surveys conducted for the YJB show a substantial reduction in the proportion of children in mainstream schooling who self-reported offending in the previous 12 months, from 26 per cent in 2004 to 23 per cent in 2008. It would thus appear that the growth in detected youth crime during this period was a function of New Labour's determination to appear tough on children who break the law. Such an interpretation is confirmed by what happened when the OBTJ target lapsed (see below).

The commitment to earlier intervention was underpinned by a rejection of the widely accepted tenet that juvenile offending is a common feature of adolescence rather than a symptom of individual pathology. Left to their own devices, the majority of children 'grow out of crime' (Rutherford, 1992). New Labour's blunt assertion that the 'evidence shows this does not happen' (Home Office, 1997: preface) again relied on the Audit Commission who offered two refutations of the maturation thesis.

First, it argued that the known rate of offending by young adults had risen significantly. No evidence was offered, however, and available Home Office data actually undermined the claim. Detected offending for 17–20 year old males fell by 7 per cent between 1984 and 1991; between 1992 (when 17 year olds were removed from youth court jurisdiction) and 1996 (the date of the Audit Commission's report), detected offending by 18–20 year olds fell by 15 per cent (Home Office, 1987, 1993, 1994, 2000).

Second, the Audit Commission contended that the peak age of male offending had risen from 15 to 18 between 1986 and 1994. But the rise was not a gradual process as this account suggested. It was already 18 years by 1988 and remained stable thereafter until the end of the following decade (Barclay and Turner, 1991; Nacro, 2008a). Further, an increase in the age at which the prevalence of offending is highest does not necessarily imply a failure to grow out of crime, since it is equally compatible with a reduction in offending by younger children. Rapid decreases in theft and handling stolen goods (offences disproportionately associated with younger children), combined with the relative stability of violent offences (more prevalent among older teenagers), would generate a rise in the peak age of offending. This is precisely what prevailed during the mid-1980s (Barclay and Turner, 1991).

# DAMAGING RESPONSES

Although the statistics fail to provide a legitimate basis for the development of an increasingly retributive climate, the material effects of that development are clearly visible in the data. Two features stand out: an increase in the use of prosecution and an expansion in the number of children incarcerated.

The rate of diversion from court declined from 73.4 to 53.7 per cent in the decade from 1992, leading to a proportionate increase in prosecution (Bateman, 2013a). While overall detected youth crime fell by more than one-quarter, the number of children convicted at court rose by almost 30 per cent. The introduction, in the CDA, of a new pre-court system of reprimands and final warnings that required, at the latest, prosecution on the third offence, however trivial and irrespective of the child's circumstances, provided an additional impetus (Bateman, 2003; Goldson, 2000b). The impact on girls was particularly pronounced: over the same 10-year period, the number of girls sentenced in court rose by more than 57 per cent, while female detected youth offending fell by almost one-third (Nacro, 2008b). The greater visibility of girls in the courts ultimately provided fertile ground for the moral panic around girls' delinquency when the sanction detection target kicked in.

Between 2002 and 2006, the rate of diversion began to climb again, but as intimated above, this rise has to be understood in the context of the OBTJ target. As large numbers of minor transgressions (that would previously have been dealt with informally) were drawn into the system, so the use of reprimands and warnings grew more rapidly than convictions (Bateman, 2013a). The apparent increase in the use of 'diversionary' measures was thus a predictable artefact of the target and evidenced extensive net-widening rather than increased diversion.

Further up the tariff, deprivation of liberty became increasingly common, with black and minority ethnic children hit particularly hard (May et al., 2010). Between 1993 and 2002, custodial sentences imposed on children rose by 85 per cent (Nacro, 2005). While such sentences began to decline thereafter, the numbers of child prisoners remained stubbornly high for a further six years (Ministry of Justice, 2013a). On one estimate, notwithstanding the difficulties of comparison (Muncie and Goldson, 2006), the level of custody in England and Wales, relative to the 10–17 population, was four times higher than that in Portugal, 12 times that in Italy and more than 100 times that in Denmark (Muncie, 2008).

The deleterious effects of incarceration on a population of already disadvantaged and vulnerable children are well documented (Goldson, 2005; Goldson and Coles, 2005). The seriously damaging nature of custody is confirmed by the level of violence associated with it: in 2011/12, there were 1,725 episodes of self-harm, 3,372 assaults, and 8,419 recorded instances of physical restraint within the juvenile secure estate in England and Wales (Ministry of Justice/YJB, 2013), and in the period between 2009 and 2011, five teenagers sustained broken bones while subject to restraint in just one establishment (Allison, 2013). The evidence that custody serves to prevent crime is also lacking: 72 per cent of children released from penal detention in 2010/11 were reconvicted within 12 months (Ministry of Justice/YJB, 2013), an outcome significantly worse than for children with similar characteristics and subject to community sentences (Ministry of Justice, 2013b). But a failure to divert children from formal processing is similarly harmful. Whereas 'much youth offending ... will fade as young people grow into adulthood, providing there is no drastic response to the offending' (Smith and McAra, 2004: 21), criminalisation inhibits the natural maturation process and is correlated with increased delinquency that, in turn, has adverse consequences for future life-chances (McAra and McVie, 2007).

There would appear to be an empirical and conceptual link between these two phenomena: an increase in prosecution and an uplift of custodial detention.

Indeed, recent analysis has revealed an inverse correlation between the rate of diversion and the use of custody (Bateman, 2012b): as the former declines, the latter rises and vice versa. During the 1980s, a trend towards increasing diversion was associated with a rapid reduction in custody (Rutherford, 1992). Developments from the early 1990s to the mid-2000s are an indication of the same relationship in reverse. How to account for this relationship? On the one hand, the criminogenic consequences of system contact are greater as children are propelled further into it (McAra and McVie, 2007). On the other hand, a reduction in recidivism might be anticipated where increased diversion offsets the prospect of prosecution and formal system contact. Delayed entry into the court system also extends the number of formal disposals available before incarceration appears 'inevitable' and reduces the perception of 'persistence', a major trigger for custody (Jacobson et al., 2010), while also lessening the potential for breach (Bateman, 2013b).

# A NON-PUNITIVE TURN?

The OBTJ was not renewed and, from 2007, the data reveal an immediate, dramatic, shift in the pattern of detected youth crime. By 2012, the statistics show a reduction in offending by children of 62 per cent (Ministry of Justice, 2013c). Some of the fall no doubt simply reflects a reversion to earlier trends, but the extent of the contraction suggests that other factors are at play (Bateman, 2013a). To be sure, police-recorded crime and CSEW data also report a recent reduction in youth offending. The YJB youth survey also demonstrates continued falls in self-reported offending to 2009, but the scale of the decline in the

**Table 5.1** First time entrants to the youth justice system 2001/02–2011/12

| Year | Number of first-time entrants |
| --- | --- |
| 2001/02 | 88,984 |
| 2002/03 | 83,374 |
| 2003/04 | 88,454 |
| 2004/05 | 96,199 |
| 2005/06 | 107,695 |
| 2006/07 | 110,826 |
| 2007/08 | 100,393 |
| 2008/09 | 80,329 |
| 2009/10 | 62,555 |
| 2010/11 | 45,910 |
| 2011/12 | 36,677 |

*Source*: Ministry of Justice/Youth Justice Board, 2013: supplementary table 2.5

proportion of children admitting an offence in the past 12 months – from 23 to 18 per cent for those in mainstream school – is not sufficient, in itself, to account for the overall reduction in detected youth crime (Anderson et al., 2010).

A government performance measure again offers the key to an adequate explanation. As the OBTJ initiative lapsed, it was replaced with an alternative target. Burgeoning workloads associated with the rapid rise in the criminalisation of children proved unsustainable and, in a pragmatic attempt to counter the inflationary impact of soaring sanctions detections, the New Labour administration introduced a target, in 2008, to reduce the number of children entering the system for the first time by 20 per cent by 2020 (HM Government, 2008).[4] Like its predecessor, the newly imposed target was met early: as shown in Table 5.1, the 20 per cent reduction was achieved in 12 months. Reducing first-time entrants (FTEs) has more recently been reaffirmed as one of the Coalition government's targets for youth justice (Ministry of Justice, 2010).

If the sanction detection directive promoted the criminalisation of minor delinquency, this new target has had the opposite effect in encouraging the police to respond informally to children with no prior system contact. A political commitment to formal early intervention was thus replaced by a focus on diversion and, predictably, this produced a deflationary impact on the overall volume of detected youth crime.

The FTE target was accompanied by, but was also a manifestation of, a less politicised environment for youth crime, reflected in the fact that in the 2010 general election issues of 'law and order scarcely figured' (Downes and Morgan 2012: 187). The shift in political mood heralded a broader rediscovery of diversion, encouraging the use of an array of informal pre-court mechanisms that are not reflected in criminal statistics (Criminal Justice Joint Inspectorates, 2012). As a consequence, recent data that show a substantial decline in the rate of diversion are again misleading. Pre-court disposals have seemingly reduced much faster than convictions: 66 compared to 17 per cent (Ministry of Justice/YJB, 2013). But according to one estimate, if just half of the fall in FTEs in 2010 represented children who would otherwise have received a formal pre-court disposal, the rate of diversion for that year would, in the absence of the FTE target, have been higher than at any point since 1993 (Bateman, 2012b). The abolition of the final warning scheme and its replacement by a system of youth cautioning – that allows considerably greater discretion to impose pre-court sanctions as an alternative to prosecution – holds the prospect that pre-court sanctions may decline further still (Hart, 2014).

Over the same period, custody has also fallen rapidly: between 2000/01 and 2008/09, the average population of child prisoners fluctuated between 2,745 and 3,029 but by October 2013 it had declined to 1,250, a reduction of 57 per cent over the equivalent month in 2008 (Ministry of Justice, 2013a).

---

[4] In fact, the YJB had introduced a version of the target from 2005 while the OBTJ indicator was still in force (Youth Justice Board, 2005).

ward trend, coinciding as it does with the 'rediscovery' of diver-
des further confirmation of the relationship described above.

# _LUSION: REASONS TO BE CAUTIOUS

The ebbs and flows evident in recent youth crime statistics are expressions not
primarily of changing patterns of delinquency but of shifts in the construction
of, and responses to, children who transgress the law. If between 1992 and 2008
such responses demonstrated a clear 'knowledge-policy rupture' (Goldson, 2010),
developments thereafter have been more closely aligned to the evidence-base.
But this welcome reorientation should not be taken to provide grounds for
complacency. Arguably, the seemingly more progressive shift in youth justice
policy – inaugurated during the concluding years of the most recent New
Labour administration and still manifest in the approach of the current Coalition
government – is pragmatic rather than principled: a response to alleviate pressures on stretched services and overcrowding of the custodial estate in a time of
austerity (the introduction of the FTE target coincided with the onset of financial
crisis). Indeed, the Coalition government, through its commitment to 'payment
by results' (whereby the risk of any penal policy is transferred to the provider of
services who is subject to monetary sanction if outcome targets are not met) has
effectively ceded from government any responsibility for developing an understanding of how better to respond to children in trouble (Yates, 2012).

If law and order is currently less politicised than it was a decade earlier, it is
apparent that punitive undertones remain close to the surface, evidenced by the
provisions in the Legal Aid, Sentencing and Punishment of Offenders Act 2012
that extend the powers of the court to subject children to curfews and permit
breach of custodial licence, and a return to custody, even after the original
order has expired (Hart, 2012); and by the revamping of anti-social behaviour
legislation in a manner that allows the imposition of positive sanctions as well
as negative proscriptions on children who have not been convicted of a crime
(Wigzell, 2014). The current conjuncture is thus fraught with contradiction.

Arguably, for instance, the three youth justice performance indicators established by the Coalition government display an inherent tension with the potential
to instigate a resurgence of punitivism. The targets to reduce FTEs and the use of
custody discussed above remain, but reducing reoffending – the third target – is
a key priority for the government: comprising the first strategic objective in the
YJB's corporate plan for 2013–2016 (YJB, 2013). But achieving this latter target
is not obviously compatible with the other two. The YJB was able to claim a 7.5
per cent reduction in recidivism between 2005 and 2007 (YJB, 2009), but this
was at the height of the OBTJ target, raising the possibility that the fall was simply a function of the dilution of the average level of risk within the youth justice
cohort as a consequence of net-widening. Indeed, the decline in reoffending was
greater for precisely those children drawn into the system as a direct consequence

of the target itself: girls, younger children, and those receiving reprimands, warnings and first-tier penalties. By contrast, reconvictions for those subject to community sentences remained stable, while proven reoffending following periods of custody actually rose (Bateman, 2010). One might anticipate, therefore, that the FTE target would generate increased reconviction since children who enter the system will on average have a more extensive history of offending behaviour than those who entered the system during the OBTJ era. There has indeed been such a rise. Between 2007 and 2011, the overall reconviction rate rose by 3.4 per cent, but for younger children the increase was higher at 4.8 per cent. Pre-court disposals have similarly contributed disproportionately to the increase as one would expect, given that lower-level 'offenders' have been diverted from formal outcomes (Ministry of Justice, 2013b).

Bernard (1992) has described a 'cycle of juvenile justice' wherein the apparent failure of, in this case, a lenient policy leads to harsher treatment of children who offend. In the event that reoffending data continue to rise, albeit as a consequence of systemic factors rather than changes in children's behaviour, the prospect that the wheel will turn again cannot be precluded. Paradoxically, were that to involve abandoning the FTE and custody targets, youth detected offending would be likely to rise.

# REFERENCES

Allison, A. (2013) 'Youth prison investigated after five inmates suffer broken bones', *Guardian*, 20 September. Available at: www.theguardian.com/society/2013/sep/20/youth-prison-investigated-inmates-broken-bones (accessed 1.10.14).

Anderson, F., Worsley, R., Nunney, F., Maybanks, N. and Dawes, W. (2010) *Youth Survey 2009: Research Study Conducted for the Youth Justice Board for England and Wales*. London: Youth Justice Board.

Armstrong, D. (2004) 'A risky business? Research, policy, governmentality and youth offending', *Youth Justice*, 4 (2): 100–16.

Audit Commission (1996) *Misspent Youth: Young People and Crime*. London: Audit Commission.

Barclay, G. and Turner, D. (1991) 'Recent trends in official statistics on juvenile offending in England and Wales', in Booth, T. (ed.), *Juvenile Justice in the New Europe*. Sheffield: Joint Unit for Social Sciences Research.

Bateman, T. (2003) 'Living with final warnings: making the best of a bad job', *Youth Justice*, 2 (3): 131–40.

Bateman, T. (2008) 'Target practice: sanction detection and the criminalisation of children', *Criminal Justice Matters*, 73 (1): 2–4.

Bateman, T. (2010) 'Reoffending as a measure of effectiveness of youth justice intervention: a critical note', *Safer Communities*, 9 (3): 28–35.

Bateman, T. (2012a) *Criminalising Children for No Good Purpose: The Age of Criminal Responsibility in England and Wales*. London: National Association for Youth Justice.

Bateman, T. (2012b) 'Who pulled the plug? Towards an explanation of the fall in child imprisonment', *Youth Justice*, 12 (1): 36–52.

Bateman, T. (2013a) *Children in Conflict with the Law: An Overview of Trends and Developments – 2012*. London: National Association for Youth Justice.

Bateman, T. (2013b) 'Encouraging compliance, maintaining credibility or fast-tracking to custody? Perspectives on enforcement in the youth justice system', in Ugwudike, P. and Raynor, P. (eds), *What Works in Offender Compliance: International Perspectives and Evidence-Based Practice*. Basingstoke: Palgrave MacMillan.

Bernard, T.J. (1992) *The Cycle of Juvenile Justice*. Oxford: Oxford University Press.

Budd, T., Sharp, C. and Mayhew, P. (2005) *Offending in England and Wales: First Results of the Crime and Justice Survey 2003*. London: Home Office.

Criminal Justice Joint Inspectorates (2012) *Facing Up to Offending: Use of Testorative Justice in the Criminal Justice System*. London: CJJI.

Downes, D. and Morgan, R. (2012) 'Overtaking on the left: the politics of law and order in the "Big Society"', in Maguire, M., Morgan, R. and Reiner, R. (eds), *The Oxford Handbook of Criminology*, 5th edn. Oxford: Oxford University Press. pp. 182–205.

Fionda, J. (2008) 'No more excuses', in Goldson, B. (ed.), *Dictionary of Youth Justice*. Cullompton: Willan. pp. 246–7.

Goldson, B. (ed.) (1999) *Youth Justice: Contemporary Policy and Practice*. Aldershot: Ashgate.

Goldson, B. (ed.) (2000a) *The New Youth Justice*. Lyme Regis: Russell House.

Goldson, B. (2000b) 'Wither diversion? Interventionism and the new youth justice', in Goldson, B. (ed.), *The New Youth Justice*. Lyme Regis: Russell House.

Goldson, B. (2005) 'Child imprisonment: a case for abolition', *Youth Justice*, 5 (2): 75–6.

Goldson, B. (2010) 'The sleep of (criminological) reason: knowledge-policy rupture and New Labour's youth justice legacy', *Criminology and Criminal Justice*, 10 (2): 155–78.

Goldson, B. (2013) 'Unsafe, unjust and harmful to wider society': grounds for raising the minimum age of criminal responsibility in England and Wales', *Youth Justice: An International Journal*, 13 (2): 111–30.

Goldson, B. and Chigwada-Bailey, R. (1999) '(What) justice for black children and young people?', in Goldson, B. (ed.), *Youth Justice: Contemporary Policy and Practice*. Aldershot: Ashgate.

Goldson, B. and Coles, D. (2005) *In the Care of the State? Child Deaths in Penal Custody in England and Wales*. London: INQUEST.

Hart, D. (2012) *Legal Aid Sentencing and Punishment of Offenders Act 2012: Implications for Children*. London: National Association for Youth Justice.

Hart, D. (2014) *Pre-court Arrangements for Children who Offend*. London: National Association for Youth Justice.

HM Government (2008) *Youth Crime Action Plan*. London: HM Government.

Home Office (1987) *Criminal Statistics – England and Wales 1986*. London: HMSO.

Home Office (1993) *Criminal Statistics – England and Wales 1992*. London: HMSO.

Home Office (1994) *Criminal Statistics – England and Wales 1993*. London: HMSO.

Home Office (1997) *No More Excuses: A New Approach to Tackling Youth Crime in England and Wales.* Cmnd 3809. London: The Stationery Office.

Home Office (2000) *Criminal Statistics – England and Wales 1998.* London: The Stationery Office.

Home Office (2002) *Narrowing the Justice Gap.* London: Home Office.

Home Office (2007) *National Community Safety Plan 2008–11.* London: Home Office.

Jacobson, J., Bhardwa, B., Gyateng, T., Hunter, G. and Hough, M. (2010) *Punishing Disadvantage: A Profile of Children in Custody.* London: Prison Reform Trust.

Jeory, T. and Douglas, H. (2009) 'The rise of the violent youth', *Sunday Express*, 12 April. Available at: www.express.co.uk/news/uk/94624/The-rise-of-the-violent-youth (accessed 1.10.14).

Jones, D. (2001) 'Misjudged youth: a critique of the Audit Commission's reports on youth justice', *British Journal of Criminology*, 41 (2): 362–80.

Kelly, P. (2008) 'Net-widening', in Goldson, B. (ed.), *Dictionary of Youth Justice.* Cullompton: Willan. pp. 244–5.

Leapman, B. (2008) 'Violent youth crime up a third', *Daily Telegraph*, 20 January. Available at: www.telegraph.co.uk/news/uknews/1576076/Violent-youth-crime-up-a-third.html (accessed 1.10.14).

Maguire, M. (2012) 'Criminal statistics and the construction of crime', in Maguire, M., Morga, R. and Reiner, R. (eds), *The Oxford Handbook of Criminology*, 5th edn. Oxford: Oxford University Press. pp. 206–44.

May, T., Gyateng, T. and Bateman, T. (2010) *Exploring the Needs of Young Black and Minority Ethnic Offenders and the Provision of Targeted Interventions.* London: Youth Justice Board.

McAra, S. and McVie, S. (2007) 'Youth justice? The impact of system contact on patterns of desistance from offending', *European Journal of Criminology*, 4 (3): 315–45.

Ministry of Justice (2010) *Breaking the Cycle: Effective Punishment, Rehabilitation and Sentencing of Offenders.* Cmnd 7972. London: The Stationery Office.

Ministry of Justice (2013a) *Youth Custody Report – October 2013.* London: Ministry of Justice.

Ministry of Justice (2013b) *Proven Re-offending Statistics Quarterly Bulletin – October 2010 to September 2011.* London: Ministry of Justice.

Ministry of Justice (2013c) *Criminal Justice Statistics 2012 – England and Wales.* London: Ministry of Justice.

Ministry of Justice/Youth Justice Board (2013) *Youth Justice Statistics 2011/12.* London: Ministry of Justice.

Muncie, J. (2008) 'The "punitive turn" in juvenile justice: cultures of control and rights compliance in Western Europe and the USA', *Youth Justice*, 8 (2): 107–21.

Muncie, J. (2009) *Youth and Crime*, 3rd edn. London: Sage.

Muncie, J. and Goldson, B. (2006) *Comparative Youth Justice.* London: Sage.

Nacro (2005) *A Better Alternative: Reducing Child Imprisonment.* London: Nacro.

Nacro (2008a) *Some Facts About Children and Young People Who Offend – 2006.* London: Nacro.

Nacro (2008b) *Responding to Girls in the Youth Justice System.* London: Nacro.

Office for National Statistics (2013) *Crime in England and Wales, Year Ending 2013.* London: Office for National Statistics.

Osborne, S. (2010) 'Extent and trends', in Chaplin, R., Flatley, J. and Smith, K. (eds), *Crime in England and Wales 2010/11.* London: Home Office.

Parfremont-Hopkins, J. (2011) 'Extent and trends', in Flatley, J., Kershaw, C., Smith, K., Chaplin, R. and Moon, D. (eds), *Crime in England and Wales 2009/10*. London: Home Office.

Pitts, J. (2000) 'The new youth justice and the politics of electoral anxiety', in Goldson, B. (ed.), *The New Youth Justice*. Lyme Regis: Russell House. pp. 1–13.

Pitts, J. (2005) 'The recent history of youth justice in England and Wales', in Bateman, T. and Pitts, J. (eds), *The RHP Companion to Youth Justice*. Lyme Regis: Russell House.

Rutherford, A. (1992) *Growing Out of Crime: The New Era*. Winchester: Waterside Press.

Sharpe, G. (2012) *Offending Girls: Young Women and Youth Justice*. Abingdon: Routledge.

Smith, D. and McAra, L. (2004) *Gender and Youth Offending*. Edinburgh: University of Edinburgh.

Smith, R. (2007) *Youth Justice: Ideas, Policy, Practice*, 2nd edn. Cullompton: Willan.

Squires, P. and Stephen, D. (2005) *Rougher Justice: Anti-Social Behaviour and Young People*. Cullompton: Willan.

Stephenson, M., Giller, H. and Brown, S. (2011) *Effective Practice in Youth Justice*, 2nd edn. Abingdon: Routledge.

Taylor, P. and Bond, S. (eds) (2012) *Crimes Detected in England and Wales 2011/12*, Home Office Statistical Bulletin 8/12. London: Home Office.

Whyte, D. (ed.) (2008) *Crimes of the Powerful: A Reader*. Maidenhead: McGraw Hill/Open University Press.

Wigzell, A. (2014) 'Moving beyond the ASBO? A review of the proposed anti-social behaviour measures and their implications for children', *Safer Communities*, 13 (2): 73–82.

Yates, J. (2012) 'What prospects youth justice? Children in trouble in the age of austerity', *Journal of Social Policy*, 46 (4): 432–47.

Youth Justice Board (2005) *Corporate and Business Plan 2005/06 to 2007/08*. London: Youth Justice Board.

Youth Justice Board (2009) *Annual Report and Accounts 2008/09*. London: Youth Justice Board.

Youth Justice Board (2013) *YJB Corporate Plan 2013–16 and Business Plan 2013/14*. London: Ministry of Justice.

# 6 WHAT EVIDENCE FOR YOUTH JUSTICE?

## DAVID SMITH

This chapter argues that the claims of successive governments since 1997 that their policies on youth justice are 'evidence-based' are, at best, only partly justified. It contends that, apart from the inherent difficulty of implementing genuinely evidence-based policies in a field as contested and politicised as youth justice, recurrent problems have arisen from misconceptions on the part of policy-makers – and sometimes of practitioners – about what evidence actually exists, and what should be expected of research intended to produce such evidence. These misconceptions lead, it is proposed, to a tendency for the government's position to swing between the poles of excessive optimism and excessive pessimism. The confusions that have resulted are illustrated by an examination of relevant material recently produced by the Youth Justice Board for England and Wales (YJB). The chapter concludes with some reflections on how far youth justice policy can be evidence-based, and what it might look like if it were informed by a realistic understanding and interpretation of the evidence.

## DIVERSION AND THE LABOUR GOVERNMENTS

When the first 'New' Labour government was elected in 1997, it was publicly committed to the 'modernisation' of the processes of government (Cabinet Office, 1999a, 1999b). Modernisation was taken to mean greater policy coherence ('joined-up' government) and the development of policies based on evidence of 'what works'. As applied to youth justice, which it enthusiastically was, 'modernisation' turned out to mean both more and less than the implementation of coherent, empirically grounded policies. As Jones (2002) demonstrated, the incoming government already knew what it wanted to do about youth justice, which was why it was able to act as quickly as it did, with a White Paper (*No More Excuses*) in 1997 and a very substantial piece of new legislation, the Crime and Disorder Act, in 1998. The Act, among much else, established the YJB to take charge of what the government apparently considered 'a fractured and immature youth justice system' (House of Commons Justice Committee, 2011: 6). Among the Board's responsibilities were 'identifying and promoting effective practice' and 'commissioning research and publishing information' (Ministry of Justice, 2011). So far, so reasonable-sounding, but these duties were to be undertaken within a culture of responsibility that was to replace the 'culture of excuses' from which youth justice had supposedly been suffering. Jones wrote of the Board's 'apparent expurgation of all youth justice knowledge and practice prior to 1998' (2002: 15); while what was to count as evidence was not specified, it was clear that the skills and experience of practitioners would not form part of it.

In particular, the YJB reversed the assumption that it was better to divert young people from the formal system if at all possible, which had been a key principle of youth justice practice from the early 1980s (Fergusson, 2007; Smith, 2010). In fact, the rate of diversion had been in decline since the early 1990s, reflecting the 'repoliticisation' of youth crime by the Conservative government (in which Labour followed), in the wake of youthful disturbances in the early 1990s (Campbell, 1993) and in particular the killing of James Bulger in 1993 (Bateman, 2012; Goldson, 1997; Hay, 1995). The principle of diversion where possible was thus already under pressure, for ideological reasons rather than considerations of effective practice; but the formal rejection of it as a principle was still a striking example of the priority of political over evidential considerations.

The subsequent history of diversion as an element of youth justice policy is interesting, however, in that it shows at least a partial rejection of, or at least a drift away from, the pro-intervention, 'no more excuses' position. Whether this further change was any more evidence-based than the original turn away from diversion is doubtful, but – without actually using the term – the YJB in 2006 introduced a new performance indicator that implied that diversion was back in favour: one of the ways youth justice was to be judged was by its success in reducing the number of 'first time entrants' to the system. This was made government policy in 2008 (Bateman, 2009, 2012) and became one of the Ministry of Justice's three key indicators for youth justice, the others being a fall in 'proven reoffending' and a decrease in the use of custody. So something like the principles that were ruthlessly disavowed by both Conservative and Labour governments in the 1990s were reinstated – and the YJB's apparent success in relation to these indicators seems to have been among the reasons why, in late 2011, the Coalition government reversed its decision to abolish it as part of its 'cull' of 'quangos' (House of Commons Justice Committee, 2011; Ministry of Justice, 2012).

This begins to look like an example of evidence-based policy-making, or at least of an evidence-based change of mind: it could have been difficult to go ahead with the abolition of the Board in the face of such apparent success (though the part played by the Board itself in contributing to these positive outcomes is not easy to identify), and the Justice Committee was told that the support of the Board was valued by members of local Youth Offending Teams (YOTs). In any case, the reinstatement of diversion and the apparent determination to drive down custody was, for many commentators and practitioners, an encouraging reversal of the previous policy, though, as Bateman (2012; this volume) argues, it would be unwise to assume that the downward trends in system involvement and in the use of custody will prove stable. They might have a better chance of being so if they were clearly and publicly defended on crime-reduction grounds, but no one involved in high-level discussions about the future of the YJB seems to have mentioned that there is strong research evidence in favour of diversion both from the system and from custody. Impressive evidence that targeted early intervention in the lives of young people 'at risk' may increase rather than reduce the prospect of serious offending, and that the best policy in some cases (if the aim is to reduce the likelihood of serious offending) is to do nothing, has come from the quasi-experimental Edinburgh Study of Youth Transitions and Crime (McAra and McVie, 2007, 2010; see also Goldson, 2008; Soothill et al., 2008). This evidence is far stronger than that available in the 1980s: then, practitioners certainly used social science – in the form of labelling theory – to guide their practice (Thorpe et al., 1980), but neither they nor the government (which supported an increase in cautioning instead of prosecution) could have claimed that there was much empirical evidence to support their preference for minimum intervention. Whether the much more persuasive evidence that emerged from the Edinburgh study and elsewhere will get the attention it deserves remains to be seen, though it would be unwise to hold one's breath; McAra and McVie draw the broad conclusion that the policy direction implied by their findings is 'the provision of services proportionate to need and offering maximum diversion' (2010: 201), implying a commitment to a welfare-based system that is in direct contradiction to dominant trends in politics and practice in Scotland as well as in England and Wales.

# USING SOCIAL SCIENCE THEORIES

Practitioners' awareness of labelling theory in the 1980s, and their success in finding space within the system to develop forms of practice that were in line with its predictions, is a (rare) example of the large-scale practical application of a social science theory, or in this case a group of theories. Their use of it might prompt reflection on the nature of knowledge in the social sciences, what counts as evidence, and how it might be used. When they look at social science, research policy-makers, understandably enough, want it to yield clear, unambiguous guidance on how to solve a problem; they tend to look for 'one best way' answers (Smith, 2004). But this expectation is based on a misunderstanding of the kind of knowledge the social sciences can be expected to produce. The misunderstanding arises from a crude version of positivism, meaning in this context 'the assumption that knowledge in the social sciences is essentially similar in kind to knowledge in the natural sciences, and that if social science is properly conducted, it can produce universal truths that are as stable and reliable as those of, for example, chemistry' (Smith, 2006: 83). There are good reasons why this is not the case, though sometimes social scientists themselves have succumbed to the temptation to give managers and bureaucrats what they demand, and claimed that their research can produce results that can be treated as certain and universal.

The essential reason why this is impossible is that the social world can never be made entirely predictable (MacIntyre, 1985). The logic of theory in the social sciences is, therefore, necessarily different from that of natural science theories. MacIntyre writes that 'What managerial expertise requires for its vindication is a justified conception of social science as providing a stock of law-like generalisations with strong predictive power' (1985: 90). But this requirement, according to MacIntyre, is unachievable. One of the examples he gives to show the difference between generalisations in the social and the natural sciences is Oscar Newman's (1973) well known and enduringly influential theory of defensible space. This predicted, among other things, that crime rates would rise with the height of residential buildings but level off when they reached 13 storeys. This was subjected to close research by positivist criminologists, who found disconfirming as well as supportive cases. But it does not follow that because a prediction of the theory is not right all the time, in every context and in every place, we should abandon the theory or at least radically modify it. It is doubtful if anyone really expects social science theories to deliver universal truths, but managers and policy-makers, including – as will be seen below – the YJB, often behave as if they do. Sensible practitioners and policy-makers meanwhile continue to draw on the social sciences as and when they find them helpful, without expecting them to be right all the time. They are able to do this because they know that human life is not and cannot be entirely predictable and controllable.

Within criminology, a helpful formulation of these ideas is found in John Braithwaite's (1993) paper on how criminologists who want their work to be useful to practitioners should move 'beyond positivism' and think in terms of 'contextual integrated strategies' as they try to deal with problems of crime. Braithwaite argues that criminologists should 'develop a range of theories that are sometimes useful' and that for purposes of practical problem-solving 'it is contextualized usefulness that counts, not decontextualized statistical power' (1993: 386–8). While recognising the importance of good positivist research, not least in exposing some theories as consistently wrong (the evaluation of 'Scared straight' programmes provides an example (Petrosino et al., 2013), though this has not led to their demise), Braithwaite contends that criminologists should 'reject the view that the ultimate value in science is discovering that single set of law-like statements that offers the best explanation of the phenomenon' (1993: 394). The same ought to apply to criminal justice managers and practitioners.

The status of knowledge in the social sciences might seem an abstract and esoteric issue, but misunderstanding of it has real practical effects. First, the inevitable failure of research on 'what works' to produce universal law-like generalisations can contribute to a rejection by policy-makers and practitioners of the very idea that research can ever be useful. At the level of policy-making, this leaves the field open for evidence-free policy motivated by ideological preferences – as in the case of 'Scared straight' programmes – and/or initiatives that appear to have an obvious populist appeal (e.g. the proposed privatisation of most probation work in England and Wales; Ministry of Justice, 2013). At the level of practice, a belief that research has (and can have) nothing to offer would leave practitioners with nothing to guide them but intuition and habit, and with no basis for reasoned resistance to ideologically driven managerial demands.

# MAKING SENSE OF WHAT WORKS

Second, and more pertinently to the discussion that follows, misunderstanding what social science can deliver leads to an erratic and irrational oscillation on the part of policy-makers (who may also be commissioners of research) between excessive optimism and excessive pessimism (the latter probably being the default position of recent years in England and Wales). Thus, following a period when the orthodox position was apparently characterised by 'nothing works' despondency, well-conducted empirical research began to appear that suggested that something might work after all (Raynor and Vanstone, 1996, 1997). The researchers themselves expressed their conclusions modestly and tentatively. But, according to Mair (2004), there was nothing tentative about the Home Office's reaction to the research: probation managers were encouraged to see cognitive-behavioural offending-focused groupwork programmes as the single answer to the question 'What works?' and to ensure that they became the core of probation practice. A sensible response to the evidence would have been cautious optimism and curiosity about what more could be learned: for example, about the contextual features which enabled such programmes to be effective (Pawson and Tilley, 1997) or the importance of individual staff characteristics (Bonta et al., 2011; Burnett and McNeill, 2005; Raynor et al., 2013). Instead, cognitive-behavioural programmes were 'rolled out' with very little attention to contexts and processes of implementation and with, eventually, a disregard for some basic messages from the 'what works' research. For example, the 'risk principle' that intensity of intervention should be proportional to the assessed risk of reoffending was apparently forgotten: since cognitive-behavioural programmes were taken to comprise *the* answer, everyone should get them – which led the chief inspector of probation to complain of 'programme fetishism' (HM Inspectorate of Probation, 2002, 2004). The research was interpreted in this way, according to Mair (2004), because of New Labour's commitment to 'modernisation' and therefore to evidence-based policy, and because people in key positions in the Home Office and the probation inspectorate were enthusiastic about the research and believed it could be straightforwardly used to make practitioners work more effectively (by following the prescribed groupwork curriculum).

This over-optimism – not so much about what the research said but about how its implications could be implemented in a changed approach to practice – was, perhaps inevitably, succeeded by over-pessimism. The Home Office's Crime Reduction Programme (CRP), launched in 1998, was the largest and best-funded crime reduction initiative ever attempted in Britain – and a product of the modernising optimism identified by Mair. It was meant to run for 10 years, but was closed down in 2002 (Maguire, 2004). Much of what was envisaged was never implemented, or not implemented as had been hoped. Maguire summarises the problems it encountered:

> Ultimately, few projects were implemented as planned, with the knock-on effect of a dearth of conclusive research findings ... it was undermined significantly by inherent risks and tensions that became increasingly prominent as circumstances (and the political climate) changed. While initially conceived as research-driven, it was 'sold' to politicians as contributing to the government's challenging crime reduction targets, an aim which progressively took priority over research ... It was over-ambitious in scale and raised unrealistic expectations of its outcomes. It suffered from major practical problems ... Low commitment to project integrity, cultural resistance among practitioners, and insufficient attention to differences between academics' and policy makers' understandings of research, also contributed to its problems. (2004: 213–4)

He concludes that 'the ideal of "evidence based policy" may be more effectively pursued as a quiet iterative process over the longer term, rather than through a risky investment in one high profile and rapidly implemented "programme" which promises more than it can guarantee to deliver' (Maguire, 2004: 213–4).

# INTERPRETING RESEARCH

The response of civil servants responsible for research was to criticise the academics involved in evaluating the programme, who were told that 'we did the wrong kind of research' (Raynor, 2004: 319). This entailed a tacit self-criticism, since the advice evaluators had been given at the start of the CRP was very different from the prescriptions for future evaluations that were given after it ended. The initial advice had mentioned randomised controlled trials (RCTs) as a method of evaluation but rejected them as 'usually ... not possible for practical reasons' (Colledge et al., 1999: 16). After the end of the CRP, the position of the Home Office was that randomised controlled trials were indisputably superior to any other method of evaluation. The Home Office review of 'what works' published in 2005 was much more sceptical than an earlier review (Goldblatt and Lewis, 1998) about the state of knowledge on the effectiveness of interventions designed to reduce reoffending. The introduction (Friendship et al., 2005) noted the difficulty of transferring findings from one setting to another (i.e. the Canadian research which had informed much of the development of cognitive-behavioural programmes in Britain might not be relevant after all). It went on to complain about the poor quality of most British evaluative research on the topic, and in particular about the lack of RCTs. The conclusion of the review reiterated this claim: Chitty complained that 'many of the results in this volume say a great deal about implementation, its problems and its effects on outcomes rather than the true effects of interventions' (though what this distinction means is obscure) and called for the use of RCTs in the 'correctional services, so that our knowledge of what works is truly improved and the existing equivocal evidence is replaced with greater certainty' (2005: 79–80). The same line was taken in the 'minimum standards for reconviction studies' produced by the Home Office in 2004 and incorporated into the YJB's Research Strategy for 2008–11 (YJB Research Team, 2008). As will be shown below, this enthusiasm for RCTs remains a feature of the latest thinking about evaluation in the YJB.

Can RCTs really produce definitive, unambiguous results, as Harper and Chitty (2005) and the YJB Research Team appear to believe they can? The experience of the last time the Home Office funded RCT research, in the late 1960s and early 1970s, is not encouraging in this respect. In that period there were four projects concerned with the effect of 'treatment' on reconvictions that used an RCT design (Nuttall, 2003). These were a study of Kingswood Approved School by Clarke and Cornish (1972; 1975); a study of social work in prison by Margaret Shaw (1974); the IMPACT study of the effects of intensive probation (Folkard et al., 1976); and what was presented as a replication of Shaw's study by Fowles (1978). None produced results that could reasonably be described as clear-cut, though taken together they were believed by policymakers to give broad support to the thesis that nothing worked (Nuttall, 2003). This was despite the fact that the most apparently definite results, from Shaw's prison study, were also the most positive, in terms of suggesting that something had worked. But this message was apparently unwelcome in official circles: the then head of the Home Office Research Unit, I.J. Croft, wrote in his Foreword that 'until they have been repeated, the experiments in social casework described in this report should not necessarily be regarded as the answer to the penologists' prayer' (Shaw, 1974: iii). And, reassuringly enough for penological pessimists, they were not repeated in the study by Fowles (1978), supposedly a replication (though in fact a very approximate one) of Shaw's research – though neither were its findings (like those of the IMPACT study) as negative as they were often presented as being (Nuttall, 2003: 276).

As a result of his experience with the Kingswood research, Ron Clarke became permanently disillusioned with 'treatment' approaches and with RCTs as an evaluation method, and turned to other forms of research on other approaches to crime reduction, notably situational preventive measures, which evolved into what is claimed as the new discipline of 'crime science' (Clarke, 2004). Nuttall (2003) gives Clarke's views as one local and specific reason for the negative interpretation of the findings of the four RCTs. It may also be that it was difficult for Home Office researchers to accept an interpretation of the findings that was contrary to the emerging orthodoxy that nothing worked (for which Martinson (1974) is usually held responsible). On a larger scale, the response to this research could be interpreted as a product of the emerging disillusionment with treatment approaches which Garland (2001) and others have identified as one element of a much broader movement away from penal modernism and faith in rehabilitative expertise towards a more populist and punitive set of policy assumptions (Pratt et al., 2005). At an intermediate level, the acceptance of the negative view by practitioners – and by most academic commentators – could be explained by their awareness that while the results were not entirely negative, they were not as positive as enthusiasts for offender 'treatment' had hoped.

Whatever level of explanation is adopted – and all are likely to be relevant – the reception of these research reports is a clear example of how research is always delivered into a particular political and ideological context, and how it is that context, and not the findings of the research alone, determines how it will be used. In other contexts the response to the findings might have been 'Interesting – let's see what more we can find out', instead of a near-total loss of interest in evaluative research on interventions with offenders on the part of the government, which lasted for over 20 years. As discussed above, its revival, when it came, was fragile, as an ostensible commitment to evidence-based policy was overtaken by what were seen as political imperatives. Still, we are not quite back to 'nothing works' even though – as the following discussion of the uses of research in youth justice shows – there is not much sign of confidence that we know what does 'work'.

# WHAT WE KNOW AND DON'T KNOW IN YOUTH JUSTICE: THE OFFICIAL STORY

It seems fair to say that at the time of writing (late 2013) the status of evidence on youth justice in official circles is not entirely clear. In late 2011 the YJB seemed to accept that it had failed to make practitioners sufficiently aware of what counts as effective practice. Giving evidence to the House of Commons Justice Committee, the Board's chief executive, John Drew, said that 'Effective practice is probably the area of the YJB where we have met our mandate least satisfactorily' (House of Commons Justice Committee, 2011: Ev. 20). He was responding to a question about the National Audit Office's (NAO) finding in the previous year that 'seventy-six per cent of YOT managers agreed with the statement, "It is difficult to find evidence on 'what works' for certain areas of our work'", from which the NAO report's authors seemed to draw the grand but doubtfully justified conclusion that 'Practitioners in the youth justice system do not know which interventions have the most impact on reducing offending' (National Audit Office, 2010: 8). It would be understandable if John Drew was on the defensive in giving his evidence, since the Justice Committee was specifically examining the proposed abolition of the YJB, but it is not clear how defensive he needed to be, since, as he told the Committee, the YJB had published 73 research studies, 31 of which were concerned with the outcomes of interventions and 'about another dozen' were 'in the pipeline'. He was surely justified in saying that the YJB's contribution to research was not 'negligible', and that 'we know quite a lot about what works'. All the same, he said that recent scrutiny of the YJB's work on effective practice (by the NAO and in the internal review chaired by Dame Sue Street; Department for Education, 2010) had been 'a real wake-up call' and that the YJB was 'in the process of reformulating our entire offer in relation to effective practice' and as a result would be 'much more focused'.

YOT staff who look at the YJB's website, as they are presumably expected to do from time to time, are unlikely to be struck by a lack of material on 'effective practice'. They might, however, be baffled by the variety of the material that they find. As well as a range of research reports on specific topics, some, as John Drew said, evaluating the results of interventions, the enquiring practitioner will find (among other things) 10 statements of the Key Elements of Effective Practice (KEEPs), each with an accompanying 'source document' that gives the basis in evaluative research findings for the brief guidance offered in the KEEP document. These KEEP statements date from 2008, when the original versions were revised (Prior and Mason, 2010). With a bit more effort, the practitioner will also find some more recent documents, which taken together make up the 'effective practice framework'. These include an account of the YJB 'Practice Classification System' (Archer, 2013a) and a statement on 'Effective Practice Identification and Dissemination' (Archer, 2013b), as well as reports from the previous two years on the 'Effective practice prioritisation exercise'. There is also an 'Effective Practice Library', which is meant to 'provide practitioners and commissioners in youth justice with easy access to examples of effective practice' and to 'allow those developing and using innovative practice to share what they have found to be effective' (Youth Justice Board, 2012). (How far it succeeds in these aims is briefly discussed below.) On the face of it, youth justice practitioners do not lack advice from the YJB on 'what works'; presumably the post-2008 documents represent part of the YJB's response to criticism by the NAO and others, but even before then there had hardly been a shortage of material. There are, however, interesting differences between the earlier and later sets of documents in the view they take of what counts as evidence of effectiveness. I look first at the earlier set, the KEEPs, and in particular their source documents.

The 10 KEEPs follow a standard format and, after suggestions on how they should be used, give general guidance to practitioners and managers on 'delivery', 'operational management' and 'strategic management and partnership working'. They reiterate the importance of monitoring and evaluation at each level and, by means of cross-referencing, they encourage their readers to refer to the relevant source documents. There is little in the KEEPs that anyone could sensibly object to, but much of the guidance seems so general as to be unlikely to be very helpful: many readers might well feel that they know all this already, and the NAO (2010: 36) found that most YOT respondents would have liked 'more practical guidance'. The source documents are a different matter, being generally authoritative statements, based on systematic reviews of the literature, on what evidence there is that could helpfully inform practice. Only 50 per cent of respondents to the NAO (2010) thought that the information they got from the YJB had a convincing evidence-base, but given the effort put into the source documents it seems unreasonable to blame the Board (or only the Board) for this.

# WHAT KINDS OF EVIDENCE COUNT?

It may be, however, that the Board's expectations of the authors of the source documents led to an unnecessary limitation on what kinds of evidence were to count as valid. As Prior and Mason (2010) explain, the brief for the source documents emphasised that authors should conduct a systematic review of research in the field following the guidelines of the Campbell Collaboration (www.campbell-collaboration.org/). In practice, Campbell Collaboration reviews of research usually include only the findings of experiments or quasi-experiments, with a strong preference for RCTs (see e.g. Strang et al. (2013) on restorative justice, and the authors' explanation in Appendix A of why even some RCTs were excluded as insufficiently rigorous). Full adherence to the Campbell position that only RCTs count as valid would have meant that the KEEP source documents – with the possible exception of the one on offending behaviour programmes (Wikström and Treiber, 2008) – would have been a good deal thinner than they are. This is not just because many topics that could in principle have been researched using RCTs or something approaching them have not been, but, as Prior and Mason say, because 'certain research questions are, in effect, rendered "unaskable" because they cannot be addressed using experimental methods' (2010: 219). One such question is their own, on how best to go about *Engaging Young People Who Offend* (Mason and Prior, 2008). They found no studies of 'engagement' that met the systematic review criteria, and, rather than producing a 'very slim' source document that would be of little help to anyone, they agreed after discussions with YJB staff that they should move beyond the Campbell principles and conduct a broader review that would include what 'robust' evidence they could find specifically on techniques of engagement, findings from other YJB reviews that were relevant to these techniques, and 'key messages' on engagement from the practice literature. As they say, the last category is of special interest because it 'opens up the possibility of a quite distinctive conception of what might count as "evidence" in attempts to establish "what works"' (Prior and Mason, 2010: 213–4). As has long been accepted in thinking about evidence-based medicine – but, oddly, less so in social work and youth justice – the skills and experience of practitioners ought to count as a valid source of evidence (Sackett et al., 1997; Smith, 2006).

It is to the credit of the YJB staff involved that they were open to the possibility that helpful evidence might be found in places other than the results of RCTs. Most of the other KEEP source documents share this view – necessarily, since if they were to confine themselves to RCTs they would have been very thin indeed. It is, therefore, slightly odd to find that the most recent (post-NAO report) material on effective practice on the YJB website looks like a strong restatement of the view that RCTs are superior to any other kinds of evaluative research. Thus Archer (2013a), in explaining how the YJB's Effective Practice Classification Panel will work, reproduces from Friendship et al. (2005: 7) the 'Scientific Methods Scale adapted for reconviction studies'. The scale ranks research from 1 to 5, with RCTs at Level 5, followed by studies with a well-matched comparison group, with an unmatched comparison group and with no comparison group (e.g. using a risk predictor to compare actual and expected outcomes), down to Level 1, which are before and after studies with no point of comparison. The scale encourages the view that anything below Level 4 is barely worthy of attention – and is certainly unlikely to be funded. What Archer does not reproduce is Friendship et al.'s (2005: 8) suggestion that for an expected reduction of 2.5 percentage points in the rate of reconviction a sample size of 5,024 is needed for both intervention and control groups – and that even on the optimistic assumption of a 10 percentage point reduction the minimum number required for each group is 325. It is not surprising that Friendship et al. remarked that few UK studies had met these requirements and concluded that Level 5 had rarely been achieved in reconviction studies – but Archer (2013a) pays no attention to this surely critical question of whether RCTs, or even Level 4 studies on a large enough scale, are practical propositions.

To be fair, the YJB does not go so far as to dismiss all other kinds of evaluation research entirely. Archer (2013a: 7–9) gives considerably more space to qualitative than to quantitative methods, and provides a sensible list of factors to be considered in appraising qualitative evaluations (a shorter and perhaps more user-friendly list than the original version in Spencer et al., 2003). He also acknowledges the limitations of quantitative methods, including their typical lack of attention to processes and the problem of how far the results of a controlled study can be generalised to different contexts. Correspondingly, he notes the virtues of qualitative methods in illuminating 'why' and 'how' questions about interventions, and he is clear about the importance of the context in which any intervention is undertaken and of practitioner variables. But he also notes that qualitative methods 'do not offer the same scientifically rigorous certainty [as RCTs, presumably] that it was the practice or programme being evaluated that produced the results seen, or to what extent those results were achieved' (Archer, 2013a: 12). Overall, the message is that quantitative methods are superior, and the more rigorously they are applied the better.

This is also the view of the YJB's partner in matters of research, the Social Research Unit at Dartington, which in turn draws inspiration from the 'Blueprints' project at the University of Colorado.[1] The Blueprints criteria are exacting: before a 'program' can be classified as 'promising' it must have been tested by one high-quality RCT or two high-quality quasi-experiment evaluations; and the requirement for a 'model program' is two high-quality RCTs or one such RCT plus a high-quality quasi-experiment. Few programmes qualify as models: eight out of over 1,100 'youth promotion programs' were reviewed. The list includes some that are so general that their implementation must vary widely across contexts and by the skills and commitment of practitioners, even if the content could somehow be controlled: Functional Family Therapy, LifeSkills Training and Multisystemic Therapy, for example. It is hard to see how this categorisation can help practitioners (or 'commissioners', in YJB-speak). It is equally unclear what they are meant to do when faced with the YJB's 'Effective Practice Library' (Youth Justice Board, 2012), which takes a similarly parsimonious position in bestowing its approval. Functional Family Therapy and Multisystemic Therapy are among eight (or so) out of 168 types of intervention (including tools or aids to intervention as well as 'programs') that are awarded 'research-proven' status; a few others are 'promising' (fortunately, the Blueprints criteria have not been applied in their full rigour to all of these); and the great majority are 'emerging', which is a polite way of saying that they have not been evaluated. Nobody could reasonably say that the YJB has not made an effort to respond to the criticisms of the NAO and others, but it is reasonable to wonder how productive this effort has been.

In particular, the cause of evidence-based practice would be seriously harmed if the idea that only RCTs can produce valid results were taken seriously. As we have seen, RCTs on interventions with offenders are in short supply everywhere, and almost non-existent in the UK. There is every reason to think that this will continue to be the case. The demands of RCTs articulated by Friendship et al. (2005) are such as to make them practically impossible to carry out – especially in a time when public sector spending is being deliberately cut. RCTs have their enthusiastic advocates, notably Farrington (1997) and Sherman (2009). The main example Sherman gives to support his case that RCTs can be executed effectively is the work of Shapland et al. (2008) on restorative justice schemes and their effects on reconviction. This was funded from 2001 under the CRP discussed above. Over four reports Shapland et al. provided rich material on both processes and outcomes and went some way towards answering the question that RCTs are often criticised for not answering (or asking): what was it about the interventions that made the difference? In many respects this research is exemplary, as good as research on criminal justice programmes is likely to get. But Sherman's (2009) claim that it shows the feasibility and value of the RCT approach is doubtful: Shapland et al. (2008) themselves say that

---

[1] See http://dartington.org.uk/projects/blueprints-for-success/.

only one of the three schemes they evaluated (though the largest of them) used random allocation to restorative justice conferencing, so for the other two schemes they had to identify a comparison group, matched as far as possible. They therefore rate their work on the largest project at Level 5 on the Scientific Methods Scale, and their work on the other two projects at Level 4. To achieve sufficient numbers for statistically significant results, cases from the different schemes had generally to be aggregated, but since 'restorative justice' meant different things in different places, the aggregated outcomes were not all produced by the same intervention. None of this is to disparage the work of Shapland et el., but it is to suggest that its results were not as clear-cut as Sherman (2009) suggests. While persuasive, and encouraging for advocates of restorative justice, they inevitably leave questions unanswered (Smith, 2012).

# CONCLUSIONS

Maguire (2004) was quoted above as arguing that evidence-based policy should be seen as a 'quiet iterative process' that will take time to achieve. Also reflecting on the CRP, Raynor concluded that 'The business of using research evidence to improve services is more incremental, provisional, iterative and gradual than big gestures would like it to be' (2004: 322). I would apply this to 'big gestures' in research as well as in offender-related programmes: to conduct an RCT in the UK with the numbers specified by Friendship et al. (2005) – even if we think of the lower figure (325 in each group) and not the higher one (5,024 in each group) – would require an almost unimaginable input of resources. It seems reasonable to conclude that it is not going to happen any time soon. So the claim that such an RCT – or several of them – would finally provide *the* answers that have previously eluded us, is to mislead policy-makers about what kind of research is feasible. It also reflects a mistaken view of the nature of evaluation, the kind of evidence it can produce, and the nature of the social sciences as a whole.

It is unrealistic to expect that youth justice policy will be shaped by research (Fergusson, 2007), but it ought to be realistic to expect that it will be informed and influenced by it (Goldson, 2010). The argument of this chapter suggests that this is most likely to be achieved if policy-makers are helped to be realistic about what they should and should not expect of research. They should not look for MacIntyre's (1985) 'law-like generalisations', but for empirically informed ideas on what approaches look promising, and what conditions are required for them to be implemented properly. Researchers, therefore, have a responsibility not to pander to politicians' demands for certainty, for single true answers. The claims they make for evaluative research should be more modest in one sense (they are not claiming that they can reveal universal truths) but in another sense they can be more confident, since they will not be trapped by the belief that only RCTs, or something very like them, can tell us anything useful.

# REFERENCES

Archer, B. (2013a) *YJB Practice Classification System*. London: Youth Justice Board.

Archer, B. (2013b) *Effective Practice Identification and Dissemination*. London: Youth Justice Board.

Bateman, T. (2009) 'Figures show a fall in the number of "first time entrants" to the Youth Justice System in England and Wales', *Youth Justice*, 9 (1): 87–8.

Bateman, T. (2012) 'Who pulled the plug? Towards an explanation of the fall in child imprisonment in England and Wales', *Youth Justice*, 12 (1): 36–52.

Bonta, J., Bourgon, G., Rugge, T., Scott, T., Yessine, A.K., Gutierrez, L. and Li, J. (2011) 'An experimental demonstration of training probation officers in evidence-based community supervision', *Criminal Justice and Behavior*, 38 (11): 1127–48.

Braithwaite, J. (1993) 'Beyond positivism: learning from contextual integrated strategies', *Journal of Research in Crime and Delinquency*, 30 (4): 383–99.

Burnett, R. and McNeill, F. (2005) 'The place of the officer-offender relationship in assisting offenders to desist from crime', *Probation Journal*, 52 (3): 221–42.

Cabinet Office (1999a) *Modernising Government*. London: The Stationery Office.

Cabinet Office (1999b) *Professional Policy Making in the Twenty-First Century*. London: The Stationery Office.

Campbell, B. (1993) *Goliath: Britain's Dangerous Places*. London: Methuen.

Chitty, C. (2005) 'The impact of corrections on re-offending: conclusions and the way forward', in Harper, G. and Chitty, C. (eds), *The Impact of Corrections on Re-offending: A Review of 'What Works'*, 2nd edn, Home Office Research Study 291. London: Home Office.

Clarke, R.V. (2004) 'Technology, criminology and crime science', *European Journal on Criminal Policy and Research*, 10 (1): 5–63.

Clarke, R. V. G. and Cornish, D.B. (1972) *The Controlled Trial in Institutional Settings: Paradigm or Pitfall for Penal Evaluators?* Home Office Research Study 15. London: HMSO.

Clarke, R. V. G. and Cornish, D.B. (1975) *Residential Treatment and its Effects on Delinquency*. Home Office Research Study 32. London: HMSO.

Colledge, M., Collier, P. and Brand, S. (1999) *Programmes for Offenders: Guidance for Evaluators*, CRP Guidance Note 2. London: Home Office.

Department for Education (2010) *Safeguarding the Future: A Review of the Youth Justice Board's Governance and Operating Arrangements*. London: Department for Education.

Farrington, D.P. (1997) 'Evaluating a community crime prevention program', *Evaluation*, 3 (2): 157–73.

Fergusson, R. (2007) 'Making sense of the melting pot: multiple discourses in youth justice policy', *Youth Justice*, 7 (3): 179–94.

Folkard, M.S., Smith, D.E. and Smith, D.D. (1976) *IMPACT Volume II: The Results of the Experiment*, Home Office Research Study 24. London: HMSO.

Fowles, A.J. (1978) *Prison Welfare: An Account of an Experiment at Liverpool*, Home Office Research Study 45. London: HMSO.

Friendship, C., Street, R., Cann, J. and Harper, G. (2005) 'Introduction: assessing the evidence', in Harper, G. and Chitty, C. (eds), *The Impact of Corrections on Re-offending: A Review of 'What Works'*, 2nd edn, Home Office Research Study 291. London: Home Office.

Garland, D. (2001) *The Culture of Control: Crime and Social Order in Late Modernity*. Oxford: Clarendon.

Goldblatt, P. and Lewis, C. (1998) *Reducing Offending: An Assessment of Research Evidence on Ways of Dealing with Offending Behaviour*, Home Office Research Study 187. London: Home Office.

Goldson, B. (1997) 'Children in trouble: state response to juvenile crime', in Scraton, P. (ed.), *'Childhood' in 'Crisis'?* London: UCL Press.

Goldson, B. (2008) 'Early intervention in the youth justice sphere: a knowledge-based critique', in Blyth, M. and Solomon, E. (eds), *Prevention and Youth Crime*, Researching Criminal Justice Series. Bristol: Policy Press.

Goldson, B. (2010) 'The sleep of (criminological) reason: knowledge-policy rupture and New Labour's youth justice legacy', *Criminology and Criminal Justice*, 10 (2): 155–78.

Harper, G. and Chitty, C. (eds) (2005) *The Impact of Corrections on Re-offending: A Review of 'What Works'*, 2nd edn, Home Office Research Study 291. London: Home Office.

Hay, C. (1995) 'Mobilization through interpellation: James Bulger, juvenile crime and the construction of a moral panic', *Social and Legal Studies*, 4 (2): 197–223.

HM Inspectorate of Probation (2002) *Annual Report 2001–2002*. London: Home Office.

HM Inspectorate of Probation (2004) *Annual Report 2003–2004*. London: Home Office.

House of Commons Justice Committee (2011) *The Proposed Abolition of the Youth Justice Board. Tenth Report of Session 2010–2012* (HC 1547). London: The Stationery Office.

Jones, D.W. (2002) 'Questioning New Labour's youth justice strategy: a review article', *Youth Justice*, 1 (3): 14–26.

MacIntyre, A. (1985) *After Virtue: A Study in Moral Theory*, 2nd edn. London: Duckworth.

Maguire, M. (2004) 'The crime reduction programme in England and Wales: reflections on the vision and the reality', *Criminology and Criminal Justice*, 4 (3): 213–37.

Mair, G. (2004) 'The origins of what works in England and Wales: a house built on sand?', in Mair, G. (ed.), *What Matters in Probation*. Cullompton: Willan.

Martinson, R. (1974) 'What works? Questions and answers about prison reform', *The Public Interest*, 35: 22–54.

Mason, P. and Prior, D. (2008) *Engaging Young People Who Offend: Source Document*. London: Youth Justice Board.

McAra, L. and McVie, S. (2007) 'Youth justice? The impact of agency contact on patterns of desistance from offending', *European Journal of Criminology*, 4 (3): 315–45.

McAra, L. and McVie, S. (2010) 'Youth crime and justice: key messages from the Edinburgh study of youth transitions and crime', *Criminology and Criminal Justice*, 10 (2): 179–209.

Ministry of Justice (2011) *Consultation on Reforms Proposed in the Public Bodies Bill* (Consultation Paper 10/2011). London: Ministry of Justice.

Ministry of Justice (2012) *Government's Response to the Justice Committee's Report: The Proposed Abolition of the Youth Justice Board*. London: Ministry of Justice.

Ministry of Justice (2013) *Transforming Rehabilitation: A Strategy for Reform* (Cm 8619). London: The Stationery Office.

National Audit Office (2010) *The Youth Justice System in England and Wales: Reducing Offending by Young People*. London: National Audit Office.

Newman, O. (1973) *Defensible Space: Crime Prevention through Urban Design*. London: Architectural Press.

Nuttall, C. (2003) 'The Home Office and random allocation experiments', *Evaluation Review*, 27 (3): 267–89.

Pawson, R. and Tilley, N. (1997) *Realistic Evaluation*. London: Sage.

Petrosino, A., Turpin-Petrosino, C., Hollis-Peel, M.E. and Lavenberg, J.G. (2013) *Scared Straight and Other Juvenile Awareness Programs for Preventing Juvenile Delinquency: A Systematic Review*. Available at: www.campbellcollaboration.org/lib/project/3/ (accessed 9.19.14). Oslo: The Campbell Collaboration.

Pratt, J., Brown, D., Brown, M., Hallsworth, S. and Morrison, W. (eds) (2005) *The New Punitiveness: Trends, Theories, Perspectives*. Cullompton: Willan.

Prior, D. and Mason, P. (2010) 'A different kind of evidence? Looking for "what works" in engaging young offenders', *Youth Justice*, 10 (3): 2121–22.

Raynor, P. (2004) 'The probation service "pathfinders": finding the path and losing the way?', *Criminal Justice*, 4 (3): 309–25.

Raynor, P. and Vanstone, M. (1996) 'Reasoning and rehabilitation in Britain: the results of the Straight Thinking on Probation (STOP) programme', *International Journal of Offender Therapy and Comparative Criminology*, 40: 279–91.

Raynor, P. and Vanstone, M. (1997) *Straight Thinking on Probation (STOP): The Mid-Glamorgan Experiment*. Oxford: Centre for Criminological Research.

Raynor, P., Ugwudike, P. and Vanstone, M. (2013) 'The impact of skills in probation work: a reconviction study', *Criminology and Criminal Justice*, July. Available online at: http://crj.sagepub.com/content/early/2013/07/14/1748895813494869.full.pdf+html (accessed 16.12.13).

Sackett, D.L., Richardson, W.S., Rosenberg, W. and Haynes, R.B. (1997) *Evidence-based Medicine: How to Practise and Teach EBM*. Edinburgh: Churchill Livingstone.

Shapland, J., Atkinson, A., Atkinson, H., Dignan, J., Edwards, L., Hibbert, J., Howes, M., Johnstone, J., Robinson, G. and Sorsby, A. (2008) *Does Restorative Justice Affect Reconviction? The Fourth Report from the Evaluation of Three Schemes*, Ministry of Justice Research Series 10/08. London: Ministry of Justice.

Shaw, M. (1974) *Social Work in Prison*, Home Office Research Study 22. London: HMSO.

Sherman, L.W. (2009) 'Evidence and liberty: the promise of experimental criminology', *Criminology and Criminal Justice*, 9 (1): 5–28.

Smith, D. (2004) 'The uses and abuses of positivism', in Mair, G. (ed.), *What Matters in Probation*. Cullompton: Willan.

Smith, D. (2006) 'Youth crime and justice: research, evaluation and "evidence"', in Goldson, B. and Muncie, J. (eds), *Youth Crime and Justice*. London: Sage.

Smith, D. (2010) 'Out of care 30 years on', *Criminology and Criminal Justice*, 10 (2): 119–35.

Smith, D. (2012) 'Arguments about methods in criminal justice evaluation', in Bowen, E. and Brown, S. (eds), *Perspectives on Evaluating Criminal Justice and Corrections*. Bingley: Emerald.

Soothill, K., Ackerley, E. and Francis, B. (2008) 'Criminal convictions among children and young adults: changes over time', *Criminology and Criminal Justice*, 8 (3): 297–315.

Spencer, L., Ritchie, J., Lewis, J. and Dillon, L. (2003) *Quality in Qualitative Evaluation: A Framework for Assessing Research Evidence*. London: Cabinet Office.

Strang, H., Sherman, L.W., Mayo-Wilson, E., Woods, D. and Ariel, B. (2013) *Restorative Justice Conferencing (RJC) Using Face-to-Face Meetings of Offenders and Victims: Effects on Offender Recidivism and Victim Satisfaction. A Systematic Review*. Oslo: The Campbell Collaboration. Available at: www.campbellcollaboration.org/lib/project/63/ (accessed 16.12.13).

Thorpe, D.H., Smith, D., Green, C.J. and Paley, J.H. (1980) *Out of Care: The Community Support of Juvenile Offenders*. London: Allen and Unwin.

Wikström, P.-O. and Treiber, K. (2008) *Offending Behaviour Programmes. Source Document*. London: Youth Justice Board.

YJB Research Team (2008) *Research Strategy 2008–11*. London: Youth Justice Board. Available at: www.justice.gov.uk/downloads/publications/yjb/2008/ResearchStrategy200811.pdf, (accessed 16.12.13).

Youth Justice Board (2012) *Purpose of the Effective Practice Library*. London: Justice. Available at: www.justice.gov.uk/youth-justice/effective-practice-library (accessed 13.10.14).

# 7 RISK MANAGEMENT AND EARLY INTERVENTION: A CRITICAL ANALYSIS

## STEPHEN CASE AND KEVIN HAINES

The concepts of risk management and early intervention have underpinned contemporary understandings of offending behaviour by young people and systemic responses to it, especially within the youth justice systems of the UK, Australasia and North America. The notion, philosophies and practices of 'risk-based early intervention' are redolent in other spheres too including: social work (Churchill, 2011), education (Ross et al., 2011) and health (Allen, 2011), although here we focus specifically on the implementation of early intervention in the youth justice field, particularly in England and Wales. We offer a critical discussion of the application of risk management through a highly structured risk assessment process that serves, we argue, to reduce, oversimplify, individualise and impute understandings of, and responses to, offending behaviour by young people based on methodologies with questionable validity and ambiguous foci. Finally, we explore and evaluate the (deleterious) outcomes that result when risk management and early intervention imperatives are melded together to form a policy and practice framework for responding to young people, before outlining a more positive alternative approach underpinned by a coherent set of philosophical principles.

## THE RISK FACTOR PREVENTION PARADIGM (RFPP)

Risk management has become embedded in the youth justice policy, practice and empirical literature and has been animated by identifying so-called 'risky' individuals and multiple 'risk factors', typically through the application of assessment instruments designed to regulate risks through appropriate preventative intervention. The internal logic of the RFPP is clear:

> The basic idea ... is very simple: Identify the key risk factors for offending and implement prevention methods designed to counteract them. There is often a related attempt to identify key protective factors against offending and to implement prevention methods designed to enhance them. (Farrington, 2007: 606)

The rise to prominence of the RFPP within youth justice policy and practice (Hawkins and Catalano, 1992; O'Mahony, 2009) reflects the growing popularity of *developmental theories* (Farrington, 2007, 2002; Thornberry and Krohn, 2003; Wikström and Butterworth, 2006) and *life course theories* (Laub and Sampson, 2003; Sampson and Laub, 2005, 1993) of the aetiology of offending by young people. There is an accompanying corpus of 'risk factor research' suggesting that exposure to risk factors in 'psychosocial' domains (individual, family, school, neighbourhood) at an early stage of life (childhood, early adolescence) can *predict* and even *determine* later offending (see Case and Haines, 2009 for a critical overview of this literature). A logical corollary of such developmental determinism has been the perceived need for early (risk-focused) preventative intervention to 'nip crime in the bud' (Blair, 2007).

# RISK MANAGEMENT IN YOUTH JUSTICE: REDUCTIONISM AND AMBIGUITY

The uncritical application of the RFPP in youth justice belies the fact that the concept of 'risk management' has not been comprehensively, clearly and/or consistently articulated in principle or practice. According to Kemshall, 'risk factors are used to predict reoffending and identify areas for intervention and management' (in Goldson, 2008: 309). Whilst this is a valid portrayal of how risk factors have been understood within risk factor research (RFR) and how they have been utilised in practice, when subjected to further scrutiny the picture becomes far messier. The research that is taken to constitute the 'evidence-base' for policy and practice guidance is reductionist, ambiguous, partial and inconclusive.[1] There has been little reflective critique of the methodologies employed and little consensus regarding the nature of the 'risk' that should be managed, its relationship with offending and/or the form of 'offending' behaviour that risk measures are allegedly able to predict. Critical questions emerge:

1. Should (can) the concept of 'risk' be *quantified and aggregated* into simplified 'factors' or does such *reductionism* produce invalid, unrepresentative, oversimplified and individualised representations of dynamic, subjective processes and interactions that are experienced and negotiated by young people?

---

[1] Space precludes a full exposition of the methodological critique of RFR, but see Case and Haines (2009).

2. What *outcomes* and risks are researchers and practitioners actually trying to measure? Is the outcome measure the risk that young people present *to themselves* (e.g. risk of *serious harm*)? The risk they present *to others* (e.g. potential *victimisation*)? The risk of *first-time offending*? The risk of *reoffending*? The risk of *reconviction*? The risk of *other problematic behaviour* associated with offending?
3. What is the *nature of the relationship* between so-called 'risk factors' and offending outcomes? Do risk factors exert a *causal* or *predictive* influence on offending? Are they merely *correlates* with it, *symptoms* of it, or *not related* in any substantive way?

## Reductionist quantification and aggregation

Risk management and risk assessment are central features of youth justice in England and Wales. Since 2000, all young people who come to the attention of the youth justice system (YJS) have been subjected to structured, standardised risk assessment via a practitioner-administered questionnaire known as 'Asset' (Youth Justice Board, 2000). The Asset tool measures/assesses risk factors in young people's lives across 12 'dynamic' (amenable to change) risk (factor) domains and one 'static' (unchangeable) risk domain, along with four additional risk-related domains,[2] thus activating a staged process of reductionism that moves understandings of young people's lives incrementally further away from their own interpretations, understandings and lived realities (see France, 2008; MacDonald, 2007). The assessment of risks in each dynamic (psychosocial) domain is further reduced and removed/distanced by requiring (adult) practitioners to identify whether each of a series of risk factors are present (by using dichotomous yes/no responses) and then provide a summative, aggregated rating for each domain of 'the extent to which the young person's lifestyle is associated with the likelihood of further offending (0 = not associated, 4 = very strongly associated)'. The final step is to require practitioners (with limited input from the young person) to total the dynamic risk domain scores across the assessment instrument (giving a possible score of 48 from 12 domains, each rated 0–4) and to add these to a total score for the static risk domain (possible score 16: each element rated 0–4), providing each young person with a risk profile score up to 64. This score is taken to signal the young person's likelihood of reoffending: low (0–14), medium (15–32) and high (33+). However, the overall *aggregated* risk score is not related to or representative of

---

[2] The 12 dynamic risk domains are: living arrangements; family and personal relationships; education, training and employment; neighbourhood; lifestyle; substance use; physical health; emotional and mental health; perception of self and others; thinking and behaviour; attitudes to offending; motivation to change. The single static risk domain relates to offending behaviour. There are four (non-quantified/rated) sections relating to positive factors, indicators of vulnerability, indicators of risk of serious harm to others and a brief 'What do you think?' self-assessment section for young people to complete.

any specific risk domain (score), nor do individual risk domain scores necessarily relate to, or represent, specific risk factor measures within that domain – because the methods of aggregation used effectively wash away sensitivity to individual risk measures.

The above process exposes deep flaws in the 'commonsense' approach to (risk) assessment and intervention, notably:

- Its reliance on reductionist and practitioner/adult-led quantifying processes render risk a practitioner-rated static 'artefact' that can only be given meaning superficially (and then only by adults).
- It incrementally moves understandings of young people's lives away from any grounding in the dynamic complexities and nuances of their self-perceived realities and experiences, to the extent that it paints a partial and distorted picture of the young person it is intended to represent.
- Every element of the risk assessment approach reduces, restricts and oversimplifies potential understandings of young people's lives due to an uncritical pursuit of risk – which ultimately, because these risks are aggregated, disconnects the assessment of specific risks from intervention planning.

The very act of oversimplifying potentially complex dynamic phenomena into readily quantifiable and targetable risk 'factors' is an exercise in crude reductionism, the results of which cannot hope to accurately represent the lived realities of young people (France et al., 2010; Kemshall, 2011).

## Reductionist individualisation

The 'flagging up' of early concerns about children's well-being and/or 'risk factors' have thus become central to government strategy and policy formation. (Chief Secretary to the Treasury, 2003: 53)

Risk assessment and management technologies invoke further reductionism through their tendencies to *individualise* responsibility for offending. Rather than offering sensitive, contextualised understandings and responses to young people's behaviour and their lives (Kemshall, 2011), Asset serves to individualise responsibility for offending by prioritising psychosocial risk domains. In this way, the responsibility (blame) for offending is placed with the young person and their inability to resist risk factors, rather than examining broader issues such as socio-structural factors (e.g. social class, poverty, unemployment, social deprivation, neighbourhood disorganisation, ethnicity), the absence of support mechanisms or the external influence of others (e.g. criminal justice agencies, schools, youth provision) in the construction of youth offending.

Paradoxically, however, the individualising nature of the risk assessment process is structured to *deindividualise* understandings of young people by aggregating risk measures across domains (producing a risk profile/score) and allocating individuals to *generic* risk categories (based on a large body of group-based empirical risk research[3]). The model of risk assessment routinely employed in the YJS in England and Wales, therefore, has engendered a contradictory relation of individualisation and deindividualisation, both of which have promoted a policy and practice agenda that inculcates children and young people with responsibility by perpetuating adult-centric understandings of them as risky, passive and in need of corrective intervention.

## Ambiguous and disparate offending outcomes

There has been a lack of consensus within RFR regarding which offending and offending-related *outcomes* might be predicted and thus targeted by risk management measures. A range of disparate RFR studies have related risk factors to differently defined offending outcomes, measured variously as: *first-time offending* (Farrington, 2000; West and Farrington, 1973), *reoffending* (Baker et al., 2005, 2002), *serious offending* (Budd et al., 2005), *frequent offending* (Flood-Page et al., 2000), *current/active offending* (Smith and McVie, 2003), *historic/ lifetime offending* (Case and Haines, 2004) or a *mixture* of these offending outcomes (Case et al., 2005). Other RFR studies have measured related, but non-offending, outcomes such as *substance use* (Case and Haines, 2008), *antisocial behaviour* (Moffitt, 2006), *social exclusion* (Johnston et al., 2000; University of Birmingham, 2004), and *school exclusion* (Beinert et al., 2002). Indeed, where RFR studies have adopted equivalent offending measures (nominally), these measures have typically been constituted in incompatible or disparate ways (see Case and Haines, 2009).

Asset risk assessment muddies these waters further by stating that the 'offending' outcome measured by the tool is 'reoffending' (Youth Justice Board, 2000), when it actually 'reconviction' (see Case, 2009). Making this misleading elision introduces a disconnect between the nature of the 'predictive' risk factors assessed and the goal of the tool to reduce reoffending, because risk factors for reconviction (assuming they actually exist in the real world) may differ markedly from those for reoffending (e.g. exposure may have been exacerbated by contact with the YJS). Indeed, the risk factors that populate Asset are derived from RFR studies of first-time offending, not reoffending or reconviction. Just as risk factors for reoffending and reconviction are likely to differ, so risk factors for reoffending may differ markedly from those for first-time offending (e.g. exposure may be exacerbated by previous offending behaviour and personal, familial and societal responses to it). Consequently, Asset risk assessment is not only ambiguous in terms of its purported outcome measure, but also this measure is not clearly linked to an appropriate, valid evidence-base, because of the application of risk factors for first-time offending to the prediction of reoffending/reconviction outcomes.

---

[3] For a further discussion of the processes and consequences of these 'actuarial' practices, see Case (2009).

# Reductionist imputation of the nature of the risk factor offending relationship

As stated, the risk assessment approaches used in the YJS in England and Wales prescribe and produce developmental understandings of young people's offending behaviours as the (irresistible) product of prior exposure to risk factors at early stages in their lives. The inevitable conclusion, on which this approach is based, is that childhood exposure to risk factors leads to/predicts adolescent offending. Such a deterministic conception of the influence of risk factors on future behaviour (offending) is highly questionable in two key forms: a critique of the evidence-base and a critical evaluation of the model.

The cross-sectional nature of much RFR precludes the identification of directional and causal relationships between two variables (e.g. risk factors and offending behaviour) as these variables tend to be measured concurrently or exposure to them measured over the same time period (e.g. the past year). Thus, the very limited sensitivity to the time of initial exposure to a given risk and its temporal relationship to the dependent variable (offending) precludes imputation of any causality (Case and Haines, 2009). Consequently, there is often no way of establishing which variable predates the other (e.g. do risk factors occur before offending behaviour?) or whether this is the case at all. Exposure to risk factors and the occurrence of offending behaviour could actually occur simultaneously/concurrently and be unconnected or both be influenced by extraneous variables. Indeed, offending behavior could actually lead to and/or exacerbate exposure to risk factors, which therefore function as *symptoms* of offending. There is a lack of conclusive evidence regarding the nature and even existence of any substantive relationship between risk factors and offending.[4] However, the absence of definitive evidence has not obstructed generalised predictions that young people exposed to certain numbers and levels of risk factors, at certain times of life, are statistically more likely to become offenders in the future and, as such, risk predictions should be used as the basis for informing preventive interventions. Overall, the evidence-base for a causal relationship between risk factors and offending is far from proven.

The most valid conclusion from RFR is that risk factors and offending behavior are statistical *correlates* with one another (i.e. they are co-related, associated, co-occurring). The developmental determinism of the RFR that underpins Asset, therefore, is highly problematic, *both* in the absence of a conclusive evidence-base regarding the nature of the risk factor–offending relationship *and* in the ambiguities surrounding the nature of the outcome to be predicted. At the practical level, it stretches credulity to assert that exposure to risk factors in early childhood is deterministic of offending behaviour in adolescence and adulthood. Such developmental determinism neglects the potential role of a host of intervening factors and influences (which may not be measured in risk

---

[4] An indeterminacy reflected in Asset risk assessment.

assessment) that may mitigate, mediate, reshape and confound any (developmental) relationships between risk factors and offending behaviour. For example, developmental RFR tends to neglect: the real-time influence of situational/environmental risk factors in the immediate lives and contexts of young people (Wikström, 2005); unpredictable critical life moments (Webster et al., 2006); and young people's ability to construct, resist and negotiate their risk-related experiences in everyday life (MacDonald, 2007). Despite such neglect, however, a conceptualisation of young people as 'crash test dummies' (Case and Haines, 2009) – on an inevitable collision course with offending outcomes – has come to dominate core aspects of youth justice policy and practice as the rationale for earlier and earlier intervention by adults has grown stronger.

# EARLY INTERVENTION IN YOUTH JUSTICE: A PROBLEMATIC CONCEPT

Prevention and early intervention for children in need has considerable appeal to policy-makers and professionals operating from health, education and social services contexts. (Little, 1999: 304)

The goal of prevention permeates children's services internationally in relation to health, education, social services, youth work, policing and youth justice (see Glass, 1999; Little, 1999). Categorising preventative practice with children offers more nuanced understanding (Little and Mount, 1999), for prevention work can be *universal* (intervening with a population to stop potential problems emerging), *early intervention* (targeting individuals who demonstrate the first signs of a problem and a 'high-risk' of developing that problem) or *treatment/intervention* (focusing on individuals who have developed most of the identifiable symptoms of a problem).

If we are not prepared to predict and intervene far more thoroughly then the children are going to grow up … a menace to society and actually threats to themselves. (Blair, 2006)

Further to the election of the first New Labour government in the UK in 1997, successive government publications and independent reviews have privileged early intervention as an ostensibly 'effective' and 'evidence-based' means of pre-empting problems and preventing and reducing levels of youth crime, whilst simultaneously supporting young people and their families to address their psychosocial deficits and 'criminogenic' needs (Home Office, 2008; Independent Commission on Youth Crime and Antisocial Behaviour, 2010; Ministry of Justice, 2010).

As we have noted, however, a range of ambiguities and uncertainties have characterised conceptions and applications of early intervention within the youth justice arena, prompting even major proponents of early intervention with young people 'at risk' of offending to concede that:

A critical question from a scientific and policy standpoint concerning child delinquency is: 'How early can we tell?' It is difficult, however, to obtain a clear answer to this question. (Loeber et al., 2003a: 6)

Despite an inconclusive and sparse evidence-base regarding how and when early intervention should be delivered in order to be effective, post-1997 youth justice in England and Wales has adopted an explicit standpoint of 'the earlier the intervention the better' (Blyth and Solomon, 2009: 3). However, the exact meaning of 'early' itself is not always clear and this gives rise to critical questions such as:

1. At which *developmental stage or age* should an individual be in receipt of intervention? Should early mean '*pre-birth*' (Blair, 2006), *0–2 years* of age (Daniel-Echols et al., 2010), *childhood* (Early Intervention Foundation, 2013), *early adolescence* (Lindsay et al., 2011), *late adolescence* (Thomas et al., 2008), *early adulthood* (Bernburg and Krohn, 2003)?

The lack of consensus around precisely what constitutes 'early' introduces further ambiguity. If the nature of the input variable (early intervention), along with the nature of the output/outcome variable (offending), cannot be defined accurately or consistently, then it is impossible to reduce valid and reliable evidence-based conclusions regarding the efficacy of early intervention. It could well be that intervention is effective at different developmental stages, but a sensitivity to this is not permitted by the uncritical generic push towards a universally applicable menu of interventions for practitioners working with children and young people.

2. What *outcome(s)* should early intervention be seeking to prevent/reduce or promote? Should the focus be the prevention/reduction of *first-time* offending (Haines et al., 2013), *reoffending* (Sherman et al., 1998), reoffending *seriousness or frequency* (Sapouna et al., 2011), *reconviction* (YJB, 2009), *other problematic behaviours and outcomes* such as school exclusion, substance use, antisocial behaviour and social exclusion (Conrad Hilton Foundation, 2012), *risk reduction* (Action for Children, 2010), promoting *resilience and desistance* (Hine, 2005), facilitating *restoration and reintegration/social inclusion* (University of Birmingham, 2004), enhancing *protective factors, strengths and capacities* (Hawkins et al., 2003), promoting *positive behaviours* (Case and Haines, 2004)?

Early intervention across children's services has become increasingly targeted (Little, 1999; Puffett, 2013), arguably as a means of filling the void in universal welfare provision with short-term interventions and programmes (Haines, 1999). This approach has been supported by a vacillating mixture of welfarist, (purportedly) evidence-based, systems management and economic (resource management, cost effectiveness) rationales. However, there is an alarming paucity of empirical support for the efficacy of early intervention with children and young people, particularly when targeted on reducing risk (see Goldson, 2005); a situation that appears to contradict successive UK governments' prioritisation of 'evidence-based' policies and practices (Case and Haines, 2009; Clarke, 2009; Squires and Stephen, 2005).

3. At which *behavioural stage* is early intervention most appropriate? Should intervention be implemented once an individual is identified to be *at risk* of problematic behaviour (Independent Commission on Youth Crime and Antisocial Behaviour, 2010; Morgan Harris Burrows, 2003), once they have demonstrated *pre-offending* risky behaviour such as school exclusion, substance use and antisocial behaviour (Walker et al., 2007), once they have come to the *official attention of the YJS* for an identified offence (YJB, 2000), once they have been assessed as *in need* of support such as welfare provision (Statham and Smith, 2010)? Should early intervention, therefore, be implemented in a *targeted* way (Clarke, 2009) or as a *universal* provision available to all young people (National Assembly Policy Unit, 2002)?

The goal of early intervention with children and young people in many areas of children services has tended towards the targeted prevention of problems and negative behaviours, as opposed to the universal promotion of strengths, capacitors, potentialities, children's rights (e.g. to support from adults, to equality of outcomes) and positive, pro-social outcomes. The prioritisation of prevention of the promotion is precipitated by a risk-averse culture of *interventionism* across services and practices that has serious ethical implications if implemented uncritically and crudely. The growing interventionist preference of government to identify as eligible for ameliorative preventative intervention growing numbers of young people at younger and younger ages demonstrating a broadening range of behaviours fuels the net-widening and control/surveillance agendas (Harrison and Wiles, 2005), whilst potentially labelling, stigmatising and marginalising incrementally larger numbers of young people at accelerating speed (Cohen, 1985; Goldson and Muncie, 2006; Matza, 1969), for example, exposing them to the negative (even if unintended) consequences of contact with the YJS (McAra and McVie, 2007). Delineating a section of the youth population as failing, helpless and hopeless enough to 'qualify' for an intervention (Goldson, 2000), regardless of whether they have ever actually demonstrated a problematic behaviour/outcome, whether they welcome the intervention or whether they have been consulted as to its content, is unethical, a restriction of liberty, punitive and non-evidenced through any robust evaluation criteria. In the youth justice context, this subverts due process and the tenet of 'innocent until proven guilty' (Case, 2006; Goldson, 2005, 2000), whilst contravening article 17 of the UN *Convention on the Rights of the Child* (UNICEF, 1989). Targeted intervention also denies a ('low-risk') proportion of that population access to intervention (and related services, information, support etc.), merely because they are not considered problematic enough to be recipients. This stands in direct contravention of the aspirations of the Children Act 2004 to provide services for all children in a universal way (Case, 2006).

# THE 'SCALED APPROACH':
# DISPROPORTIONALITY, REDUCTIONISM
# AND NEGATIVITY

The government believes that risk factors can be clearly identified, justifying intervention from a very early age, and that it can and does work. (Blyth and Solomon, 2009: 3)

An attempt to peddle simplistic, but politically acceptable, solutions to remarkably complex social, economic and cultural problems. (Pitts, 2003: 14)

In practice, much early intervention in the youth justice arena takes place once a young person has been officially identified as 'anti-social' or as an 'offender'. Typically, such intervention is thought to be risk-focused, preventative and developmental (in accordance with the RFPP) and it is predicated on the master status of the young person as an offender, employing a range of offence and offender focused approaches. Risk-focused early intervention offers a common-sense, purportedly effective, efficient and economical preventative approach that has been central to the development of youth justice in England and Wales since the Crime and Disorder Act 1998. The central 'key element of effective practice' for youth justice practitioners has been *Assessment, Planning Interventions and Supervision* (APIS): the 'foundation activities which guide and shape all work with young people who offend' (YJB, 2003: 6). However, concerns have been expressed that practice has not been consistent or assiduous enough in linking Asset scores to planned interventions for young people. Rather than review or replace the assessment and intervention process, however, the government chose to revamp and expand its commitment to risk by introducing the 'Scaled Approach' in November 2009. Under the Scaled Approach assessment and intervention framework, youth justice practitioners are required to tailor or scale the frequency, duration and intensity of planned interventions to levels of risk assessed by the young person's Asset score: standard intervention/low likelihood (0–14), enhanced intervention/medium likelihood (15–32) and intensive intervention/high likelihood (33+). However, the Scaled Approach has been subject to serious critique.

A notable criticism has been the potential for young people to receive *disproportionate intervention* (excessive or insufficient) on the basis of measured risk and predicted (not actual) behaviour, such that a young person displaying low risk may receive minimal intervention, regardless of the actual need for support, whilst young people assessed as high risk could be exposed to excessive and prolonged intervention in a quite unappropriate and unnecessary form (Bateman, 2011; Paylor, 2010; Sutherland, 2009). It is an approach that privileges a process of dealing with young people on the basis of what they '*might do*' as opposed to what they '*have done*' (Goldson, 2005: 264), thus placing an inordinate amount of faith in a body of RFR evidence that is: lacking in validity (e.g. full of uncertain conclusions regarding the nature of the risk factor-offending relationship), unreliable (e.g. exemplified by a lack of consensus regarding appropriate input and output variables) and practically non-existent (e.g. there is very little empirical evidence that risk focused interventions are effective in youth justice).

The validity of the risk-based assessment and intervention of the Scaled Approach is further undermined by its preference for *reductionist aggregation*. Consequently, individual young people subject to the Scaled Approach receive intervention based on their (risk) group affiliation rather than on their individual profile or circumstances. Such intervention may not only be disproportionate to their assessed level of risk and the actual offence they have committed (as above), but also inappropriate (invalid, ineffective) because the intervention fails to target the real-life influences on their offending, meet their welfare needs and/or provide their human rights entitlements as children.

Indeed, the Scaled Approach ultimately pursues a *negative and retrospective agenda*, seeking to prevent problem behaviours and to reduce risks that have already been experienced by young people, at the expense of prospectively promoting young people's capacities, strength, potential for positive outcomes and children's rights (see also Bateman, 2011; Haines and Case, 2012; Paylor, 2010). The underpinning logic of risk-based assessment and intervention portrays young people as risky, flawed individuals suffering the irresistible effects of 'deficits' in their past and current lives; 'crash test dummies' exposed to risk and hurtling towards inevitable offending outcomes (Case and Haines, 2009). Young people are depicted as passive victims of deterministic (risk) factors in their lives as opposed to agentic, resilient and resourceful individuals with the capacity to resist and avoid risks. Such a negative view of young people serves as justification for correctional (early) intervention, whilst simultaneously neglecting an entire body of alternative RFR that offers an empirical rejection of such negative and restricted conceptualisations (France and Homel, 2007; Hine, 2005; MacDonald, 2007).

Despite assertions that the risk-focused early intervention of the Scaled Approach is 'evidence-based' (YJB, 2009) and grounded in a long-standing, reliable and validated body of empirical RFR (see Loeber et al., 2003b), there is, in fact, an alarming paucity of evidence that risk-focused early intervention actually achieves its objectives in practice[5] (see Case and Haines, 2009; Goldson, 2005; Haines and Case, 2008; McAra and McVie, this volume). Indeed, the founders of RFR, Glueck and Glueck (1950), concluded that 'maturation' had the greatest influence upon desistance, providing a cogent argument for minimal/non-intervention with young people. Other noted RFR studies have evaluated the impact of long-term, risk-focused (early) interventions, with only very limited and inconsistent evidence of success (Bottoms and McClintock, 1973; Hawkins et al., 2003; Tremblay et al., 2003). The implication here is that the Scaled Approach has been promoted as an evidence-based intervention, when it is actually bereft of any substantive or coherent evidence-base at all. Worse still, it can be argued that there is empirical evidence linking risk-focused

---

[5] There is even evidence that assiduous adherence to the Scaled Approach has produced detrimental outcomes for young people (see Haines and Case, 2012).

early intervention to net-widening, the labelling, stigmatisation and criminalisation of young people and the exacerbation of attending behaviour (Goldson, 2000, 2008; McAra and McVie, this volume).

# ASSETPLUS: A WAY FORWARD?

Whilst the echoes of the risk assessment, risk management and early intervention relationship continue to be heard in youth justice practice in England and Wales, there are encouraging signs of change in the form of the planned revision to the government's assessment and intervention framework. The 'AssetPlus' model, due to be fully introduced by September 2014, challenges (in part at least) traditional conceptions of risk assessment, risk management and early intervention within youth justice practice and reintroduces more holistic, sensitive and positive assessments and interventions with young people. AssetPlus represents an ongoing assessment cycle that spans the entire youth justice spectrum (from prevention to custody), driven by practitioner completion of a 'core record' for each young person, consisting of three stages: information gathering and description; explanations and conclusions; and pathways and planning.

The proposed 'information gathering and description' stage contains four inter-related quadrants/sections: personal, family and social factors; offending/antisocial behaviour; foundations for change; and self-assessment. Moreover, the ratings and measures used in each of the sub-sections will not rely on crude numerical scores and instead signal a move away from the reductionist elements of Asset by avoiding the over-simplistic quantification of potentially complex life experiences and circumstances. Equally, the conceptual emphasis shifts towards prioritising a prospective focus on problems, needs and strengths (as opposed to risks) and resilience, desistance, engagement, participation and other positive outcomes (as opposed to the prevention of negative behaviours/outcomes). A more holistic assessment model containing a detailed exploration of 'foundations for change' and greater emphasis on 'self-assessment' is also evident. These step changes offer prospects for departing from adulterised and adult-centric assessments and the neglect of young people's voices and perspectives in the assessment process.

'Information gathering and description' data will feed into the 'explanations and conclusions' section of AssetPlus. The explicit intention is for practitioners to use the information to develop a more holistic understanding of young people's offending behaviour by considering both *contextual information* and temporally-sensitive *interactions* between the past and the present, life events, needs, positive factors and the various contexts in which young people demonstrate problems (YJB, 2013). Notwithstanding such welcome developments, problems potentially remain. It is unclear, for example, how the 'information gathering and description' data will avoid the psychosocial biases and inevitable individualisation/responsibilisation focusing, as it does, on predominantly psychological and immediate social (family, education, neighbourhood) issues at the expense of structural and socio-economic influences. There is also a creeping re-emergence (by stealth) of quantification in terms of the extent to which different factors will be rated on a three-point scale: 'high', 'medium' or 'low' (YJB, 2013). This section, as currently conceived, signals the danger of regression into risk management and its attendant problems, a retreat incongruous with the more holistic, prospective and positive emphasis promised in the opening data gathering section of AssetPlus.

The final section, 'pathways and planning', is intended to use the 'explanations and conclusions' information to assist practitioners in designing interventions to achieve positive outcomes for young people, including young people's engagement, participation and positive behaviours, all appropriate to their assessed circumstance, experiences and perceptions (YJB, 2013). However, these progressive objectives also face the prospect of being compromised by proposals to retain the three levels of intervention prescribed by the Scaled Approach – 'standard', 'enhanced' and 'intensive' (YJB, 2013).

In sum, on one hand the proposed AssetPlus assessment and intervention framework could constitute a major shift in focus away from the measurement of (psychosocial) risk factors and the prevention of offending through risk-focused early intervention, towards a more clearly defined emphasis on *needs* in personal, family and social domains, *strengths* that promote desistance and change, and *positive* outcomes such as well-being, safety, engagement and participation. On the other hand, however, the enduring presence of risk/likelihood of reoffending assessments appears contradictory to this shift. Despite its potential, AssetPlus is particularly vulnerable to the problems outlined above because, like the Asset tool that preceded it, it is a technique without an overarching purpose or philosophy (see Haines and Drakeford, 1998 for a broader discussion). It is to the broader question of philosophy that we now turn by way of conclusion.

# CHILDREN FIRST, OFFENDERS SECOND: CHILD-FRIENDLY YOUTH JUSTICE

Criminologists are frequently criticised, particularly by those in policy and practice domains, for always being negative: for saying what is wrong (with a particular policy or practice), but never saying what should be done instead. Although much of this chapter has engaged in a critical analysis of existing notions and practises associated with risk management and early intervention, we also want to say something about how we think youth justice policy and practice generally, and AssetPlus specifically, can be progressed along a more positive trajectory.

Risk, as we have shown in this chapter, is now largely discredited – in academic, policy and practice realms – and is no longer sufficient theoretically, empirically, in policy or practice terms to animate youth justice. Instead, we wish to argue the case for a broader philosophical approach underpinned by the principles of 'children first, offenders second' (Haines and Drakeford, 1998; see also Drakeford, 2010; Haines et al., 2013; Welsh Assembly Government and YJB, 2004).

Children first, offenders second (CFOS) de-emphasises offence/offender-focused youth justice guided by risk assessment, instead prioritising a focus on the inherent 'child' status of children in conflict with the law (hence 'children first'). All youth justice practices (including assessment and intervention) should therefore be *child-appropriate* and focused on the *whole child*, examining the full complexity of their lives, experiences, perspectives and needs. It is imperative that offending be seen as a part of the child's broader social identity (Drakeford, 2010) rather than their defining master status and that any responses are appropriately whole-child as a consequence. This necessitates seeing *children as part of the solution, not part of the problem* – with practitioners and policy-makers working in *partnership with children* to hold their interests, needs, rights and views as paramount throughout the youth justice process. CFOS demands that adult practitioners view themselves as working for the children they engage with, rather than as representatives of other interest groups (the YJS, community, victims). Thus, the priority for adults must be to engage closely and regularly with children to ensure that they are facilitated in expressing their views on issues that affect them (cf. Article 12 of the UNCRC), that they can participate equitably in decision-making regarding their futures and that they are enabled to access their universal entitlements as set out in progressive policy statements and international conventions. These features coalesce to produce a model of partnership working that can be viewed as *legitimate* to children, thus increasing the likelihood of them investing in, and committing to, the approach. In this way, children's engagement with youth justice practitioners goes deeper than the fundamentals of voluntarism, trust, respect and fairness (although these remain essential building blocks of the engagement relationship) and moves towards more progressive notions of partnership, reciprocity, investment and legitimate participation in decision-making processes.

Reductionist, retrospective, risk assessment, risk management and risk-based early intervention strategies are anathema to child-friendly, child-appropriate youth justice. However, the CFOS approach is not a clarion call for radical non-intervention, but rather for principled diversionary responses that focus on promoting positive behaviour and outcomes for children and enabling access to universal entitlements to services, opportunities, support and information (Goldson and Muncie, this volume). Therefore, we are not arguing for non-intervention per se, we are arguing for non-*formal* intervention. CFOS enables children to participate in and contribute to assessment outcomes and intervention plans that are future-orientated and that address their self-assessed needs, rights, strengths and potentialities. CFOS posits an approach to youth justice working with children that has a coherent *philosophy* (children first), an explicit sense of *purpose* (prevention is better than cure, children are part of the solution not part of the problem), clear *goals* (responsibilising adults, evidence-based partnership working) and clearly articulated, desirable *outcomes* for children (positive behaviour, access to rights/ entitlements). Practitioners must understand why they come into work every day, what it is that they are employed to do, to have singularity of purpose – but an essential element is freedom in selecting what methods they employ in achieving this purpose. At its core, CFOS seeks to establish key principles for youth justice policy and practice that establish a consistency to *how* practitioners and the YJS can work with children in ways that are appropriate, principled, valid and legitimate from the perspectives of children and thus can increase the chances of creating effective assessment practices and responsive, appropriate interventions.

# REFERENCES

Action for Children (2010) *Deprivation and Risk: The Case for Early Intervention.* Watford: Action for Children.

Allen, G. (2011) *Early Intervention: Next Steps. An Independent Report to Her Majesty's Government.* London: Department for Work and Pensions and Cabinet Office. Available at: www.dwp.gov.uk/docs/early-intervention-next-steps.pdf (accessed January 2013).

Baker, K., Jones, S., Roberts, C. and Merrington, S. (2002) *Validity and Reliability of Asset.* London: Youth Justice Board.

Baker, K., Jones, S., Roberts, C. and Merrington, S. (2005) *Further Development of Asset.* London: Youth Justice Board.

Bateman, T. (2011) 'Punishing poverty: the scaled approach and youth justice practice', *Howard Journal of Criminal Justice*, 50 (2): 171–83.

Beinert, S., Anderson, B., Lee, S. and Utting, D. (2002) *Youth at Risk? A National Survey of Risk Factors, Protective Factors and Problem Behaviour Among Young People in England, Scotland and Wales.* London: Communities that Care.

Bernburg, J.G. and Krohn, M. (2003) Labeling, life chances, and adult crime: the direct and indirect effects of official intervention in adolescence on crime in early adulthood. *Criminology*, 41 (4): 1287–1318.

Blair, T. (2006) '"We can clamp down on antisocial children before birth", says Blair', *Guardian*, 1 September.

Blair, T. (2007) 'I've been tough on crime, now we have to nip it in the bud', *Daily Telegraph*, 28 April.

Blyth, M. and Solomon, E. (2009) *Prevention and Youth Crime: Is Early Intervention Working?* Bristol: Policy Press.

Bottoms, A.E. and McClintock, F.H. (1973) *Criminals Coming of Age: A Study of Institutional Adaptation in the Treatment of Adolescent Offenders.* London: Heinemann.

Budd, T., Sharp, C. and Mayhew, P. (2005) *Offending in England and Wales: First Results from the 2003 Crime and Justice Survey.* London: Home Office.

Case, S.P. (2006) 'Young people "at risk" of what? Challenging risk-focused early intervention as crime prevention', *Youth Justice*, 6 (3): 171–9.

Case, S.P. (2009) 'Preventing and reducing risk', in Taylor, W., Earle, R. and Hester, R. (eds), *Youth Justice Handbook.* Cullompton: Willan.

Case, S.P. and Haines, K.R. (2004) 'Promoting prevention: evaluating a multi-agency initiative of youth consultation and crime prevention in Swansea', *Children and Society*, 18 (5): 355–70.

Case, S.P. and Haines, K.R. (2008) 'Factors shaping substance use by young people', *Journal of Substance Use*, 13 (1): 1–15.

Case, S.P. and Haines, K.R. (2009) *Understanding Youth Offending: Risk Factor Research, Policy and Practice.* Cullompton: Willan.

Case, S.P., Clutton, S. and Haines, K.R. (2005) 'Extending entitlement: a Welsh policy for children', *Wales Journal of Law and Policy*, 4 (2): 187–202.

Chief Secretary to the Treasury (2003) *Every Child Matters*, Cm 5860. London: The Stationary Office.

Churchill, H. (2011) *Wither the Social Investment State? Early Intervention, Prevention and Children's Services Reform in the New Policy Context.* Paper presented at the Social Policy Association International conference 'Bigger Societies, Smaller Governments?', 4–6 July, University of Lincoln, England.

Clarke, K. (2009) 'Early intervention and prevention: lessons from the Sure Start programme', in Blyth, M. and Solomon, E. (eds), *Prevention and Youth Crime: Is Early Intervention Working?* Bristol: Policy Press.

Cohen, S. (1985) *Visions of Social Control: Crime, Punishment and Classification.* London: Polity Press.

Conrad Hilton Foundation (2012) *Screening, Brief Intervention and Referral to Treatment.* Agoura Hills, CA: Conrad N. Hilton Foundation. Available at: www.hiltonfoundation.org/enewsletter/353-initiative-supports-prevention-and-early-intervention-to-reduce-substance-use-and-abuse (accessed November 2013).

Daniel-Echols, M., Sawyers, K. and Williams-Bishop, R. (2010). *Ready Children and Ready Schools: Combining Developmentally Appropriate Early Childhood Practice and Elementary School Improvement in the Mississippi Delta.* Session presented at the National Association for the Education of Young Children Annual Conference and Expo, November, Anaheim, CA.

Drakeford, M. (2010) 'Devolution and youth justice in Wales', *Criminology and Criminal Justice*, 10 (2): 137–54.

Early Intervention Foundation (2013) www.earlyinterventionfoundation.org.uk/ (accessed November 2013).

Farrington, D.P. (2000) 'Explaining and preventing crime: the globalization of knowledge', *Criminology*, 38 (1): 1–24.

Farrington, D.P. (2002) 'Developmental criminology and risk-focused prevention', in Maguire, M., Morgan, R. and Reiner, R. (eds), *The Oxford Handbook of Criminology*, 3rd edn. Oxford: Oxford University Press.

Farrington, D.P. (2007) 'Childhood risk factors and risk-focused prevention', in Maguire, M., Morgan, R. and Reiner, R. (eds), *The Oxford Handbook of Criminology*, 4th edn. Oxford: Oxford University Press.

Flood-Page, C., Campbell, S., Harrington, V. and Miller, J. (2000) *Youth Crime: Findings from the 1998/99 Youth Lifestyles Survey*, Home Office Research Study 209. London: Home Office.

France, A. (2008) 'Risk factor analysis and the youth question', *Journal of Youth Studies*, 11 (1): 1–15.

France, A. and Homel, R. (2007) *Pathways and Crime Prevention: Theory, Policy and Practice.* Cullompton: Willan.

France, A., Freiberg, K. and Homel, R. (2010) 'Beyond risk analysis: towards a more holistic approach to prevention', *British Journal of Social Work*, 40 (4): 1192–1210.

Glass, N. (1999) 'Sure Start: the development of an early intervention programme for young children in the United Kingdom', *Children & Society*, 13 (4): 257–64.

Glueck, S. and Glueck, E. (1950) *Unraveling Juvenile Delinquency.* New York: Commonwealth Fund.

Goldson, B. (2000) 'Wither diversion: interventionism and the new youth justice', in Goldson, B. (ed.), *The New Youth Justice*. Lyme Regis: Russell House.

Goldson, B. (2005) 'Taking liberties: policy and the punitive turn', in Hendrick, H. (ed.), *Child Welfare and Social Policy*. Bristol: Policy Press.

Goldson, B. (2008) 'Early intervention in the youth justice sphere: a knowledge-based critique', in Blyth, M. and Solomon, E. (eds), *Prevention and Youth Crime*, Researching Criminal Justice Series. Bristol: Policy Press.

Goldson, B. and Muncie, J. (2006) *Youth Crime and Justice*. London: Sage.

Haines, K.R. (1999) 'Crime as a social problem', *European Journal on Criminal Policy and Research*, 17 (2): 263–75.

Haines, K.R. and Case, S.P. (2008) 'The rhetoric and reality of the Risk Factor Prevention Paradigm approach to preventing and reducing youth offending', *Youth Justice*, 8 (1): 5–20.

Haines, K.R. and Case, S.P. (2012) 'Is the scaled approach a failed approach?', *Youth Justice*, 12 (3): 212–28.

Haines, K.R. and Drakeford, M. (1998) *Young People and Youth Justice*. Basingstoke: Macmillan.

Haines, K.R., Case, S.P., Charles, A.D. and Davies, K. (2013) 'The Swansea Bureau: a model of diversion from the youth justice system', *International Journal of Law, Crime and Justice*, 41 (2): 167–87.

Harrison, R. and Wiles, C. (2005) *Working with Young People*. London: Sage.

Hawkins, J.D. and Catalano, R.F. (1992) *Communities that Care*. San Francisco, CA: Jossey-Bass.

Hawkins, J.D., Smith, B.H., Hill, K.G., Kosterman, R., Catalano, R.F. and Abbott, R.D. (2003) 'Understanding and preventing crime and violence: findings from the Seattle Social Development Project', in Thornberry, T.P. and Krohn, M.D. (eds), *Taking Stock of Delinquency: An Overview of Findings from Contemporary Longitudinal Studies*. New York: Kluwer.

Hine, J. (2005) 'Early intervention: the view from On Track', *Children and Society*, 19 (2): 117–30.

Home Office (2008) *Youth Crime Action Plan*. London: Home Office. Available at: www.homeoffice.gov.uk/documents/youth-crime-action-plan/ (accessed December 2013).

Independent Commission on Youth Crime and Antisocial Behaviour (2010) *Time for a Fresh Start*. London: Police Foundation. Available at: www.youthcrimecommission.org.uk/_(accessed December 2013).

Johnston, J., MacDonald, R., Mason, P., Ridley, L. and Webster, C. (2000) *Snakes & Ladders: Young People, Transitions and Social Exclusion*. Bristol: Policy Press.

Kemshall, H. (2011) 'Crime and risk: contested territory for risk theorising', *International Journal of Law, Crime and Justice*, 39 (4): 218–29.

Kemshall, K. (2008) 'Risk factors', in Goldson, B. (ed.), *Dictionary of Youth Justice*. Cullompton: Willan.

Laub, J. and Sampson, R. (2003) *Shared Beginnings, Delinquent Lives: Delinquent Boys to Age 70*. London: Harvard University Press.

Lindsay, G., Strand, S., Cullen, M.A., Band, S. and Cullen, S. (2011) *Parenting Early Intervention Programme*. London: Department for Education and Skills.

Little, M. (1999) 'Prevention and early intervention with children in need: definitions, principles and examples of good practice', *Children and Society*, 13 (4): 304–16.

Little, M. and Mount, K. (1999) *Prevention and Early Intervention with Children in Need*. London: Ashgate.

Loeber, R., Farrington, D.P. and Petechuk, D. (2003a) *Child Delinquency: Early Intervention and Prevention*, Bulletin. Washington, DC: US Department of Justice, Office of Justice Programs, Office of Juvenile Justice and Delinquency Prevention.

Loeber, R., Farrington, D.P., Stouthamer-Loeber, M., Moffitt, T.E., Caspi, A., White, H., Wei, E. and Beyers, J.M. (2003b) 'The development of male offending: key findings from fourteen years of the Pittsburgh Youth Study', in Thornberry, T.P. and Krohn, M.D. (eds), *Taking Stock of Delinquency: An Overview of Findings from Contemporary Longitudinal Studies*. New York: Kluwer.

MacDonald, R. (2007) 'Social exclusion, youth transitions and criminal careers: five critical reflections on "risk"', in France, A. and Homel, R. (eds), *Pathways and Crime Prevention: Theory, Policy and Practice*. Cullompton: Willan.

Matza, D. (1969) *Becoming Deviant*. New York: Prentice-Hall.

McAra, L. and McVie, S. (2007) 'Youth justice? The impact of system contact on patterns of desistance from offending', *European Journal of Criminology*, 4 (3): 315–45.

Ministry of Justice (2010) *Breaking the Cycle: Effective Punishment, Rehabilitation and Sentencing of Offenders*. London: Ministry of Justice.

Moffitt, T.E. (2006) 'Life-course persistent versus adolescence-limited antisocial behaviour', in Cicchetti, D. and Cohen, D. (eds), *Developmental Psychopathology*, 2nd edn. New York: Wiley.

Morgan Harris Burrows (2003) *Evaluation of the Youth Inclusion Programme*. London: Morgan Harris Burrows.

National Assembly Policy Unit (2002) *Extending Entitlement: Support for 11 to 25 year olds in Wales: Direction and Guidance*. Cardiff: National Assembly for Wales.

O'Mahony, P. (2009) 'The risk factors paradigm and the causes of youth crime: a deceptively useful analysis?', *Youth Justice*, 9 (2): 99–115.

Paylor, I. (2010) 'The scaled approach to youth justice: a risky business', *Criminal Justice Matters*, 81 (1): 30–1.

Pitts, J. (2003) *The New Politics of Youth Crime: Discipline or Solidarity?* Lyme Regis: Russell House.

Puffett, N. (2013) 'DfE data shows funding shift from universal to targeted services', *Children and Young People Now*, 15 October.

Ross, A., Duckworth, K., Smith, D.J., Wyness, G. and Schoon, I. (2011) *Prevention and Reduction: A Review of Strategies for Intervening Early to Prevent or Reduce Youth Crime and Anti-Social Behaviour*. London: DfES and Centre for Analysis of Youth Transitions.

Sampson, R.J. and Laub, J.H. (1993) *Crime in the Making: Pathways and Turning Points through Life*. Harvard: Harvard University Press.

Sampson, R.J. and Laub, J.H. (2005) 'A general age-graded theory of crime: lessons learned and the future of life-course criminology', in Farrington, D.P. (ed.), *Integrated Developmental and Life-Course Theories of Offending*. New Brunswick: Transaction.

Sapouna, M., Bissett, C. and Conlong, A.M. (2011) *What Works to Reduce Reoffending: A Summary of the Evidence Justice Analytical Services*. Edinburgh: Scottish Government.

Sherman, L., Gottfredson D., MacKenzie, D., Eck, J., Reuter, P. and Bushway, S. (1998) *Preventing Crime: What Works, What Doesn't, What's Promising*.

Baltimore, MD: Department of Criminology and Criminal Justice, University of Maryland.

Smith, D.J. and McVie, S. (2003) 'Theory and method in the Edinburgh study of youth transitions and crime', *British Journal of Criminology*, 43 (1): 169–95.

Squires, P. and Stephen. D. (2005) *Rougher Justice: Anti-social Behaviour and Young People*. Cullompton: Willan.

Statham, J. and Smith, M. (2010) *Issues in Earlier Intervention: Identifying and Supporting Children with Additional Needs*. London: Department for Children, Schools and Families.

Sutherland, A. (2009) 'The "scaled approach" in youth justice: fools rush in …', *Youth Justice*, 9 (1): 44–60.

Thomas, J., Vigurs, C.A., Oliver, K., Suarez, B., Newman, M., Dickson, K. and Sinclair, J. (2008) *Targeted Youth Support: Rapid Evidence Assessment of Effective Early Interventions for Youth at Risk of Future Poor Outcomes*. London: EPPI Centre Social Science Research Unit.

Thornberry, T.P. and Krohn, M.D. (2003) *Taking Stock of Delinquency: An Overview of Findings from Contemporary Longitudinal Studies*. New York: Kluwer.

Tremblay, R.E., Vitaro, F., Nagin, F., Pagani, L. and Seguin, J. (2003) 'The Montreal longitudinal experimental study: rediscovering the power of descriptions', in Thornberry, T.P. and Krohn, M.D. (2003) *Taking Stock of Delinquency: An Overview of Findings from Contemporary Longitudinal Studies*. New York: Kluwer.

UNICEF (1989) *United Nations Convention on the Rights of the Child*. London: UNICEF.

University of Birmingham (2004) *National Evaluation of the Children's Fund*. London: Department for Education and Skills.

Walker, J., Thompson, C., Laing, K., Raybould, S., Coombes, S., Proctor, S. and Wren, C. (2007) *Youth Inclusion and Support Panels: Preventing Crime and Antisocial Behaviour?* London: Department for Education and Skills.

Webster, C., MacDonald, R. and Simpson, M. (2006) Predicting criminality: risk/protective factors, neighbourhood influence and desistance, *Youth Justice*, 6 (1): 7–22.

Welsh Assembly Government and Youth Justice Board (2004) *All Wales Youth Offending Strategy*. Cardiff: Welsh Assembly Government.

West, D.J. and Farrington, D.P. (1973) *Who Becomes Delinquent?* London: Heinemann.

Wikström, P.-O. (2005) 'The social origins of pathways in crime: towards a developmental ecological action theory of crime involvement and its changes', in Farrington, D.P. (ed.), *Integrated Developmental and Life-Course Theories of Offending*. New Brunswick: Transaction.

Wikström, P.-O. and Butterworth, D. (2006) *Adolescent Crime: Individual Differences and Lifestyles*. Cullompton: Willan.

Youth Justice Board (2000) *ASSET: Explanatory Notes*. London: YJB.

Youth Justice Board (2003) *Assessment, Planning Interventions and Supervision*. London: YJB.

Youth Justice Board (2009) *Youth Justice: The Scaled Approach. A Framework for Assessment and Interventions. Post-Consultation Version Two*. London: YJB.

Youth Justice Board (2013) Assessment and Planning Interventions Framework – AssetPlus, Model Document. London: YJB.

# 8 THE CASE FOR DIVERSION AND MINIMUM NECESSARY INTERVENTION

## LESLEY McARA AND SUSAN McVIE

Over the past 40 years there has been a gradual decoupling of the study of crime from the study of punishment (Hamilton, 2014; Tonry, 2007). The process began with the 'critical turn' in criminology during the 1970s, which had the effect of focusing the attention of more radical criminologists on the political dimensions of crime control and penal processes rather than offender aetiology (Armstrong and McAra, 2006). It gained momentum with the invocation of 'penality' in the study of punishment in the 1980s by scholars who aimed to set an academic as well as a political agenda by critically engaging with social theory (as the principal lens through which to 'read' contemporary penal systems) and identifying the preconditions necessary for the development of a grounded praxis (Blomberg and Cohen, 1995; Cohen and Scull, 1983; Garland and Young, 1983).

This decoupling process has culminated in a series of methodological schisms within criminology between, inter alia: those who research crime control and penal practice in late modernity (whose analytical focus is primarily institutional dynamics or state level actors) (Garland, 2001; Simon, 2007; Wacquant, 2001); grounded accounts of penal transformation based on analysis of policy (Barker, 2009; Jones and Newburn, 2007; Miller, 2009); a growing body of developmental and life-course criminology, predicated on scientific rationalism (Farrington, 2005; Laub, 2006; Tremblay, 2012); and cultural criminologists and ethnographers who highlight the significance of 'edgework' and lived cultural practices and eschew both positivism and crime science (Hayward and Young, 2012; Young, 2011).

In our contribution to this book we will argue that there is a strong and enduring relationship between punishment and offender identity, which has been understated in much contemporary theorising about what works in crime reduction and how offending behaviour is understood (in both the academic and policy worlds). If we wish to build a juvenile justice system which protects the rights of children, promotes the well-being of young people who come into contact with official agencies, reduces crime and promotes social justice, then it behoves us to address and challenge more explicitly the criminogenic nature of variant modes of agency intervention and the ways in which offending pathways are aggravated by the very institutions which have been set up to reduce or eradicate troublesome behaviour. In sum, there is a need to evolve a 'diversionary paradigm' for juvenile justice.

The evidence-base for our argument derives from the Edinburgh Study of Youth Transitions and Crime (the Edinburgh Study), a longitudinal programme of research on pathways into and out of offending. The chapter begins with an overview of the research and policy context. This is followed by a brief description of the aims and methods of the Edinburgh Study. Drawing from over 15 years of fieldwork, the chapter then sets out key findings relating to the inter-relationships between offending and juvenile justice interventions. The chapter concludes with a review of the implications of the findings for the development of a grounded praxis, and more specifically with a call for enhanced and purposeful diversion and minimum necessary intervention. Whilst acknowledging that there is always a need to maintain a secure estate for the very small number of young people who are a danger to others, the findings of the Edinburgh Study indicate that, for the vast majority of offenders, minimal intervention is the most effective course of action.

# THE RESEARCH AND POLICY CONTEXT

## Theoretical framings

The link between offending and regulatory practices was most famously promulgated by labelling theorists such as Becker (1997) and Lemert (1967). The epistemological and ontological foundations of labelling lie in symbolic interactionism which posits that self-identity is a product of the ways in which an individual perceives that he/she is perceived by others (Blumer, 1969). Symbolic indications of self-hood are read from the behaviour of others within specific encounters, absorbed by the individual involved and then reflected back in a series of role adaptations. Labelling theorists contend that repeated (negative) encounters with authority have damaging consequences for self-identity. Lemert, for example, argued that the process of labelling (particularly when harsh and unwarranted) can lead individuals to reconstruct their identity around the deviant label (a process he terms as secondary deviation; Lemert, 1967). In a similar

**Table 8.1** Juvenile justice paradigms

| | Just deserts | Welfare | Restorative | Actuarial | Diversionary |
|---|---|---|---|---|---|
| **Personhood** | Child as rights bearer | Child as bearer of entitlements | Child as bearer of entitlements and rights | Child qualified bearer of rights | Child as bearer of rights |
| | Individuals constitutionally self-interested | Individuals a product of experience | Individuals constitutionally 'good' | Individuals potentially 'bad' | Individuals product of social encounters |
| | Offender as rational and responsible | Offender as non-rational, irresponsible | Offender as rational and responsible | Offender as dangerous | Offenders adapt to ascribed identities |
| | The rational man | The patient | The penitent | The commodity | The deviant status |
| **Social relations** | Core relationship: contractual: state vs. individual citizen | Core relationships: nested model of state: community, family, child | Core relationships: inclusive: child, victim and community | Core relationship: adversarial community vs. potential offender | Core relationship: reflexive |
| | | | | | Regulatory practices shaping individual sense of self |
| | Didactic | Transformative | Integrationist | Protective | Preventative |
| | Audience: citizens | Audience: offender and family | Audience: community and victims | Audience: public | Audience: the child |
| | Sensibility: retribution (vengeance) | Sensibility: philanthropy (paternalism) | Sensibility: connection (infliction of shame) | Sensibility: fear (hate) | Sensibility: rational calculus (managerialist) |
| **Intervention** | Aim to deter and punish | Aim to diagnose and to rescue | Aim to support victims, to restore harm, to reconnect child to community, to build more cohesive peaceful community | Aim to diminish current and future risk, safeguard victims and the wider community | Aim to diminish negative effects of regulatory practises and support inclusion |
| | Proportionality to deeds, parsimony | Proportionality to needs | Proportionality to harm caused | Proportionality to risk | Proportionality to pernicious consequences of agency impact |

*Source*: Adapted from McAra, 2010

vein, Becker (1997) argued that an 'outsider' status can become a self-fulfilling prophecy as moral entrepreneurs construct and apply labels which the 'deviant' subsequently finds hard to shrug off (the deviant label becoming the individual's 'master-status'). Goffman (1961) too asserted that identity is shaped by the dynamics of regulation. According to Goffman, an individual's actions in public are governed by a set of unwritten, but commonly understood, modes of regulation or sets of rituals. Individuals have to be constantly alert to things which will disturb the equilibrium of their social appearance and be ready to adapt. In public life the individual is vulnerable (and particularly vulnerable when acting alone rather than in a group), required to display the correct situational proprieties in a variety of encounters. Goffman describes an intricate network of ritual behaviour patterns and appropriate responses to social encounters and cross-encounters which together contribute to a reciprocally sustained sense of identity.

The main implication of labelling theory in terms of offender management is that interventions should be kept to a minimum, to avoid stigmatisation and the pernicious consequences of secondary deviation: in Shur's (1973) terms there is a need for 'radical non-intervention'. A further implication is the need for institutions to be more reflexive, acknowledging that their practices, no matter how benign in orientation, can contribute to the imposition of modes of identity which sustain and reproduce patterns of behaviour (including offending behaviours in some instances).

Such implications have a significant bearing on our understanding of the modes of juvenile justice and the narratives that frame contemporary systems, which are complex in orientation and varied in implementation. McAra (2010) has outlined four paradigms that dominate contemporary juvenile justice discourse (just deserts, welfare, restorative and actuarial). In acknowledging the implications of labelling theory, a fifth aspect, the 'diversionary paradigm', may be evolved. By deconstructing each of these paradigms, as shown in Table 8.1, we can begin to interrogate the core assumptions about the nature of personhood and the relationship between the citizen, the community and the state which inhere in current policy. More importantly we can open up for critical discussion the philosophical and empirical basis on which to construct the evidence-base for a more effective and 'just' system for dealing with children and young people who come into conflict with the law.

As indicated in Table 8.1, a diversionary paradigm conceives of the Child as a bearer of rights, but one whose identity and sense of self is predominantly a product of social encounters. Where social encounters impose negative or 'spoiled' versions of self-hood, then this undermines the Child's right to develop in dignity and diminishes respect for their 'natural worth as human beings' (as per the United Nations Convention on the Rights of the Child). The deviant status is a conferred identity that can become all-consuming in specific contexts (see McAra and McVie, 2012a). Regulatory practices, therefore, are inherently reflexive: enforcement and implementation always have consequences in terms of shaping an individual's sense of self. In evolving a diversionary practice, the aim is to prevent the emergence and reproduction of deviance as an identity. This involves careful systems management and a rational calculation of the harms of intervening for the child. In this paradigm, managerialism is no longer an aphilosophical approach to offender management, rather it is strongly imbued with the values of social justice, a principled approach to supporting the rights of the child.

## Policy framings

The radical implications of labelling theory (and by extension, the diversionary paradigm) have rarely shaped juvenile justice policy: recognising that less is more is a somewhat difficult message to sell to an electorate, particularly in contexts where crime control has become a key mechanism through which governments build political capacity (McAra, 2011; Simon, 2007). However, two key examples stand out. The first of these occurred during the 1980s in England and Wales with the implementation of 'systems management'. This approach was pioneered by the Lancaster Group[1] and was characterised by multi-agency diversion. The aim was to keep youngsters out of the juvenile justice system (through a major increase in the use of cautioning if offending was very low level and of limited seriousness), or minimising the level of intervention (or degree of system penetration) for those more serious and persistent offenders captured by the system (with a major expansion of intermediate treatment as an alternative to custody) (see Goldson, 1997; Pitts, 2001; Smith, 2010). Systems management contributed to a reduction in the use of custody over the decade, with the proportion of children aged between 14 and 16 sentenced to custody dropping from 12 per cent in 1985 to 7 per cent by 1990 (Newburn, 2002). However, it was largely abandoned during the 1990s when 'prison works' became the dominant mantra (in the latter days of Conservative government), followed by New Labour's 'tough on crime' rhetoric which increasingly infused policy and practice (Smith, 2010).

The second example relates to Scotland. The original ethos of the children's hearing system (the Kilbrandon Committee philosophy, 1964) was aimed at avoiding criminalisation, but it is only now (in the wake of the passage of the Children's Hearing (Scotland) Act 2011) that offences admitted by children within this system count as alternatives to prosecution rather than convictions.[2] In addition to this, the Scottish government has recently committed to

---

[1] The Lancaster Group comprised academics from Lancaster University's Centre of Youth, Crime and Community, Norman Tutt, David Thorpe and David Smith. Members of the group had links with Social Information Systems, a private consultancy which advised local social services on how to implement systems management techniques.

[2] There are some exceptions – those offences for which DNA evidence can be retained, mostly sexual and violent offences. Prior to the 2011 Act any offences that were admitted in a children's hearing could be disclosed to future employers up to the age of 40, which arguably undermined the Kilbrandon ethos (see McAra and McVie, 2014).

a new 'whole system approach' to young people who offend. A key focus of this approach is to maximise the use of diversion and to keep 16 and 17 year olds out of the criminal justice system (formerly the vast majority of 16 and 17 year olds were dealt with in the adult court system; see McAra, 2010). This new system advocates the streamlining of planning, assessment and decision-making processes, with resources being directed at services beyond the formal juvenile and criminal justice systems. Early indications suggest that the approach is having some success; in particular, the number of young people committing crime between 2011 and 2012 fell by 9 per cent and offence referrals to the Children's Reporter over the same period dropped by 31 per cent (MacQueen and McVie, 2013), although further research is needed. The evidence-base on which the whole system approach was developed was informed by the Edinburgh Study of Youth Transitions and Crime, to which we now turn.

# THE EDINBURGH STUDY: AIMS AND METHODS

The Edinburgh Study of Youth Transitions and Crime tracks the lives of a single cohort of around 4,300 young people who started secondary school in the City of Edinburgh in 1998.[3] Core aims of the Study are: (i) to explore from the early teenage years onwards the factors leading to criminal offending and desistance from it; and (ii) to examine the impact of interactions with formal agencies of control, such as the police, social work, the children's hearings system and the courts, on subsequent behaviour. Young people from all school sectors (both state funded and independent, and mainstream and special education) were included in the study and response rates were consistently high (see McAra and McVie, 2007b).

Data about the whole cohort were collected from multiple sources including: self-completion questionnaires (six annual waves from age 12 to 17)[4]; school, police, social work, and children's hearings records (the latter two from birth up to age 18); and conviction data from Scottish criminal records (up to age 24). Complementing the quantitative dimension of the Study, semi-structured interviews were also carried out with sub-samples of the cohort at ages 13 and 18.[5]

---

[3] The Edinburgh Study has been funded by grants from the Economic and Social Research Council (R000237157; R000239150), the Scottish Government and the Nuffield Foundation.

[4] A range of strategies were employed to enhance response rates (see McVie, 2001, 2003). Missing data were dealt with using a combination of multiple imputation and weighting. Further information on the Study can be found in Smith and McVie, 2003 and on data handling in McAra and McVie, 2010.

[5] At age 13, 40 youngsters were interviewed. The sub-sample was stratified by gender, socio-economic status and involvement in offending. At age 18, interviews were carried out with 18 youngsters who continued to be involved in serious offending and illegal drug use.

A further wave of fieldwork was conducted at age 24 with those who had any offence referral to the children's hearing system and two matched groups.

Drawing on these data, the next sections of the chapter provide a conspectus of the evidence from the Study which is supportive of the diversionary paradigm.

# THE LINKS BETWEEN JUVENILE JUSTICE INTERVENTIONS AND OFFENDING BEHAVIOUR

## Selection effects within the system

The process for dealing with young people who were engaged in offending (at the time the fieldwork was conducted) is set out in Figure 8.1. The key gatekeepers to the juvenile justice system were the police. The Study found that selection effects operated with the system that resulted in the construction of a population of 'usual suspects' which was continually recycled by agencies (McAra and McVie, 2005). Rather than diminishing the likelihood of future offending, system intervention served to inhibit the natural process of desistence from offending exhibited by the vast majority of the cohort in the mid-to-late teenage years (see Smith, 2006).

In order to determine the existence, and longer-term impacts, of selection effects within the system, we used the longitudinal design of the study to examine the three crucial decision-making stages within the Scottish juvenile justice process (see Figure 8.1): the decision of police officers to 'charge' a young person with committing a crime; the decision of police officers to refer a young person to the Children's Reporter on offending grounds[6]; and the decision of

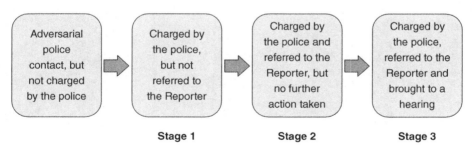

| Adversarial police contact, but not charged by the police | Charged by the police, but not referred to the Reporter | Charged by the police and referred to the Reporter, but no further action taken | Charged by the police, referred to the Reporter and brought to a hearing |
|---|---|---|---|
| **Stage 1** | **Stage 2** | **Stage 3** |

**Figure 8.1**  Juvenile justice decision-making process in Scotland

---

[6] Within the Scottish juvenile justice system, the Children's Reporter is the paid official of the Children's Hearings System who has responsibility for investigating all referrals and making a decision about whether to refer cases to a hearing or take no further action. For further information see www.chscotland.gov.uk (accessed 7.10.14).

the Children's Reporter to bring a young person to a formal hearing to determine whether there were grounds for compulsory measures of care and supervision (see McAra and McVie, 2007a). Quasi-experimental analysis – using propensity score matching – was conducted which allowed individuals who had experienced these three progressively more intensive forms of intervention to be paired up with a control group of similar young people, statistically matched on a range of characteristics (including frequency of self-reported serious offending) who had not had formal system intervention.

Analysis showed that selection effects were operating at each of these three stages in a way that ensured that a small sub-population of young people who offended were being propelled into a repeated cycle of referral to the children's hearing system, whereas other young people who were equally serious offenders escaped the attention of formal agencies altogether. Change in offending was measured between age 15 (the point of intervention) and age 16 (one year later). Figure 8.2 compares the percentage of those in the three intervention and comparison groups who reported engaging in serious offending one year post intervention (at age 16). There was no

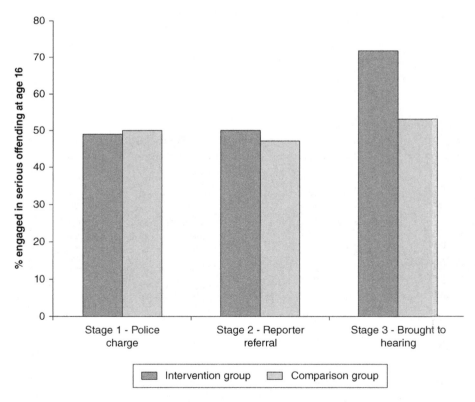

**Figure 8.2** Comparing prevalence of serious offending at age 15 between intervention and comparison groups

significant difference in prevalence of offending between the matched groups at stages 1 and 2, with around half of the young people in these groups still reporting some engagement in serious offending. However, those who were brought to a hearing and placed on supervision were significantly more likely to be involved in serious offending subsequently than their matched counterparts with no such hearings contact. In other words, those who had experienced the most intervention were most likely to still be offending seriously one year later.

In line with the broad pattern of desistance amongst the cohort as a whole, all groups showed a decline in their average frequency of self-reported serious offending one year post intervention. As shown in Table 8.2, the reduction in volume of offending was significant within all groups with the exception of *those brought to a hearing*. Generally speaking, the deeper 'the usual suspects' penetrated the juvenile justice system, the more likely it was that their pattern of desistance from involvement in serious offending was *inhibited*. Those who were charged by the police reduced their serious offending by 50 per cent on average, compared to only 39 per cent for those who were referred to the Reporter, and a non-significant reduction of 31 per cent for those who were brought to a hearing. Meanwhile, the reduction in serious offending amongst the comparison groups was broadly equal for stages 1 and 2, and slightly higher for stage 3. These findings indicate that, far from addressing their engagement in serious offending, being made subject to compulsory measures of care appears to have hindered the desistance process.

These findings provide support for a growing body of international literature (see Huizinga et al., 2003; Wiley et al., 2013; Ward et al., 2014), which suggests that repeated and more intensive forms of contact with agencies of juvenile justice may be criminogenic, even within the confines of a predominantly welfare-based juvenile justice system. As we have shown, forms of diversion that serve to caution without recourse to formal intervention may encourage, or at least maintain, desistance from serious offending; however, many of those who are pushed furthest over the threshold of intervention run the risk of engaging in further offending. We turn next to an exploration of the longer-term impact of such intervention and the potentially damaging outcomes for those who experience it.

**Table 8.2** Average change in frequency of offending from age 15 to age 16 within intervention and comparison groups

|  | Intervention group | Comparison group |
| --- | --- | --- |
| **Stage 1: Charged by the police** | −50% *** | −43% ** |
| **Stage 2: Referred to the Reporter** | −39% ** | −42% *** |
| **Stage 3: Brought to a hearing** | −31% | −49% ** |

*Source*: McAra and McVie, 2007a: 334

*Notes*: *** $p<.001$, ** $p<.01$, *$p<.05$

# The long-term impact of intervention

Evidence from the Edinburgh Study shows that far from nipping criminal justice careers in the bud, many of those with involvement with the juvenile justice system are rapidly 'up-tariffed' in the adult criminal justice system once they reach the transition point of 16 (see McAra and McVie, 2007b). A high proportion (56 per cent) of those who had been referred to the Reporter on offence grounds at any point up to age 16 had a conviction in the adult criminal justice system by age 22, which was five times higher than for those with no such referral. Youngsters who made the transition between the hearings system and the adult criminal justice system were generally assessed by agencies as having a high volume of needs (relating to personal, family and school adversities) at the point of transition. And yet, such youngsters were up-tariffed relatively quickly, with disproportionate numbers being placed in custody by their 22nd birthdays (19 per cent as contrasted with just 3 per cent of those with convictions who had no hearings history).

While the risk of a negative outcome for those experiencing intervention is high, it is important to recognise that it is not inevitable. We know, from the ubiquitous age–crime curve, that desistance from offending is a common trend in the late teenage years and it is clear that while many who experience juvenile justice make the transition into the adult system, some do not. What is less well understood is what are the drivers of desistance and where the gaze of policymakers and practitioners should be focused in order to maximize the impact of diversion.

Using data from the Scottish Criminal Records Office (SCRO), we applied semi-parametric group-based (or trajectory) modelling to identify common trajectories of conviction amongst the Edinburgh Study cohort (see McAra and McVie 2010). This statistical technique was used to identify an optimum number of developmental trajectories within the cohort based on the number of convictions recorded at each year of age (see McAra and McVie, 2012b). Discrete groups of offenders, which were internally homogeneous (i.e. individuals within groups were similar to each other) but externally heterogeneous (i.e. the groups differed from each other), were estimated based on the probability of conviction. Every individual had a probability of belonging to each group; however, they were assigned to the group with the highest probability. The modelling estimated four typical conviction trajectories, which are shown graphically in Figure 8.3. The largest of the groups, to which 85 per cent of the cohort were assigned, had little or no probability of conviction. Most of the remaining cohort members (13 per cent) were assigned to a 'late onset decliner' group, whose probability of conviction began to rise from age 15 and peaked around age 20 before starting to decline. At its peak, individuals within this group had around a 30 per cent chance of conviction on average. This group reflects the typical age curve found when analysing aggregate convictions data. What is normally concealed within such aggregate data are the two much smaller 'early onset' groups whose probability of conviction started to rise from around age 9–10. These two groups exhibited very similar trajectories until the age of 13, before diverging dramatically. The 'early onset chronic' group's probability of conviction rose steeply to their early twenties (at which point individuals had an 80 per cent chance of conviction on average) before starting to decline slightly. Meanwhile, the probability of conviction amongst the 'early onset desister' group stabilised at around 30 per cent from age 14–16 before declining and becoming almost zero by age 22.

The emergence of the two early onset groups raises important questions about why some individuals begin their 'criminal justice careers' so much earlier than others and what causes such a divergence of trajectories in the early teenage years, leading one to a long-term pattern of conviction and the other to an apparent pathway of desistance. In order to answer these questions, we compared the two early onset trajectory groups at age 12 on a broad range of study measures (including socio-economic status, early history of system contact, school experience, family dynamics, leisure activities, substance use,

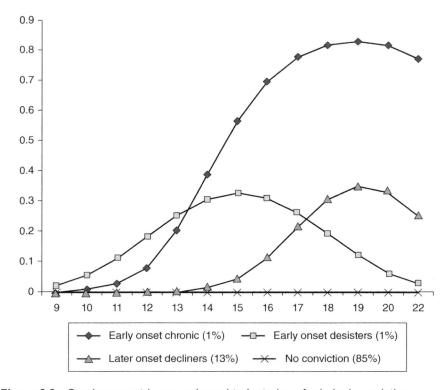

**Figure 8.3** Semi-parametric group-based trajectories of criminal conviction

personality measures and self-reported offending behaviour). Both groups were identified as being significantly more disadvantaged, vulnerable and problematic than all other groups within the cohort. However, we found *no significant difference* between the two early onset groups on any of these measures at age 12.

The significant point of divergence for the two early onset groups appeared to occur between age 13–15, so we examined which of the measures included in the comparative analysis at age 12 showed significant within-group change (for either the chronics or the desisters) over this period. Several key factors emerged as changing significantly amongst the chronic group, but not the early onset desisters. The chronic group significantly increased their level of truancy and their likelihood of school exclusion. And they significantly increased their frequency of adversarial police contact, police warnings and charges and referral to the Children's Reporter on offence grounds. On all other measures, there was no other significant difference in change between the two groups. Taken together, these findings suggest that the chronic conviction trajectory was aggravated by increased truancy and exclusion from school and increased police contact and system intervention. Importantly, the divergence of the two early onset conviction trajectories was *not accounted for* by differential involvement in serious offending as both groups were indistinguishable in respect of their self-reported offending over the period from age 12 to age 17, as shown in Figure 8.4.

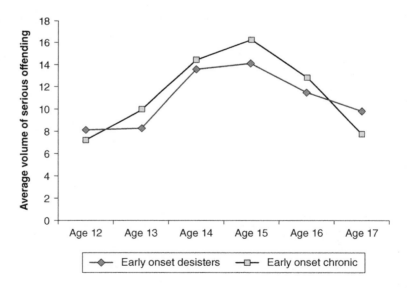

**Figure 8.4** Comparison of volume of serious offending amongst the early onset conviction groups

# The deleterious consequences of offender identities

From our analysis of the Edinburgh Study data, a theory of offending pathways based on the concept of 'negotiated order' has emerged (for a full discussion of the findings, see McAra and McVie, 2012a). This theory focuses on the roles that formal and informal regulatory orders play in the creation and ontogeny of offender and non-offender identities. We argue that the day-to-day regulatory practices of both formal agencies (such as schools, police, social work and courts) and informal orders (including parents, peers and street-based cultures) impose a set of (sometimes competing) identities on young people. The individual must then negotiate a pathway through these complex orders and actively engage with the ascribed identities, either absorbing or transforming them in order to retain their own sense of self. The regulatory practices of formal and informal orders, while different in nature, mirror each other in terms of their core dynamics – they are both animated by an inclusionary-exclusionary logic which impacts on the creation of the offender identity.

We found evidence that patterns of both convictions and self-reported offending were underpinned by three complex and intertwining sets of exclusionary imperatives that operated at the level of the school, the police and the street. Each of these three regulatory mechanisms contributed to the development of an offender identity in interconnected ways. Within schools, exclusionary practices operated to ascribe troublemaker identities not only on the basis of contemporaneous behaviour that was labelled 'bad', but as a result of multi-layered labelling processes which took account of class and gender, previous history and wider family reputations and community identities. While tolerance was shown to the majority within school systems, a minority were systematically singled out and subjected to repeated forms of disapprobation which compounded the troublemaker identity. For example, those who were excluded from school and those labelled as troublemakers by teachers in their early teenage years had around three times greater odds of being excluded from school at age 15 when other factors were held constant. Discipline within the school context resulted in further discipline and confrontation, thus reinforcing the impulsion to repeatedly exclude, a process within which labelled youngsters had limited capacity to negotiate a new or improved identity.

The labelling process in respect of schools was similarly evident in young people's encounters with the police. Exploring what predicted police warnings and charges at age 15, engagement in serious offending and wider adversarial contact with the police were significant. However, even when controlling for these factors, deprived, disadvantaged and vulnerable youngsters were at far greater risk of police intervention. In addition, previous police history and association with others labelled as offenders by police significantly increased the likelihood of further formal discipline. Like schools, the police appear to operate exclusionary practices that ascribe a troublemaker status to young people based on a process of multi-layered labelling, resulting in a cycle of repeated and amplified police contact that propels people further into the juvenile justice system. Our modelling showed that those who had been warned or charged in previous years had twice the odds of being warned or charged at age 15, when holding constant their involvement in serious offending and other factors. The narratives of young people confirmed that they were often repeatedly and unjustly targeted and highlighted the difficulty of shrugging off their ascribed offender identity. The long-term effect of perceived unfair labelling was a strong sense of civil rights violation and a deep distrust and lack of belief in the police and the justice system as a whole.

Informal orders that operate at the level of the 'street' (defined in social rather than geographical terms) operate by an alternative set of complex rules and codes of practice, which both influence and constrain behaviour at the individual level. Unlike formal orders, young people have greater input to rule construction and reproduction, and indeed their routine activities serve to sustain and reinforce the network of rules to which they are both subject and object. And yet, such orders mirror their more formal counterparts in the sense that they are animated by the same inclusionary-exclusionary imperatives, and processes of secondary labelling are also evident. We found that peer exclusion was not class based in the sense that formal orders were exclusionary; however, it was targeted towards particular types of young people who could be defined as both vulnerable and challenging. Those subjected to peer exclusion tended to be impulsive and perceive violence as a normal response to solving problems, which was reinforced by high levels of conflict in the home environment. They were also frequently victims of crime themselves. Involvement in serious offending and troublemaking within the school environment did not lead to greater inclusivity, rather such individuals were more likely to be expelled from the peer group and become socially isolated, with early experience of expulsion increasing the odds of later expulsion by a factor of two. Indeed, the entrenched troublemaker identity offered limited rewards for young people, with those who were labelled risky and troublesome being shunned and excluded.

Broadly speaking, young people who do not exhibit the appropriate appearance, demeanor or broader lifestyle of culturally constructed insiders (whose parameters are determined by majority or legal rules) are ruthlessly expelled or excluded through a process of *secondary labelling* – a multi-layered labelling process which results in the young person being perceived by those in 'authority' only in terms of the ascribed identity and not in terms of the whole person beneath. The process of expulsion can be manifested physically and temporally, for example exclusion from school or from friendship groups; or at a more perceptual or symbolic level, such as where the individual is labelled by insiders as 'other'. We do not contend that offender identities become fully embedded or fixed at the individual level – there is always choice and the capacity to change, which diminishes the value of deterministic theories; nevertheless, such labelling results in increased likelihood of marginalisation, intervention and sanction (including criminalisation) in respect of formal regulatory practices; and diminishes opportunities for friendship, inclusivity and group solidarity in respect of informal regulatory practices. Our theory suggests that identity negotiation lies at the heart of impulsions to offend, it shapes the contexts and situational dynamics in which offending takes place, and it forms a key dimension of institutional encounters and cross-encounters which result in different conviction and offending pathways.

## CONCLUDING THOUGHTS: THE PROMISE OF A DIVERSIONARY PARADIGM

The route to diminishing offender identities, and hence reducing crime, lies in minimal intervention and maximal diversion from formal systems of social control and supporting young peoples' capacity to negotiate complex social interactions in their teenage years. Those young people who have repeated and intensive forms of contact with agencies of justice have the worst long-term outcomes, not just in terms of further offending and convictions but also in social, familial, economic and health terms (Sampson and Laub, 1993; Schnittker and John, 2007; Wacquant, 2001). The factors that determine system intervention are not only individual and behavioural, but systematically biased and evidence repeated cycles of practice through which the police and other justice agencies create their own client population. A key challenge for juvenile justice professionals and politicians in delivering justice is to balance the needs of the offender against the rights of the community and the broader public interest. In a politicised agenda, concern for the community and wider public has manifested itself in tough talk about youth crime within the UK that has rarely been conducive to a 'do less' approach (McAra, 2006; Muncie and Goldson, 2006). Indeed, an evidence-base that suggests that minimal intervention is likely to be effective in reducing offending is often deemed to be politically unpalatable (Goldson, 2010). In this chapter we have set out the philosophical and empirical basis for a diversionary paradigm. Our claim is that this paradigm has the greatest promise in terms of enhancing the dignity of human thinking and protecting the rights of the child. Moreover, it is fundamental to our capacity to support communities, to promote social justice, and to construct a praxis which is theoretically informed and effective in practice.

## REFERENCES

Armstrong, S. and McAra, L. (2006) 'Audiences, borders, architecture: the contours of control', in Armstrong, S. and McAra, L. (eds), *Perspectives on Punishment: The Contours of Control*. Oxford: Oxford University Press.
Barker, V. (2009) *The Politics of Imprisonment*. Oxford: Oxford University Press.

Becker, H. (1997) *Outsiders: Studies in the Sociology of Deviance*. New York: Free Press.

Blomberg, T. and Cohen, S. (eds) (1995) *Punishment and Social Control*. Hawthorne, NY: Aldien de Gruytere.

Blumer, H. (1969) *Symbolic Interactionism: Perspective and Method*. Englewood Cliffs, NJ: Prentice-Hall.

Cohen, S. and Scull, A. (1983) *Social Control and the State*. Oxford: Robertson.

Farrington, D.P. (ed.) (2005) *Integrated Developmental and Life-Course Theories of Offending: Advances in Criminological Theory*, Vol. 14. New Brunswick, NJ: Transaction.

Garland, D. (2001) *The Culture of Control*. Oxford: Oxford University Press.

Garland, D. and Young, P. (eds) (1983) *The Power to Punish: Contemporary Penality and Social Analysis*. Aldershot: Ashgate.

Goffman, E. (1961) *Asylums: Essays on the Social Situation of Mental Patients and Other Inmates*. Garden City, NY: Doubleday.

Goldson, B. (1997) 'Children in trouble: state response to juvenile crime', in P. Scraton (ed.), *'Childhood' in 'Crisis'?* London: UCL Press.

Goldson, B. (2010) 'The sleep of (criminological) reason: knowledge-policy rupture and New Labour's youth justice legacy', *Criminology and Criminal Justice*, 10 (2): 155–178.

Hamilton, C. (2014) *Reconceptualising Penality: A Comparative Perspective on Punitiveness in Ireland, Scotland and New Zealand*, Ashgate Advances in Criminology Series (ed. David Nelken). Farnham: Ashgate.

Hayward, K. and Young, J. (2012) 'Cultural criminology', in Maguire, M., Morgan, R. and Reiner, R. (eds), *The Oxford Handbook of Criminology*. Oxford: Oxford University Press.

Huizinga, K., Schumann, K., Ehret, B. and Elliot, A. (2003) *The Effects of Juvenile Justice Processing on Subsequent Delinquent and Criminal Behaviour: A Cross-National Study*. Washington, DC: National Institute of Justice.

Jones, T. and Newburn, T. (2007) *Policy Transfer and Criminal Justice: Exploring US Influence Over British Crime Control Policy*. Maidenhead: Open University Press.

Kilbrandon Committee (1964) *Report on Children and Young Persons*. Edinburgh: HMSO.

Laub, J.H. (2006) 'Edwin H. Sutherland and the Michael-Adler Report: searching for the soul of criminology seventy years later', *Criminology*, 44 (2): 235–58.

Lemert, E. (1967) *Human Deviance, Social Problems and Social Control*. Englewood Cliffs, NJ: Prentice-Hall.

MacQueen, S. and McVie, S. (2013) *The Whole System Approach for Children and Young People who Offend: An Evaluation of Early Stage Implementation*. Glasgow: SCCJR Briefing Paper.

McAra, L. (2006) 'Welfare in crisis? Youth justice in Scotland', in Muncie, J. and Goldson, B. (eds), *Comparative Youth Justice*. London: Sage.

McAra, L. (2010) 'Models of youth justice', in Smith, D.J. (ed.), *A New Response to Youth Crime*. Cullompton: Willan.

McAra, L. (2011) 'The impact of multi-level governance on crime control and punishment' in Crawford, A. (ed.), *International and Comparative Criminal Justice and Urban Governance*. Cambridge: Cambridge University Press.

McAra, L. and McVie, S. (2005) 'The usual suspects? Street-life, young offenders and the police', *Criminal Justice*, 5 (1): 5–36.

McAra, L. and McVie, S. (2007a) 'Youth justice? The impact of system contact on patterns of desistance from offending', *European Journal of Criminology*, 4 (3): 315–45.

McAra, L. and McVie, S. (2007b) *Criminal Justice Transitions*, Edinburgh Study of Youth Transitions and Crime, Research Digest No. 14. Edinburgh: Centre for Law and Society.

McAra, L. and McVie, S. (2010) 'Youth crime and justice: key messages from the edinburgh study of youth transitions and crime', *Criminology and Criminal Justice*, 10 (2): 179–209.

McAra, L. and McVie, S. (2012a) 'Negotiated order: towards a theory of pathways into and out of offending', *Criminology and Criminal Justice*, 12 (4): 347–76.

McAra, L. and McVie, S. (2012b) 'Critical debates in developmental and life-course criminology', in Maguire, M., Morgan, R. and Reiner, R. (eds), *The Oxford Handbook of Criminology*, 5th edn. Oxford: Oxford University Press.

McAra, L. and McVie, S. (2014) 'The Scottish juvenile justice system: policy and practice', in Winterdyk, J. (ed.), *Juvenile Justice: International Perspectives, Models and Trends*. Boca Raton, FL: CRC Press.

McVie, S. (2001) *Technical Report: Sweeps 1 and 2*. Available at: www2.law.ed.ac.uk/cls/esytc/findings/technical.htm (accessed 7.10.14).

McVie, S. (2003) *Technical Report: Sweeps 3 and 4*. Available at: www2.law.ed.ac.uk/cls/esytc/findings/technical.htm (accessed 7.10.14).

Miller, L. (2009) *The Perils of Federalism: Race, Poverty and the Politics of Crime Control*. Oxford: Oxford University Press.

Muncie, J. and Goldson, B. (2006) *Comparative Youth Justice*. London: Sage.

Newburn, T. (2002) 'Young people, crime and youth justice', in Maguire, M., Morgan, R. and Reiner, R. (eds), *The Oxford Handbook of Criminology*, 3rd edn. Oxford: Oxford University Press.

Pitts, J. (2001) 'Korrectional karaoke: New Labour and the zombification of youth justice', *Youth Justice*, 1 (2): 3–16.

Sampson, R.J. and Laub, J.H. (1993) *Crime in the Making: Pathways and Turning Points through Life*. Cambridge, MA: Harvard University Press.

Schnittker, J. and John, A. (2007) 'Enduring stigma: the long-term effects of incarceration on health', *Journal of Health and Social Behaviour*, 48 (2): 115–30.

Shur, E. (1973) *Radical Non-intervention – Rethinking the Delinquency Problem*. Englewood Cliffs, NJ: Prentice-Hall.

Simon, J. (2007) *Governing through Crime: How the War on Crime Transformed American Democracy and Created a Culture of Fear*. Oxford: Oxford University Press.

Smith, D. (2006) *Social Inclusion and Early Desistance from Crime*, Edinburgh Study of Youth Transitions and Crime, Research Digest No. 12. Edinburgh: Centre for Law and Society.

Smith, D.J (2010) 'The need for a fresh start', in Smith, D.J. (ed.), *A New Response to Youth Crime*. Cullompton: Willan.

Smith, D. and McVie, S. (2003) 'Theory and method in the Edinburgh study of youth transitions and crime', *British Journal of Criminology*, 43: 169–95.

Tonry, M. (ed.) (2007) *Crime, Punishment and Politics in Comparative Perspective*, Vol. 36 of *Crime and Justice: A Review of Research*. Chicago, IL: University of Chicago Press.

Tremblay, R.E. (ed.) (2012) *Handbook of Life-Course Criminology: Emerging Trends and Directions for Future Research*. New York: Springer.

Wacquant, L. (2001) 'Deadly symbiosis: when ghetto and prison meet and mesh', *Punishment and Society*, 3: 95–134.

Ward, J.T., Krohn, M.D. and Gibson, C.L. (2014) 'The effects of police contact on trajectories of violence: a group-based, propensity score matching analysis', *Journal of Interpersonal Violence*, 29 (3): 440–75.

Wiley, S.A., Slocum, L.E. and Esbensen, F.-A. (2013) 'The unintended consequences of being stopped or arrested: an exploration of the labelling mechanisms through which police contact leads to subsequent delinquency', *Criminology*, 51 (4): 927–66.

Young, J. (2011) *The Criminological Imagination*. Cambridge: Polity.

# 9 RESTORATIVE JUSTICE? A CRITICAL ANALYSIS

## CHRIS CUNNEEN AND BARRY GOLDSON

Attempts have long been made to introduce degrees of informalism into youth justice systems. Such initiatives were especially evident throughout the decades of the 1970s and 1980s. During this period, many youth justice researchers, policy analysts and practitioners – particularly across North America, Europe and Australia – advocated radical alternatives to, or departures from, formal justice. Diversion, decriminalisation, decarceration, deprofessionalisation, decentralisation, delegalisation and, ultimately, decarceration, formed the conceptual foundations for a movement towards less criminalising, more child-centred and more human-rights compliant responses to children in conflict with the law. Such movement was embedded, more generally, within a 'destructuring impulse' relating to 'all parts of the machine' which challenged orthodox 'justice' and the concomitant hegemony of state, bureaucratic and professional power (Cohen, 1985: 36).

More recently, variants of informalism have been encapsulated within a significantly broader restorative justice 'movement' (McLaughlin et al., 2003: 2):

> Global and regional policy exchange in the field of criminal justice knowledge, information and expertise is not new but its current proliferation and intensification is unprecedented and restorative justice is located at the centre of many of these contemporary exchanges. (Ibid.: 1)

Indeed, it seems as though virtually everybody with an interest in youth justice believes that restorative justice is beneficial. It is typically presented as a commonsense approach that respects both 'victims' and 'offenders'. Similarly, it is claimed that restorative justice takes a social problem (youth crime) away from the state – and its impersonal, bureaucratic processes of dealing with human conflict, harm and pain – and returns it to those most affected (the 'community'). Even the fact that many academics, policy-makers and practitioners employ the acronym 'RJ' gives it a kind of folksy, feel-good flavour; a theory of justice for the common people. Yet it is precisely this taken-as-given commonsense that begs critical analysis. What precisely is 'restorative justice' and to what extent do its various claims stand up to rigorous scrutiny?

# RESTORATIVE JUSTICE: DEFINITIONS, ORIGINS AND CONTEMPORARY MANIFESTATIONS

There is no single definition of restorative justice, nor any exhaustive narrative of its foundational principles or constituent elements. Restorative justice covers a range of practises that might occur at various points within criminal justice processes generally, and youth justice processes more particularly. In the youth justice sphere restorative justice is typically expressed via pre-court diversion and restorative cautioning, family group conferencing, various victim-offender mediation initiatives and/or sentencing circles. Beyond youth/criminal justice processes, the technologies of restorative justice can increasingly also be found in workplaces, schools and child welfare/child protection systems and, beyond this, in post-conflict and transitional justice contexts including, as an especially notable example, the South African Truth and Reconciliation Commission (Tutu, 1999).

At a generic level, restorative justice might be defined in a number of ways: as a process; as a set of values, principles and/or goals or, more broadly; as a social movement seeking specific change in the way in which youth and criminal justice systems – and other conflict-resolution processes – operate. Paradoxically, given its well-established presence and widespread application(s), however, there remains contention around *precisely* what 'restorative justice' might be taken to mean (Vaandering, 2011). Indeed, Daly and Proietti-Scifoni (2011) have observed that even the most prominent contributors to both the theory and practice of restorative justice have failed to reach agreement with regard to exact definitions and absolute meanings. Some perspectives even appear to imply that restorative justice embraces almost any 'alternative' approach to conventional 'justice' and, as a consequence, it has developed in a rather incoherent and piece-meal manner, both nationally and internationally.

Perhaps the most frequently cited definition is offered by Marshall, who conceptualises restorative justice as a 'process whereby parties with a stake in a specific offence collectively resolve how to deal with the aftermath of the offence and its implications for the future' (1996: 37). Indeed, notions of reciprocity, dialogue, collectivity, community, problem solving, reparation and future-oriented healing are embedded within much restorative justice discourse. Similar concepts often appear in 'official' government reports and other youth/criminal justice publications. A report published by the Australian

Institute of Criminology, for example, states that: 'restorative justice ... is about repairing harm, restoring relationships and ultimately, it is about strengthening those social bonds that make a society strong' (Larsen, 2014: viii). Equally, a joint thematic report by Her Majesty's Inspectorates of Constabulary, Probation, Prisons and the Crown Prosecution Service in England and Wales refers to restorative justice as: 'processes which bring those harmed by crime or conflict, and those responsible for the harm, into communication, enabling everyone affected by a particular incident to play a part in repairing the harm and finding a positive way forward' (Criminal Justice Joint Inspection, 2012: 4). In such ways, restorative justice is presented in an unequivocally positive – even idealised – light; as an exclusively benign and unquestionably progressive mechanism for facilitating inclusivity, reparation, resolution and, ultimately, healing and satisfactory closure.

A key element of the restorative justice 'story', as part of its wider appeal for authenticity and legitimacy, derives from its claimed longevity and, in particular, its purported origins within pre-modern indigenous 'justice'. Weitekamp, for example, observes that:

> Some of the new ... programs are in fact very old ... [A]ncient forms of restorative justice have been used ... by early forms of humankind. [F]amily group conferences [and] ... circle hearings [have been used] by indigenous people such as the Aboriginals, the Inuit, and the native Indians of North and South America ... It is kind of ironic that we have ... to go back to methods and forms of conflict resolution which were practiced some millennia ago by our ancestors. (1999: 93)

But just as the unequivocally positive idealisation of restorative justice is open to challenge and critique, the claims that link contemporary restorative approaches to indigenous peoples are also problematic. At one end of a continuum such assertions are trivialising and patronising. At the other end of the continuum, the same romantic contentions not only appear to disavow the complex and corrosive effects of colonialism and imperialism – that at various historical junctures have sought to exterminate, assimilate, 'civilise' and 'Christianise' indigenous peoples in Australia, Canada, New Zealand and the USA through warfare, the imposition of reservations, the denial of citizenship, forced removal and institutionalisation (particularly of children), the prohibition and problematisation of cultural and spiritual practices and systemic criminalisation and exposure to an externally imposed criminal justice apparatus – but they also disavow the diverse and multifarious nature of indigenous approaches to conflict resolution by aggregating them crudely within a monolithic construction of 'restorative justice' (for a fuller discussion see Cunneen, 2003, 2010).

Notwithstanding such contested definitions, meanings and origins, however, it is no exaggeration to suggest that what we have seemingly learnt to call 'restorative justice' – in all its heterogeneity – has induced a paradigm shift in global criminal justice (in general) and transnational youth justice (in particular). Restorative justice has become an international business that has, in turn, spawned widespread and multi-faceted policy and practice experimentation, massive research interest and a monumental literature. Of particular note, when considering its contemporary manifestations, is the extent to which the Council of Europe and the United Nations have each offered enthusiastic support for restorative justice in the youth justice sphere.

# RESTORATIVE JUSTICE, THE COUNCIL OF EUROPE AND THE UNITED NATIONS

The Council of Europe has recommended that restorative approaches should be made more available within the territorial jurisdictions of each of its 47 member states, to cover all stages of the youth justice process. Perhaps more significantly, it further recommends that such approaches should form autonomous mechanisms for conflict resolution and operate independently from conventionally formal means of judicial processing. By way of illustration, the Committee of Ministers has stated that:

> Alternatives to judicial proceedings such as mediation, diversion (of judicial mechanisms) and alternative dispute resolution should be encouraged. (Council of Europe, 2010: para. 24)

and the same Committee subsequently observed that:

> in several member states attention has been focused on the settlement of conflicts outside courts, *inter alia* by family mediation, diversion and restorative justice. This is a positive development and member states are encouraged to ensure that children can benefit from these procedures. (Council of Europe, 2011: para 81)

Similarly, in 2002, the United Nation's Economic and Social Council (ECOSOC) formulated a number of foundational universal principles relating to restorative justice, including non-coercive 'offender' and 'victim' participation, voluntarism and confidentiality. A number of accompanying procedural safeguards – informed by human rights imperatives – were also expressed:

> 6. Restorative justice programmes may be used at any stage of the criminal justice system, subject to national law.
>
> 7. Restorative processes should be used only where there is sufficient evidence to charge the offender and with the free and voluntary consent of the victim and the offender. The victim and the offender should be able to withdraw such consent at any time during the process. Agreements should be arrived at voluntarily and should contain only reasonable and proportionate obligations.
>
> 8. The victim and the offender should normally agree on the basic facts of a case as the basis for their participation in a restorative process. Participation of the offender shall not be used as evidence of admission of guilt in subsequent legal proceedings.
>
> 9. Disparities leading to power imbalances, as well as cultural differences among the parties, should be taken into consideration in referring a case to, and in conducting, a restorative process.

10. The safety of the parties shall be considered in referring any case to, and in conducting, a restorative process.

11. Where restorative processes are not suitable or possible, the case should be referred to the criminal justice authorities and a decision should be taken as to how to proceed without delay. In such cases, criminal justice officials should endeavour to encourage the offender to take responsibility vis-à-vis the victim and affected communities, and support the reintegration of the victim and the offender into the community. (United Nations Economic and Social Council, 2002: paras 6–11)

Three years later, the Eleventh United Nations Congress on Crime Prevention and Criminal Justice (United Nations, 2005: 3) undertook to 'enhance restorative justice' and urged member states to recognise the importance of further developing restorative justice policies, procedures and programmes. It follows that numerous variants of 'restorative justice' have proliferated globally with the inevitable effect of both diversifying and intensifying multiple and often competing definitions, operational practises and legitimising logics.

Before we begin to explicitly subject such phenomena to critical analysis, we turn first to a brief sketch of the application of restorative approaches within the contemporary youth justice spheres in Australia and in England and Wales.

# RESTORATIVE JUSTICE IN THE CONTEMPORARY YOUTH JUSTICE SPHERE

Australia and England and Wales comprise interesting 'case studies' of the application(s) of restorative justice, not least because they encompass jurisdictional sites where restorative approaches have been extensively trialled within the youth justice sphere. Cunneen and White (2011: 355) observe that 'restorative justice approaches have been institutionalised' through the corpora of Australian youth justice law, policy and practice. Similarly, Muncie (2009: 331) alludes to the 'political popularity' of restorative justice in England and Wales, where 'it has been incorporated into several aspects of the youth justice system' (Haines and O'Mahony, 2006: 110).

## Australia

Perhaps the most significant example of the restorative justice approach in Australia is the Family Group Conference (or juvenile conferencing), originally pioneered in New Zealand following the implementation of the Children, Young Persons and their Families Act 1989. Family Group Conferences comprise the coming together of the child 'offender', their family and their 'victim' with a view to repairing the harm caused. In addition to juvenile conferencing – which is available 'for young offenders in *all Australian states and territories*' (Larsen, 2014: vi, our emphases), victim-offender mediation programmes and circle sentencing are also commonly applied variants of restorative justice (see Richards, 2010, for an overview of the legislative and policy context within which restorative justice is framed in Australia; see Larsen, 2014, for a detailed description of the range of restorative approaches in the contemporary Australian youth justice sphere).

## England and Wales

In 2010, the Independent Commission on Youth Crime and Antisocial Behaviour published a major report in which it subjected the youth justice system in England and Wales to a level of analytical scrutiny (Goldson, 2011; Independent Commission on Youth Crime and Antisocial Behaviour, 2010). During the course of its inquiries the Commission consulted with, and/or received 'evidence' from, over 170 individuals and organisations. At the conclusion of their investigations, the Commissioners detected the need to make a 'fresh start' in responding to youth crime and delivering youth justice in England and Wales. More significantly, for present purposes, they placed heavy emphasis on restorative justice. In his Introduction to the report, the Chairperson of the Commission stated:

> At the heart of our intended reforms are proposals for a *major expansion of ... restorative justice* ... Our recommendation is that restorative justice should become the *standard means* of resolving the majority of cases. (Salz, 2010: 5, our emphases)

and the Commission itself explained:

> Our principles, objectives and the evidence we have studied ... have drawn us increasingly towards the concept and practice of restorative justice. (Independent Commission on Youth Crime and Antisocial Behaviour, 2010: 55)

The extent to which the Independent Commission itself directly influenced the direction of subsequent youth justice policy is a matter for conjecture. What is more clear is that not long after the Commission published its findings, 'official' reports and government policy statements appeared to echo its recommendations. For example, a joint thematic report by Her Majesty's Inspectorates of Constabulary, Probation, Prisons and the Crown Prosecution Service in England and Wales referred to a 'renewed focus on restorative justice' (Criminal Justice Joint Inspection, 2012: 4). Similarly and in the same year, the Parliamentary Under-Secretary of State and Minister for Prisons and Rehabilitation stated that restorative justice will 'be accessible at *every stage of the criminal justice process* ... this action plan sets out a series of actions which the Government will drive forward ... to bring about *real change in the delivery and provision of restorative justice* across England and Wales' (Wright, 2012: 1, our emphases). Such pledges were accompanied by additional funding and, in 2013, the government announced that 'at least £29 million is being made available ... to help deliver restorative justice ... a further £10 million will be made available for 2014–15 ... [and] in 2015–16 at least £14 million has been set aside (Ministry of Justice, 2013: np).

Indeed, since the implementation of the Youth Justice and Criminal Evidence Act 1999 – that provided for the near mandatory application of (a variant of) restorative justice (via the Referral Order) (Goldson, 2000) – more recent policy and practice developments including the Youth Restorative Disposal (Rix et al., 2011), Restorative Youth Cautions (Ministry of Justice and Youth Justice Board, 2013) and Pre-Sentence Restorative Justice (Ministry of Justice, 2014) have served to deepen the penetration and widen the reach of restorative approaches within the youth justice sphere in England and Wales.

# A CRITICAL ANALYSIS OF RESTORATIVE JUSTICE

## The 'victim'–'offender' binary

The contemporary popularity of restorative justice – and both its political and policy attraction – derives, in large part, from its promise to enable moral clarification and deliver moral pedagogy (see Bottoms, 2003). This is particularly resonant in the youth justice sphere, given the widespread belief that children and young people are especially impressionable and responsive and, as such, most likely to benefit from moral pedagogy. What this requires, however, at least in its 'pure' form, is the union of an 'ideal victim' (a representative subject and model citizen who has been victimised by a, preferably unknown, 'offender' engaging in a predatory and acquisitive offence such as a robbery, car theft or house burglary) and an 'ideal offender' (a child or young person who readily acknowledges culpability and guilt, regrets their offence to the point of remorse, and who is readily susceptible to remoralisation). If this borders on caricature, it also exposes a major theoretical problem with restorative justice: its fundamental claim to universalism. Indeed, such universalism reaches down into the very concepts of 'victim' and 'offender', abstracted and essentialised constructs devoid of particularised socio-economic circumstances and stripped of individualised identities and unique biographies. To put it another way, 'victim' and 'offender' are effectively conceptualised as uncomplicated and homogeneous categories of self: universal classifications that appear to subsume all other possible identities. In this way, and not unlike the wider corpus of criminal law, restorative justice narratives tend to construct subjectivity with reference to a 'victim'–'offender' binary. In fact, the capacity to articulate a particular narrative (a scripted role) as a 'victim' or as an 'offender' is fundamental to the restorative process. The ascription of such 'fixed or singular meanings' (Stubbs, 2010: 974) and their abstraction from social reality is deeply problematic, however.

The reality is that most children in conflict with the law (young 'offenders') are also, at one and the same time, 'victims'. On one hand, and wherever we may care to look in the world, youth justice systems typically sweep up children and young people who are routinely 'victimised' by their exposure to profound and myriad social injustices and harms. For such children and young people – especially those most deeply embroiled in youth justice processes – the fabric of life invariably stretches across poverty, family discord, public care, drug and alcohol misuse, mental distress, ill-health, emotional, physical and sexual abuse, self-harm, homelessness, isolation, loneliness, circumscribed educational and employment opportunities, 'hollowed-out' communities and the most pressing sense of distress and alienation (Goldson, this volume). On the other hand, child 'offenders' are often also 'victims' of conventional 'crimes', as evidenced by systematic crime victimisation surveys (see e.g. Muncie, 2009: 165–9).

Indeed, the child's 'offender self' and 'victim self' are invariably intrinsically intertwined in complex forms that deny neat compartmentalisation and dichotomised classification. Thus, restorative justice is ultimately trapped by its own variant of 'binary and foundational thinking' (Cook et al., 2006: 6; see also Walklate, 2006). If the 'offender' in one situation is a 'victim' in another, 'restorative' processes effectively require the child to be one person and its 'opposite' at the same time; a curious duality of identity and self that is not only conceptually flawed but also raises pressing questions with regard to natural justice. To what extent, for example, might it be considered 'just' to require a child to assume an 'offender' identity in a formal 'restorative' process whilst harbouring knowledge of the same child's 'victim' status (often chronic) in their wider milieu? And, if the 'offender-victim' child is subjected to 'shaming' rituals, how certain can we be that such processes will produce 'reintegrative' (positive) as distinct from 'disintegrative' (corrosive) outcomes? Rather than offering resolution and 'healing', as imagined within restorative justice discourse, therefore, such processes may just as readily be conceptualised as abusive and harmful.

## The inclusive community

Fundamentally restorative justice is underpinned by, and rests upon, an imagined consensual and inclusive community and civil society that enables benign, mutually engaged and balanced processes; a coming together of remorseful child 'offenders' and receptive (often adult) 'victims', each keenly engaged in discourses of moral pedagogy and repair. Cook explains:

> First, empowering participants to express themselves authentically is one piece of elegant genius behind restorative justice ... Second, restorative justice ideally encourages remorse and shame from the offender and social integration ... Gestures of remorse ... are, it is hoped, embraced with gestures of connection and reconciliation. Third, ideally, restorative justice breaks down barriers between victims, offenders and the community by encouraging all to participate equally in developing resolutions to the harms done. (2006: 110)

But, in reality, communities – with their multiple and contested meanings – are contingent, fluid and unstable entities. Furthermore, they evolve in relation to, and are constructed by, historical, social, economic and political conditions that reflect, maintain and reproduce conflicts, inequalities and differentiated distributions of power. The defining imagery of the inclusive, consensual and readily forgiving community, that lies at the core of restorative justice, therefore, not only sidesteps the prospect of profound – and potentially unreconcilable – inter-generational and inter-personal tensions between 'victims' and 'offenders' but, more fundamentally, it airbrushes-out the antagonistic structural divisions (particularly those deriving from class, 'race', gender, generation) that give rise to deep contradictions in the social order (inequality, poverty, social and economic injustice). The same divisions and contradictions are played out through the infrastructure of everyday life, and the (disfigured) relations that they forge define the lived realities of 'community'. But by privileging a largely unrealised 'nirvana story' (Daly, 2002: 70), restorative justice overlooks the likelihood of it becoming precisely what it claims to oppose: a practice that excludes individuals because they are without community or without the *right* community. Ultimately, restorative justice relies upon a communitarian ideal that is the stuff of fiction and, in so doing, it simulates something that has never really existed: a kind of hyper-reality of the inclusive community and the wider consensual civil society and, more specifically, a youth justice system that is fair and equitable and offers redemption for all, where 'offenders' are free agents who are now contrite and where 'victims' are engaged civic personalities who forgive and forget.

Exposing the apparently naive domain assumptions that inform restorative justice discourses also invokes questions concerning the relation of restorative justice technologies to broader impositions of coercive state power. In many western jurisdictions, for example, restorative justice initiatives are situated within the legislative and administrative architecture of youth justice systems that also embrace deeply problematic – and overtly anti-restorative – practices and routinely violate children's human rights (Goldson, 2009; Goldson and Muncie, 2012; Goldson and Muncie, this volume). The key point here is that any comprehensive analysis of restorative justice requires that it be situated within the broader operational frameworks of youth justice with which it co-exists, including recognisably coercive and punitive dimensions.

The centrality of the police in restorative justice practices is particularly interesting, especially as it has evolved in tandem with significant legislative extensions of police powers in a range of other areas, from anti-social behaviour orders and increased stop-and-search mandates, for example, through to the raft of interventions provided by surveillance, 'security' and 'anti-terrorist' legislation. Policing and the youth justice system have a determining role in constituting identifiable groups of children and young people as problematic threats and in reproducing a society built on racialised (Webster, this volume), gendered (Sharpe and Gelsthorpe, this volume) and class-based injustices (White and Cunneen, this volume). In other words, the processes of criminalisation play a significant part in the reproduction of social marginalisation and the intensification of exclusion. In this respect, increased police powers, public order interventions over minor transgressions, the discriminatory application of stop-and-search, targeted surveillance and a consolidating spectre of suspicion based on 'race' are as much part of the fabric of policing as restorative justice. It follows that 'racial', ethnic and indigenous minorities may have good reason to be sceptical about any claims that the police act as independent arbiters in restorative justice processes. Indeed, the empirical evidence shows that specific groups of minoritised children and young people are much less likely to be dealt with via diversionary options such as restorative justice, and are significantly more likely to be processed via the most punitive avenues available (Cunneen and White, 2011; Webster, this volume).

## The imputation of responsibility

We have noted the tendency for restorative justice to seek to universalise legal subjects with certain attributes of individual responsibility, accountability and civic obligation. Furthermore – and despite the rhetorical constructions of restorative justice that privilege notions of reciprocity, inclusivity, reparation, resolution, healing and closure – much official policy discourse reconfigures such meanings and presentations in ways that emphasise responsibility and responsibilisation. We take two examples from England and Wales.

First, in the introduction to the report published by the Independent Commission on Youth Crime and Antisocial Behaviour (2010), the Chairperson of the Commission states:

> [W]e recommend an approach that will encourage young offenders to *face up to the consequences* of their actions and *accept responsibility* for them ... At the heart of our intended reforms are proposals for a major expansion of ... restorative justice ... Young offenders themselves acknowledge just how tough it [is] to have to *face up to the harm and misery they have caused* their victims, their families and the community. (Salz, 2010: 5, our emphases)

Second, similar responsibilising logics appear in the Ministerial Foreword to the government's 'restorative justice action plan' (Ministry of Justice, 2012):

> For many victims, seeing the perpetrator punished for their crime helps to bring closure, enabling them to get on with their lives. For others, the judicial process is not enough. Rather than relief, victims may feel frustrated that they were not able to describe the hurt, stress and anxiety caused by the crime to the one individual who needed to hear it most; the offender. Restorative justice can help in this respect ... I want restorative justice to become something that victims feel comfortable and confident requesting at any stage of the criminal justice system. But this process has to be led by the victim and be on their terms. If it doesn't work for the victim, then it should not happen. Restorative justice is not an alternative to sentencing; a way of an offender getting a lighter sentence by expressing insincere remorse. I'm very clear that restorative justice will not lead to offenders escaping proper punishment ... Restorative justice has the potential to break the destructive pattern of behaviour of those that offend by forcing them to confront the full extent of the emotional and physical damage they have caused to their victims. (Wright, 2012: 1)

In such respects restorative justice is framed not as 'an escape from proper punishment' but rather as a form of punishment: as a compensatory mechanism for the perceived shortcomings of the 'judicial process' and the means by which the 'frustrations' that 'victims may feel' might be rectified by imposing responsibility on the 'offender' to 'confront the full extent of the … damage they have caused' (ibid.).

The imputation of unmitigated responsibility not only betrays the more benign and progressive imperatives with which restorative justice is conventionally associated, it also raises serious questions with regard to the legitimacy of such responsibilising strategies. This is particularly problematic in jurisdictions where criminal responsibility is ascribed to children at a young age. In Australia and in England and Wales, for example, the minimum age of criminal responsibility stands at 10 years. This implies fundamental incoherence regarding the manner in which the legal personality of the child is constructed and social rights and responsibilities are statutorily assigned. Rightly or wrongly, the law serves to mediate the transition from 'childhood' to 'adulthood' whereby rights and responsibilities tend to accumulate incrementally with age. The legitimacy of such legal regulation is open to debate, but if its defence rests with notions of maturational process then it is difficult to claim legitimacy for statutorily responsibilising children in criminal proceedings – via restorative justice or any other means – when, in many other areas of civil law, social responsibilities (and rights) are reserved exclusively for adults (Goldson, 2013).

A further problem associated with the responsibilising impulses of restorative justice relates to the question of communication. It goes almost without saying that effective reciprocal communication is crucial if restorative processes are to operate in the form that is desired. It follows that child 'offenders' need to be able to articulate reflective narrative accounts of their offending and their remorse. But the evidence suggests that children and young people, in particular, encounter difficulties in this respect: low levels of confidence and self-esteem, educational deficits, learning and other disabilities, mental health issues and patterns of drug and alcohol misuse are all likely to impact negatively on the child's ability to adjust communicative styles to meet differing contexts (Cunneen, 2010). Such difficulties are only likely to be compounded in an unfamiliar social context where the overarching tone emphasises child responsibilisation. These problems can be exacerbated further still, if the restorative justice programme is in a language other than the first language of the 'offender', or if the 'offender' speaks a dialect of the programme language. As noted with Aboriginal children and young people, for example, problems communicating in what linguists refer to as 'standard English' can result in silence which, in turn, might be interpreted as sullenness, disregard, disrespect and/or an unwillingness to recognise and assume responsibility. The end result is that the 'victim' feels anger and the 'offender' feels alienated (Dodson, 1996). We are not arguing that traditional court processes provide more effective opportunities for 'offenders' or 'victims' to provide narrative accounts of youth crime and its contexts; what we are contending, however, is that the claim that restorative justice processes offer opportunities for 'dialogic encounters' in the youth justice sphere is overstated. Although both 'offenders' and 'victims' may get to tell their stories, there are also various impediments that might just as readily serve to compromise the capacity for either party to participate effectively. Some of these factors will relate to communicative competencies. Others will derive from the institutional setting, the expectations of a set script and/or the role of key operational players such as convenors and police officers. Neither will be assisted by any determination to impute responsibility by 'forcing [children and young people] to confront the full extent of the emotional and physical damage they have caused to their victims'.

A final concern here relates to the sex of the 'offender'. A great deal of discussion of the 'victim'–'offender' relationship in restorative justice tends to rest on the assumption – which is valid in the majority of cases – that the 'offender' is male. However, what implications are raised when the 'offender' – the subject of the (responsibilising) restorative justice process – is a girl or young woman? It is well-established that girls' behaviour is judged, controlled and disciplined through gendered scripts in the youth justice sphere (Sharpe and Gelsthorpe, this volume). Can we be confident that processing girls and young women through restorative justice programmes will necessarily be more benign? What, if any, grounds are there for supposing that 'informal' restorative processes will be any less likely than 'formal' court interventions to operate within circumscribed and gender-defined contexts where limited visions of what is appropriate/inappropriate behaviour for girls prevail (Alder, 2003)? Cook, for example, concludes that class, gender and ethnicity are prisms through which restorative justice conferences operate and, for the most part, the 'socially constructed categories of difference are not eliminated but instead are used as subtle devices of domination' (2006: 121).

## Alternative justice

It is not unknown for restorative justice to be presented as a replacement discourse. Indeed, if framed within the more radical traditions of abolitionist (Christie, 1986) and peacemaking (Pepinsky and Quinney, 1991) criminologies, restorative justice might be imagined as a form of alternative justice; as a means of displacing – if not completely replacing – conventional modes of adversarial and retributive justice. Such imaginaries are nowhere to be found within contemporary youth justice systems, however. It is more common to hear the claim that an expansion of 'restorative youth conferencing ... would reduce the need for conventional prosecutions, court proceedings and sentencing, but it would not remove it entirely' (Independent Commission on Youth Crime and Antisocial Behaviour, 2010: 71).

The first part of this claim – the promise of reducing the need for 'conventional' justice – comprises a speculative and, almost certainly, over-optimistic reading. There can be no guarantee that incorporating restoration into an otherwise retributive youth justice system will serve to reduce recourse to 'conventional prosecutions, court proceedings and sentencing' (ibid.). In fact, quite the opposite is, at least, just as likely. To apply restorative justice as a non-exclusive technique (one intervention among many) implies a form of 'spliced justice' (Daly, 2002: 64); a bifurcated approach whereby restorative interventions are reserved for low-level child 'offenders': the 'respectable', the readily compliant, those deemed to be 'deserving'; whilst the more conventional retributive apparatus remains open for the 'heavy-enders': the recalcitrant, the persistent and those judged to be 'undeserving' (decision-making processes that, as stated, are mediated through the structural relations of class, 'race' and gender).

The second part of the same claim – the acceptance that restorative justice, however rigorously applied, does not 'remove' the need for parallel processes of retributive justice – is widely recognised and explicitly stated within numerous official youth justice policy statements. By way of illustration, a report published by the Australian Institute of Criminology, a government agency, states:

> In the two decades since youth conferencing was first used by the NSW [New South Wales] Police Service in Wagga Wagga, restorative justice has *largely been incorporated into existing criminal justice systems*. As the Justice and Community Directorate states in relation to the ACT [Australian Capital Territory] Scheme, 'it [restorative justice] *augments the criminal justice system without replacing it*' ... Across the country, *restorative justice processes now run alongside existing criminal justice responses*. (Larsen, 2014: 5, our emphases)

Similarly, in England and Wales, the government's stated imperative is to 'embed' restorative justice within wider youth/criminal justice processes:

> Through this action plan we are seeking to establish the necessary levers to enable *RJ to be embedded* ... This action plan acknowledges that there are evolving strategies for restorative justice across the National Offender Management Service (NOMS), the Youth Justice Board, the police forces ... The actions underpin and support those strategies in considering how *RJ can be integrated within existing systems*. (Ministry of Justice, 2012: 5, our emphases)

This is not a recipe for alternative justice, therefore, but rather an invitation for net-widening, system expansion and the co-existence of diversified (but inter-dependent) technologies of criminalisation, control and, ultimately, punishment. In other words, the restorative is subsumed by the retributive; it becomes nested within a pre-existing architecture of repressive 'justice'.

In these ways, ostensibly informal and restorative processes might do more to re-legitimise rather than to challenge formal adversarial and retributive systems of youth justice. Indeed, in many jurisdictions, restorative justice has been widely articulated and applied at precisely the same time as youth justice has taken a decidedly punitive turn. This poses pressing questions regarding the popularisation of restorative justice in tandem with consolidating modes of neo-liberal governance. Developments in late modern states have witnessed a decline of welfarism and a diminished focus on the social context of youth 'crime', together with a corresponding emphasis on individual, familial and community responsibility and accountability. In Europe where, as we have seen, the Council of Europe has pushed for the development of restorative approaches within each of the territorial jurisdictions of its 47 member states, Bailleau et al. observe:

> Social intolerance in various States is rising against a backdrop of a drift to hard-line law-and-order policies and practices. The deviant youth is perceived first and foremost as a social problem ... to the detriment of a vision that saw the 'child in danger' as someone whom society also had to protect ... a greater tendency to hold the youth's 'entourage' accountable for his/her actions by shifting responsibility to his or her family and the local community (either the geographic community or cultural or ethnic community) ... There has also been a shift in the State's orientations and strategies in the public management of youth deviance ... The main consequence of this new orientation is the increased surveillance of young people and families by a host of entities and the extension of criminalisation to include certain types of behaviour that used to be considered to be mere deviations from the norm and/or petty delinquency. (2010: 8–9)

It follows that the emphasis on actuarialism and the prediction of risk (Case and Haines, this volume) is not necessarily contradictory to the simultaneous development of restorative justice initiatives; rather, the two can be seen as complementary strategies within penal regimes. Indeed, risk assessment becomes a fundamental technology for dividing child and youth populations, between those who are deemed to deserve the benefit of restorative justice and those who are conceptualised as undeserving and/or unsuitable and, as a consequence, are channelled through more retributive (read punitive) processes. Risk assessment instruments apply a veneer of science to the categorisation and classification of children and young people. The focus on individual factors such as the age of the 'offender' at first conviction, offence record and compliance with court orders is used to predict the likelihood of future offending. Various familial and socio-economic factors are also indexed into such assessments including household composition, education and employment status. Through the miracles of science and statistics, the most disadvantaged, distressed and marginalised children and young people are invariably also those deemed to present the greatest risks; the 'problem cases' unlikely to respond to the opportunities offered by restorative justice and, consigned instead, to more restrictive and coercive interventions. There is no alternative for such children.

## Effectiveness and impact

To conclude our critical review of restorative justice we turn to the pragmatic question: does it 'work'? Many politicians, policy-makers and restorative justice 'evangelists' incline towards hyperbole in addressing this matter. For example, in 2012 the then Parliamentary Under-Secretary of State and Minister for Prisons and Rehabilitation in the UK Parliament stated:

> The benefits of restorative justice are well known by those working within the sector. 85 per cent of victims who go through restorative justice conferences find it helpful. For offenders who take part in restorative justice, there is a 14 per cent reduction in reoffending rates. (Wright, 2012: 1)

Whilst no sources were cited to substantiate this statement, the available research literature provides strong grounds for doubting its validity. On the matter of 'victim satisfaction', surveys may well reveal some positive outcomes but the reality is that levels of 'victim' participation in restorative processes within the youth justice system are often exceptionally low (see e.g. Crawford and Newburn, 2003). Concerning the specific question of 'reoffending rates', Larsen notes that 'the evidence for restorative justice remains mixed' (2014: viii) and that 'the ability of restorative justice to reduce reoffending is still contested' (ibid.: vii).

Restorative justice initiatives have been applied extensively in Northern Ireland:

> A wide range of groups now employ restorative justice approaches in Northern Ireland, using a wide range of techniques – conferencing (including both youth conferencing and family group conferencing), mediation, circles, restitution, community service and other processes. Restorative justice is deployed systematically in Northern Ireland's youth justice system. Aside from diversionary disposals, youth conferencing is the means by which a large proportion of young people's offending is dealt with, either through a diversionary youth conference directed by the prosecutor for less serious offences or through a court-ordered conference. Each year youth conferencing services receive around 1,800 referrals (15 per cent of all young offenders), of which about half come from the prosecution service. (Muir, 2014: 6–7)

Notwithstanding this, it is important to acknowledge that the 'evidence' available is limited, incomplete and ambiguous. Even Jacobson and Gibbs – in their optimistic, schematic and methodologically suspect report – concede that 'it is too early to reach definitive conclusions about the effectiveness of youth conferencing' (2009: 18). Moreover, whilst the most detailed study available (Campbell et al., 2006) provides a range of interesting and important insights into implementation 'process' issues and the varied experiences of participants, it offers little with regard to 'hard outcomes' beyond observing that 'as the system of youth conferencing develops it will be interesting to consider [its] impact on recidivism' (ibid.: 144).

The most nuanced qualitative messages with regard to youth restorative conferencing in Northern Ireland can be drawn from the relatively small-scale study undertaken by Maruna and his colleagues, provided that, as the researchers themselves (wisely) advise, the findings are 'treated cautiously and sweeping generalisations are avoided' (Maruna et al., 2007: 8). The research team report that 'many of the post-conference "outcomes" ... are positive' and in 'relatively rare, best-case scenarios, reparative conference plans actually led to ... a new direction in a young person's life' (ibid.: 2). But the research also communicates contrary messages:

> A number of the conferencing outcomes were less than positive ... In some of these cases, the conferencing experience might have simply had no impact at all. In others, however, the young person's self-reported conferencing experiences were so negative that they might have exacerbated ... problems through either labelling or provoking defiance ... several interviewees ... felt that they were being expected to accept complete blame and responsibility for the crime ... This insistence that the offender be held entirely responsible for criminal conflicts appears to further their sense of resentment and anger. (Ibid.: 3)

And, with explicit regard to the question of 'desistance':

> most of those who avoided offending entirely after the conference had not been involved in much serious delinquency prior to the conference itself, and many were first-time offenders. It could be argued that a good number of these would have desisted regardless of the conferencing experience. (Ibid.: 24)

In other words, restorative conferencing is no silver bullet. At the heavy end, the available evidence suggests that over-zealous modes of responsibilisation may serve to consolidate 'antisocial' responses from 'persistent young offenders', whilst at the light end restorative conferencing might, at best, produce neutral outcomes.

Restorative justice is also widely applied in New South Wales in Australia where there is a very well-developed system of restorative conferencing for children and young people. It is established in legislation. It has a dedicated team of conference managers and local conference convenors, and there are clearly articulated legislative and administrative procedures for the use of conferences. The system has been in place since the later 1990s, developed after various trials of restorative justice in the youth justice sphere that date back to the early 1990s. But, after two decades, what has been the net outcome? Depending on the year, between 2 and 4 per cent of police interventions involving children and young people result in referral to a youth justice conference. Police prefer all other forms of intervention, including police warnings, cautions, infringement notices (on-the-spot fines), summons to appear in court, or legal process by way of arrest and charge. In hindsight, while a small army of criminologists has been discussing and arguing the merits of restorative justice, police have decided that the most efficient way of dealing with 'young offenders' is simply to write out a ticket and enforce a monetary payment. At the other end of the legal process – the courts – restorative justice has not faired any better. For every one young person who appears in a restorative justice conference, about 15 appear in court, and the great growth area in court has been an expanding use of child imprisonment, both for those sentenced and those held on remand (Cunneen, 2010).

Such examples are not uncommon. At best, the international 'evidence-base' is inconclusive. In providing what is probably the most comprehensive and systematic review of the restorative justice 'effectiveness' literature currently available, Sherman and Strang (2007: 15) note that the 'short answer' to the 'why restorative justice works when it does work' question is: 'we cannot tell much from the available evidence'. Similarly, informed by her wide-ranging and long-term research project on restorative initiatives within youth justice systems, Daly concludes:

> The conference effect everyone asks about is, does it reduce reoffending? Proof (or disproof) of reductions in reoffending from conferences (compared *not only to court*, but to other interventions such as formal caution, other diversion approaches or no legal action at all) will not be available for a long time, if ever. The honest answer to the reoffending question is 'we'll probably never know'. (2002: 71, original emphasis)

Furthermore, when the evidence is presented more conclusively it is not encouraging. Returning to New South Wales, Smith and Weatherburn (2012) reviewed a range of studies that compared the impact of reoffending amongst children and young people who were referred to youth conferencing with those who only appeared in the Children's Court, together with studies that compared restorative conferencing with other responses including cautions, mediation and orders to pay restitution. Following their rigorous analysis, the authors concluded that there was 'little basis for the confidence that conferencing reduces re-offending at all' (ibid.: 6). They also identified a range of design problems and methodological flaws in various research studies on conferencing, including a failure to adjust for differences between control and treatment groups, small sample sizes and restricted definitions of reoffending. In order to rectify such methodological shortcomings, Smith and Weatherburn applied propensity score matching to compare patterns of reoffending between children and young people participating in restorative conferences with those who were eligible for a conference but were nonetheless processed through the Children's Court. The researchers found no significant differences between the two groups regarding: the proportion who reoffended; the length of time to first (proven) reoffence; the level of seriousness of reoffending; or the number of proven offences and concluded that restorative conferencing 'is no more effective than the NSW [New South Wales] Children's Court in reducing juvenile offending among young person's eligible for a conference' (ibid.: 1).

# CONCLUSION

In concluding our critical analysis of restorative justice it is important to recognise that many progressive activists within both the youth justice sphere and the broader human rights arena – particularly minority and indigenous groups – conceptualise restorative justice as an infinitely preferable alternative to the adversarial and retributive nature of conventional youth justice. Whilst we share a sense of enthusiasm for the restorative justice that *might be*, we are profoundly sceptical of the restorative justice *that is*, however. In this sense our analysis centres restorative justice within a context of unfulfilled possibilities. As it is currently constituted within the contemporary youth justice sphere, there is little, if anything, inherent to restorative justice that prevents it from co-existing with, being accommodated by and, ultimately, lending legitimacy to repressive youth justice systems and youth crime control strategies.

Salz, along with many others, claims that 'restorative justice is an approach whose time has come' (2010: 5). But perhaps Blagg's (2008: 74) suggestion that restorative justice was a good idea 'whose time has gone' is more fitting? We remain alive to the prospect, indeed the necessity, of 're-imagining' the delivery of justice for children and young people (Goldson, 2015), but the project requires substantially more than existing variants of restorative justice appear able to provide.

# REFERENCES

Alder, C. (2003) 'Young women offenders and the challenge for restorative justice', in McLaughlin, E., Fergusson, R., Hughes, G. and Westmarland, L. (eds), *Restorative Justice: Critical Issues*. London: Sage.

Bailleau, F., Cartuyvels, Y. and de Fraene, D. (2010) 'The criminalisation of youth and current trends: the sentencing game', in Bailleau, F. and Cartuyvels, Y. (eds), *The Criminalisation of Youth: Juvenile Justice in Europe, Turkey and Canada*. Brussels: VUBPress (Brussels University Press).

Blagg, H. (2008) *Aboriginality and the Decolonisation of Justice*. Sydney: Hawkins Press.

Bottoms, A. (2003) 'Some sociological reflections on restorative justice', in Hirsch, A., Roberts, J., Bottoms, A., Roach, K. and Schiff, M. (eds), *Restorative Justice and Criminal Justice: Competing or Reconcilable Paradigms*. Oxford: Hart.

Campbell, C., Devlin, R., O'Mahony, D., Doak, J., Jackson, J., Corrigan, T. and McEvoy, K. (2006) *Evaluation of the Northern Ireland Youth Conference Service*. Belfast: Statistics and Research Branch, Northern Ireland Office.

Christie, N. (1986) 'The ideal victim', in Fattah, E. (ed.), *From Crime Policy to Victim Policy: Reorienting the Justice System*. London: Macmillan.

Cohen, S. (1985) *Visions of Social Control*. Cambridge: Polity.

Cook, K. (2006) 'Doing difference and accountability in restorative justice conferences', *Theoretical Criminology*, 10 (1): 107–24.

Cook, K., Daly, K. and Stubbs, J. (2006) 'Introduction', Special Issue: 'Gender, Race and Restorative Justice', *Theoretical Criminology*, 10 (1): 5–7.

Council of Europe (2010) *Guidelines of the Committee of Ministers of the Council of Europe on Child Friendly Justice* (adopted by the Committee of Ministers on 17 November 2010 at the 1098th meeting of the Ministers' Deputies). Strasbourg: Council of Europe.

Council of Europe (2011) *Committee of Ministers of the Council of Europe on Child-friendly Justice: Explanatory Memorandum*. Strasbourg: Council of Europe.

Crawford, A. and Newburn, T. (2003) *Youth Offending and Restorative Justice: Implementing Reform in Youth Justice*. Cullompton: Willan.

Criminal Justice Joint Inspection (2012) *Facing Up To Offending: Use of Restorative Justice in the Criminal Justice System*. London: CJJI.

Cunneen, C. (2003) 'Thinking critically about restorative justice', in McLaughlin, E., Fergusson, R., Hughes, G. and Westmarland, L. (eds), *Restorative Justice: Critical Issues*. London: Sage.

Cunneen, C. (2010) 'The limitations of restorative justice', in Cunneen, C. and Hoyle, C. (eds), *Debating Restorative Justice*. Oxford: Hart.

Cunneen, C. and White, R. (2011) *Juvenile Justice: Youth and Crime in Australia*, 4th edn. Melbourne: Oxford University Press.

Daly, K. (2002) 'Restorative justice: the real story', *Punishment and Society*, 4 (1): 55–79.

Daly, K. and Proietti-Scifoni, G. (2011) 'Reparation and restoration', in Tonry, M. (ed.), *Oxford Handbook of Crime and Criminal Justice*. New York: Oxford University Press.

Dodson, M. (1996) *Aboriginal and Torres Strait Islander Social Justice Commissioner Fourth Report*. Canberra: Australian Government Printer Service.

Goldson, B. (2000) 'Wither diversion? Interventionism and the new youth justice', in Goldson, B. (ed.), *The New Youth Justice*. Lyme Regis: Russell House.

Goldson, B. (2009) 'Child incarceration: institutional abuse, the violent state and the politics of impunity', in Scraton, P. and McCulloch, J. (eds), *The Violence of Incarceration*. London: Routledge.

Goldson, B. (2011) 'Time for a fresh start, but is this it? A critical assessment of the report of the Independent Commission on Youth Crime and Antisocial Behaviour', *Youth Justice: An International Journal*, 11 (1): 3–27.

Goldson, B. (2013) "Unsafe, unjust and harmful to wider society": grounds for raising the minimum age of criminal responsibility in England and Wales', *Youth Justice: An International Journal*, 13 (2): 111–30.

Goldson, B. (2015 in press) *Re-imagining Juvenile Justice*. Abingdon: Routledge.

Goldson, B. and Muncie, J. (2012) 'Towards a global "child friendly" juvenile justice?', *International Journal of Law, Crime and Justice*, 40 (1): 47–64.

Haines, K. and O'Mahony, D. (2006) 'Restorative approaches, young people and youth justice', in Goldson, B. and Muncie, J. (eds), *Youth Crime and Justice*. London: Sage.

Independent Commission on Youth Crime and Antisocial Behaviour (2010) *Time for a Fresh Start: The Report of the Independent Commission on Youth Crime and Antisocial Behaviour*. London: The Police Foundation.

Jacobson, J. and Gibbs, P. (2009) *Out of Trouble: Making Amends – Restorative Youth Justice in Northern Ireland*. London: Prison Reform Trust.

Larsen, J.J. (2014) *Restorative Justice in the Australian Criminal Justice System*, AIC Reports Research and Public Policy Series 127. Canberra: Australian Institute of Criminology.

Marshall, T. (1996) 'The evolution of restorative justice in Britain', *European Journal on Criminal Policy and Research*, 4 (4): 21–43.

Maruna, S., Wright, S., Brown, J., van Merle, F., Devlin, R. and Liddle, M. (2007) *Youth Conferencing as Shame Management: Results of a Long-Term Follow-up Study*. Cambridge: ARCS.

McLaughlin, E., Fergusson, R., Hughes, G. and Westmarland, L. (eds) (2003) *Restorative Justice: Critical Issues*. London: Sage.

Ministry of Justice (2012) *Ministry of Justice Restorative Justice Action Plan for the Criminal Justice System*. London: Ministry of Justice.

Ministry of Justice (2013) Press Release: 'New victims' funding for restorative justice', 19 November. London: Ministry of Justice. Available at: www.gov.uk/government/news/new-victims-funding-for-restorative-justice (accessed 7.10.14).

Ministry of Justice (2014) *Pre-sentence Restorative Justice (RJ)*. London: Ministry of Justice.

Ministry of Justice and Youth Justice Board (2013) *Youth Cautions: Guidance for Police and Youth Offending Teams*. London: Ministry of Justice.

Muir, R. (2014) *Everyday Justice: Mobilising the Power of Victims, Communities and Public Services to Reduce Crime*. London: Institute for Public Policy Research.

Muncie, J. (2009) *Youth and Crime*, 3rd edn. London: Sage.

Pepinsky, H. and Quinney, R. (eds) (1991) *Criminology as Peacemaking*. Bloomington, IN: Indiana University Press.

Richards, K. (2010) *Trends & Issues in Crime and Criminal Justice: Police-referred Restorative Justice for Juveniles in Australia*, No. 398, August. Canberra: Australian Institute of Criminology.

Rix, A., Skidmore, K., Self, R., Holt, T. and Raybould, S. (2011) *Youth Restorative Disposal Process Evaluation*. London: Youth Justice Board.

Salz, A. (2010) 'Chair's introduction', in Independent Commission on Youth Crime and Antisocial Behaviour, *Time for a Fresh Start: The Report of the Independent Commission on Youth Crime and Antisocial Behaviour*. London: The Police Foundation and Nuffield Foundation.

Sherman, L. and Strang, H. (2007) *Restorative Justice: The Evidence*. London: The Smith Institute.

Smith, N. and Weatherburn, D. (2012) 'Youth justice conferences verses children's court: a comparison of re-offending', *Crime and Justice Bulletin: Contemporary Issues in Crime and Justice*, No. 160, February. Sydney: New South Wales Bureau of Crime Statistics and Research.

Stubbs, J. (2010) 'Relations of domination and subordination: challenges for restorative justice in responding to domestic violence', *UNSW Law Journal*, 33 (3): 970–86.

Tutu, D. (1999) *No Future Without Forgiveness*. London: Rider.

United Nations (2005) *United Nations A/Conf.203/1: Eleventh United Nations Congress on Crime Prevention and Criminal Justice, Bangkok 18–25 April*. New York: United Nations.

United Nations Economic and Social Council (2002) *ECOSOC Resolution 2002/12: Basic Principles on the Use of Restorative Justice Programmes in Criminal Matters*. New York: United Nations.

Vaandering, D. (2011) 'A faithful compass: rethinking the term "restorative justice" to find clarity', *Contemporary Justice Review*, 14 (3): 307–28.

Walklate, S. (2006) *Imagining the Victim of Crime*. Maidenhead: Open University Press.

Weitekamp, E. (1999) 'The history of restorative justice', in Bazemore, G. and Walgrave, L. (eds), *Restorative Juvenile Justice: Repairing the Harm of Youth Crime*. Monsey, NY: Criminal Justice Press.

Wright, J. (2012) 'Ministerial foreword', in Ministry of Justice Restorative Justice Action Plan for the Criminal Justice System. London: Ministry of Justice.

# 10 DESISTANCE FROM CRIME IN THE TRANSITION TO ADULTHOOD

## SHADD MARUNA, BRENDAN COYLE AND BRENDAN MARSH

I would that there were no age betweene ten and three and twenty, or that youth would sleep out the rest: for there is nothing (in the betweene) but getting wenches with childe, wronging the Ancientry, stealing, fighting.

Shakespeare, *The Winter's Tale*, Act III, iii

In a recent article with the provocative title 'Why crime went away', the American news weekly *Time Magazine* tries to grapple with the sharp drop in the rates of murder and violent crime in the USA over the past 20 years (Von Drehle, 2010). The article begins by quoting a number of police chiefs who, of course, claim (perhaps not surprisingly) that all the credit goes to police chiefs. Yet, when the article surveys academic criminologists they point instead to a less heroic explanation: the changing age demographics of American society. These criminologists argue that one explanation for the rise in crime during the 1970s and 1980s in the USA was the high number of young people in the population correlating with the coming of age of the 'baby boomer' generation. Yet, with the baby boom generation now approaching retirement – and even their children approaching middle age! – the current American age profile has shifted discernibly. Whereas the median age for Americans at the peak of the crime wave was 32 years old, by 2010, the median age of Americans had risen to over 36 years old. Criminologists see this correlation as far more than coincidence. The *Time Magazine* article concludes that, regardless of what the criminal justice system attempts in its efforts to reduce crime, it may be that 'the most effective crime-fighting tool is a 30th birthday' (ibid.: 24).

Indeed, for most individuals, participation in so-called 'street crimes' like burglary, robbery and drug sales – the types of offenses that are of particular concern to criminologists – generally begins in the early teenage years, peaks rapidly in late adolescence or young adulthood, and dissipates before the person reaches 30 years of age (Farrington, 1986). From longitudinal research that follows cohorts of young people over the life course and periodically asks them to self-report their criminal activities, it has been estimated that something like 85 per cent of those people to whom we assign the label 'young offenders' will have fully desisted from crime by the time they turn 28 (Blumstein and Cohen, 1987). These findings have been repeated so often in the empirical literature that the relationship between age and crime has been described as one of the 'brute facts' (Hirschi and Gottfredson, 1983: 552) and 'surest things' (Griffin, 2006: 1) in all of criminology.

In fact, the sheer consistency of this finding has led many observers over the centuries to conclude that desistance from crime with age is a 'natural' process akin to puberty (Goring, 1919). In one of the first empirical analyses of criminological statistics, for instance, Adolphe Quételet concluded that the apparent diminution of criminality over time was 'due to the enfeeblement of physical vitality and the passions', and that 'among all the causes that influence the growth and abatement of criminality, age is without question the most energetic' (1833: 75). One hundred years later, Sheldon and Eleanor Glueck (1937: 15) would also argue that 'Father Time' has an 'inevitable effect upon biologic and psychologic processes', and that 'aging is the only factor which emerges as significant in the reformative process' (Glueck and Glueck, 1940: 105). Even by the end of the twentieth century, criminology's understanding of age and crime had 'not progressed appreciably beyond [the Gluecks'] work', according to Shover (1985: 77). Indeed, in their influential theory of crime, Gottfredson and Hirschi argued that 'Crime declines with age. This ... spontaneous desistance is just that, change in behaviour that cannot be explained and change that occurs regardless of what else happens' (1990: 136).

In this account, if delinquency was seen as a problem of youth, then desistance was viewed as a benefit of adulthood. The logic here, although simplistic, is also elegant. Why do some people commit antisocial acts? Because they are young and immature. Why do they cease committing crimes when they get older? Because they grow up. Indeed, the process of desistance from crime was traditionally referred to as a process of 'maturational reform' (Matza, 1964), and the terms 'maturity' and 'maturation' are frequently applied to efforts to explain the relationships between age, crime and desistance. This, of course, corresponds to 'commonsense' understandings about crime among the general public as well.

However, there are real problems with this explanation for the age–crime relationship. As every first-year social science student knows, correlation does not equate to causation. Moreover, age is simply a number that indexes a range of complicated variables, including biological changes, social transitions and life experiences. Explaining the age–crime curve by concluding 'it is all down to age' is really no explanation at all. Indeed, as recently as 1993, leading scholars in developmental criminology largely agreed that the relationship between age and crime remains 'at once the most robust and least understood empirical observation in the field of criminology' (Moffitt, 1993: 675).

It is also potentially dangerous from a policy perspective. In many ways, the presumption that 'boys will be boys' (and 'girls will be girls' as well, presumably) has benign consequences and should logically encourage leniency within the criminal justice system for the young (see e.g. Rutherford, 1992; Schur and Maher, 1973). This may not always be the case, however. For instance, consider the words of the prison governor that sociologist John McKnight (1995) quotes in his book *The Careless Society*. McKnight describes a tour he took of a huge penal 'warehouse' where hundreds of young male prisoners, all in their early 20s or younger, sat idly in a massive room, watching television screens and essentially wasting away. Shocked at what he saw, McKnight asked his tour guide why there was not any constructive rehabilitative activity taking place. The governor's response was priceless:

> You may not realise this but you are observing the only method of rehabilitation that we are sure works. These men are ageing. When they reach a certain time in their late twenties and early thirties, they will stop engaging in the behaviour that brought them here. You see, the one thing we know for sure is that as people grow older their tendency to engage in most types of violent crimes rapidly declines. (McKnight, 1995: 135–6)

This rather Shakespearean solution to sleeping through the tribulations of youth in the name of crime control (or locking away all the young males) is a shockingly literal interpretation of the 'maturational reform' idea, but it is perfectly logical as well, if indeed the theory is correct.

Moffitt (1993) and other critics in the early 1990s were clearly right. Criminology needs to do better at explaining the age–crime connection. While biological ageing certainly plays some role in the process of desistance, maturational reform explanations fail to 'unpack' the 'meaning' of age (Sampson and Laub, 1992). For age to be a meaningful explanation of social behaviour, according to this argument, one must ask which features indexed by age 'constitute the mediating mechanisms' at work in this process (Rutter, 1996: 608).

The primary response from criminology to this challenge has been the development of a multi-method research literature on the process of 'desistance from crime' that seeks to understand how and why people are able to move away from criminal behaviours. Prior to this point, academic criminology had tended almost exclusively to focus on answering the question 'Why do individuals start offending?' (Laub and Sampson, 2001), and had largely neglected the issue of why people stop (Sampson and Laub, 1993). Even by 2004, Mulvey et al. could still lament the dearth of research into desistance from serious adolescent offending and antisocial behaviour: 'Social Scientists know far more about the factors that lead adolescents into antisocial activity than about the factors that lead antisocial adolescents out of it' (2004: 3). More than a decade later and the situation has improved considerably, thanks in large measure to ground-breaking research into youth desistance in the UK. In fact, Paternoster and Bushway argue that 'theorising and research about desistance from crime is one of the most exciting, vibrant, and dynamic areas in criminology today' (2009: 1156).

In this chapter, we briefly review this growing body of research into the mediating mechanisms underlying the relationship between ageing and desistance from crime. We start with those social changes such as employment and personal relationships that are typically associated with the move into adulthood. Next, we review some of the more internal or subjective changes in cognition or self-identity associated with a 'mature' personality. We conclude with the youth justice policy and practice implications of this new body of desistance research. Before doing so, however, we first seek to define desistance. After all, although the term is easily understood in theory, it is highly difficult to operationalise in research.

# WHAT IS DESISTANCE?

desistance, n. The action of desisting, leaving off, or forbearing to proceed; cessation, discontinuance of action. (Oxford English Dictionary)

Despite the burgeoning recognition of desistance as a central focus in criminological research, there remains a significant degree of uncertainty with regard to the appropriate definition of the term (Bottoms et al., 2004; Bushway et al., 2001). For example, Farrall and Calverley state that distance is 'something of an enigma in modern criminology', while Uggen and Massoglia argue that this definitional uncertainty makes it 'difficult to draw empirical generalisations from the growing literature on desistance from crime' (2003: 317). Much of this uncertainty is due to the difficulty of ascertaining precisely when desistance has occurred (Barry, 2006).

Whereas the early theoretical perspectives on behavioural reform initially portrayed desistance as 'an event – an abrupt cessation of criminal behaviour' (Maruna, 2001: 22), prevailing studies most frequently characterise desistance as a 'maintenance process' (ibid.: 26). Following from Fagan's (1989: 380) description of desistance as the 'process of reduction in frequency and severity' of offending, 'leading to its eventual end', other commentators have gradually come to define desistance in a similar fashion. For instance, Bushway et al. depict desistance as a 'developmental process that unfolds over time rather than a static state that is achieved' (2003: 133). Similarly, Laub and Sampson distinguish between the terms 'desistance' and 'termination', arguing that the cessation of offending behaviour is distinct 'from the dynamics underlying the process of desistance' (2001: 11).

Several of the qualitative accounts of desistance demonstrate that the process of maintaining abstinence from offending behaviours is not as smooth or gradual a process as the typical age–crime curve might suggest (Burnett, 2004; Maruna, 2001). Rather, desistance is widely considered an uncertain and challenging process for the majority of individuals, involving periods of 'drifting' (Matza, 1964) between social conformity and offending activity. As Bottoms et al. note, when it comes to desistance, 'Damascene conversions may happen for a few, but we suspect that, for many people, the progression is faltering, hesitant and oscillating' (2004: 383).

In furthering this understanding of desistance as a complex process, Maruna and Farrall (2004) use Lemert's (1951) notion of primary and secondary deviance to submit a distinction between two phases of desistance. Whereas primary desistance involves a (possibly temporary) hiatus from offending behaviour, secondary desistance involves 'the movement from the behaviour of non-offending to the assumption of the role or identity of a "changed person"' (Maruna et al., 2004: 19). Maruna and Farrall summarise their distinction as follows:

> Primary desistance, like primary deviation, could be expected to occur only sporadically, for short periods – a week here, two months there. Secondary desistance, on the other hand, involves a more sustained pattern of demonstrable conformity – a measurable, reflective and more *self-conscious* break with previous patterns of offending. (2004: 174–5, emphasis in the original)

Although some authors argue that this is an unnecessary distinction (see e.g. Bottoms et al., 2004), this conceptualisation of desistance serves to highlight the significance of 'identifiable and measurable changes at the level of personal identity' (Maruna and Farrall, 2004: 174).

Even if criminologists could agree on a basic definition of desistance, there remains considerable difficulty in operationalising and measuring the concept in our research studies. After all, desistance from crime is not something that one can see or touch, and it is not even an event one can witness like a crime. It is essentially an abstract concept that refers to a lack of tangible events across a period of time. At the most basic level, then, it is often asked how many months or years of this non-event (i.e. non-offending) are required before we can label the non-behaviour 'desistance from crime' (Bushway et al., 2001; Laub and Sampson, 2001)? Farrington argues that 'even a five-year or ten-year crime-free period is no guarantee that offending has terminated' (1986: 201). Most researchers who use terms like 'desistance', 'cessation' or 'termination' seem to imply that this is a permanent change. Yet, such permanence can only be determined retrospectively, presumably after the ex-offender is deceased (Blumstein et al., 1982; Elliott et al., 1989; Farrington and Wikström, 1994). Otherwise, patterns of intermittency, which are common in offending career trajectories (see Piquero, 2004), may be misinterpreted as 'desistance.'

Because limiting one's research to deceased desisters from crime is highly impractical, academic researchers have crafted a number of different operational definitions for what they label 'desistance'. Several of these definitions involve some uncertainty as to whether this state of desistance is temporary or permanent. In this research, 'desistance' is more likely to refer to a state of 'temporary non-offending' than a permanent change from one state to another

(Bushway et al., 2001). Yet, because these conceptual and operational definitions of desistance vary across existing studies, 'it is difficult to draw empirical generalizations from the growing literature on desistance from crime' (Uggen and Massoglia, 2003: 316–17). These conceptual controversies and methodological impediments to the study of desistance should be born in mind when reviewing the following section on the social and psychological factors thought to be associated with desistance in both the theoretical and the empirical literatures.

# SOCIAL FACTORS INFLUENCING DESISTANCE

'Good' things sometimes happen to 'bad' actors, and when they do desistance has a chance. (Laub et al., 1998: 237)

A large body of research on desistance has drawn attention to the importance of social bonds in the process of desistance. According to these theories, desistance from crime is said to be gradual, resulting from an accumulation of social bonds and changing social associations (Horney et al., 1995). Irwin (1970) identifies three key dimensions in the explanation of desistance from crime: a good job; a good relationship; and involvement in prosocial hobbies and interests. Likewise, Trasler writes: 'as they grow older, most young men gain access to other sources of achievement and social satisfaction—a job, a girlfriend, a wife, a home and eventually children—and in doing so become gradually less dependent upon peer-group support' (1980: 10, cited in Gottfredson and Hirschi, 1990: 135). Giordano et al. (2002) refers to this as a 'respectability package', arguing that relationships and job stability exert a more substantial impact on desistance if they occur jointly.

Sampson and Laub's (1993) theory of informal social control is by far the best developed and best known theory of desistance. They argue that desistance is largely the result of social bonds developed in adulthood. Following the control theory axiom that a person who is attached to mainstream institutions will be less likely to risk the consequences of offending, the theory suggests that new opportunities for attachments in young adulthood (especially to a spouse or a career) account for the process of desistance. They provide the individual with 'something to lose' by offending.

Warr (1998, 2002) has provided the best developed sociological alternative to Sampson and Laub's theory. Warr counters that changes in post-adolescent peer relations, rather than the development of adult institutional attachments, are at the heart of the desistance process. In his social learning or differential association-based reinterpretation, Warr argues that changes in social networks (e.g. exposure to offending or delinquent peers, time spent with peers and loyalty to peers) can account for the decline in crime with age. When a person drifts away from criminal peer networks who promote and rationalise deviant behaviours, they lose both the motivation and the means of committing most types of criminal behaviour. Warr does not doubt that adults who are employed and in stable marriages are most likely to desist from crime, but he argues that this is because married and employed individuals have the least amount of time on their hands to associate with their rowdy friends. Therefore, it is the associations, rather than the informal social control factors that are driving desistance.

# INTERNAL FACTORS INFLUENCING DESISTANCE

The other well known rejoinder to the informal social control theory originates in a critique of the claim that salient life events like marriage and employment are mainly exogenous occurrences. Gottfredson and Hirschi, for instance, scoff at the notion that 'jobs somehow attach themselves' to individuals, and emphasize that 'subjects are not randomly assigned to marital statuses' (1990: 188). Similarly, in her review of Sampson and Laub's (1993) *Crime in the Making*, Joan McCord argues that the authors' own qualitative case histories 'seem to show that attitude changes precede the attachments which Sampson and Laub emphasize in their theory' (1994: 415). In what Uggen and Kruttschnitt (1998) refer to as 'motivational models of desistance', desistance theorists have started to focus on what specific changes – on the level of personal cognition (Giordano et al., 2002; Zamble and Quinsey, 1997) or self-identity (Burnett, 2004; Shover, 1996) – might precede or coincide with changes in social attachments. Often emerging from a symbolic interactionist tradition, these models suggest that 'turning point' events may have a different impact depending on the actor's level of motivation, openness to change or interpretation of the events (Maruna, 2001).

In fact, drawing on qualitative, often narrative data, a series of studies have provided evidential support for the theoretical position that desistance at least partially involves 'symbolic reorganisation at the level of … self-identity' (Maruna et al., 2004: 19; see also Paternoster and Bushway, 2009; Shover, 1996; Stevens, 2012). For instance, exploring the narratives of individuals in the Liverpool Desistance Study, Maruna (2001) found marked differences in the 'life scripts' of those persisting in, or desisting from, criminal activity. While those persisting in offending behaviours followed an archetypal 'condemnation script', characterised by 'blocked opportunities and insurmountable obstacles' (Terry, 2002: 227), the narratives of desisting individuals played out a 'redemption script', cognitively transforming 'a seemingly intractable pattern of deviance into a life of benevolence and social contribution' (ibid.: 228). In this way, desistance is maintained by the narrative reconstruction of the 'true self' in developing a desisting identity (Maruna, 2001: 89).

Likewise, Peggy Giordano et al.'s (2002) four-part 'theory of cognitive trans-formation' suggests that the desistance process involves four stages:

1. A 'general cognitive openness to change' (ibid.: 1000).
2. Exposure and reaction to 'hooks for change' or turning points (ibid.: 1000).
3. The envisioning of 'an appealing and conventional "replacement self"' (ibid.: 1001).
4. A transformation in way the actor views deviant behaviour (ibid.: 1002).

The 'replacement self' most often described in the literature is that of the par-ent, 'family man' or provider (Burnett, 2004; Shover, 1996). Gove, for instance, argues that desistance results at least in part from:

> a shift from self-absorption to concern for others; increasing acceptance of societal values ...; increasing comfort with social relations; increasing concern for others in their community; and increasing concern with the issue of the meaning of life. (1985: 128)

Maruna et al. (2003) refer to this as the development of generativity or a con-cern for promoting and nurturing the next generation – a process that is thought to be a normative aspect of adult development as individuals mature.

Following from the work of Maruna (2001) and Giordano et al. (2002), Paternoster and Bushway (2009) propose that processes of desistance are started and maintained by an interaction between individuals' changing concep-tions of self and identity, and their subsequent engagement with a series of prosocial institutions. They argue that this interaction acts as the primary cata-lyst in behavioural reform:

> When these life dissatisfactions become linked to one's criminal identity, they are more likely to be projected into the future, and the person begins to think of his or her 'self' as one who would like to change to be something else. This perceived sense of a future or possible self as a non-offender coupled with the fear that without change one faces a bleak and highly undesirable future provides the initial motivation to break from crime. Movement toward the institutions that support and maintain desistance (legitimate employment or association with conventional others, for example) is unlikely to take place until the possible self as non-offender is contemplated and at least initially acted upon. (Paternoster and Bushway, 2009: 1105)

Massoglia and Uggen (2010: 571) argue that desistance represents a 'distinct dimension of the transition to adulthood' and a critical element in the creation and maintenance of an adult identity. Following a symbolic interactionist view-point, the authors argue that desistance is a constituent part of the constellation of markers and milestones associated with adulthood and adult status, along with marriage, parenthood and full-time employment, among others. Thus, an engagement with these social processes, including desistance, are purported to contribute to the transformation of an individual's identity and their attainment of subjective adult status.

Although studies of this nature have been criticised for a lack of generalisa-bility due to the prioritisation of subjective accounts and perceptions of desistance (Massoglia and Uggen, 2007), research focusing upon the interaction between cognitive transformations, narrative identity developments and social environments has produced detailed and valuable exploratory insights into individual lived experiences and understandings of desistance (see also Farrall and Calverley, 2006; LeBel et al., 2008; Nagin and Paternoster, 1991).

# IMPLICATIONS FOR POLICY AND PRACTICE

The point of arguing that 'the most effective crime-fighting tool is a 30th birthday' (Von Drehle, 2010: 24) is that maturation is more powerful than any 'programme' designed by the police, youth justice agencies, the prison service or other correctional bodies to reduce crime. One way to interpret this is to decide that there is therefore no point in investing in rehabilitation. Yet, as the above review demonstrates, there is nothing 'natural' or automatic about desistance from crime. That is, there is nothing magical about the candles on a 30th birthday cake that instantly transforms individuals away from lives of crime. The desistance process is far more nuanced and dependent upon a number of complex external and internal shifts.

As such, the idea that has animated desistance researchers at least since Sheldon and Eleanor Glueck's time was whether or not 'educators, psychologists, correctional workers, and others [can] devise means of "forcing the plant," as it were, so that benign maturation will occur earlier than it seems to at present' (1937: 205). This is a unique way to approach the issue of correctional rehabilitation. A desistance-focused approach to rehabilitation starts by asking what is empirically known about why some individuals persist in criminal behaviour over time and others desist from criminal behaviour. Then it seeks to determine how interventions can support or accelerate approximations of these 'organically' occurring processes (see e.g. Farrall, 2004; Halsey, 2006; Maguire and Raynor, 2006; Raynor and Robinson, 2005; Ward and Maruna, 2007).

McNeill, for instance, explains this 'desistance paradigm' thus: 'put simply, the implication is that offender management services need to think of themselves less as providers of correctional treatment (that belongs to the expert) and more as supporters of desistance processes (that belong to the desister)' (2006: 46). Likewise, Porporino writes: 'the desistance paradigm suggests that we might be better off if we allowed offenders to guide us instead, listened to what they think might best fit their individual struggles out of crime, rather than continue to insist that our solutions are their salvation' (2010: 80). Farrall (2004) distinguishes 'desistance-focused' perspectives from 'offending-related' approaches on the basis that whereas the latter concentrates on targeting or correcting offender deficits, the former seeks to promote those things thought to be associated with desistance (including strong social bonds, pro-social involvements and social capital) (Farrall 2002). Others have argued for a shift from 'deficit-based' interventions (focusing on risk factors and 'needs' as defined by the experts) to 'strengths-based' approaches that seek to promote 'good lives' as defined by the person him or herself (Burnett and Maruna, 2006; Ward and Maruna, 2007).

All of these differences make the desistance paradigm distinct from traditional approaches to rehabilitation. Indeed, these differences may be the most apparent where they matter the most: from the perspective of young people themselves. Harris (2005) argues that 'many people who are currently or were formerly in prison embrace the self-change, empowerment, and desistance perspective'. At the same time, however, she argues 'they hold negative attitudes toward the concept of rehabilitation and correctional treatment programs'. She writes:

> In general, the distaste for such programs is linked to a sense that such interventions involve things being 'done to' or 'prescribed for' passive recipients who are characterized as deficient, ineffectual, misguided, untrustworthy, possibly dangerous, and almost certain to get into trouble again. Although people who have been incarcerated often believe that some staff members or other outside parties and some types of programs can be helpful, their effectiveness stems from the potential they offer for empowering participants rather than trying to compel them to change. Most argue, 'No one else can rehabilitate you. You rehabilitate yourself'. (Harris, 2005: 318)

This view, articulated by prisoners, precisely captures the fundamental idea behind desistance research and theory.

# REFERENCES

Barry, M. (2006) *Youth Offending in Transition: The Search for Social Recognition.* London: Routledge.

Blumstein, A. and Cohen, J. (1987) 'Characterizing criminal careers', *Science*, 237 (4818): 985–91.

Blumstein, A., Cohen, J. and Hsieh, P. (1982) *The Duration of Adult Criminal Careers: Final Report to National Institute of Justice.* Pittsburgh, PA: Carnegie-Mellon University.

Bottoms, A., Shapland, J., Costello, A., Holmes, D. and Muir, G. (2004) 'Towards desistance: theoretical underpinnings for an empirical study', *The Howard Journal of Criminal Justice*, 43 (4): 368–89.

Burnett, R. (2004) 'To reoffend or not to reoffend? The ambivalence of convicted property offenders', in Marun, S. and Immarigeon, R. (eds), *After Crime and Punishment: Pathways to Offender Reintegration.* Cullompton: Willan. pp. 152–80.

Burnett, R. and Maruna, S. (2006) 'The kindness of prisoners: strength-based resettlement in theory and in action', *Criminology and Criminal Justice*, 6: 83–106.

Bushway, S.D., Piquero, A.R., Broidy, L.M., Cauffman, E. and Mazerolle, P. (2001) 'An empirical framework for studying desistance as a process', *Criminology*, 39 (2): 491–515.

Bushway, S.D., Thornberry, T.P. and Krohn, M.D. (2003) 'Desistance as a developmental process: a comparison of static and dynamic approaches', *Journal of Quantitative Criminology*, 19 (2): 129–53.

Elliott, D.S., Huizinga, D. and Menard, S. (1989) *Multiple Problem Youth: Delinquency, Substance Use, and Mental Health Problems*. New York: Springer.

Fagan, J. (1989) 'Cessation of family violence: deterrence and dissuasion', in Ohlin, L. and Tonry, M. (eds), *Family Violence*, Vol. 11. Chicago, IL: University of Chicago Press. pp. 377–425.

Farrall, S. (2002) *Rethinking What Works with Offenders*. Cullompton: Willan.

Farrall, S. (2004) 'Social capital and offender reintegration: making probation desistance focused', in Maruna, S. and Immarigeon, R. (eds), *After Crime and Punishment: Pathways to Offender Reintegration*. Cullompton: Willan. pp. 57–82.

Farrall, S., and Calverley, A. (2006) *Understanding Desistance from Crime: Theoretical Directions in Resettlement and Rehabilitation*. Buckingham: Open University Press.

Farrington, D.P. (1986) 'Age and crime', in Morris, N. and Tonry, M. (eds), *Crime and Justice*, Vol. 7. Chicago, IL: Chicago University Press. pp. 189–250.

Farrington, D.P. and Wikström, P.-O. (1994) 'Criminal careers in London and Stockholm: a cross-national comparative study', in Weitekamp, E.G.M. and Kerner, H.-J. (eds), *Cross-National Longitudinal Research on Human Development and Criminal Behavior*. Dordrecht: Kluwer Academic. pp. 65–89.

Giordano, P.C., Cernkovich, S.A. and Rudolph, J.L. (2002) 'Gender, crime, and desistance: toward a theory of cognitive transformation', *American Journal of Sociology*, 107 (4): 990–1064.

Glueck, S. and Glueck, E. (1937) *Later Criminal Careers*. New York: Kraus.

Glueck, S. and Glueck, E. (1940) *Juvenile Delinquents Grown Up*. New York: Commonwealth Fund.

Goring, C. (1919) *The English Convict*. London: His Majesty's Stationery Office.

Gottfredson, M.R. and Hirschi, T. (1990) *A General Theory of Crime*. Stanford, CA: Stanford University Press.

Gove, W. (1985) 'The effect of age and gender on deviant behavior: a biopsychosocial perspective', in Rossi, A.S. (ed.), *Gender and the Life*. New York: Aldine. pp. 115–44.

Griffin, P. (2006) *National Overviews: State Juvenile Justice Profiles*. Pittsburgh, PA: National Centre for Juvenile Justice.

Halsey, M. (2006) 'Negotiating conditional release: juvenile narratives of repeat incarceration', *Punishment and Society*, 8: 147–81.

Harris, M.K. (2005) 'In search of common ground: the importance of theoretical orientations in criminology and criminal justice', *Criminology and Public Policy*, 4: 311–28.

Hirschi, T. and Gottfredson, M. (1983) 'Age and the explanation of crime', *American Journal of Sociology*, 89: 553–84.

Horney, J., Osgood, D.W. and Marshall, I.H. (1995) 'Criminal careers in the short-term: intra-individual variability in crime and its relation to local life circumstances', *American Sociological Review*, 60: 655–73.

Irwin, J. (1970) *The Felon*. Englewood Cliffs, NJ: Prentice Hall.

Laub, J.H. and Sampson, R.J. (2001) 'Understanding desistance from crime', in Tonry, M. (ed.), *Crime and Justice*, Vol. 28. Chicago, IL: University of Chicago Press. pp. 1–69.

Laub, J.H., Nagin, D.S. and Sampson, R.J. (1998) 'Trajectories of change in criminal offending: good marriages and the desistance process', *American Sociological Review*, 63: 225–38.

LeBel, T.P., Burnett, R., Maruna, S. and Bushway, S. (2008) 'The "chicken and egg" of subjective and social factors in desistance from crime', *European Journal of Criminology*, 5 (2): 130–58.

Lemert, E.M. (1951) *Social Pathology: Systematic Approaches to the Study of Sociopathic Behavior*. New York: McGraw-Hill.

Maguire, M. and Raynor, P. (2006) 'How the resettlement of prisoners promotes desistance from crime: or does it?', *Criminology and Criminal Justice*, 6: 19–38.

Maruna, S. (2001) *Making Good: How Ex-convicts Reform and Rebuild their Lives*. Washington, DC: American Psychological Association.

Maruna, S. and Farrall, S. (2004) 'Desistance from crime: a theoretical reformulation', *Kölner Zeitschrift für Soziologie und Sozialpsychologie*, 43 (1): 171–94.

Maruna, S., Immarigeon, R. and LeBel, T. P. (2004) 'Ex-offender reintegration: theory and practice', in Maruna, S. and Immarigeon, R. (eds), *After Crime and Punishment: Pathways to Ex-Offender Reintegration*. Cullompton: Willan. pp. 1–26.

Maruna, S., LeBel, T. P. and Lanier, C. (2003) 'Generativity behind bars: some "redemptive truth" about prison society', in de St. Aubin, E., McAdams, D. and Kim, T. (eds), *The Generative Society*. Washington, DC: American Psychological Association.

Massoglia, M. and Uggen, C. (2007) 'Subjective desistance and the transition to adulthood', *Journal of Contemporary Criminal Justice*, 23 (1): 90–103.

Massoglia, M. and Uggen, C. (2010) 'Settling down and aging out: toward an interactionist theory of desistance and the transition to adulthood', *American Journal of Sociology*, 116 (2): 543–82.

Matza, D. (1964) *Delinquency and Drift*. New York: Wiley.

McCord, J. (1994) 'Crimes through time: review of R.J. Samson and J.H. Laub "Crime in the Making: Pathways and Turning Points through Life", *Contemporary Sociology*, 23: 414–15.

McKnight, J. (1995) *The Careless Society: Community and its Counterfeits*. New York: Basic Books.

McNeill, F. (2006) 'A desistance paradigm for offender management', *Criminology and Criminal Justice*, 6: 39–62.

Moffitt, T.E. (1993) 'Adolescence-limited and life-course-persistent antisocial behavior: a developmental taxonomy', *Psychological Review*, 100 (4): 674–701.

Mulvey, E.P., Steinberg, L., Fagan, J., Cauffman, E., Piquero, A.R., Chassin, L. and Losoya, S.H. (2004) 'Theory and research on desistance from antisocial activity among serious adolescent offenders', *Youth Violence and Juvenile Justice*, 2 (3): 213–36.

Nagin, D.S. and Paternoster, R. (1991) 'On the relationship of past and future participation in delinquency', *Criminology*, 29: 163–190.

Paternoster, R. and Bushway, S. (2009) 'Desistance and the "feared self": toward an identity theory of criminal desistance', *The Journal of Criminal Law and Criminology*, 99 (4): 1103–56.

Piquero, A. (2004) 'Somewhere between persistence and desistance: the intermittency of criminal careers', in Maruna, S. and Immarigeon, R. (eds), *After Crime and Punishment: Pathways to Offender Reintegration*. Cullompton: Willan. pp. 102–25.

Porporino, F. (2010) 'Bringing sense and sensitivity to corrections: from programmes to "fix" offenders to services to support desistance', in Brayford, J., Cowe, F. and Deering, J. (eds), *What Else Works? Creative Work with Offenders*. Cullompton: Willan.

Quételet, A. (1833) *Recherches Sur le Penchant au Crime aux Differents Ages*. Brussels: Hayez.

Raynor, P. and Robinson, G. (2005) *Rehabilitation, Crime and Justice*. Basingstoke: Palgrave.

Rutherford, A. (1992) *Growing Out of Crime: The New Era*. Winchester: Waterside Press.

Rutter, M. (1996) 'Transitions and turning points in developmental psychopathology: as applied to the age span between childhood and mid-adulthood', *Journal of Behavioral Development*, 19 (3): 603–26.

Sampson, R.J. and Laub, J. (1992) 'Crime and deviance in the life course', *Annual Review of Sociology*, 18: 63–84.

Sampson, R.J. and Laub, J. (1993) *Crime in the Making: Pathways and Turning Points through Life*. Cambridge, MA: Harvard University Press.

Schur, E.M. and Maher, V. (1973) *Radical Nonintervention: Rethinking the Delinquency Problem*. Englewood Cliffs, NJ: Prentice-Hall.

Shakespeare, W. (1611/2005) 'The Winter's Tale', in Montgomery, J.W., Taylor, G. and Wells, S.W. (eds), *The Oxford Shakespeare: The Complete Works*, 2nd edn. Oxford: Oxford University Press. pp. 1123–52.

Shover, N. (1985) *Aging Criminals*. Beverly Hills, CA: Sage.

Shover, N. (1996) *Great Pretenders: Pursuits and Careers of Persistent Thieves*. Boulder, CO: Westview Press.

Stevens, A. (2012) '"I am the person now I was always meant to be": identity reconstruction and narrative reframing in therapeutic community prisons', *Criminology and Criminal Justice*, 12 (5): 527–47.

Terry, C.M. (2002) 'Book review: Making Good: How Ex-Convicts Reform and Rebuild their Lives', *Theoretical Criminology*, 6 (2): 227–34.

Trasler, G.B. (1980) *Aspects of Causality, Culture, and Crime*. Paper presented at the Fourth International Seminar at the International Centre of Sociological, Penal and Penitentiary Research and Studies, Messina, Italy.

Uggen, C. and Kruttschnitt, C. (1988) 'Crime in the breaking: gender differences in desistance', *Law and Society Review*, 32: 339–66.

Uggen, C. and Massoglia, M. (2003) 'Desistance from crime and deviance as a turning point in the life course', in Mortimer, J. and Shanahan, M. (eds), *Handbook of the Life Course*. New York: Springer. pp. 311–29.

Von Drehle, D. (2010) 'Why crime went away: the murder rate in America is at an all-time low. Will the recession reverse that?', *Time Magazine*, 22 February, pp. 22–5.

Ward, T. and Maruna, S. (2007) *Rehabilitation: Beyond the Risk Paradigm*. London: Routledge.

Warr, M. (1998) 'Life-course transitions and desistance from crime', *Criminology*, 36: 183–215.

Warr, M. (2002) *Companions in Crime*. Cambridge: Cambridge University Press.

Zamble, E. and Quinsey, V.L. (1997) *The Criminal Recidivism Process*. Cambridge: Cambridge University Press.

# 11

# THE CIRCULAR MOTIONS OF PENAL POLITICS AND THE PERVASIVE IRRATIONALITIES OF CHILD IMPRISONMENT

## BARRY GOLDSON

Mapping the historical trajectory of youth justice law, policy and practice in England and Wales exposes the jurisdiction's persistent affinity with custodial institutions (Goldson, 2015; Hagell and Hazel, 2001). Following the separation of child from adult prisoners in the hulks of ships in the early nineteenth century, and the establishment of the first land-based penal institution exclusively for children at Parkhurst Prison in 1838, an array of policy initiatives, statutory reforms and carceral experiments have created and sustained a panoply of institutional forms. The Youthful Offenders Act 1854 provided the *Reformatory*; the Prevention of Crime Act 1908 ushered in *Borstals*; the Children and Young Persons Act 1933 created *Approved Schools*; the Criminal Justice Act 1948 established *Remand Centres* and *Detention Centres*; the Criminal Justice Act 1982 set up *Youth Custody Centres*; the Criminal Justice Act 1988 introduced *Young Offender Institutions*; the Criminal Justice and Public Order Act 1994 prefaced the opening of *Secure Training Centres*; the Crime and Disorder Act 1998 served to 'modernise' the 'juvenile secure estate' and, more recently, the Ministry of Justice (2013: 17) has outlined its 'vision for a youth estate of "Secure Colleges"', claiming that it will provide 'a new model of youth custody'

(Ministry of Justice, 2014a: 5). In other words, penal custody, in various forms, has retained a permanent foothold in the youth justice system: from the 'invention' of 'juvenile delinquency' in the early-mid nineteenth century (Magarey, 1978), through the establishment of child-specific legislation, court structures, policies, procedures and practices at the beginning of the twentieth century, to the present day when 'secure colleges' are currently being mooted as the latest innovation in child imprisonment.

Despite the omnipresent nature of penal institutions, however, the actual size and shape of child prisoner populations have fluctuated – and continue to fluctuate – over both time and place. The related claims that the ebbs and flows of child imprisonment are symptomatic of variations in the volume and/or gravity of youth crime, and that penal custody is a necessary and effective institutional mechanism for reducing – if not preventing – youth crime and protecting the public, are not uncommon. Such claims are essentially fallacious, however. As Hagell observes, 'it is clear from a range of statistics and research that levels of custody ... do not necessarily reflect levels of juvenile crime nor do they particularly reflect evidence of its effectiveness' (2005: 157). To elaborate further:

> One axiom of the sociological literature is that punishment and penal measures are, to a considerable degree, independent of crime. Punishment, it has been pointed out, is a social process with social causes and social effects and not – or 'not merely' – a reaction to crime. (The sociological insight here is that neither individual crimes nor aggregate crime rates determine the nature and extent of penal measures. It is not 'crime' that dictates penal laws, penal sentences, and penal policies but the ways in which crime is socially perceived and problematized and the *political* and *administrative decisions* to which these perceptions give rise) ... Penal processes develop in a complex relation to crime processes, and one does not directly or immediately determine the other. 'Crime problems' are subject to competing definitions and are sometimes proxies for other issues; penal 'solutions' are contested both pragmatically and ideologically; and punishments may be selected for symbolic rather than instrumental effect. (Garland, 2013: 486–87, emphases added)

In building upon and extending such propositions, and by focusing explicitly on the application of penal custody within the youth justice sphere over the last 20 years or more – principally in England and Wales – this chapter seeks to develop two core contentions. First, the extent to which the practices of child imprisonment are applied at any given time (the punitiveness or otherwise of law, policy and practice) are best explained by reference to the deliberate and calculated politicisation or depoliticisation of youth crime, rather than to the volume and/or gravity of youth crime itself. To put it another way, rates of child imprisonment tend to be driven, in circular motions, by *penal politics* ('political and administrative decisions') as distinct from the nature and scale of *youth offending*. Second, penal custody is spectacularly counter-productive – even iatrogenic – when measured against its capacity to either meet the needs of children, prevent (or even to reduce) youth crime, or offer best value for public money.

Indeed, volumes of empirical data testify to the harmful and damaging impositions of child imprisonment, to high rates of post-custodial recidivism and reconviction and to the enormous financial costs that penal custody imposes, rendering it's application profoundly *irrational* on all counts.

# THE CIRCULAR MOTIONS OF PENAL POLITICS: FROM A 'REDUCTIONIST AGENDA' TO A 'RUSH TO CUSTODY' AND BACK ROUND AGAIN

## A 'reductionist agenda': 1982–1992

Newburn described the 1979 Conservative Party Manifesto as 'the most avowedly "law and order" manifesto in British political history': it 'promised, among many other measures, to strengthen sentencing powers with respect to juveniles' (1997: 642). Indeed, the 1980 White Paper *Young Offenders* proposed the re-introduction of Detention Centres with tough regimes designed to deliver a 'short, sharp, shock' and William Whitelaw, the Home Secretary at the time, warned that the children and young people 'who attend them will not ever want to go back' (cited in Newburn, 1997: 642; see also Muncie, 1990). Paradoxically, however, the decade that followed comprised what Rutherford (1995: 57) has described as 'one of the most remarkably progressive periods of juvenile justice policy', during which a 'reductionist agenda' consolidated (Rutherford, 1984).

A coincidence of four otherwise disparate developments combined to legitimise a significant reduction in the number of children held in penal detention. First, a substantial volume of academic research revealed the counter-productive consequences of over-zealous criminal justice intervention, particularly custodial sanctions (Goldson, 1997a). Second, juvenile/youth justice practice innovations – especially the expansion of community-based 'alternative to custody' schemes – demonstrated the efficacy of non-institutional responses to youth offending (Haines and Drakeford, 1998). Third, notwithstanding early Conservative Party Manifesto statements, the fiscal constraints imposed by specific policy objectives of 'Thatcherism' created the conditions within which decarceration suited the wider political objective of radically scaling back public expenditure. As Pratt observed, 'to reduce the custodial population on the grounds of cost effectiveness ... led to a general support for alternative to custody initiatives' (1987: 429). Fourth, there was increasing, if uneven, recognition that such initiatives were consistent with the stated aims of the police and the courts to reduce the incidence of youth crime. Indeed, whilst some reservations remained, many senior police officers and court officials positively embraced the 'reductionist agenda' (Gibson, 1995) in the light of 'the plethora of Home Office research ... that evidenced the discernible success of such policies' (Goldson, 1994: 5).

The combination of permissive statute[1] and innovatory 'alternative to custody' practice was not insignificant. The number of custodial sentences imposed on children fell from 7,900 in 1981 to 1,700 in 1990 (Allen, 1991). Furthermore, the 'reductionist agenda' was effective not only in terms of substantially moderating child imprisonment but also, according to David Faulkner, the Head of the Home Office Crime Department between 1982 and 1990, it was 'successful in the visible reduction of known juvenile offending' (cited in Goldson, 1997b: 79). Indeed, faith in the effectiveness of decarceration was such that penal reform organisations confidently advocated 'phasing out prison department custody for juvenile offenders' and 'replacing custody' (Nacro, 1989a and 1989b). Government support for the 'reductionist agenda' was always conditional and contingent, however, and its fortunes ultimately depended upon the extent to which it continued to suit wider political priorities.

## A 'rush to custody': 1993–2007

Throughout the 1980s the strength of successive Conservative governments' electoral mandates and parliamentary majorities were such that the Party was both able and willing to relax its long-established attachment to a punitive 'law and order' politics. Between 1989 and 1992, however, Britain experienced a major economic recession that indirectly, but no less dramatically, served to subvert political support for the 'reductionist agenda'. The opinion polls appeared to signal that public confidence in the government was abating and, as a consequence, the triumphalism of 'Thatcherism' finally looked vulnerable. In particular, 'with ... a prison population falling from 50,000 to 42,000 ... the Conservative lead over Labour as the party best able to guarantee law and order' appeared tenuous 'for the first time in over 30 years' (Downes, 2001: 69). With a General Election looming, leading figures in the Conservative Party became conscious of the need to take corrective action. The Party reacted in 1990 by deposing Margaret Thatcher and installing John Major as Leader and Prime Minister and, alongside senior colleagues, he set about restoring electoral viability. Restating the Party's traditional 'hard line' on 'law and order' comprised a key plank of the recovery strategy. In his 'Foreword' to the Conservative Party's General Election Manifesto in 1992, Major expressed a commitment to 'protect law-abiding people from crime and disorder' and, under a sub-heading

---

[1] For example: the Criminal Justice Act 1982 imposed tighter criteria for custodial sentencing and introduced the 'Specified Activities Order' as a direct alternative to custodial detention; the Criminal Justice Act 1988 tightened the criteria for custodial sentencing further; the Children Act 1989 abolished the Criminal Care Order; and the Criminal Justice Act 1991 abolished prison custody for 14 year old boys and provided for the similar abolition of penal remands for 15–17 year olds (although this provision has never been implemented). For a fuller discussion, see Goldson, 2002b and Goldson and Coles, 2005.

'Freedom Under Law', the Manifesto drew particular attention to children and young people:

> The Conservative Party *has always stood for* the protection of the citizen and the defence of the rule of law ... Our policies on law and order, and the rights of individuals, are designed to protect the people of this country and their way of life ... And the challenge for the 1990s is to *step up the fight against lawlessness* ... We must tackle crime at its roots. Two-thirds of the offences dealt with by our courts are committed by only seven per cent of those convicted. *Most of these constant offenders started down the path of crime while still of school age.* (Conservative Party, 1992: np, emphases added)

The 1992 General Election result took many commentators by surprise. Polling leading up to the day of the election – 9 April – had shown the Labour Party to be consistently, if narrowly, ahead, but the electorate returned the Conservative Party to government for a fourth consecutive term. Within months following the election youth crime came into sharp focus. With increasing regularity and developing force, the media drew attention to car crime, youth disorder, children and young people offending whilst on court bail and the activities of so-called 'persistent young offenders'. There was minimal effort to distinguish, and thus account for, the various forms of 'anti-social behaviour', youth 'disorder' and/or the different 'types' of child 'offender'; rather, every troublesome child was portrayed as 'out of control' and a 'menace to society'. Indeed, there was a burgeoning sense that 'childhood' was in 'crisis' (Scraton, 1997), and any lingering doubts were seemingly extinguished by a single case, in February 1993, when two 10 year old boys where charged with the murder of 2 year old James Bulger. The 'Bulger case' imposed enormous symbolic purchase and activated processes of moral panic and child demonisation (Davis and Bourhill, 1997; Goldson, 1997a; Goldson, 2001), as 'myth and fantasy [began] to replace objectivity and detachment and conjure monsters that seem to lurk behind the gloss and glitter of everyday life' (Pratt, 2000: 431). Troublesome children were 'essentialised as other' (Young, 1999) and an 'ecology of fear' (Davis, 1998) was awakened and mobilised. For a recently elected government determined to establish its 'tough' credentials with regard to law and order, reactive political posturing was predictable. The Prime Minister, John Major, argued that the time had arrived for society 'to condemn a little more and understand a little less' (cited in Goldson, 1997a: 130–31), and at the Conservative Party Conference in 1993 the Home Secretary, Michael Howard, announced that 'we shall no longer judge the success of our system of justice by a fall in our prison population', proceeding to proclaim that 'prison works' and, as such, 'more people will go to prison' (Conservative Party Conference, 6 October 1993).

The Labour Party – that had effectively been consigned to the political wilderness since the Conservative Party's victory in the General Election of 1979, and now faced the prospect of a further five years in opposition – was deeply wounded by the outcome of the 1992 election. The failure of the Party to seize power from the Conservatives provided succour for a radical 'rebranding' initiative – the New Labour project – that had been emerging under the steadily increasing influence of Tony Blair. New Labour broke away from the conventionally moderate position of the Labour Party on questions of penal policy and, just three days after returning from a visit to the USA in 1993, Blair, Opposition Home Secretary at the time, declared his intention to be 'tough on crime, tough on the causes of crime' (Labour Party Conference, 30 September 1993). Blair had seemingly been persuaded by what he had seen and learnt in the USA where Bill Clinton's New Democratic Coalition had re-politicised crime to positive electoral effect in the 1992 Presidential campaign (Tonry, 2004). The 'Americanisation' of New Labour's position on criminal justice in general, and their approaches to youth justice in particular, came to operate *both* at the symbolic level of 'tough' political rhetoric *and*, more significantly, at the formal level of legislation and policy (Jones and Newburn, 2004; Muncie, 2002; Pitts, 2000).

Throughout the period 1993–97, New Labour policy-makers published a wide range of documents focussing on youth justice and related matters, within which a creeping punitivity was increasingly evident (Goldson, 2010; Jones, 2002). It was not until the election of the first New Labour government in May 1997, however, that the full weight of its 'toughness' agenda was practically realised. Within months of coming to office, the newly elected government produced a raft of consultative documentation in relation to youth justice (Home Office, 1997a, 1997b, 1997c), followed by a White Paper ominously entitled *No More Excuses: A New Approach to Tackling Youth Crime in England and Wales* (Home Office, 1997d). Clinton adopted and applied the notion of 'zero tolerance' in the USA. Blair settled for 'no more excuses' in England and Wales. Just as 'the rise of "law-and-order" politics and the mobilization of cross-party support for tough-on-crime measures' (Garland, 2013: 480) came to characterise the criminal justice landscape in the USA, so it was in England and Wales. Political opportunism had trumped criminological rationality, the 'reductionist agenda' was abandoned and, instead, a 'rush to custody' concretised (Rutherford, 2002: 102).

Taken together, in the period 1993–2007 both Conservative and successive New Labour governments translated 'tough' political rhetoric into a seemingly relentless stream of youth justice legislation and policy (for a fuller discussion, see Goldson, 2002a, 2010). Hough et al. noted that the combined effect of 'tough' legislative provisions, framed within contexts of heightened media attention and politicisation, precipitated significant penal expansion:

> The increases in custody rates and sentence length strongly suggest that sentencers have become more severe. This greater severity undoubtedly reflects, in part, a more punitive legislative and legal framework of sentencing. Legislation, guideline judgements and sentence guidelines have all had an inflationary effect on sentences passed. At the same time, the climate of political and media debate about crime and sentencing has become more punitive, and is also likely to have influenced sentencing practice. (2003: 2)

The 'inflationary effect' was plain to see as imprisonment in England and Wales escalated significantly. In 1994, just months after Michael Howard's 'prison works' claim and Tony Blair's 'tough on crime' pledge, the average prison population was 48,631 (Prison Reform Trust, 2004: 3). By the time that New Labour came to government in May 1997, however, the average prison population had risen to 60,131 (ibid.), and by 2007 it stood at 80,216 (Berman and Dar, 2013: 20). The trends specific to child imprisonment followed similar contours. In the 10-year period 1992–2001 inclusive, the *total number* of custodial sentences imposed upon children rose from approximately 4,000 per annum to 7,600, a 90 per cent increase (Nacro, 2003, 2005). During the same decade the child remand population grew by 142 per cent (Goldson, 2002b). Whilst such trends commenced prior to the election of the first New Labour government in 1997, they simply consolidated afterwards (Hagell, 2005). The *average* 'juvenile secure estate' population for the year 2000/01, for example, was 2,807, but by 2007/08 it had risen to 2,932 (Youth Justice Board, 2014).

At least five additional observations help to further contextualise the 'rush to custody' and to comprehend its impacts. First, whilst it is difficult to engage truly comparative analyses of youth justice systems – not least because accurate international data with regard to child imprisonment are not readily available (Goldson and Muncie, 2006, 2009; Muncie, 2005; Muncie and Goldson, 2006) – it appears that during this period greater use of penal custody for children was being made in England and Wales than in most other industrialised democratic countries in the world (Youth Justice Board for England and Wales, 2004). Second, in addition to substantial increases in the number of child prisoners, periods of penal detention also increased in length (Home Office, 2003b), and proportionately more children were sentenced to long-term detention (Graham and Moore, 2004). Third, law and policy provided for the imprisonment of younger children and 'as a result the detention of children under the age of 15 years [became] routine' (Nacro, 2003: 12). Fourth, the expansionist drift was disproportionately applied in terms of gender and the rate of growth was higher for girls than for boys (Nacro, 2003). Furthermore, girls were regularly detained alongside adult prisoners, a practice that was seriously problematised by penal reform organisations (Howard League for Penal Reform, 2004) and Her Majesty's Chief Inspector of Prisons (2004) alike. Fifth, racism continued to pervade youth justice sentencing processes and custodial regimes. For example, black (African-Caribbean) boys were 6.7 times more likely than their white counterparts to have custodial sentences in excess of 12 months imposed upon them in the Crown Court (Feilzer and Hood, 2004), and black child prisoners were more likely than white detainees to encounter additional adversity within custodial institutions owing to racist practices (Cowan, 2005).

## And back round to a 'reductionist agenda': 2008–?

Following 15 years of cross-party punitivity it seemed that high rates of child imprisonment had become an immovable feature of the youth justice policy landscape but, in 2008, the circular motions of penal politics turned again.

In the period 2000–08, the annual average number of child prisoners in England and Wales fluctuated between a low of 2,745 and a high of 3,029. By December 2008, however, the number stood at 2,715, the lowest it had been in almost a decade (Bateman, 2012: 37). Three years later, Allen (2011: 3) reported that child imprisonment had fallen 'by a third ... from about 3,000 in the first half of 2008 to around 2,000 in the first half of 2011' and, in 2013, Her Majesty's Chief Inspector of Prisons observed that it 'fell by almost 30 per cent again from 1,873 to 1,320 in one year alone between February 2012 and February 2013' (Hardwick, 2014: 22). By April 2014, the number of child prisoners had dropped further still, to 1,177 (Ministry of Justice, 2014b). Penal reduction was clearly back on the political agenda, but why?

To re-state one of the core propositions underpinning this chapter: rates of child imprisonment cannot necessarily be taken to comprise either accurate reflections of, and/or proportionate responses to, the incidence or severity of youth crime at any given moment. It follows that the contemporary 'reduction-ist turn' – and the substantial diminution of the child prisoner population in England and Wales from 2008 – simply cannot be accounted for by any singular reference to the volume or nature of youth crime over the same period of time (Allen, 2011; Bateman, 2012; Bateman, this volume). It seems equally implausible to posit that either 'practitioner activism', of which there are 'few signs' (Bateman, 2012: 39), or any deliberative actions taken by the Youth Justice Board have imposed any determinative bearing on such trends. Indeed, Allen (2011: 9) points to the paradox that when 'reducing the use of custody was one of the Youth Justice Board's corporate targets from 2005–8' there was actually 'no decline in numbers', but after 'the target was dropped in the corporate plan for the following three year period (2008–11)' the size of the child prisoner population, as we have noted, began to shrink quite significantly. In other words, the irony lies in the fact that the number of child prisoners began to fall at precisely the same time that the Board *withdrew* its explicit and publically stated commitment to penal reduction. Furthermore, despite the best efforts of academic researchers, non-governmental organisations and authoritative human rights agencies to influence government policy in the direction of penal reduction, there is little, if any, evidence to suggest that the combined effect of such interventions have, in and of themselves, realised significant political purchase (Goldson, 2010; Goldson and Kilkelly, 2013; Goldson and Muncie, 2012; Goldson and Muncie, this volume).

Just as Pratt (1987: 429) had argued that 'cost effectiveness' was a key driver during the period of penal reduction in the 1980s, Faulkner (2011: 80) detected that the 'crisis in public debt' – that emerged some 20 years later – also provided 'opportunity for progress in penal practice'. Indeed, if the relatively generous investment in public services during the decade following the general election of 1997 (Chote et al., 2010) had, paradoxically, been accompanied by penal expansion and the consolidation of 'new punitiveness' (Goldson, 2002a), the global financial crisis of 2008 triggered a discernible shift in political mood, not least because 'authoritarianism is very costly' (Sanders, 2011: 15).

In this way, it is no coincidence that the latest reductionist turn has been, and remains, framed within a context of deep cuts in public expenditure and conditions of austerity (Muncie, 2015; Yates, 2012). In the period between February 2008 and August 2010, for example, the Youth Justice Board 'decommissioned 710 places' from within the 'juvenile secure estate' producing 'estimated savings of £30 million per year' (House of Commons Justice Committee, 2013: 38). Whatever other influences are at play, therefore, it seems likely that it is the instrumental imperatives of cost reduction, as distinct from any intrinsic priorities of progressive reform, that ultimately provide the key to comprehending the substantial fall in child imprisonment in the post-2008 period.

Although the New Labour government's comprehensive spending review in 2007 was 'tighter than its predecessors' (Chote et al., 2010: 5), it was the economic recession in the second quarter of 2008 that prompted unparalleled cuts in public expenditure. It follows that the Conservative Party's 2010 election pledge to 'create strong financial discipline at all levels of government' (Conservative Party, 2010: 27) soon translated into a sweeping 'austerity programme'. Whilst the impact of 'austerity' has produced devastating consequences for young people – for example, 'youth services have been disproportionately hit by government-imposed public spending cuts, with more than £100m axed from local authority youth services by April 2011 [and] some councils cutting 70%, 80% or even 100% of youth services' (Williams, 2011: np) – it has also produced conditions within which youth crime and youth justice have been steadily depoliticised. Even in cases where 'grave and newsworthy incidents involving children' have occurred, therefore, they have generally not 'led to the calls for tough responses that might have been expected' (Allen, 2011: 23). More significantly, on the limited number of occasions when such 'calls' have been heard, 'politicians have hesitated to rush to make changes, aware perhaps that the costs of a more expansive use of prosecution or custody would have been unaffordable' (ibid.: 23). So, although the government has fallen short of making explicit policy statements favouring child decarceration, dramatic penal reduction has evolved by stealth, under the public radar and largely as a result of manoeuvres 'behind the scenes' (ibid.: 10).

If, as noted at the outset of this chapter, child imprisonment retains a permanent foothold in the youth justice system, the level and extent of its application are, as stated, subject to the vagaries of political, economic and administrative conditions. In this way, and as we have seen, the logics underpinning decision-making processes in the youth justice sphere are rarely, if ever, exclusively driven by the nature of offending or the incidence of crime. To put it another way, the power to punish and/or imprison children is variously applied, or reserved, in accordance with ulterior motives; political calculations that ultimately operate independently of crime. This gives rise to circular motions, to ebbs and flows of punitivity and to low points and high points of child imprisonment. Notwithstanding such *inconsistency*, however, the imposition of imprisonment is strikingly *consistent* in failing to attend to the needs of child prisoners, to prevent (or even to reduce) youth crime and/or to offer best value for public money. Indeed, whilst particular – essentially disingenuous – *political rationalities* might well drive penal trends upwards or downwards, the corrosive impact of custodial institutions, their lack of success in 'preventing youth offending' (the 'principal aim' of the youth justice system as provided by s37 Crime and Disorder Act 1998), and the enormous financial burden that they impose on the public purse, are indicative of an interrelated complex of *penological irrationalities*.

# THE PERVASIVE IRRATIONALITIES OF CHILD IMPRISONMENT

## Meeting the needs of children?

Wherever we might care to look in the world, child prisoners are routinely drawn from some of the most disadvantaged, distressed and impoverished families, neighbourhoods and communities (Goldson, 2002b, 2009; Goldson and Coles, 2005; Goldson and Kilkelly, 2013). In the jurisdiction of England and Wales, Her Majesty's Chief Inspector of Prisons (1999: 3) has noted that penal custody often marks 'just one further stage in the exclusion of a group of children who between them, have already experienced almost every form of social exclusion on offer', subsequently adding:

> Before any work can be done to sensitise [child prisoners] to the needs of others and the impact of their offending on victims, their own needs as maturing adolescents for care, support and direction have to be met. (Her Majesty's Chief Inspector of Prisons, 2000: 25)

Many child prisoners are, or will have been, 'open cases' to statutory child welfare agencies as a result of neglect and/or other child protection concerns and a significant proportion have biographies scarred by adult abuse and violation (Association of Directors of Social Services et al., 2003; Challen and Walton, 2004; Holmes and Gibbs, 2004; Prison Reform Trust, 2004; Social Exclusion Unit, 2002; Social Services Inspectorate et al., 2002). Although no centralised records are maintained by either Her Majesty's Prison Service or the Youth Justice Board, the House of Commons Justice Committee (2013: 44) has reported that 'children in care … are over-represented in the prison population; [d]espite accounting for less than 1 per cent of the total population, the most recent survey of 15–18 year olds in custody found that 30 per cent [of boys] and 44 per cent [of girls] had spent time in care', and a further study of 200 child prisoners revealed that 39 per cent had been on local authority child protection registers and/or had experienced abuse (Jacobson et al., 2010).

In a major review of the educational needs of children in penal custody, Her Majesty's Chief Inspector of Prisons and the Office for Standards in Education (2001: 10) found that: 84 per cent of child prisoners had been excluded from school; 86 per cent had regularly not attended school; 52 per cent had left school aged 14 years or younger; 29 per cent had left school aged 13 years or younger; and 73 per cent described their educational achievement as 'nil'. Over 25 per cent of child prisoners have literacy and numeracy skills equivalent to a 7 year old (Social Exclusion Unit, 2002) and 'most' have 'very significant learning needs and problems' (Social Services Inspectorate et al., 2002: 70). Over 10 years later, Her Majesty's Inspectorate of Prisons and the Youth Justice Board (2013) and the Ministry of Justice (2014a) presented strikingly similar data.

Turning to health, the British Medical Association, commenting upon the relationship between poverty, disadvantage and poor health, has observed that

> patients within prison are amongst the most needy in the country in relation to their health care needs. Over 90 per cent of patients who reside in our jails come from deprived backgrounds ... 17 per cent of young offenders were not registered with a general practitioner and generally the young people had a low level of contact with primary health care. (2001: 1 and 5)

Again, more than a decade later Murray (2012) found that 27 per cent of boys in prison reported emotional and mental health problems, perhaps a predictable finding given that the experience of imprisonment itself is known to impose deleterious effects on the physical and mental well-being of children (Farrant, 2001; Goldson, 2002b; Goldson and Coles, 2005; Leech and Cheney, 2001; Mental Health Foundation, 1999).

In sum, when taking account of the personal/familial, educational and health profiles of child prisoners, 'it is evident that on any count this is a significantly deprived, excluded, and abused population of children, who are in serious need of a variety of services' (Association of Directors of Social Services et al., 2003: 6) and the 'Juvenile Secure Estate' is 'not equipped to meet their needs' (Her Majesty's Chief Inspector of Prisons, 2000: 69–70).

In 2012/13, 74 per cent of child prisoners in England and Wales were detained in Young Offender Institutions (state and/or privately managed prisons), 16 per cent were confined in Secure Training Centres (privately managed jails) and the remaining 9 per cent were held in Secure Children's Homes (smaller and more 'child-centred' facilities managed by local authorities) (Ministry of Justice and Youth Justice Board, 2014: 41). The fact that the substantial majority of child prisoners are held in Young Offender Institutions raises important issues with regard to conditions and treatment:

> One of the most important factors in creating a safe environment is size. The other places where children are held – Secure Units and Secure Training Centres – are small, with a high staff–child ratio. The Prison Service, however, may hold children in what we regard as unacceptably high numbers and units. Units of 60 disturbed and damaged adolescent boys are unlikely to be safe ... There are therefore already significant barriers to the Prison Service being able to provide a safe and positive environment for children; and the question whether it should continue to do so is a live one. (Her Majesty's Chief Inspector of Prisons, 2002: 36–7)

The Children's Rights Alliance for England (2002: 49–137) undertook a detailed analysis of the conditions and treatment experienced by children in

Young Offender Institutions, drawing on reports prepared by Her Majesty's Inspectorate of Prisons. The results were illuminating: widespread neglect in relation to physical and mental health; endemic bullying, humiliation and ill-treatment (staff-on-child and child-on-child); racism and other forms of discrimination; systemic invasion of privacy; long and uninterrupted periods of cell-based confinement; deprivation of fresh air and exercise; inadequate educational and rehabilitative provision; insufficient opportunities to maintain contact with family; poor diet; ill-fitting clothing in poor state of repair; a shabby physical environment; and, in reality, virtually no opportunity to complain and/or make representations. Such conditions led Mr Justice Munby, a High Court Judge, to conclude that:

> They ought to be – I hope they are – matters of the very greatest concern to the Prison Service, to the Secretary of State for the Home Department and, indeed, to society at large. For these are things being done to children by the State – by all of us – in circumstances where the State appears to be failing, and in some instances failing very badly, in its duties to vulnerable and damaged children ... [these are] matters which, on the face of it, ought to shock the conscience of every citizen. (Munby, 2002: paras 172 and 175)

Penal custody for children, therefore, can never be a neutral experience. Apart from the emotional and psychological harms that are typically endured by child prisoners, standards of safety and physical integrity are also compromised. Her Majesty's Chief Inspector of Prisons (2005: 56) surveyed children in one Young Offender Institution and found that 56 per cent reported that they had felt 'unsafe', 'nearly a quarter said they had been hit, kicked or assaulted' and there 'had been 150 proven assaults in eight months'. Similarly, having surveyed 942 boys and young men in prisons, Her Majesty's Inspectorate of Prisons and the Youth Justice Board reported that '30 per cent ... said they had felt unsafe at their establishment ... 22 per cent said they had been victimised by other young men and 22 per cent said that they had been victimised by staff' (2013: 11). Only 29 per cent of the boys and young men said that they would tell a member of staff if they were being victimised and, in his annual report for the year 2012/13, Her Majesty's Chief Inspector of Prisons noted that, even when reported, 'the quality of investigations into alleged violence was poor' (2013: 59). Physical assault – or physical abuse – is clearly commonplace, under-reported and inadequately investigated in penal custody. Child prisoners are also exposed to other forms of 'bullying' including sexual assault; verbal abuse (including name-calling; threats; racist, sexist and homophobic taunting); extortion and theft; and lending and trading cultures – particularly in relation to tobacco – involving exorbitant rates of interest that accumulate on a daily basis (Goldson, 2002b). Moreover, random violence is framed within a context in which physical force is formally institutionalised:

> The Office of the Children's Commissioner found evidence ... of a tendency in youth custody to focus on physical controls ... rather than on relationships. Restraint is supposed to be a 'last resort', to prevent individuals from causing harm to themselves or others. However, there were 8,419 incidents of restrictive physical intervention used in the youth

secure estate in 2011/12, up 6 per cent from 2008/09 and 17 per cent from 2010/11. 254 of these restraints involved injury to young people. (House of Commons Justice Committee, 2013: 42)

For some child prisoners, their troubled lives together with the treatment and conditions that they experience in penal custody are literally too much to bear. Between 1998 and 2002, for example, there were 1,659 reported incidents of self-injury or attempted suicide by child prisoners in England and Wales (Howard League for Penal Reform, 2005). At the sharpest extremes, 33 children died in penal custody in England and Wales between 1990 and October 2012; all but two of the deaths were apparently self-inflicted (Goldson and Coles, 2005; the Prison Reform Trust and INQUEST, 2012).

As Miller has observed, penal institutions 'have always been, and continue to be, neglectful, demeaning, frequently violent and largely ineffective' (1991: 3). Indeed, the corrosive effects of child imprisonment have been recognised and reported for decades. Despite this, however, and irrespective of the harmful impositions of penal institutions and the publication of 'critical report after critical report', there is little evidence of 'fundamental change' (Hardwick, 2014: 23). Indeed, whilst *rates* of child imprisonment might ebb and flow, the *practices* of imprisoning children appear to be irrevocable. Ultimately this implies, to paraphrase Cohen (2001: 1), that children's suffering is being 'denied', 'evaded', 'neutralised' or 'rationalised away'.

## Preventing and/or reducing crime?

It is a well-established criminological 'fact' that, when measured in terms of crime prevention and/or crime reduction, child imprisonment fails miserably. In this way, Miller has noted that 'the hard truth is that ... juvenile penal institutions have minimal impact on crime ... incapacitation as the major tenet of crime control is a questionable social policy' (1991: 181–2). Similarly, Hagell and Hazel (2001) have observed that concern with 'poor performance' (with regard to reconviction rates) is a recurring theme in penal discourse.

The enduring failure of penal custody as a measure of crime reduction is clearly illustrated by analyses of the 'the proportion of [child] prisoners discharged from prisons [who] are convicted on a further occasion within a given period' (Home Office, 2003a: 150). An evaluation of nearly 6,000 children subject to custodial sentences, for example, reported high rates of reoffending, particularly in the first few weeks following release (Hazel et al., 2002). This echoed the results from earlier research that had revealed that 11 per cent of children were arrested for a further offence within 7 days of their discharge from a Secure Training Centre, 52 per cent were similarly arrested within 7 weeks and 67 per cent were arrested within 20 weeks of release (Hagell et al., 2000). The Chairperson of the House of Commons Committee of Public Accounts (2004: Ev. 1) referred to what he termed 'an absurdly high reconviction rate' of 84 per cent following children's 'release from prison'. Almost a decade later, the Prison Reform Trust (2013: 26) noted 'that 72.3 per cent of children (10–17) released from custody … reoffended within a year', and the Ministry of Justice (2013: 8) reported institutionally variable reconviction rates ranging from 70 per cent to 76 per cent.

The persistent failure of penal custody in this respect is conspicuously at odds with the statutory 'principal aim' of the youth justice system in England and Wales – to 'prevent offending' (and re-offending) – as provided by the Crime and Disorder Act 1998, s.37. To put it another way, the practices of child imprisonment are irrational when set against the failure of custodial institutions to prevent (or even to reduce) youth crime in accordance with the provisions of statute. Such irrationality is only exacerbated when account is taken of the extraordinary costs – human and fiscal – that such practices impose.

## Offering best value for public money?

Although estimates vary, an enormous amount of public money is spent on imprisoning children in England and Wales. The Audit Commission (2004: 2) reported that to 'place' a single child in a young offender institution (a state or privately managed prison) costs £977.00 per week or £50,800 per year. Almost a decade later and the corresponding costs had risen to £1,250 and £65,000 respectively (Ministry of Justice, 2013: 8). In 2004, the costs of a similar 'placement' in a Secure Training Centre (a private jail) were substantially higher, standing at £3,168 per week or £164,750 per year (House of Commons Committee of Public Accounts, 2004: 4). By 2013, significant inflation was again evident, with the weekly cost of imprisoning a child in a private jail standing at £3,423 and the yearly cost amounting to £178,000 (Ministry of Justice, 2013: 8). According to the Chairperson of the Youth Justice Board for England and Wales the gross costs of imprisoning children amounted to £293.5 million in the financial year 2003–04 alone (Morgan, 2004) and, despite the substantial reduction in the numbers of child prisoners in the post-2008 period, child imprisonment continues to absorb millions of pounds of public money:

> In 2012/13 the Ministry of Justice and the YJB have budgeted that £245m will be spent on commissioning the youth secure estate. This estimates to an average cost of almost £100,000 a place per annum … and in some cases we are paying more than £200,000 per annum [a]t a time of particular financial challenge … but in spite of such excessively high costs reoffending outcomes are consistently unacceptable. (Ministry of Justice, 2013: 13–14)

Indeed, it remains the case that 'large sums of money' are being spent 'to achieve poor outcomes' or, to put it another way, 'places in the secure estate … [are] five times the cost of sending a child to a top private boarding school … [but] we see many of the same young faces back at the gate within a matter of months' (Grayling and Gove, 2013: 4). In actual fact, such figures tell only part of the fiscal story in that they exclude the considerable public expense incurred in processing children through the courts. The Social Exclusion Unit reported, for example, that: 'the average cost of a prison sentence imposed at a crown court is roughly £30,500, made up of court and other legal costs' (2002: 2). When the annual gross costs of child imprisonment are calculated, therefore, the £245 million that the government budgeted in 2012/13 for directly 'commissioning' places from penal institutions will only have paid for part of the total bill.

# CONCLUSION

Garland contends that:

> Social currents may ebb and flow, but they have no penal consequence unless and until they enlist state actors and influence state action. It follows that the character of the penal state and the processes whereby it responds to social forces, translating (or not translating) political pressures into specific penal outcomes, are always the proximate causes of penal action and penal change. (2013: 494)

To focus more sharply, the ebbs and flows of child imprisonment are, ultimately, best understood as adaptations and responses to 'political pressures' rather than reactions to the incidence and nature of youth crime. In other words, the circular motions of penal politics, the politicisation or depoliticisation of youth crime, high rates or low rates of child imprisonment – the extent to which the penal state might 'translate (or not translate) political pressures into specific penal outcomes' – are ultimately driven by ulterior motives that are situated beyond the immediate governance and regulation of youth crime itself. It follows that rates of child imprisonment are contingent; subject to the vagaries of social, economic and political conditions.

If penal politics give rise to unpredictable and inconsistent *rates* of child imprisonment, the *outcomes* of custodial interventions are, by contrast, strikingly predictable and consistent. Penal institutions reliably and persistently fail to meet the needs of child prisoners, prevent (or even reduce) youth crime and/ or offer best value for public money. In this way – and irrespective of whether child imprisonment is moderated by a 'reductionist agenda' or applied excessively via a 'rush to custody' – it typically comprises a harmful, ineffective and expensive response to children in trouble.

Stern describes her experience of a conference in Brooklyn, New York, attended by people living in disadvantaged neighbourhoods:

> They were talking about housing, employment, health and education and they were adding up dollars. They had done some geographical plotting. They had analysed where the prisoners lived, where the poor people lived, where the victims lived, where the most social services were needed and were not available in sufficient quantity. They found, not surprisingly, that where the poor people lived and where the services are needed is also where the prison population comes from. Some blocks, single streets, consume one million dollars worth of imprisonment in a year ... Now those people in Brooklyn were asking, 'Can we have that money and spend it on the people here ... instead of sending them to prison?' (2005: 83)

Bearing in mind all that is known about the adverse social circumstances from which child prisoners are routinely drawn, the damaging conditions and treatment to which they are typically exposed, the failings of penal institutions to deliver in terms of crime prevention, crime reduction and/or community safety, and the enormous expense that child imprisonment imposes on the public purse, serious questions have to be asked. Stern's account of her conference experience conveys a persuasive logic. But such logic is muted within a context in which the circular motions of penal politics continue to turn, the pervasive irrationalities of child imprisonment endure and the government has announced its intention to:

> Bring forward legislation to create Secure Colleges as a new form of youth detention ... This legislation will pave the way for the development of a first pathfinder Secure College ... [a] 320-place establishment ... It is envisaged that construction of the Secure College will commence in 2015, with the establishment opening in spring 2017 ... the Government's long-term ambition is the complete transformation of the youth custodial estate through the introduction of a network of Secure College[s] across England and Wales ... demonstrating the strength and appetite of the market to deliver a new form of youth custodial provision. (Ministry of Justice, 2014a: 6–8)

If and when youth crime is next politicised, therefore – in such a way to invoke a further wave of repenalisation – a 'network' of '320-place establishments' will seemingly be at hand to meet demand and reproduce failure.

# REFERENCES

Allen, R. (1991) 'Out of jail: the reduction in the use of penal custody for male juveniles 1981–1988', *The Howard Journal of Criminal Justice*, 30 (1): 30–52.

Allen, R. (2011) *Last Resort? Exploring the Reduction in Child Imprisonment 2008–11*. London: Prison Reform Trust.

Association of Directors of Social Services, Local Government Association, Youth Justice Board for England and Wales (2003) *The Application of the Children Act (1989) to Children in Young Offender Institutions*. London: ADSS, LGA and YJB.

Audit Commission (2004) 'Youth justice 2004: a review of the reformed youth justice system', *Criminal Justice Briefing*. London: Audit Commission.

Bateman, T. (2012) 'Who pulled the plug? Towards an explanation of the fall in child imprisonment in England and Wales', *Youth Justice*, 12 (1): 36–52.

Berman, G. and Dar, A. (2013) *Prison Population Statistics*. London: House of Commons Library.

British Medical Association (2001) *Prison Medicine: A Crisis Waiting to Break*. London: British Medical Association.

Challen, M. and Walton, T. (2004) *Juveniles in Custody*. London: Her Majesty's Inspectorate of Prisons.

Children's Rights Alliance for England (2002) *Rethinking Child Imprisonment: A Report on Young Offender Institutions*. London: Children's Rights Alliance for England.

Chote, R., Crawford, R., Emmerson, C. and Tetlow, G. (2010) *Public Spending Under Labour*. London: Nuffield Foundation.

Cohen, S. (2001) *States of Denial*. Cambridge: Polity Press.

Conservative Party (1992) *Conservative Party General Election Manifesto: The Best Future for Britain*. London: Conservative Party.

Conservative Party (2010) *Invitation to Join the Government of Britain: The Conservative Manifesto 2010*. London: The Conservative Party.

Cowan, R. (2005) 'Juvenile jail staff accused of racism', *Guardian*, 14 June.

Davis, H. and Bourhill, M. (1997) '"Crisis": the demonization of children and young people', in Scraton, P. (ed.), *'Childhood' in 'Crisis'?* London: UCL Press.

Davis, M. (1998) *Ecology of Fear: Los Angeles and the Imagination of Disaster*. New York: Metropolitan Press.

Downes, D. (2001) 'The *macho* penal economy: mass incarceration in the USA – a European perspective', *Punishment and Society*, 3 (1): 61–80.

Farrant, F. (2001) *Troubled Inside: Responding to the Mental Health Needs of Children and Young People in Prison*. London: Prison Reform Trust.

Faulkner, D. (2011) 'Criminal justice reform at a time of austerity: what needs to be done?', in Silvestri, A. (ed.), *Lessons for the Coalition: An End of Term Report on New Labour and Criminal Justice*. London: Centre for Crime and Justice Studies.

Feilzer, M. and Hood, R. (2004) *Differences or Discrimination?* London: Youth Justice Board for England and Wales.

Garland, D. (2013) 'Penality and the penal state', *Criminology*, 51 (3): 475–517.

Gibson, B. (1995) 'Young people, bad news, enduring principles', *Youth and Policy*, 48: 64–70.

Goldson, B. (1994) 'The changing face of youth justice', *Childright*, 105: 5–6.

Goldson, B. (1997a) 'Children in trouble: state responses to juvenile crime', in Scraton, P. (ed.), *'Childhood' in 'Crisis'?* London: UCL Press.

Goldson, B. (1997b) 'Children, crime, policy and practice: neither welfare nor justice', *Children and Society*, 11 (2): 77–88.

Goldson, B. (2001) 'The demonisation of children: from the symbolic to the institutional', in Foley, P., Roche, J. and Tucker, S. (eds), *Children in Society: Contemporary Theory, Policy and Practice*. Basingstoke: Palgrave.

Goldson, B. (2002a) 'New punitiveness: the politics of child incarceration', in Muncie, J., Hughes, G. and McLaughlin, E. (eds), *Youth Justice: Critical Readings*. London: Sage.

Goldson, B. (2002b) *Vulnerable Inside: Children in Secure and Penal Settings*. London: The Children's Society.

Goldson, B. (2009) 'Child incarceration: institutional abuse, the violent state and the politics of impunity', in Scraton, P. and McCulloch, J. (eds), *The Violence of Incarceration*. London: Routledge.

Goldson, B. (2010) 'The sleep of (criminological) reason: knowledge-policy rupture and New Labour's youth justice legacy', *Criminology and Criminal Justice*, 10 (2): 155–178.

Goldson, B. (2015 in press) *Re-imagining Juvenile Justice*. London: Routledge.

Goldson, B. and Coles, D. (2005) *In the Care of the State? Child Deaths in Penal Custody in England and Wales*. London: INQUEST.

Goldson, B. and Kilkelly, U. (2013) 'International human rights standards and child imprisonment: potentialities and limitations', *International Journal of Children's Rights*, 21 (2): 345–71.

Goldson, B. and Muncie, J. (2006) 'Rethinking youth justice: comparative analysis, international human rights and research evidence', *Youth Justice*, 6 (2): 91–106.

Goldson, B. and Muncie, J. (eds) (2009) *Youth Crime and Juvenile Justice, Vol. 2: Juvenile Corrections*. London: Sage.

Goldson, B. and Muncie, J. (2012) 'Towards a global "child friendly" juvenile justice?', *International Journal of Law, Crime and Justice*, 40 (1): 47–64.

Graham, J. and Moore, C. (2004) *Trend Report on Juvenile Justice in England and Wales*, European Society of Criminology Thematic Group on Juvenile Justice. Available at: www.esc-eurocrim.org/workgroups.shtml#juvenile_justice (accessed 24.8.04).

Grayling, C. and Gove, M. (2013) 'Ministerial Foreword', in Ministry of Justice *Transforming Youth Custody: Government Response to the Consultation*. London: Ministry of Justice.

Hagell, A. (2005) 'The use of custody for children and young people', in Bateman, T. and Pitts, J. (eds), *The RHP Companion to Youth Justice*. Lyme Regis: Russell House.

Hagell, A. and Hazel, N. (2001) 'Macro and micro patterns in the development of secure custodial institutions for serious and persistent young offenders in England and Wales', *Youth Justice*, 1 (1): 3–16.

Hagell, A., Hazel, N. and Shaw, C. (2000) *Evaluation of Medway Secure Training Centre*. London: Home Office.

Haines, K. and Drakeford, M. (1998) *Young People and Youth Justice*. Basingstoke: Macmillan.

Hardwick, N. (2014) 'Feltham: time for a new start', *Criminal Justice Matters*, 95 (1): 22–3.

Hazel, N., Hagell, A., Liddle, M., Archer, D., Grimshaw, R. and King, J. (2002) *Detention and Training: Assessment of the Detention and Training Order and its Impact on the Secure Estate across England and Wales*. London: Youth Justice Board for England and Wales.

Her Majesty's Chief Inspector of Prisons (1999) *Suicide is Everyone's Concern: A Thematic Review by HM Chief Inspector of Prisons for England and Wales*. London: Home Office.

Her Majesty's Chief Inspector of Prisons (2000) *Unjust Deserts: A Thematic Review by HM Chief Inspector of Prisons of the Treatment and Conditions for Unsentenced Prisoners in England and Wales*. London: Her Majesty's Inspectorate of Prisons for England and Wales.

Her Majesty's Chief Inspector of Prisons (2002) *Annual Report of HM Chief Inspector of Prisons for England and Wales, 2001–2002*. London: The Stationery Office.

Her Majesty's Chief Inspector of Prisons (2004) *Report on an Announced Inspection of HMP Eastwood Park 22–26 September 2003 by HM Chief Inspector of Prisons*. London: Home Office.

Her Majesty's Chief Inspector of Prisons (2005) *Annual Report of HM Chief Inspector of Prisons for England and Wales, 2003–2004*. London: The Stationery Office.

Her Majesty's Chief Inspector of Prisons (2013) *HM Chief Inspector of Prisons for England and Wales Annual Report 2012–13*. London: The Stationery Office.

Her Majesty's Chief Inspector of Prisons and The Office for Standards in Education (2001) *A Second Chance: A Review of Education and Supporting Arrangements Within Units for Juveniles Managed by HM Prison Service*. London: Home Office.

Her Majesty's Inspectorate of Prisons and the Youth Justice Board (2013) *Children and Young People in Custody 2012–13*. London: The Stationery Office.

Holmes, C. and Gibbs, K. (2004) *Perceptions of Safety: Views of Young People and Staff Living and Working in the Juvenile Estate*. London: Her Majesty's Prison Service.

Home Office (1997a) *Tackling Youth Crime: A Consultation Paper*. London: Home Office.

Home Office (1997b) *Tackling Delays in the Youth Justice System: A Consultation Paper*. London: Home Office.

Home Office (1997c) *New National and Local Focus on Youth Crime: A Consultation Paper*. London: Home Office.

Home Office (1997d) *No More Excuses: A New Approach to Tackling Youth Crime in England and Wales*. London: The Stationery Office.

Home Office (2003a) *Prison Statistics England and Wales*. London: The Stationery Office.

Home Office (2003b) *World Prison Population List*, Findings 234. London: Home Office.

Hough, M., Jacobson, J. and Millie, A. (2003) *The Decision to Imprison: Key Findings*. London: Prison Reform Trust.

House of Commons Committee of Public Accounts (2004) *Youth Offending: The Delivery of Community and Custodial Sentences*, Fortieth Report Of Session 2003–04. London: The Stationery Office.

House of Commons Justice Committee (2013) *Youth Justice: Seventh Report of Session 2012–13*. London: The Stationery Office.

Howard League for Penal Reform (2004) *Girls Held in Adult Prisons Against their 'Best Interest'* Press Release, 20 January. London: The Howard League for Penal Reform.

Howard League for Penal Reform (2005) *Children in Custody: Promoting the Legal and Human Rights of Children*. London: The Howard League for Penal Reform.

Jacobson, J., Bhardwa, B., Gyatang, T., Hunter, G. and Hough, M. (2010) *Punishing Disadvantage: A Profile of Children in Custody*. London: Prison Reform Trust.

Jones, D. (2002) 'Questioning New Labour's youth justice strategy: a review article', *Youth Justice*, 1 (3): 14–26.

Jones, T. and Newburn, T. (2004) 'The convergence of US and UK crime control policy: exploring substance and process', in Newburn, T. and Sparks, R. (eds), *Criminal Justice and Political Cultures: National and International Dimensions of Crime Control*. Cullompton: Willan.

Leech, M. and Cheney, D. (2001) *The Prisons Handbook*. Winchester: Waterside Press.

Magarey, S. (1978) 'The invention of juvenile delinquency in early nineteenth-century England', *Labour History*, 34: 11–25.

Mental Health Foundation (1999) *Bright Futures: Promoting Young People's Mental Health*. London: Salzburg-Wittenburg.

Miller, J. (1991) *Last One Over the Wall: The Massachusetts Experiment in Closing Reform Schools*. Columbus, OH: Ohio State University Press.

Ministry of Justice (2013) *Transforming Youth Custody: Putting Education at the Heart of Detention*. London: Ministry of Justice.

Ministry of Justice (2014a) *Transforming Youth Custody: Government Response to the Consultation*. London: Ministry of Justice.

Ministry of Justice (2014b) *Youth Custody Data: Youth Custody Report – March 2014*. London: Ministry of Justice. Available at: www.gov.uk/government/publications/youth-custody-data (accessed 2.6.14).

Ministry of Justice and Youth Justice Board (2014) *Youth Justice Statistics 2012/13 England and Wales*. London: Ministry of Justice.

Morgan, R. (2004) 'Where does child welfare fit into youth justice', paper presented at *Children First, Offending Second?*, Nacro Youth Crime Conference, April. Loughborough University: unpublished.

Munby, The Honourable Mr Justice (2002) *Judgment Approved by the Court for Handing Down in R (on the application of the Howard League for Penal Reform) v. The Secretary of State for the Home Department, 29 November*. London: Royal Courts of Justice.

Muncie, J. (1990) 'Failure never matters: detention centres and the politics of deterrence', *Critical Social Policy*, 28: 53–66.

Muncie, J. (2002) 'Policy transfers and what works: some reflections on comparative youth justice', *Youth Justice*, 1 (3): 27–35.

Muncie, J. (2005) 'The globalization of crime control – the case of youth and juvenile justice: neo-liberalism, policy convergence and international conventions', *Theoretical Criminology*, 9 (1): 35–64.

Muncie, J. (2015) *Youth and Crime*, 4th edn. London: Sage.

Muncie, J. and Goldson, B. (eds) (2006) *Comparative Juvenile Justice: Critical Issues*. London: Sage.

Murray, R. (2012) *Children and Young People in Custody 2011/12: An Analysis of the Experiences of 15–18-year-olds in Prison*. Norwich: The Stationery Office.

Nacro (1989a) *Phasing Out Prison Department Custody for Juvenile Offenders*. London: Nacro.

Nacro (1989b) *Replacing Custody: Findings from Two Census Surveys of Schemes for Juvenile Offenders Funded Under the DHSS Intermediate Treatment Initiative Covering the Period January to December 1987*. London: Nacro.

Nacro (2003) *A Failure of Justice: Reducing Child Imprisonment*. London: Nacro.

Nacro (2005) *A Better Alternative: Reducing Child Imprisonment*. London: Nacro.

Newburn, T. (1997) 'Youth, crime and justice', in Maguire, M., Morgan, R. and Reiner, R. (eds), *The Oxford Handbook of Criminology*, 2nd edn. Oxford: Clarendon.

Pitts, J. (2000) 'The new youth justice and the politics of electoral anxiety', in Goldson, B. (ed.), *The New Youth Justice*. Lyme Regis: Russell House.

Pratt, J. (1987) 'A revisionist history of intermediate treatment', *British Journal of Social Work*, 15.

Pratt, J. (2000) 'Emotive and ostentatious punishment: its decline and resurgence in modern society', *Punishment and Society*, 2 (4): 417–39.

Prison Reform Trust (2004) *Prison Reform Trust Factfile: July 2004*. London: Prison Reform Trust.

Prison Reform Trust (2013) *Bromley Briefings Prison Factfile Autumn 2013*. London: Prison Reform Trust.

Prison Reform Trust and INQUEST (2012) *Fatally Flawed: Has the State Learned Lessons from the Deaths of Children and Young People in Custody?* London: The Prison Reform Trust.

Rutherford, A. (1984) *Prisons and the Process of Justice*. London: Heinemann.

Rutherford, A. (1995) 'Signposting the future of juvenile justice policy in England and Wales', in Howard League for Penal Reform (ed.), *Child Offenders: UK and International Practice*. London: Howard League for Penal Reform.

Rutherford, A. (2002) 'Youth justice and social exclusion', *Youth Justice*, 2 (2): 100–107.

Sanders, A. (2011) 'What was New Labour thinking? New Labour's approach to criminal justice', in Silvestri, A. (ed.), *Lessons for the Coalition: An End of Term Report on New Labour and Criminal Justice*. London: Centre for Crime and Justice Studies.

Scraton, P. (ed.) (1997) *'Childhood' in 'Crisis'?* London: UCL Press.

Social Exclusion Unit (2002) *Reducing Re-offending by Ex-prisoners*. London: Social Exclusion Unit.

Social Services Inspectorate, Commission for Health Improvement, Her Majesty's Chief Inspector of Constabulary, Her Majesty's Chief Inspector of the Crown Prosecution Service, Her Majesty's Chief Inspector of the Magistrates' Courts Service, Her Majesty's Chief Inspector of Schools, Her Majesty's Chief Inspector of Prisons and Her Majesty's Chief Inspector of Probation (2002) *Safeguarding Children: A Joint Chief Inspectors' Report on Arrangements to Safeguard Children*. London: Department of Health.

Stern, V. (2005) 'The injustice of simple justice', in Conway, D. (ed.), *Simple Justice*. London: CIVITAS.

Tonry, M. (2004) *Punishment and Politics: Evidence and Emulation in the Making of English Crime Control Policy*. Cullompton: Willan.

Williams, R. (2011) 'Teens are left to their own devices as council axes all youth services', *Guardian*, 23 August. Available at: www.theguardian.com/society/2011/aug/23/norfolk-axes-youth-services-effect (accessed 8.6.14).

Yates, J. (2012) 'What prospects youth justice? Children in trouble in the age of austerity', *Social Policy and Administration*, 46 (4): 432–47.

Young, J. (1999) *The Exclusive Society*. London: Sage.

Youth Justice Board (2014) *Youth Custody Report – March 2014*. London: Youth Justice Board. Available at: www.gov.uk/government/publications/youth-custody-data (accessed 2.6.14).

Youth Justice Board for England and Wales (2004) *Strategy for the Secure Estate for Juveniles: Building on the Foundations*. London: Youth Justice Board for England and Wales.

# 12 COMMUNITY SAFETY AND THE POLICING OF YOUNG PEOPLE IN AUSTERE TIMES

## ADAM EDWARDS, GORDON HUGHES AND RACHEL SWANN

This chapter focuses on the key continuities and shifts in the porous policy field of community safety and crime prevention and the changing modes of both policing young people and promoting their safety. Our focus is largely on the current context of governing safety and the 'policing' (in a broad sense, Hughes, 2007) of crime and anti-social behaviour in austere times in England and Wales. However, there will also be some discussion of the wider European trends regarding young people and what, in Europe, is more often termed 'public safety' and 'urban security' (Edwards et al., 2013a). Given the breadth and scope of the discussion, the chapter is necessarily synoptic with regard to the specific implications of developments in governing safety for young people and 'youth justice'. In attempting to write a 'history of the present', we will reflect on the claims and insights made in the chapter on community safety published in the first edition of this book (Hughes and Follett, 2006) that focused on the policy agenda of the New Labour government. In particular, we compare what, in retrospect, was the high watermark of the 'preventive turn' with more recent, post-2010 politics, policy and practice in austere times. In so doing we argue for the need for a programme of comparative local case study research to help us better understand the ways in which government policy is being implemented and, as crucially, contested and fought over in localities across England

and Wales. In particular, we take the current debate surrounding the Mayor of London's strategic vision for policing and crime in the metropolis as an exemplar of the Coalition government's agenda and how it is being contested. The chapter concludes by calling for greater engagement from the critical social scientific community with questions of the nature of state and public power, both malign and benign, and how our work as critical criminologists may help reconstitute the public debate on what is possible in the governance of young people, including enhancing the conditions for their safety and flourishing.

# MAPPING THE RISE AND (POSSIBLE) DEMISE OF COMMUNITY SAFETY IN ENGLAND AND WALES[1]

The development of the policy field of community safety in England – and in large measure Wales – has been widely charted in previous commentary and may be said to represent one of the most renowned, long-term experiments in multi-agency, partnership-based crime prevention across the world (Hughes, 2007). Put briefly, it is possible to identify, following Gilling et al. (2013), three broad phases:

- the 'voluntary' (1982–97),
- the 'national mandatory' (1998–2010), and
- the still unfolding 'localised and devolved' (2010–?).

A brief overview of the constituent elements of these phases reveals the contested and unstable nature of a policy terrain that has principally focused on *young people*, street crime and public disorder.

## The 'voluntary' phase (1982–97)

In England and Wales, the emergence of community safety strategies in the voluntary phase signified a 'reaction discourse' initially among radical left local authorities in the larger municipalities against a relatively narrow, police-led and central- government-led definition of what is to be prevented (recordable crimes) and how (by situational measures for reducing the opportunities for

---

[1] This chapter focuses primarily upon England and Wales and, as such, it does not address community safety and policing developments across the UK as a whole (see Gilling et al., 2013 for an innovative comparative analysis of the polities of the UK (England, Northern Ireland, Scotland and Wales) and the Republic of Ireland and the varying politico-constitutional settlements and uneven institutionalisation of community safety initiatives across these countries).

specific crimes to be committed). Counterpoised to this, community safety discourse has also identified how various environmental conditions impact upon the perception and experience of safety (such as leisure and educational provision for young people) and how this entails interventions beyond the expertise of the police (such as employment, training and education schemes, and youth work).

Following the publication of Home Office Circular 8/84 (Home Office, 1984), an increasing number of community safety partnerships (CSPs) were established by municipal authorities throughout England and Wales. This circular provided the first official acknowledgement that the police could not tackle problems of crime without the support of other statutory organisations and the active involvement of local citizens in promoting their own safety. This multi-agency approach to crime prevention was reiterated and expanded upon subsequently in an independent report on safer communities headed by James Morgan but commissioned by the Home Office (Home Office, 1991). The 'Morgan Report' is renowned in the recent history of policing for promoting the role of social and economic policy responses to problems of crime and violence. The social democratic ethos of the Report did not appeal to the Conservative administrations of the early-1990s who rejected Morgan's recommendations that local government leaders should be statutorily obliged to consult local communities about their policing priorities, and to build the same priorities into local community safety strategies. As a consequence, local authorities were left to decide themselves whether or not they established community safety partnerships and, of course, whether they were willing to adequately fund them. At this time, much of the innovation in community safety work occurred in the provinces, in particular Merseyside, Northumbria and the Thames Valley (Edwards and Hughes, 2002).

## The 'national mandatory' phase (1998–2010)

The major turning point in the national institutionalisation of community safety was the election of the first New Labour government in 1997, which was committed to modernising policing by emphasising the role that local authorities and other 'responsible authorities' (such as health boards, probation services and fire and rescue services) had to play in 'partnership' with the police in delivering 'safer communities'. This conception of community safety included providing improvements in people's 'quality of life' by tackling 'anti-social behaviour' in addition to preventing crime. New Labour had been enthusiastic supporters of the Morgan Report whilst in opposition to the Conservative governments of the early-1990s and, once elected, moved very quickly to legislate – the Crime and Disorder Act 1998 – for statutory crime and disorder reduction partnerships (CDRPs), alongside multi-agency Youth Offending Teams (YOTs). The statutory duty obliged every municipal authority throughout England and Wales to establish CDRPs, to conduct public consultations about local problems of crime and disorder and to formulate three-yearly strategies to address the same problems. Throughout this period, tackling the 'problem of youth' held an absolutely pivotal place in driving the partnership work underpinning local strategies (Hughes and Follett, 2006).

Hughes and Follett (2006: 157) have noted the exclusionary and punitive consequences of the national government's drive to both prioritise and address the problem of youthful anti-social behavior.[2] At the same time, the evaluation of the actual local implementation of community safety and crime and disorder reduction strategies – including anti-social behaviour management – remained complex and uncertain: 'compromise, contestation, even resistance, are all present in the day-to-day realities of the local implementation and delivery of community safety strategies that focus upon the perennial youth issue' (Hughes and Follett, 2006: 158). Significantly uneven developments of *localised* policy and practice were found across England and Wales, despite the intended *national* project envisaged by central government (ibid.). In retrospect, it is also clear that alongside the punitive exclusion of 'anti-social youth', the period was also marked by significant central government investment, albeit *sotto voce*, in primary, secondary and tertiary crime prevention.[3] At the local level Hughes and Follett (ibid.) also pointed to the persistent influence of conditionally inclusive strategies towards the problem both *with* and *of* 'at risk' children and young people (see e.g. the projects associated with the Welsh Government's Safer Communities Fund, Hughes et al., 2009). Rigorous empirical intranational research studies are also necessary in order to comprehend the Coalition government's policy outcomes, rather than relying on textual analysis of its rhetoric on policing, 'anti-social behaviour' management, youth justice and community safety. Indeed, it is fair to say that we currently lack rigorous research evidence pertaining to post-2010 developments in these overlapping fields.[4]

With the benefit of hindsight, the first decade of the twenty-first century can be seen as the pinnacle of an attempt to realise the broader conception of multi-agency policing and crime prevention envisaged in the Morgan Report. Community Safety Partnerships (CSPs) benefitted from the significant expansion of public expenditure following the New Labour administration's first

---

[2] We should also note the increasing political and policy salience of the relationship between an alcohol-fuelled night-time economy and the 'anti-social behaviour' of both male and female young people (see Swann, 2012).

[3] As the terms are currently understood in the youth crime prevention field, 'primary prevention' operates at a broad level to address economic, social or other conditions which could over the longer term lead to the development of crime, 'secondary prevention' focuses more specifically on groups that are directly 'at risk' of becoming offenders, and 'tertiary prevention' seeks to prevent further offending by individuals already defined as offenders (Hughes et al., 2009)

[4] Indeed, in retrospect it is striking how little comparative empirical case study research on the local governance of community safety was undertaken during the whole of the New Labour period (for an early exception, see Hughes and Edwards (eds) 2002).

comprehensive spending review in 1999. However, the CSPs were criticised for their bureaucracy, their anonymity and consequently their failure to effectively engage local citizens in a more democratic form of policing. A report entitled *Engaging Communities in the Fight Against Crime*, led by Louise Casey (Cabinet Office, 2008), identified a culture of professionalism in which local civil servants staffing CDRPs/CSPs had insulated community safety work from public priorities and concerns – especially over issues of anti-social behaviour – whilst pursuing their own agendas or those of particularly forceful local politicians. However, civil servants argued that the insulation of the CSPs was a consequence, in part, of the way in which they were funded and performance managed by national government. To draw down the funding provided to them by the Treasury, local CSPs had to enter into 'Public Service Agreements' (PSAs) that contained nationally-set targets for crime reduction. Progress towards meeting these targets was monitored on a quarterly basis and this led to a proliferation of additional bureaucracy, including posts dedicated to monitoring and auditing performance. In turn, local practitioners noted the limitations that this forensic performance management placed on their ability to respond to the priorities of local citizens or plan longer-term preventive interventions beyond the annual budgetary cycle (see e.g. Edwards and Hughes, 2008).

It should also be noted, however, that alongside the 'downside' of excessive bureaucracy and performance management, the national mandatory phase also witnessed local policy innovation with the institutionalisation of multi-agency teams and new community safety managers in many municipalities. Such actors played a key role in coordinating the partnership work of the contributing statutory agencies and public authorities and in establishing new and distinct forms of community safety expertise, particularly with regard to marginalised young people (see Edwards and Hughes, 2008; Hughes, 2007: ch. 4; Hughes et al., 2009).

Again in retrospect an important tendency throughout this period from proponents of multi-agency approaches was the ambitious and radical ambition to rethink how to govern social problems such as the criminalisation of young people. In calling for 'joined up thinking for joined up government', a radical challenge was being made to the 150-year long tradition of departmentalism and narrow institution-based approaches to dealing with problems (the police, as an institution, 'owning' the problem of crime). This led to attempts in a number of larger cities to govern the locality as a locality rather than a number of discrete problems and departmental silos. At their most successful, Local Area Agreements represented the beginning of a political programme of city governance, the radicalism of which should not be under-estimated (Hughes, 2007: 178–85).

## The 'localised and devolved' phase (2010–?)

The financial crisis of 2008 and the severe economic downturn acted as a catalyst for another phase of policing and community safety reform. The 2010 general election saw Labour ejected from power but there was no overall control of Parliament by the other political parties. To secure power, the Conservatives and the Liberal Democrats formed the Coalition government. Central to this Coalition is a shared belief that Britain's economic ills were a consequence of its over-bureaucratised government and bloated public expenditure on, as a number of Coalition government politicians claimed, 'non-jobs', not least the army of performance managers in local government. The Coalition government promised a 'bonfire of the quangos' in an attempt to replace 'big government' with a 'big society', one in which local authorities would be freed from Public Service Agreements and allowed to set their own agendas. Of course, the *quid pro quo* of this new 'localism' is that local authorities must set their agendas on the basis of very severe cuts to their budgets as the Coalition government has proceeded to reduce public expenditure on local government by over one-third of its pre-2010 rate.

In this third phase – that at the time of writing is still unfolding – there remains great uncertainty regarding both the changing terrain in which community safety is now operating and the consequences for young people at risk of criminalisation and social exclusion. Economic crisis and the election of the Coalition government have certainly brought about harsh public expenditure cuts, seriously threatening the sustainability of what was, in any case, regarded by many agencies as a relatively peripheral area of activity. On the basis of our research there is emerging evidence from localities across England and Wales that the cuts are working in the same way as performance management frameworks, generating a centripetal force that encourages a focus on 'core business' and, therefore, a climate that is less supportive of experimental partnership working in areas outside of old-established departmental boundaries (including health, education, police, education and housing). The stricture that public services are now expected to 'do more with less' may tilt the balance in CSPs more in the direction of voluntary sector and private bodies, that may be 'cheaper' or more 'cost-effective' than statutory alternatives. Indeed, in some areas there is evidence that the CSP model has been effectively abandoned as cash-strapped local authorities seek only minimal compliance with Section 17 of the Crime and Disorder Act 1998, which legally requires them to integrate crime and disorder reduction strategies across their routine core activities.

Research undertaken at Cardiff University with the National Community Safety Network has highlighted the abolition of many community safety posts and the 'downsizing' of community safety teams, alongside the collapse of multi-agency partnership working and the retreat of agencies back to their departmental silos (Cartwright, 2012). Initial developments across the crime control complex (including policing, prisons and probation) suggest that the Conservative Party's 'Big Society' vision is in fact a misnomer for a Big Business vision of service delivery. Maguire (2012), for example, has noted the increasing commercialisation and marketisation of what were once national probation service activities into a mixed economy of offender management with payment by results, in large measure controlled by powerful private and international companies such as G4S and several 'super' charities, such as Nacro, themselves run largely along business lines. With regard to the implications of such developments for young people and youth justice, it is likely that projects associated, for example, with youth work and primary prevention schemes will be sacrificed and abolished. We might also speculate (in the absence of hard evidence) that the austerity programme may also signify a shift towards less expensive and less accountable police informal action and diversion or, in the worse case scenario, abandonment of young people in the most marginalised communities.

The Coalition government's Police Reform and Social Responsibility Act 2011 expressed the core ideological and policy themes of reducing the size and influence of the state sector through the abolition of Public Service Agreements and the establishment of elected Police and Crime Commissioners (PCCs) (who were granted control over the much reduced funding programmes for community safety that had previously been provided directly to the CSPs). PCCs have been heralded by leading politicians in the Coalition government as the expression of local democratic voice, connecting policing back to the public, in place of the previous control of community safety by unelected bureaucratic-professional elites in the 'bloated' public sector. PCCs are elected in each of the 42 police force areas of England and Wales except the Metropolitan Police area. Their primary role is to facilitate the local governance of policing (this is the role of the Mayor of London in the case of the Metropolitan Police). What is unclear at present are the considerations that will guide this role. There are concerns that, in the large urban areas, PCCs may succumb to populist political pressure that will result in deploying resources first and foremost for reactive, old-fashioned police-led 'crime-fighting' and easy wins such as punitive responses to youth offending and anti-social behaviour. In this eventuality many of the progressive multi-agency based, preventive gains associated with local community safety partnership work over the last 15 years could be vulnerable to reversal.

At their most extreme then, the current economic and political challenges across England, and to a large extent Wales, offer a substantial threat to the future of community safety expertise. In the words of one community safety manager from North Yorkshire interviewed by Cartwright (2012: n.p.):

> [W]e're now seeing a break up, of multi agency, community safety groups, people leaving not being replaced. Always had poor engagement with health, terrible engagement from health, and we're seeing other agencies walk away now, not walk away from their own volition, but walk away because they've got other things to do, or that person who represented that agency has retired, been made redundant, or left and they haven't been replaced. It's a splintering of partnerships. The fact [is] that I know one area community safety manager who left and his job was split in four between four other individuals, so the town centre manager got a quarter of his work, a community development manager got another quarter of his work, and they didn't have either the experience or knowledge or the availability to go and represent community safety for their organization at a multi-agency meeting.

Given the financial constraints and the possibility that new PCCs will bypass local authority-based CSPs to commission services from business and the third sector, much of the institutional architecture and accumulated expertise of the past decade and a half (especially with regard to youth crime prevention and social inclusion initiatives) could be dismantled and lost.

# COMMUNITY SAFETY AND THE POLICING
# OF YOUNG PEOPLE

Throughout the history of community safety and crime and disorder reduction, and despite its undoubted progressive potential, the social control of young people has remained the dominant tendency. In truth, community safety policy and practice has all too often been pulled back to the logic of policing and the 'criminalization of social policy'. The latter logic, alongside the resort to 'punitive display' (Garland, 2001) has tended to win out over the competing logic of the 'socialization of criminal justice'. The disproportionate focus on young people and families and the preoccupation with youth crime and anti-social behaviour looks set to continue under the Coalition government and whichever government may be elected in 2015.[5] In part, a sense of continuity across New Labour and the Conservative-dominated Coalition government seems plausible. But we would also point to the Coalition government's retreat from the social programmes of primary and secondary prevention associated with New Labour (see e.g. Hughes et al., 2009) and the almost exclusive prioritisation of tertiary youth crime prevention at the acute end of offending in, for example, the Youth Justice Board's corporate plan 2013–16 (YJB, 2013). A more sombre reading of future developments suggests the likelihood of failed local 'public safety regimes' (Edwards and Hughes, 2012) in which the very poorest communities will face virtual abandonment by the state, 'out of sight, out of mind', in an increasingly divided society of safe 'haves' and increasingly vulnerable and isolated 'have-nots'. In such a scenario, the role of the laissez faire state is limited to providing control at the hard end via coercive policing and incarceration.

As Hughes and Follett (2006) noted, the study of policy and practice in community safety generally, and youth crime prevention specifically, cannot be restricted to national government policy talk. In essence the key focus needs to be about the interaction between national government policy projects and their local implementation, including the localised negotiation, mode of implementation, and at times failure, subversion and/or resistance to national government intentions. London's official policing and community safety plan provides a good case study in this regard.

## Local matters: young people, policing and community safety in London

As noted previously, further to the election of the Coalition government in 2010, there remains a serious absence of comparative local case studies of the

---

[5] Ostensibly anti-social behaviour has slipped down the policy agenda since the Coalition government came into office. However, whilst it is no longer prioritised with a similar level of crusading zeal, and indeed investment, associated with New Labour, at the time of writing there have been some signs of its resurrection, most notably by the Anti-social Behaviour, Crime and Policing Act 2014.

actual politics and practice of policing and community safety and the consequences for young people. However, the work of Edwards and Prins (2014) on
the official construction of policing and community safety in London provides
us with some important initial evidence (drawing on the digitalisation of data
from a public consultation process) as to how matters may unfold elsewhere,
despite the obvious geo-historical uniqueness of London and its boroughs as the
UK's 'global city'. In particular, we take the current debate surrounding the
Mayor of London's strategic vision for policing and crime control in the metropolis as an exemplar of the Coalition government's agenda and how it is being
contested. More broadly, this particular illustration exemplifies our long-standing
call for local case studies that are a critical test for macro-theories and over-
generalisations of tendencies in social control in much existing criminological,
intellectual and political traditions (Edwards and Hughes, 2012).

The incumbent Mayor of London – the equivalent of the PCC elsewhere
across the country – has made a safer city one of his core ambitions and
announced that the mission for policing London is to create 'a metropolis considered the safest global city on the planet' (Mayor's Office for Policing and
Crime (MOPAC), 2013a: 9). To this end, Mayor Johnson introduced the
'20:20:20 Challenge' as his 'bold strategic objective' to be realised in three
years – by the end of his second term of office – in 2016:

> The policing challenge is to cut seven key, high-volume neighbourhood crimes by 20%,
> boost public confidence in the police by 20%, and cut costs at the MPS (Metropolitan Police
> Service) by 20% and save £500 million; and the criminal justice goal [is] to seek swifter
> justice for victims by reducing delays in the criminal justice system by 20%, achieve surer
> justice by increasing compliance with community sentences by 20%, and to reduce reoff-
> ending by young people leaving custody in London by 20%. (MOPAC, 2013a: 9)

Beyond the symbolic, rhetorical appeal and electoral device of the '20:20:20
Challenge', Edwards and Prins (2014) note that it is not clear from the first
MOPAC annual report how these targets have been arrived at, nor what underpins the logic of reducing high volume crimes by one-fifth and also reducing
expenditure on the Metropolitan Police Service by one-fifth and, incredulously,
expecting public confidence in policing to increase by one-fifth in the space of
three years. As an agenda-setting statement, however, Edwards and Prins (ibid.)
contend that the 'Challenge' neatly encapsulates the strategic dilemma of
achieving ambitious targets in the context of austerity budgeting. Implicit
then is the view that – in keeping with the grand narrative of the Coalition
government – such severe budgetary reductions can act as a catalyst for more
effective governance, rather than the more intuitive conclusion that they will
result in a serious degradation of governing capacity and the abandonment of
vulnerable populations, including poor young people (Edwards and Hughes,
2012). The presumption from the Mayoral office is that previous expenditure
was inflated by investment in self-serving 'big government' and that there is
plenty of slack in the budgets of public services (such as policing and community safety) which can be substantially cut without any deleterious effect on the

quality of (youth) service provision. On the contrary, austerity compels 'smarter' public services that will deliver much more for much less.

Central to this claim is the official construction of crime trends in London – and elsewhere in England and Wales – that have registered year-on-year falls despite the substantial cutbacks in expenditure under the Coalition government. In welcoming the national figures on reductions in officially recorded crime in July 2013 the Prime Minister, David Cameron, identified the adoption of 'smarter policing' (that makes greater use of information technologies to better monitor and target the geographical and temporal distribution of crime) as a key factor behind the apparent success story.

In addition to elementary criminological objections to inferring actual crime trends from the reporting and recording practices registered in official crime statistics, another reservation noted by Edwards and Prins (2014) arises out of inferring localised trends from data that is aggregated at the city-wide level of Greater London and covers a population of 7.5 million. Research into the distribution of volume crime in the 1990s has, for example, identified the concentration of multiple and repeat victimisation in the top decile of high crime neighbourhoods which also scored high on the Index of Multiple Deprivation (Hope, 1996; Trickett et al., 1992). An implication of this research is that data on crime trends that is aggregated at the city-wide level, is likely to obscure the grossly uneven distribution of volume crimes across neighbourhoods at the more localised level of different London boroughs. In these terms, the official construction of policing and crime in London currently lacks the level of 'granularity' that could reveal concentrations of particular offences – and patterns of victimisation – amongst especially vulnerable populations such as children and young people in the most deprived neighbourhoods. This recalls key insights from the localised 'left realist' surveys of victimisation in Islington in North London in the 1980s, which similarly identified elevated victimisation for personal and property crimes amongst low-income households (Jones et al., 1986).

Edwards and Prins (2014) also highlight that the problem of using city-wide data on crime to drive public policy was a key theme arising out of the submissions that London boroughs made to the public consultation on the first MOPAC Policing and Crime Plan (Mayor's Office for Policing and Crime, 2013b). For example, in his detailed critique of this plan, Livingstone – a cabinet member of the Borough of Southwark's Finance, Resources and Community Safety Committee – questioned the broader narrative of a successful reduction in crime because it obscured crucially the diversity of community safety challenges across London and thus the need to tailor the allocation of resources accordingly:

> Southwark has the highest level of knife crime and youth related crime and robbery is significantly on the increase, against a London wide overall reduction. Bearing in mind that the plan sets the target of a 20% reduction in a basket of crime indicators, including violence with injury and robbery, we feel that there should be a much clearer correlation between these targets and the police numbers. The crime levels in Southwark, combined

with its high density and footfall demand a much greater allocation of resources. (Livingstone, 2013: 3)

To this end, Southwark and other boroughs have re-emphasised the importance of borough-level CSPs that are more cognisant of, for example, youth offending and victimisation 'hot-spots' in particular neighbourhoods. In turn Livingstone (ibid.) criticises the MOPAC Plan (Mayor's Office for Policing and Crime, 2013b) for withdrawing effective support for this element of local governance, particularly in the context of the severe impact of austerity budgeting on welfare support, combined with economic recession and migration patterns, that generate increased demand for public services:

[I]t has long been recognised that effective crime reduction is more effective through a strong partnership approach. The changing dynamics for London through the economic recession, migration, immigration and the changes to welfare reform will have a significant impact on crime and anti social behaviour. Community Safety Partnerships will play a crucial role in establishing long term intervention and preventative plans to reduce the impact of the above, ensuring they inform our priorities and goals. Whilst the importance of partnership working is recognised in the overarching priority to, 'Ensure that all of London's public service agencies work together and with communities to prevent crime, seek swift and sure justice for victims, and reduce re-offending', this does not appear to be ... recognised in the objectives and goals. (Livingstone, 2013: 1)

In summary, Edwards and Prins (2014) conclude that submissions to the public consultation on the MOPAC Plan further clarify the key elements of the political argument about policing and community safety, not least of/for young people, in London in a context characterised by increasing demands on public services and major reductions in governing capacity.

# URBAN SECURITY REGIMES AND THE CRISIS OF YOUTH IN EUROPE

The preferred concept of 'community safety' in the Anglophone world – to signify a 'preventive turn' in policy responses to crime and incivilities – is indicative of the purchase that communitarian thinking has had on the broader spectrum of public policy and particularly on issues of 'law and order' (Hughes, 1996). This contrasts with the preferred concepts of 'public safety' and 'urban security' that are found in European countries retaining an *Etatiste* tradition of both conservative corporatist and social democratic state interventions consistent with national-popular notions of the public sphere (Edwards et al., 2013a).

As a policy construct, 'urban security' reflects particularly the persistence and continued influence of social democratic thinking across Europe at both national and municipal policy levels, albeit in the context of globally dominant neoliberal discourses and politics. This social democratic tendency is most notably associated with the European Forum for Urban Security (EFUS), established by the French socialist mayor of Épinay-sur-Seine, Gilbert Bonnemaison in 1987. Initially, the Forum employed the concept of urban security to promote crime prevention as an issue of economic and social policy, as well as criminal justice policy. The latest EFUS manifesto of 2012 reiterates the importance of understanding problems of crime and civil unrest as problems of social justice, especially in the context of economic recession and public expenditure retrenchment in European countries experiencing crises of sovereign debt. The 2012 manifesto also signals the development of the concept of urban security across many key policy domains in Europe, signifying both a broadening of policy responses to conventional problems of street crime (beyond criminal justice), and a corresponding broadening of the perceived threats to the security of urban populations (beyond street crimes) to social cohesion and the critical infrastructure of European cities.

The concern with critical infrastructure arose out of research undertaken as part of an EU-funded project entitled 'Urbis', and in particular the 'policy Delphi' and its expert panels (Edwards et al., 2013b). Expert respondents who were sampled in this project identified threats to critical infrastructure – including threats to food, water and energy and the capacity for governing rapid population changes (as a consequence of dramatic outward as well as inward migration, particularly of young people) in European cities – as issues that might displace the conventional focus on street crimes as priorities for urban security. The same expert opinion also anticipated a trend towards an increased organisation of serious crimes, exploiting the surplus labour of young people excluded from legitimate labour markets, particularly in southern Europe.

Concerns about social cohesion and critical infrastructure reflect a complex combination of tendencies. Particular tensions identified by expert respondents to the Urbis policy Delphi include, crucially for our purposes here, those between generations and migrant populations. In Southern European cities – struggling with 'the perfect storm' of severe reductions in public expenditure and governing capacity during an economic depression – there is the perceived threat of mass emigration of younger generations suffering 50–60 per cent rates of unemployment in their home countries and with the consequent abandonment of ageing populations, whilst the young people who remain may be tempted into illicit markets, particularly for vice and narcotics. The destinations for many young southern European migrants, along with those from Eastern Europe and the Balkans, are the more prosperous cities in the North West of the continent.

In this context it is important to consider how concerns about social cohesion and civil unrest centre on the capacity of local governing arrangements to cope with rapid, high-volume, inward migration and the consequent competition for housing, schooling, healthcare and employment. It is also evident that an imagined compromised security is being racialised as populist movements construe (often young) immigrant populations as the primary 'outsider' threat to social cohesion. An extreme case of this can be found in Greek cities through the activities of the far-right-wing movement, the 'Golden Dawn', and concerns over its close association with state security personnel, particularly in the local police. It is also vital to consider the less extreme, but no less pertinent, rise of populist anti-immigrant politics in northern Europe, including the Netherlands and Scandinavia – countries that were previously known for their tolerance and inclusivity (see Edwards and Hughes, 2013).

European conceptions of 'public safety', 'urban security' and 'community safety' are frequently represented as having a strong preventive orientation, which underpins their claim to legitimacy. However, the conceptual elasticity of notions of prevention, safety and security has also generated a strong dynamic of 'mission creep' that makes it difficult to contain them within any particular policy boundaries or domains of expertise (Gilling et al., 2013). We suggest that what we prefer to term 'public safety' encapsulates the following broad goals and agendas:

1. *Criminal justice*: the augmentation of criminal law enforcement through community intelligence gathering, surveillance (particularly for counter-terrorism), post-release monitoring of serious offenders, and the sanctioning of perpetrators of anti-social behaviour.
2. *Risk management*: situational opportunity reduction, early intervention with those 'at risk', and prudential advice and support for citizens' self-protection.
3. *Restorative justice*: reintegration of offenders and conflict resolution through diversionary activities, reparation and mediation.
4. *Social justice*: seeking social and political inclusion improved education, training, employment, housing, health, leisure and family support; improving health and safety at work; targeting corporate and environmental crimes, and facilitating citizen engagement with government.[6] (Edwards and Hughes, 2012)

In the present climate certainly in England and Wales and perhaps also across Europe, social justice may appear to be the least stable policy agenda.

In England, for example, over the first weekend in August 2011 major incidents of civil unrest escalated first across London – following a public protest

---

[6] It is important to emphasise that these are sensitising devices aimed at diagnosing the principal orientation and focus of a local public safety 'regime' as, and if, it is stabilised around particular policy goals. In practice, public safety regimes may incorporate inchoate, potentially contradictory, admixtures of a number of these policy concerns. Inchoate agendas may, in turn, reflect the ongoing political struggles (of ideological and instrumental motivation) to steer a regime away from one policy direction to another and the consequent failure to negotiate an agreed agenda around which a governing Coalition can coalesce and in which a regime can be stabilized. An outcome of such struggle can be policy drift and regime failure, so there is no presumption that regimes are accomplished. This is a moot point for empirical research, off the back of which this preliminary characterisation of public safety regimes can be further refined (for a fuller discussion of the uses of regime analysis in public safety research, see Edwards and Hughes, 2012).

against a fatal police shooting of a young African-Caribbean male in Tottenham – and subsequently in provincial English cities including Birmingham, Wolverhampton, Manchester and Liverpool. Popular accounts of these incidents included a focus on the 'sheer criminality' and opportunism of largely young people involved in widespread arson and looting, the role of criminal gangs in organising this unrest, and on a broader moral malaise in which young urban populations were thought to have followed the example of feckless finance capitalists and corrupt politicians in helping themselves to desired goods that could not be secured legally. More sober reflection from the social scientific community awaits the outcome of ongoing empirical investigation into the actual sentiments and motivations behind these events (see, however, Newburn, 2013). We also await social scientific analysis of the significance of such events for clarifying the formation, sustainability and failure of particular local public safety regimes. It remains, for example, a moot point whether the criminal justice and risk management policy agendas – rather than restorative justice and social justice – will suffice as a response to urban populations that are being ejected from formal labour processes precisely at a time when draconian public expenditure cuts (in the region of 20–30 per cent) are being made to the police and other public authorities. In these terms, the English 'riots' and their aftermath provide an acid test of whether it is possible to so degrade the governing capacity of public authorities – particularly in a context of economic stagnation and structural unemployment for whole cohorts of Britain's poorest and most marginalised young people – while simultaneously seeking to remoralise civil society and relegitimise public authority.

How public safety regimes will form and fare in the 'age of austerity' is thus a key subject for critical social scientific analysis. There is, perhaps, understandable scepticism about notions of the 'big society' and of self-regulation, as surrogate forms of governance for state intervention, particularly in localities whose political-economic histories have left them relatively dependent on the public sector. From the perspective of regime analysis, though, the context of austere public finances places an even greater onus on leveraging inward corporate investment to localities, with the consequence of increasing the structural power of business to set local policy agendas. This emerging structural context promises to make regime analysis – hitherto criticised as an ethnocentrically American form of political analysis (Davies, 2002) – even more commensurate with the conditions of European liberal democracies. An obvious proposition is that such structural conditions will further reduce the scope for social justice agendas, and possibly also for the resource-intensive agendas of criminal justice, while prioritising risk management strategies that claim to minimise both the opportunities for crime and the costs of crime reduction for indebted local states. Another plausible scenario is the abandonment of non-profitable populations and localities by both the state and the market; in other words, a 'hollowing-out' of governing capacity, providing opportunities for predatory forms of governance from below, including forms of 'authoritarian gangsterism'. Commenting on recent evidence of London criminal gangs using children as drug mules, Paul Olaitan, the former head of youth services in east London, pointed to the consequences of the simultaneous retreat of the state, cuts to youth services and few jobs for young people: 'As local authorities and government have removed themselves from communities, what is left behind is a group of people left to fend for themselves' (cited in Topping, 2014).

As in the mid-2000s (Hughes and Follett, 2006: 169), the dominant discourse today on 'youth' and 'community' sees the latter as needing protection from the former, rather than driving a politics of recognition whereby young people are also seen as victims (as well as perpetrators) of crime and disorder and as citizens 'in waiting'. Rather than concluding with a sermon of doom and gloom, it is important to note that different agendas co-exist and the struggle for political ascendancy continues and is far from settled.

# CRITICAL SOCIAL SCIENCE, JUSTICE FOR YOUNG PEOPLE AND THE QUESTION OF PUBLIC POWER

Whilst much critical social scientific commentary on state power and its impact on the lives of young people understandably focuses on malign, despotic and oppressive features, we suggest that this approach is itself limiting, both conceptually and politically. Rather, we wish to make the case for the rebalancing of critical interventions in criminology by engaging with both the regressive *and* progressive policies and practices with regard to youth justice, safety and control. What are the conditions and powers necessary to enable the most 'at risk' young people to flourish rather than suffer? More specifically, we believe that a fruitful means of working through the limitations of much existing political analysis in criminology is by promoting middle range political-economic analysis associated with regime theory (see Edwards and Hughes, 2012). In particular, it is vital for critical social science to highlight how power 'constructs' as well as 'constrains' and to acknowledge the negotiation, not just the command, of social orders. This is an analytical position widely associated with Foucault's work. However, unlike Foucault and in line with critical realist thinkers like Sayer (2011: 242), we contend that the crucial next step in discussing the nature of public power is to distinguish between its 'benign and malign forms' and to study their effects on both human flourishing and suffering. In taking such a conceptual position, the possibility of deploying critical social scientists to provoke political and policy change may be opened up. Such a challenge, given the widespread abandonment of vulnerable communities and their young people, is vital to a truly public 'youth criminology' (Goldson and Hughes, 2010).

Multi-agency partnerships for the prevention of youth crime and disorder have become a loud refrain in public policy, certainly in Western European democracies, over the past three decades. Whether such policy talk represents a genuine alignment of elite and non-elite actors in the politics of public safety, or merely a new 'liberal speak' mystifying a more efficient and penetrating form of authoritarian state power, is the subject of lively, ongoing debate among traditions of political analysis in criminology. For example, the liberal tradition of demarcating politics from administration is evident in the representation of crime prevention as an enlightened, evidence-driven exercise in 'problem solving'. Studies of governance have further documented how the opening-out of the policy process to partnerships of state and non-state actors creates opportunities for the advancement and integration of more diverse and positive policy agendas (Edwards and Hughes, 2002, 2009, 2012). A more sceptical account of partnerships documents how they enhance authoritarian state projects, enrolling state and non-state actors in elitist programmes aimed at the repression of young, marginalised, street populations whilst ignoring the crimes of the powerful (Coleman et al., 2009).

The specific contribution of regime analysis to this debate is to switch the analytical focus onto issues of governing capacity: to question what policy agendas exist for public safety and social justice for young people, and how the variegated governing arrangements indicated by partnerships of state and non-state actors in local political economies enable or frustrate these agendas. This implies an ambitious programme of both conceptual analysis and empirical comparative case study research, comparing the formation of governing Coalitions at the municipal level – where public safety partnerships and suchlike are organised – the resources and schemes of cooperation they employ and considering what this tells us about the possibilities for different kinds of political action ('power to'). Such a project, by its very nature, implies collective collaboration by critical social scientists across the UK and, more ambitiously, across European localities and beyond.

# REFERENCES

Cabinet Office (2008) *Engaging Communities in the Fight Against Crime*. London: Her Majesty's Government.

Cartwright, T. (2012) *Surveying Community Safety Practitioners of the NCSN: Demography, Priorities, Responsibility and Expertise*. Unpublished MSc Dissertation, Cardiff School of Social Sciences, University of Cardiff.

Coleman, R., Sim, J., Tombs, S. and Whyte, D. (2009) 'Introduction: state, power, crime', in Coleman, R., Sim, J., Tombs, S. and Whyte, D. (eds), *State, Power, Crime*. London: Sage.

Davies, J.S. (2002) 'Urban regime theory: a normative-empirical critique', *Journal of Urban Affairs*, 24 (1): 1–17.

Edwards, A. and Hughes, G. (2002) 'Introduction: the community governance of crime control', in Hughes, G. and Edwards, A. (eds), *Crime Control and Community: The New Politics of Public Safety*. Cullompton: Willan.

Edwards, A. and Hughes, G. (2008) *The Role of the Community Safety Officer in Wales*. Cardiff: Welsh Association of Community Safety Officers (WACSO).

Edwards, A. and Hughes, G. (2009) 'The preventive turn and the promotion of safer communities in England and Wales: political inventiveness and governmental instabilities', in Crawford, A. (ed.), *Crime Prevention Policies in Comparative Perspective*. Cullompton: Willan.

Edwards, A. and Hughes, G. (2012) 'Public safety regimes: negotiated orders and political analysis in criminology', *Criminology and Criminal Justice*, 12 (4): 433–58.

Edwards, A., Hughes, G. and Lord, N. (2013a) 'Crime prevention and public safety in Europe: challenges for comparative criminology', in Body-Gendrot, S., Levy, R. and Hough, M. (eds), *The European Handbook of Criminology*. London: Routledge.

Edwards, A., Hughes, G. and Lord, N. (2013b) 'Urban security in Europe: translating a concept in public criminology', *European Journal of Criminology*, 10(3): 260–83.

Edwards, A. and Prins, R. (2014) 'Policing and crime in contemporary London: a developmental agenda?', *European Journal of Policing Studies*, 2 (1): 403–35.

Garland, D. (2001) *The Culture of Control*. Oxford: Oxford University Press.

Gilling, D., Hughes, G., Bowden, M., Edwards, A., Henry, A. and Topping, J. (2013) 'Powers, liabilities and expertise in community safety: comparative lessons for "urban security" from the United Kingdom and the Republic of Ireland', *European Journal of Criminology*, 10 (3): 326–40.

Goldson, B. and Hughes, G. (2010) 'Sociological criminology and youth justice: comparative policy analysis and academic intervention', *Criminology and Criminal Justice*, 10 (2): 211–30.

Home Office (1984) *Crime Prevention*, Circular 8/84. London: Home Office.

Home Office (1991) *Safer Communities* (The Morgan Report). London: Home Office.

Hope, T. (1996) 'Communities, crime and inequality in England and Wales', in Bennett, T. (ed.), *Preventing Crime and Disorder: Targeting Strategies and Responsibilities*. Cambridge: Institute of Criminology.

Hughes, G. (1996) 'Communitarianism and law and order', *Critical Social Policy*, 16 (4): 17–41.

Hughes, G. (2007) *The Politics of Crime and Community*. Basingstoke: Palgrave Macmillan.

Hughes, G. and Edwards, A. (eds) (2002) *Crime, Control and Community: The New Politics of Public Safety*. Collumpton: Willan Publishing.

Hughes, G. and Follett, M. (2006) 'Community safety, youth and the "anti-social"', in Goldson, B. and Muncie, J. (eds) *Youth Crime and Justice*. London: Sage.

Hughes, G., Case, S., Edwards, A., Haines, K., Liddle, M., Smith, A. and Wright, S. (2009) *Evaluation of the Effectiveness of the Safer Communities Fund 2006–9*. Cardiff: Welsh Assembly Government.

Jones, T., MacLean, B. and Young, J. (1986) *The Islington Crime Survey: Crime, Victimisation and Policing in Inner-city London*. Aldershot: Gower.

Livingstone, R. (2013) *MOPAC Police and Crime Plan – Southwark Submission*. London: Southwark Council. Available at: www.london.gov.uk/sites/default/files/Southwark%20Council.pdf (accessed 15.12.13).

Maguire, M. (2012) 'Big Society, the voluntary sector and the marketization of criminal justice', *Criminology and Criminal Justice*, 12 (5): 483–93.

Mayor's Office for Policing and Crime (2013a) *Annual Report 2012–13*. London: MOPAC.

Mayor's Office for Policing and Crime (2013b) *Police and Crime Plan 2013–16*. London: MOPAC.

Newburn, T. (2013) 'Counterblast: young people and the August 2011 riots,' *Howard Journal of Criminal Justice*, 51 (3): 331–35.

Sayer, A. (2011) *Why Things Matter to People: Social Science, Values and Ethical Life*. Cambridge: Cambridge University Press.

Swann, R. (2012) *Class, Status and Partying: An Exploration of Women's Responsibilisation for their Safety in the Night-time Economy*. Unpublished PhD thesis, Cardiff School of Social Sciences, Cardiff University.

Trickett, A., Osborn, D.R., Seymour, J. and Pease, K. (1992) 'What is different about high crime areas?', *British Journal of Criminology*, 32: 81–9.

Topping, A. (2014) 'London gangs using children as drug mules as they seek to expand markets', *The Guardian*, 5 January, available at: www.theguardian.com/society/2014/jan/05/drug-gangs-using children-as-mules (accessed 17.12.14).

Youth Justice Board (2013) *Corporate Plan 2013–16*. London: Youth Justice Board.

# 13 YOUTH TRANSITIONS, CRIMINAL CAREERS AND SOCIAL EXCLUSION

## ROBERT MacDONALD

The problems of social science, when adequately formulated, must include both troubles and issues, both biography and history, and the range of their intricate relations. (Mills, 1959: 226)

'Exclusion' is something that is done by some people to other people. (Byrne, 2005: 2)

These two quotations are ones that my colleagues and I have kept coming back to as, over the years and several empirical studies, we have sought to describe and theorise the transitions to adulthood of young people who have grown up in some of England's poorest and most deprived neighbourhoods.[1] C. Wright Mills' challenge for scholars that practice 'the sociological imagination' is an ambition that has guided our endeavours. Similarly, following Dave Byrne, we see exploring the who or what that is doing the excluding (MacDonald and Marsh, 2005) as a crucial goal for any study that seriously wants to move beyond individualistic and sometimes victim-blaming accounts of social exclusion. This chapter has two aims:

---

[1] I am grateful to the Economic and Social Research Council and the Joseph Rowntree Foundation for funding these studies and to the several co-authors who have taken part in them: Jane Marsh, Paul Mason, Donald Simpson, Les Johnston, Louise Ridley, Mark Simpson, Andrea Abbas, Mark Cieslik, Colin Webster and Tracy Shildrick. Thanks in particular to Tracy for her comments on this chapter.

- First, to show the value of a broad, long-term and in-depth sociological analysis of youth transitions with regard to understanding youth offending. For instance, we could not understand the 'criminal careers' of young people, our participants, without simultaneously attending to, and examining, their 'school to work', 'leisure' and 'drug-using careers'.
- Second, to demonstrate, through a brief but critical engagement with orthodox risk factor approaches to understanding youth crime, that these sometimes lack power in a context of multiple, shared risks and can down-play the significance of macro-level 'risks' in creating the exclusionary conditions in which criminal careers form. 'Risk factors' *beyond* the individual are critical in understanding the biographies – criminal or otherwise – of young people.

Before entering these discussions, it is important to outline the methods and aims of the Teesside studies of Youth Transitions of Social Exclusion that underpin the argument and analysis presented here.

## YOUTH TRANSITIONS AND SOCIAL EXCLUSION

Since the late 1990s a group of researchers based at Teesside University in the North East of England have, in a series of connected studies supported by the Joseph Rowntree Foundation and the ESRC, examined the way that young people make transitions to adulthood in contexts of multiple deprivation and poverty. The research has been located in the most deprived neighbourhoods of Middlesbrough, which during this period was itself one of the poorest and most deprived towns in England. At the time of fieldwork in the late 1990s and early 2000s, the seven wards that comprised our research sites all featured in the top 5 per cent most deprived nationally (DETR, 2000). Theoretically, and in general, the research has been motivated by a desire to critically engage with powerful but controversial theories and novel but abstract concepts (such as neo-conservative underclass theory or the idea of social exclusion) via a qualitative, critical case study approach that puts these ideas to the empirical test. For instance, when challenged to say where one might find 'the new rabble welfare underclass' central to his theory, Murray (1994) identified Middlesbrough as a likely location (because of its high rates of crime, unemployment and 'illegitimacy'). Although the research has focused on Middlesbrough, similar findings might be expected from any town or city in England, or elsewhere, with comparable socio-economic and demographic profiles.

The first two studies – *Snakes and Ladders* (Johnston et al., 2000) and *Disconnected Youth?* (MacDonald and Marsh, 2005) – each carried out biographical interviews (Chamberlayne et al., 2002) with working-class 15–25 year olds. The combined sample totalled 186 young people (82 females and 104 males), from the predominantly white, (ex)-manual working-class population resident in one of the most de-industrialised localities in the country (Byrne, 1999). Both studies also used participation observation and together interviewed around 50 practitioners who worked in some capacity with young people. The third study – *Poor Transitions* (Webster et al., 2004) – followed up a proportion of the 186 interviewees (34 in total: 18 females and 16 males) to see where earlier transitions had led these individuals in their mid- to late-twenties (aged 23 to 29 years). A particular focus of *Poor Transitions* was on the longer-term experiences and outcomes of people with serious involvement in drugs and crime at earlier interviews. It is these three youth-oriented studies that form the basis of the discussion in this chapter; the later studies had more of a focus on adults and less of a direct interest in youth transitions. Thus, a fourth study, *Poverty and Insecurity* (Shildrick et al., 2012b), had a primary interest in longer-term experiences of the 'low-pay, no-pay cycle' – that is, of churning between insecure, low-paid jobs and time unemployed and on benefits. The sample included 30 people who had participated in the earlier Teesside studies and who were, at the time, now aged over 30 years (in addition, we talked to 30 new interviewees, aged over 40 years). The fifth study – *Are Cultures of Worklessness Passed Down the Generations?* (Shildrick et al., 2012a) – investigated the value of the idea of 'intergenerational cultures of worklessness' in explaining concentrations of poverty and unemployment in the UK. This involved a new sample of 47 interviewees from 20 families in Middlesbrough and Glasgow.

Longitudinal qualitative youth research, as found in these Teesside studies, is quite rare. Gunter and Watt have described the 'Teesside School' as providing the 'most intensive example of youth transitions research in the UK' (2009: 516). Studying youth transitions in the long-term brings analytical benefits, as does taking a broad view of the nature of these transitions, which has been another feature of this research. The value of the concept of 'youth transition' has been much debated in youth studies (see e.g. Cohen and Ainley, 2000; MacDonald et al., 2001), with one facet of critique being the alleged narrowness and economic determinism of the conceptual frame. A broad conceptualisation of transition, going beyond the common focus on 'school to work careers' is necessary, therefore. 'Housing careers' (including the movement to independent living) and 'family careers' (including the movement from 'family of origin' to 'family of destination') have increasingly been included in sociological studies of youth transition. The Teesside studies have added to this triumvirate by also investigating 'leisure careers' (changing patterns of free-time association and activity), 'criminal careers' and 'drug-using careers'. Although 'school to work', 'housing' and 'family careers' are now commonplace features of sociological research in youth studies, unfortunately the same cannot be said for the study of drug and criminal careers which remain the preserve of some criminologists.[2] Bridging intellectual divides between

---

[2] Studies of youth leisure are still largely undertaken by scholars interested in youth culture, not youth transitions.

disciplines and fields of study has been one aim of the Teesside studies, an endeavour aided by the inclusion of youth sociologists and criminologists in the research teams for the various studies.

# YOUTH TRANSITIONS AND CRIMINAL CAREERS

To recap, the combined sample of the first two Teesside studies numbered 186 young adults. Of these, 18 interviewees gave accounts of offending that were not detailed or clear enough to use;[3] 21 described very short-lived offending in their early teens (e.g. shop-lifting or criminal damage); and 100 reported no offending whatsoever. Forty-seven reported recurrent offending, all of whom had convictions, and 33 had been imprisoned; 26 of the 47 were, or had been, opiate users of whom 3 were young women.[4] It is the 44 young men who provide the basis for this illustration of typical, more serious, longer-term criminal careers. A fuller discussion of young people's criminal careers and desistance from them can be found in MacDonald et al. (2011).

A first key process in the establishment of the criminal careers was rooted in participants' 'school to work careers'. In general our interviewees had negative, 'disappointing' experiences of formal education that were not untypical of the way that many working-class young people have fared in UK secondary schools for decades (Brown, 1987; Willis, 1977). For those who are the subject of this chapter, 'disappointment' evolved into 'disaffection' which, in time, graduated into 'disengagement' (typified by persistent truancy and/or school exclusion). Simultaneously, developments in their 'leisure careers' (specifically, fuller engagement with sub-cultural forms of street life and 'hanging around' the public spaces of their estates with other similarly placed young men) further entrenched oppositional identities and emergent criminal careers. This 'street-corner society' (MacDonald and Shildrick, 2007) underpinned and defined the evolution of most careers of crime that extended beyond early to mid-teenage years:

> [J]ust me and this other lad used to nick off all the time … just go and hang about the town … that was me starting days of crime and that, yeah. Shoplifting and pinching bikes, that's what it was. (Danny, 21, YOI inmate)

---

[3] Whilst it is important to state that these were not statistically representative samples, we can sketch out the *nature* and *shape* of typical criminal careers. The numbers are for qualitative, not quantitative, argument.

[4] The young women in the studies told a different story of their criminal and drug-using involvement; of abusive relationships with male partners and family members, of sexual exploitation and street prostitution entwined with 'heavy end' heroin use (see MacDonald and Marsh, 2005).

As Corrigan (1976) described in *Resistance through Rituals*, truanting ('doing nothing') can be boring in the extreme. It was spiced up by the camaraderie of shop-lifting jaunts, petty thieving and 'joy-riding': 'crime as leisure' for bored, out-of-school teenagers. For *some*, this period marked the early phases of criminal apprenticeships, such as learning the routines of more acquisitively oriented offending and local criminal markets. For *many*, though, these sorts of infringements – coupled with underage drinking and recreational use of drugs such as cannabis, amphetamines and ecstasy – marked the extent, and end-point, of criminal careers.

The second key process that extended a smaller number of individuals' criminal careers related to their drug careers, namely a shift in personal drug use from the sort of recreational use noted above to addicted, 'problematic' use of heroin. Criminal careers became more determined, destructive and drug-driven as a consequence.

Parker et al. (1998) mapped the 'second wave of heroin outbreaks' in Britain during the mid-1990s (with 'first wave' outbreaks tending to be to the west of the Pennine around a decade earlier). Middlesbrough provides a classic case of this second-wave outbreak. Prior to the mid-1990s it had a negligible heroin 'footprint'. During numerous, lengthy interviews with young people in Teesside at the end of the 1980s – as part of a different research project (see MacDonald and Coffield, 1991) – *not once* was heroin mentioned. Returning to the field for the Teesside studies in the late 1990s, heroin was referred to in *all* inter-views, regardless of whether the interviewee used the drug or not. In the interim, it had become a fact of life in these communities. Local police and drugs workers reported how very cheap heroin had flooded into Teesside's working-class housing estates and how marginalised young people in particular, who previously participated in the recreational dance drug scene, seemed unprepared to resist the temptations of this 'poverty drug' (MacDonald and Marsh, 2002; Simpson, 2003). Rebecca, a local drugs worker, said:

> I see a lot of heroin users who went through that thing in the late '80s/early '90s when E [ecstasy] was out, who did the dance thing, who did that rave scene, and did all that and then fell into heroin use later on. They say 'I can't believe I'm here, I'm so ashamed of being here because, you know, I used to call them [verbally abuse heroin users] and now I am one'. If I had a pound for every time they say that! They really honestly think that they can [just] try it; it's the trying, the trying.

Thus, daily, dependent use of heroin became the significant next stage in the hardening up of criminal careers. Heroin dependency drove exclusionary tran-sitions and entangled them in damaging careers of drug-driven crime. Increasingly chaotic acquisitive criminality (most often shop-lifting and bur-glary) was fuelled by the need for daily drug money:

> That's the way it goes. Start off smoking a bit of ganga [marijuana], breaking into cars and pinching car radios and then you end up on heroin and that and it fucks you up. (Jason, 21, YOI inmate)

> Prior to 16 I'd had a few cautions. It just got worse as I was getting older. I went from ecstasy to heroin. Doing it daily to feed my habit so I was robbing everything in sight.

> Whatever I could sell, I'd rob. It did for me, heroin. Shoplifting, thefts, then burglary and robbery. (Barney, 20, YOI inmate)

Heroin use became central to any adequate understanding of such young men's unfolding biographies and downward social trajectories. Furthermore, the interviews were replete with stories of family estrangement, homelessness, joblessness, ill-health, bereavement, failed desistance, successive imprisonment, loss, regret and shame.

So it was not possible to understand the onset and consolidation of the most serious forms of criminal career revealed in these studies without attending to wider aspects of youth transition. The same applied to processes of desistance from crime. This was demonstrated well in our follow up study, *Poor Transitions* (Webster et al., 2004), that reported how many of the men previously engaged in 'heavy end' crime and drug use were now on paths to desistance, albeit fragile ones. Factors well-known in the research literature (Farrall and Calverley, 2006; Laub and Sampson, 2003; Maruna, 2001) were all reported as significant by these young men in the process of moving away from crime: getting a job, forming a new partnership (normally a steady, loving relationship with a woman outside of the criminal and drug-using social network, sometimes moving away from the immediate neighbourhood as part of this), and becoming a father.[5] Although, as noted, such processes have been widely acknowledged as aids to desistance, their significance as *the* central elements and symbolic markers of youth transitions to adulthood has not (and is another example, we would suggest, of the benefit of bringing together sociological youth studies with the criminological analysis of youth offending) (Coles, 1995). In other words, 'growing out of crime' (Rutherford, 1992) draws upon exactly those normal processes typically associated with the movement from youth to adulthood.

In a context where 'respectable', traditional working-class routes to adulthood have diminished along with the cutting back of the mainstays of the local economy, achieving 'normal steps' is difficult – even for those *without* the burdensome disadvantage of criminal and drug-using careers (MacDonald and Marsh, 2005). Such young men are unlikely to appear attractive as potential employees, partners and fathers. Although we found that criminal careers did *not* completely exclude individuals from employment, it made it more difficult to obtain even the low-quality jobs that were 'normal' to the non-offenders in the studies. Similarly, using a probation hostel or bed-sit address can deter employers, and renting or taking out a mortgage on a house is especially difficult, as is obtaining a bank loan, because of a singular lack of credit history. The ability to move away from Teesside for employment or other reasons is thus curtailed. Harry was 23 when we interviewed him for *Poor Transitions*. He had a long record of offending but was now determined to go straight. He spoke of a factory operative job he had managed to get:

---

[5] In addition, access to decent drug treatment and disconnection from powerful peer groups were also identified as key factors aiding desistance.

I started the job. I wasn't late once, I wasn't sick once, hadn't missed a shift ... And basically, when they found out I did have a [criminal] record, he shot us out the door without even an explanation ... I was more reliable than some of the people he had in there ... So, that's what bugs me.

The shadow of a criminal record also inhibited his housing career:

I went for a house [to rent], a couple of month back. I was in full-time employment ... I hadn't committed a criminal offence since 2000, since my release. So that was, like, three year without an offence ... Basically, they said 'No, because of your list of offences'. I mean, I told them I had a criminal record. I volunteered all the information ... They just kept turning me down for a house. It's, basically, no one wants to give you a chance. That's what I've come across.

It also had implications for his *family career* (in the sense of a new relationship he was committed to):

Her [his partner's] Mam and Dad used to hate me! The first words I got out of her Mam's mouth were, when I seen her, were 'stay away from my daughter and my doorstep!'.

To sum up this part of the discussion, it is clear from the research that wider aspects of youth transition are highly significant in shaping criminal careers for young people and, potentially, highly significant in shaping desistance from them. Legitimate opportunities that might help further encourage and facilitate the movement away from crime are difficult to come by. A social-psychological, autobiographical turn away from offending (sometimes sparked by dramatic 'critical moments', as discussed later) could be greatly aided by the provision of second chances and purposeful activities to take the place of the structures, imperatives and purpose of daily drug-driven offending. These conclusions chime directly with criminological research that focuses on desistance from drug use and the rehabilitation of offenders (see e.g. Farrall, 2004; Farrall and Sparks, 2006; Maruna et al., 2004).

# RISK FACTORS AND YOUTH OFFENDING: CRITICAL REFLECTIONS

One of the most influential criminological approaches to understanding youth offending – that employs a more deterministic conceptualisation of 'criminal career' – is the 'risk factor paradigm' (see Case and Haines, 2009; France and Homel, 2007). David Farrington has been its key exponent in the UK and 'globally' (Muncie, 2004: 277). A classic form of positivistic social science, the appeal of this approach lies with its promise that we can know with some certainty the factors that lead to individuals developing criminal careers and seek to intervene to control and limit those risks. For instance, Farrington suggests that a small group of chronic offenders is responsible for a large proportion of crime and that 'these chronics might have been identified with reasonable accuracy at age 10' (1994: 566). Longitudinal, quantitative studies (usually of young men) are used to identify, measure and model the early life influences on offenders. Individual psychopathology, from an early age, is said to be predictive of later forms of anti-social behaviour and crime:

> [H]yperactivity at age 2 may lead to cruelty to animals at 6, shoplifting at 10, burglary at 15, robbery at 20, and eventually spouse assault, child abuse and neglect, alcohol abuse, and employment and accommodation problems later on in life. Typically, a career of childhood anti-social behaviour leads to a criminal career, which often coincides with a career of teenage anti-social behaviour and leads to a career of adult anti-social behaviour. (Farrington, 1994: 512)

Different lists of the 'major risk factors for juvenile offending' (Farrington, 1996: 2–3) can be found but they usually include factors related to individual personality and intelligence, parental supervision, parental conflict and separation, school, peer and community influences and socio-economic status. This positivist, 'actuarial' conceptualisation of offending (Young, 1999) has found favour with governments as they seek scientific explanations of 'what works' in reducing offending (i.e. underpinning the UK Probation Service's risk assessment systems; Horsefield, 2003). Coles worries that this risk factor approach

> employs a remarkably 'deductive', 'positivistic' and 'normative' approach to problem identification and problem solving. It suggests that social science is supremely confident that it knows the causes of problem behaviours and poor outcomes during youth transitions. This might be a very questionable assumption. (2000: 194)

We have sympathy with this view, but the Teesside research was not designed to test or critique the assumptions of 'the risk factor paradigm'. Nevertheless, the substantial body of qualitative, longitudinal (and quasi-longitudinal) research represented in the Teesside studies can be drawn upon to offer some critical reflections and to raise some conceptual and methodological questions about particular aspects of risk factor approaches. Three issues are pivotal (see MacDonald, 2006; Webster et al., 2006 for fuller discussion).

First, the studies suggest that it is possible that in a context where very many of the youth population possess commonly identified 'risks' then actuarial approaches lose some of their predictive and explanatory power. For instance, poor educational qualifications, school disaffection and truancy are widely cited risk factors for youth offending (Graham and Bowling, 1995; Social Exclusion Unit, 1997). The majority of those with sustained criminal careers in the Teesside research *did* have low or no qualifications, negative experiences of school and had truanted. But virtually the entire sample had low/no qualifications and negative experiences of school and many had truanted – but the majority of the sample were *not* offenders. In fact, our studies were unable to identify *any* earlier single, individual or family-level factor that would predict confidently those who might follow 'delinquent' transitions. The sample as a whole shared many socio-economic, educational and familial 'risk factors' but this fails to explain why a minority of such individuals pursued criminal careers and a majority did not. This problem of how to explain why some people with a heavy burden of 'criminogenic risk factors' do *not* evolve criminal careers is also identified by Smith and McVie: 'the substantial limitation' of childhood risk predictions is 'that there are many "false positives" … [for example] among children who are difficult to control there are many who turn out not to have criminal careers as adolescents or adults' (2003: 170).

Second, a further problem suggested by our studies relates to the assumption that criminal careers are predicted, and set in train, specifically by childhood experiences. Yet biographical interviews highlight the significance of contingent, unpredictable events and experiences in the creation of *youth* transitions of different sorts. 'Youth' is emphasised here because, like Smith and McVie (2003), we are interested in *post-childhood* influences on criminal careers (such as the role of leisure lifestyles and social networks). Contrary to the implications of the 'risk factor paradigm', we argue that criminal – and non-criminal – destinies are not set in stone in childhood. Teenage years and young adulthood present unpredictable 'critical moments', with unpredictable consequences for some transitions (MacDonald and Shildrick, 2013; Thomson et al., 2002). Events and encounters in one sphere can have dramatic repercussions in another. For instance, traumatic critical moments sometimes spur desistance and cause people to re-orient their lives. Lisa used to be 'in with a crowd getting into trouble and doing drugs' until she was raped by one of them. Zack explained how 'the turning point' in his life was when 'my best mate hung 'imself'. He had now 'calmed down now' and given up 'all sorts of mad stuff'. 'Stuff happens' and more 'stuff happens' as the years pass, remarks Webster (2005: 1). Physical and mental ill health was widespread amongst our interviewees and their families, unsurprisingly so given what we know about the socio-spatial concentration of health inequalities (Macintyre et al., 2002; Mitchell et al., 2000). Experiences of loss – particularly of bereavement and parental separation – proved to be especially important in shaping the course of individuals' lives thereafter (MacDonald and Shildrick, 2013), sometimes turning young people towards offending, sometimes away from it. In other words, very often it was things other than '*childhood* risk factors' that seemed to play a substantial role in directing transitions to and from crime.

Third, and very importantly, proponents of the risk factor paradigm seem to elevate individual and family-level risk factors and down-play the risks that are presented to young people at the more macro-level. The socio-geographic and historical contexts in which young people are born and grow up themselves present different levels of risk (that a young person will develop a criminal career) (Smith and McVie, 2003). Webster asks:

> Has political expediency and scientific attrition narrowed down risk factors to the family, parenting, truancy and peer groups because these individualised factors are amenable to early micro interventions, thus ignoring the more intractable influences of social exclusion and neighbourhood destabilisation resulting from social and economic change? (2005: 2)

It is impossible properly to understand the lives of disadvantaged young people without locating them in the socio-economic landscapes in which such lives are made. Being born and bred in one of England's poorest towns, in some of that town's most deprived neighbourhoods, in the aftermath of possibly the swiftest and deepest process of deindustrialisation to affect any old industrial region of the UK (Byrne, 1999; Shildrick et al., 2012a), *inevitably* generates a set of circumstances – we could call them 'risks' – that frame how lives may shape themselves. Crises at the macro level, in the economic basis and rationale of Teesside as a place, are shifted on to lives of its working-class inhabitants, particularly onto young adults attempting to make transitions to adulthood amongst the industrial wreckage of their region (Webster et al., 2004). Teesside, a prosperous locality of 'full employment' and relatively well-paid, skilled jobs in the 1960s, within the space of a generation became notorious for its high, structural unemployment, poverty and concomitant social problems. The young people in our research were born into this social and economic transformation, a transformation that made it harder for *all* young people here to make neat, 'respectable', conventional transitions to working-class adulthood.

A particular flavour to the Teesside story of criminal careers is added by a secondary development; the historically unprecedented influx of cheap heroin in the mid-1990s. The testimonies of drugs workers, police officers, adult residents and young people all point to the devastating and localised effects of 'poverty drugs' (MacDonald and Marsh, 2002) in enmeshing some young people in the most damaging forms of criminal career. In other words, with the advent of a new heroin-crime economy, imported risks bore down on young people's lives in Teesside; risks which were unknown just a few years earlier. The relevance of the history and local geography of the UK's 'heroin outbreaks' was brought home to us by the fifth in our series of studies (Shildrick et al., 2012a). Many of the middle-aged men we interviewed *in Glasgow* had commenced highly personally damaging careers of intravenous heroin use in their teens in the 1980s. These were all linked to long careers of acquisitive offending. None of the middle-aged men *in Middlesbrough* has this sort of biography: when they passed through their teenage years, and the prime time to develop drug careers, heroin was not easily available via drug markets in their town. It 'arrived' about 10 years later, affecting a younger cohort.

Of course, it would be foolish to argue that youth crime is *de facto* rooted in drug dependency. Craine (1997) provides just one study that shows how economically marginal transitions can readily generate minority 'alternative careers' of crime, regardless of any contact with 'poverty drugs'. Nevertheless, the form of drug-crime career sketched earlier in this chapter explains much of, and the most pernicious examples of, youth offending uncovered by the Teesside studies. The implication of this argument is that in emphasising childhood experiences and ingrained personality factors, criminal career research within the risk factor paradigm can underestimate the influence of *changing* community conditions (specific to particular places and times) and how these are encountered in *youth* transitions in generating the most serious forms of criminal career.

# CONCLUSION – BIOGRAPHY AND HISTORY: 'PRIVATE TROUBLES' AND 'PUBLIC ISSUES'

The chapter has argued two main points. First, that a proper understanding of how criminal careers commence and desist for young people necessitates a broad investigation of youth transitions that incorporate not just aspects of offending but also encompass elements of school to work, housing, family, leisure and drug-using careers. There are benefits in trying to incorporate this sort of youth sociology into youth criminology. Second, as an example of the value of a broad, sociological investigation that looks in depth and over time at young people's lives and which includes the lives of non-offenders as well as offenders, the chapter reflects critically on orthodox risk factor approaches to predicting youth offending. In the context of multiple deprivation where many individuals carry many of the objectively defined 'risks' that might 'predict criminality', this individual-level risk factor approach appears to lose its predictive power. Three problems suggested by the Teesside studies have been discussed, perhaps the most significant of which is the apparent downplaying of the macro-level 'risks' for young people inherent in the socio-economic landscapes in which they make their lives.

By mapping the transitions of young people with sustained criminal careers we invoke what C. Wright Mills called the 'personal troubles of individual milieu'. As Mills warns us, 'no social study that does not come back to the problems of biography, of history, and of their intersections within society, has completed its intellectual journey' (1959: 12). To do this, we must turn more forcibly towards 'public issues of social structure' (ibid.:14). For a moment let us swap the problem of youth crime for the problem of mass unemployment about which Mills famously wrote:

> In these terms, consider unemployment. When, in a city of 100,000, only one man is unemployed, that is his personal trouble, and for its relief we properly look to the character of the man, his skills, and his immediate opportunities. But when in a nation of 50 million employees, 15 million men are unemployed, that is an issue, and we may not hope to find its solution within the range of opportunities open to any one individual. *The very structure of opportunities has collapsed. Both the correct statement of the problem and the range of possible solutions require us to consider the economic and political institutions of the society, and not merely the personal situation and character of a scatter of individuals.* (1959: 9, emphasis added)

Similarly, we cannot present a 'correct statement' (or hope for 'possible solutions') of the multiple 'personal troubles' experienced by young people – involvement in crime, imprisonment, addiction to destructive drugs, personal and family ill-health, poor schooling, homelessness, low-quality and poorly paid jobs, unemployment and so on – by focusing 'merely' on the 'personal situation' or 'character' of 'this scatter of individuals'. This sort of individualist approach is, of course, exactly the one currently, and recurrently, in favour with government. Youth policy has been *defined* by its targeting of the alleged individual-level 'deficits' and 'lacks' of young people (Coles, 2000) and, invariably, their parents too (Goldson and Jamieson, 2002). In the UK, a contemporary favourite of politicians is to 'explain' youth unemployment and stagnant social mobility as an outcome of a lack of aspiration amongst young people (as did the UK Prime Minister recently; see Mason and Wintour, 2013). Closer to home for the research profiled in this chapter, the Mayor of Middlesbrough recently identified lack of aspiration amongst children and young people as the 'major problem' behind extremely high local rates of poverty (Hetherington, 2013).

Such an approach reflects what John Veit-Wilson calls the 'weak' conceptualisation of social exclusion in which 'the solutions lie in altering excluded peoples' [alleged] handicapping characteristics' (1998: 45). A 'strong' understanding of social exclusion encourages us, instead, to look to 'those who are doing the excluding' (ibid.). In other words, combining C. Wright Mills' call to connect biography with history and to 'consider the economic and political institutions of the society' with the emphasis of writers like Veit-Wilson and David Byrne on social exclusion as a *process* of power and inequality, brings us to a fuller understanding of the social exclusion of young people. This combination turns our attention from the figures in the landscape to the landscape itself and to the massive economic and social damage that has been inflicted on places and populations by deep and rapid deindustrialisation. This perspective throws into question attempts to understand youth exclusion and youth crime as outcomes of micro-level, personal decision-making and agency of individual young people. In Teesside, and elsewhere, it alerts us to the role of the state and the economy in creating the conditions in which exclusionary youth transitions become possible: how the distant decisions of trans-national corporations and governments have resulted in the 'wrecking of a region' (Hudson, 1989); the transformation of part of the local, skilled working-class into an industrial reserve army 'condemned to continued precariousness' (Byrne, 1999; Murad, 2002: 51; Standing, 2010); the scrapping of the 'economic scaffolding' that previously enabled transitions to stable and secure working-class adult life (Salo, 2003) and the new vagaries of 'getting by' in the lack of these; and the concentration of the hardships of poverty onto these lives.

# REFERENCES

Brown, P. (1987) *Schooling Ordinary Kids*. London: Tavistock.
Byrne, D. (1999) *Social Exclusion*. Milton Keynes: Open University Press.
Byrne, D. (2005) *Social Exclusion*, 2nd edn. Maidenhead: Open University Press.
Case, S. and Haines, K. (2009) *Understanding Youth Offending: Risk Factor Research, Policy and Practice*. Cullompton: Willan.

Chamberlayne, P., Rustin, M. and Wengraf, T. (eds) (2002) *Biography and Social Exclusion in Europe*. Bristol: Policy Press.

Cohen, P. and Ainley, P. (2000) 'In the country of the blind? Youth studies and cultural studies in Britain', *Journal of Youth Studies*, 3 (1): 79–95.

Coles, B. (1995) *Youth and Social Policy*. London: UCL Press.

Coles, B. (2000) *Joined Up Youth Research, Policy and Practice*. Leicester: Youth Work Press.

Corrigan, P. (1976) 'Doing nothing', in Hall, S. and Jefferson, T. (eds), *Resistance through Rituals*. London: Hutchinson.

Craine, S. (1997) 'The black magic roundabouts', in MacDonald, R. (ed.), *Youth, the 'Underclass' and Social Exclusion*. London: Routledge.

DETR (2000) *Index of Multiple Deprivation*. London: Department of the Environment, Transport and the Regions.

Farrall, S. (2004) 'Social capital and offender re-integration: making probation desistance focused', in Maruna, S. and Immarigeon, R. (eds), *After Crime and Punishment*. Cullompton: Willan.

Farrall, S. and Calverley, A. (2006) *Understanding Desistance from Crime: Theoretical Directions in Resettlement and Rehabilitation*. Maidenhead: Open University Press.

Farrall, S. and Sparks, R. (2006) 'Introduction', *Criminology and Criminal Justice*, 6 (1): 7–17.

Farrington, D. (1994) 'Human development and criminal careers', in Maguire, M., Morgan, R. and Reiner, R. (eds), *Oxford Handbook of Criminology*. Oxford: Oxford University Press.

Farrington, D. (1996) *Understanding and Preventing Youth Crime*, Joseph Rowntree Foundation Social Policy Findings 93. York: Joseph Rowntree Foundation.

France, A. and Homel, R. (2007) *Pathways and Crime Prevention: Theory, Policy and Practice*. Cullompton: Willan.

Goldson, B. and Jamieson, J. (2002) 'Youth crime, the "parenting deficit" and state intervention: a contextual critique', *Youth Justice*, 2 (2): 82–99.

Graham, J. and Bowling, B. (1995) *Young People and Crime*. Home Office Research Study 145. London: HMSO.

Gunter, A. and Watt, P. (2009) 'Grafting, going to college and working on road: youth transitions and cultures in an East London neighbourhood', *Journal of Youth Studies*, 12 (5): 515–29.

Hetherington, G. (2013) 'Mayor accepts there is no "silver bullet" to eradicate child poverty', *Northern Echo*, 3 December. Available at: www.thenorthernecho. co.uk/news/council/middlesbroughcouncil/10852378.Mayor_accepts_there_is_ no__silver_bullet__to_eradicate_child_poverty_in_Middlesbrough/ (accessed 10.10.14).

Horsefield, A. (2003) 'Risk assessment: who needs it?', *Probation Journal*, 50 (4): 374–9.

Hudson, R. (1989) *Wrecking a Region: State Policy, Party Politics and Regional Change in North-east England*. London: Pion Press.

Johnston, L., MacDonald, R., Mason, P., Ridley, L. and Webster, C. (2000) *Snakes and Ladders: Young People, Transitions and Social Exclusion*. Bristol: Policy Press.

Laub, J.H. and Sampson, R.J. (2003) *Shared Beginnings, Divergent Lives: Delinquent Boys to Age 70*. London: Harvard University Press.

MacDonald, R. (2006) 'Social exclusion, youth transitions and criminal careers: five critical reflections on risk', *Australian and New Zealand Journal of Criminology*, 39 (3): 371–83.

MacDonald, R. and Coffield, F. (1991) *Risky Business? Youth and the Enterprise Culture*. Lewes: Falmer Press.

MacDonald, R. and Marsh, J. (2002) 'Crossing the rubicon: youth transitions, poverty drugs and social exclusion', *International Journal of Drug Policy*, 13: 27–38.

MacDonald, R. and Marsh, J. (2005) *Disconnected Youth? Growing up in Britain's Poor Neighbourhoods*. Basingstoke: Palgrave.

MacDonald, R. and Shildrick, T. (2007) 'Street corner society', *Leisure Studies*, 26 (3): 339–55.

MacDonald, R. and Shildrick, T. (2013) 'Youth and wellbeing: experiencing bereavement and ill health in marginalised young people's transitions', *Sociology of Health and Illness*, 35 (1): 147–161.

MacDonald, R., Mason, P., Shildrick, T., Webster, C., Johnston, L. and Ridley, L. (2001) 'Snakes and ladders: in defence of studies of transition', *Sociological Research On-line*, 5: 4.

MacDonald, R., Shildrick, T., Webster, C. and Simpson, M. (2011) 'Paths of exclusion, inclusion and desistance: understanding marginalized young people's criminal careers', in Farrell, S., Hough, M., Maruna, S. and Sparks, R. (eds), *Escape Routes: Contemporary Perspectives on Life After Punishment*. London: Routledge.

Macintyre, S., MacIver, S. and Sooman, A. (2002) 'Area, class and health', in Nettleton, S. and Gustaffson, U. (eds), *The Sociology of Health and Illness Reader*. Cambridge: Polity.

Maruna, S. (2001) *Making Good: How Ex-Convicts Reform and Rebuild Their Lives*. Washington, DC: American Psychological Association Books.

Maruna, S., Immarigeon, R. and LeBel, T. (2004) 'Ex-offender reintegration: theory and practice', in Maruna, S. and Immarigeon, R. (eds), *After Crime and Punishment*. Cullompton: Willan.

Mason, R. and Wintour, P. (2013) 'David Cameron admits ministers must "do far more" to increase social mobility', *Guardian*, 14 November. Available at: www.theguardian.com/society/2013/nov/14/david-cameron-social-mobility-major (accessed 10.10.14).

Mills, C. Wright (1959) *The Sociological Imagination*. New York: Oxford University Press.

Mitchell R., Shaw, M. and Dorling, D. (2000) *Inequalities in Life and Death: What if Britain were More Equal?* Bristol: Policy Press.

Muncie, J. (2004) *Youth and Crime*, 2nd edn. London: Sage.

Murad, N. (2002) 'The shortest way out of work', in Chamberlayne, P., Rustin, M. and Wengraf, T. (eds), *Biography and Social Exclusion in Europe*. Bristol: Policy Press.

Murray, C. (1994) *Underclass: The Crisis Deepens*. London: Institute of Economic Affairs.

Parker, H., Bury, C. and Eggington, R. (1998) *New Heroin Outbreaks Amongst Young People in England and Wales*, Police Research Group, Paper 92. London: Home Office.

Rutherford, A. (1992) *Growing Out of Crime: The New Era*. London: Waterside Press.

Salo, E. (2003) 'Negotiating gender and personhood in new South Africa', *European Journal of Cultural Studies*, 6 (3): 345–565.

Shildrick, T., MacDonald, R., Furlong, A., Roden, J. and Crow, R. (2012a) *Are Cultures of Worklessness Passed Down the Generations?* York: Joseph Rowntree Foundation.

Shildrick, T., MacDonald, R., Webster, C. and Garthwaite, K. (2012b) *Poverty and Insecurity: Life in Low-Pay, No-Pay Britain*. Bristol: Policy Press.

Simpson, M. (2003) 'The relationship between drug use and crime: a puzzle inside an enigma', *International Journal of Drug Policy*, 14 (4): 307–19.

Smith, D.J. and McVie, S. (2003) 'Theory and method in the Edinburgh study of youth transitions and crime', *British Journal of Criminology*, 43: 169–95.

Social Exclusion Unit (1997) *Tackling Truancy*. London: Social Exclusion Unit.

Standing, G. (2010) *The Precariat*. London: Bloomsbury.

Thomson, R., Bell, R., Holland, J., Henderson, S., McGrellis, S. and Sharpe, S. (2002) 'Critical moments: choice, chance and opportunity in young people's narratives of transition', *Sociology*, 36 (2): 335–54.

Veit-Wilson, J. (1998) *Setting Adequacy Standards*. Bristol: Policy Press.

Webster, C. (2005) *Predicting Criminal Careers Through Risk Assessment*, British Society for Criminology Annual Conference, July, University of Leeds.

Webster, C., MacDonald, R. and Simpson, M. (2006) 'Predicting criminality? Risk assessment, neighbourhood influence and desistance', *Youth Justice*, 6 (1).

Webster, C., Simpson, D., MacDonald, R., Abbas, A., Cieslik, M., Shildrick, T. and Simpson, M. (2004) *Poor Transitions*. Bristol: Policy Press.

Willis, P. (1977) *Learning to Labour: How Working Class Kids Get Working Class Jobs*. London: Saxon House.

Young, J. (1999) *The Exclusive Society*. London: Sage.

# PART THREE
# FUTURE DIRECTIONS

# 14 CHILDREN'S HUMAN RIGHTS AND YOUTH JUSTICE WITH INTEGRITY

## BARRY GOLDSON AND JOHN MUNCIE

Since the early twentieth century, most youth justice[1] legislation in the UK – and elsewhere in much of the world – has largely been based on the foundational principle that children and young people in conflict with the law should be processed separately from adults and protected from the full weight of the criminal law (and criminal justice system). Such legislative developments are underpinned by the fundamental presumption that children under a specified age are *doli incapax* (deemed incapable of forming the intent to commit a crime) and, accordingly, should not necessarily be held fully responsible for their actions. Furthermore, the rebuttable presumption of *doli incapax* is accompanied by a more-or-less universal commitment to act in the 'child's best interests' and to protect and promote children's human rights within all systems of youth justice. A key driver of this phenomenon is the United Nations Convention on the Rights of the Child (UNCRC) (United Nations General Assembly, 1989), that entered into force in September 1990 and, following the implementation of a re-stated commitment to ratify the UNCRC from Somalia in November 2013 and a similar undertaking from South Sudan's Parliament in the same month, the Convention will have been ratified by every United

---

[1] Each of the three UK jurisdictions – England and Wales, Northern Ireland and Scotland – now prefer the term 'youth justice' to 'juvenile justice'. Furthermore, the term 'youth justice' has also been adopted in several other jurisdictions internationally, whilst 'juvenile justice' remains in common use throughout much of the world. In this chapter we use the terms 'youth justice' and 'juvenile justice' interchangeably.

Nations member state with the single exception of the USA. Similarly representative, within the European context at least, are the authoritative human rights-informed guidelines on 'child friendly justice' that have been formulated by the Council of Europe (2009, 2010). Taken together, therefore, international human rights standards would appear to provide a unifying framework for youth justice systems on a near-global scale. A key question, however, is whether, and to what extent, nation states operationalise the rhetoric of human rights by applying it, in reality, to law, policy and practice in the youth justice sphere? To pose it another way, do national jurisdictions comply with their 'child friendly justice' obligations, and if not, how might they be made to do so? The question is crucial given the evidence of disjuncture between the promise of international rights discourse on the one hand and the political resistance to, and the cultural limitations of, territorial jurisdictional implementation on the other (Goldson and Kilkelly, 2013; Goldson and Muncie, 2012; Muncie, 2013). Whilst explicitly recognising such limitations, this concluding chapter explores the means by which international law, standards, treaties, rules, guidelines and conventions (that provide for children's human rights) might comprise a vital building block in the codification and construction of a youth justice with integrity.

# THE HUMAN RIGHTS FRAMEWORK

The formalisation of universal human rights was consolidated with the creation of the United Nations in 1945 and the adoption of the Universal Declaration of Human Rights in 1948. Subsequently, the United Nations General Assembly adopted five further pivotal human rights treaties: the International Convention on the Elimination of All Forms of Racial Discrimination (1965); the International Covenant on Economic, Social and Cultural Rights (1966); the International Covenant on Civil and Political Rights (1966); the Convention on the Elimination of All Forms of Discrimination against Women (1979); and the Convention Against Torture and Other Cruel, Inhuman or Degrading Treatment or Punishment (1984). Each and all of these treaties apply to children, young people and adults, but it was not until 1989 when the UNCRC was adopted by the United Nations General Assembly – and 1990 when the Convention came into force – that a universal human rights instrument focused exclusively and comprehensively on protecting and promoting children's specific interests.

Article 1 of the UNCRC provides that the term 'child' refers to 'every human being below the age of eighteen years'. The Convention comprises 54 articles bringing together children's economic, social, cultural, civil and political rights. General measures incorporated within the UNCRC include a fundamental obligation on governments (referred to as 'States parties') to develop and sustain a children's human rights infrastructure within their jurisdictional spheres comprising, for example: the right to non-discrimination (Article 2); the primacy of the child's best interests (Article 3); the right to life and maximum development (Article 6); and the right of children and young people to have their views given due weight in all matters affecting them (Article 12). The UNCRC also provides a range of 'civil rights' including: the child's right to freedom of expression and association; the right to receive information; and the right to protection from all forms of violence, abuse, neglect and mistreatment. The Convention further provides for every child's right to an adequate standard of living and the right to the best possible health care and educational services.

The Universal Declaration of Human Rights (1948), the UNCRC (1989) and each of the intervening human rights instruments cited above, have a bearing on youth justice law, policy and practice, be it direct or indirect. Economic, social and cultural rights; civil and political rights; the elimination of all forms of discrimination; safeguards against torture and other cruel, inhuman or degrading treatment or punishment; protection from violence, abuse, neglect and mistreatment; a recognition of the 'special status' of childhood; 'best interest' principles; the right to life and maximum development; the right to be informed; and the right to be heard, all have salience regarding the treatment of children in conflict with the law. Furthermore, specific and identifiable provisions of these instruments, together with an additional range of more 'specialist' international human rights law, standards, treaties, rules, guidelines and conventions, relate more explicitly still to youth justice.

# CHILDREN'S HUMAN RIGHTS AND YOUTH JUSTICE

International human rights rules, guidelines and standards with specific regard to youth justice were initially formulated via three key instruments.

First, the *United Nations Standard Minimum Rules for the Administration of Juvenile Justice* (the 'Beijing Rules') were adopted by the United Nations General Assembly in 1985. The 'Rules' provide guidance for the protection of children's human rights in the development of separate and specialist youth justice systems. They were a direct response to a call made by the Sixth United Nations Congress on the Prevention of Crime and the Treatment of Offenders that convened in 1980. Rule 4.1 provides: 'juvenile justice shall be conceived as an integral part of the national development process of each country, within a comprehensive framework of social justice for all juveniles' (United Nations General Assembly, 1985).

Second, the *United Nations Guidelines on the Prevention of Delinquency* (the 'Riyadh Guidelines') were adopted by the United Nations General Assembly in 1990. The Guidelines are underpinned by diversionary and non-punitive imperatives: 'the successful prevention of juvenile delinquency requires efforts on the part of the entire society to ensure the harmonious development of adolescents' (para. 2); 'formal agencies of social control should only be utilized as a means of last resort' (para. 5); and 'no child or young person should be subjected to harsh or degrading correction or punishment measures at home, in schools or in any other institutions' (para. 54) (United Nations General Assembly, 1990a).

Third, the *United Nations Rules for the Protection of Juveniles Deprived of their Liberty* (the 'Havana Rules') were adopted by the United Nations General Assembly in 1990. The 'Rules' centre a number of core principles including: that deprivation of liberty should be a disposition of 'last resort' and used only 'for the minimum necessary period' and, in cases where children are deprived of their liberty, the principles, procedures and safeguards provided by international human rights law, standards, treaties, rules, guidelines and conventions must be seen to apply (United Nations General Assembly, 1990b).

These core provisions were bolstered in 1990 when the UNCRC (United Nations General Assembly, 1989) came into force. Furthermore, as stated, human rights based principles governing youth justice were reiterated – in a European context – with the publication of *European Rules for Juvenile Offenders Subject to Sanctions or Measures* (Council of Europe, 2009) and the *Guidelines of the Committee of Ministers of the Council of Europe on Child Friendly Justice* (Council of Europe, 2010).

## The UNCRC

The 'Articles' of the UNCRC that have most direct bearing on youth justice include:

- In all actions concerning children ... the best interests of the child shall be a primary consideration (Article 3).
- States parties (governments) should recognise the rights of the child to freedom of association and to freedom of peaceful assembly (Article 15).
- No child shall be subjected to arbitrary or unlawful interference with his or her privacy, family, home or correspondence (Article 16).
- No child shall be subjected to torture or other cruel, inhuman or degrading treatment or punishment (Article 37a).
- No child shall be deprived of his or her liberty unlawfully or arbitrarily. The arrest, detention or imprisonment of a child shall be in conformity with the law and shall be used only as a measure of last resort and for the shortest appropriate period of time (Article 37b).
- Every child deprived of liberty shall be treated with humanity and respect for the inherent dignity of the human person, and in a manner that takes into account the needs of persons of his or her age. In particular, every child deprived of liberty shall be separated from adults unless it is considered in the child's best interest not to do so (Article 37c).
- Every child deprived of his or her liberty shall have the right to prompt access to legal and other appropriate assistance, as well as the right to

challenge the legality of the deprivation of his or her liberty before a court or other competent, independent and impartial authority, and to a prompt decision on any such action (Article 37d).

- States parties recognize the right of every child alleged as, accused of, or recognized as having infringed the penal law to be treated in a manner consistent with the promotion of the child's sense of dignity and worth, which reinforces the child's respect for the human rights and fundamental freedoms of others and which takes into account the child's age and the desirability of promoting the child's reintegration and the child's assuming a constructive role in society (Article 40(1)).
- States parties shall seek to promote the establishment of laws, procedures, authorities and institutions specifically applicable to children alleged as, accused of, or recognized as having infringed the penal law, and, in particular: (a) The establishment of a minimum age below which children shall be presumed not to have the capacity to infringe the penal law; (b) Whenever appropriate and desirable, measures for dealing with such children without resorting to judicial proceedings, providing that human rights and legal safeguards are fully respected (Article 40(3)). (see United Nations General Assembly, 1989: passim)

## The Council of Europe guidelines for 'child friendly justice'

Extending the human rights principles that informed the 'European rules for juvenile offenders subject to sanctions or measures' (Council of Europe, 2009), the Council of Europe Committee of Ministers have issued formal 'guidelines' for 'child friendly justice' (Council of Europe, 2010). The Guidelines echo core provisions of the UNCRC in stating that 'a "child" means any person under the age of 18 years' (ibid.: section II(a)) and that they apply 'to all ways in which children are likely to be, for whatever reason and in whatever capacity, brought into contact with ... bodies and services involved in implementing criminal, civil or administrative law' (ibid.: section I: para. 2). Moreover, 'child friendly justice' aims to guarantee respect for, and the effective implementation of, all children's human rights, including the right to: due process; to participate in, and to understand, legal proceedings; to respect for private and family life; and to integrity and dignity. In particular the guidelines stipulate how children's human rights should be recognised and promoted in five key areas:

### Participation

- The right of all children to be informed about their rights, to be given appropriate ways to access justice and to be consulted and heard in proceedings involving or affecting them should be respected.
- Children should be considered and treated as full bearers of rights and should be entitled to exercise all their rights in a manner that takes into account their capacity to form their own views and the circumstances of the case.

### Best interests of the child

- Member states should guarantee the effective implementation of the right of children to have their best interests be a primary consideration in all matters involving or affecting them.
- In assessing the best interests of the involved or affected children, a comprehensive approach should be adopted by all relevant authorities so as to take due account of all interests at stake, including psychological and physical well-being and legal, social and economic interests of the child.

### Dignity

- Children should be treated with care, sensitivity, fairness and respect throughout any procedure or case, with special attention for their personal situation, well-being and specific needs, and with full respect for their physical and psychological integrity.
- Children shall not be subjected to torture or inhuman or degrading treatment or punishment.

### Protection from discrimination

- The rights of children shall be secured without discrimination on any grounds such as sex, race, colour or ethnic background, age, language, religion, political or other opinion, national or social origin, socio-economic background, status of their parent(s), association with a national minority, property, birth, sexual orientation, gender identity or other status.
- Specific protection and assistance may need to be granted to more vulnerable children, such as migrant children, refugee and asylum seeking children, unaccompanied children, children with disabilities, homeless and street children, Roma children, and children in residential institutions.

### Rule of law

- The rule of law principle should apply fully to children as it does to adults.
- Elements of due process such as the principles of legality and proportionality, the presumption of innocence, the right to a fair trial, the right to legal advice, the right to access to courts and the right to appeal, should be guaranteed for children as they are for adults and should not be minimised or denied under the pretext of the child's best interests. (See Council of Europe, 2010: 4–5)

It follows that the European guidelines for 'child friendly justice' echo many of the provisions of United Nations human rights instruments including: 'the minimum age of criminal responsibility should not be too low and should be determined by law'; 'alternatives to judicial proceedings ... should be encouraged whenever these may serve the child's best interests'; 'respect for children's rights as described in these guidelines and in all relevant legal instruments on the rights of the child should be guaranteed to the same extent in both in-court and out-of-court proceedings' (ibid.: section IV(B): paras 23–26), and 'any form of deprivation of liberty of children should be a measure of last resort and be for the shortest appropriate period of time' (ibid.: section IV(A): para. 19).

Collectively, therefore, international law, together with United Nations and Council of Europe standards, treaties, rules, guidelines and conventions provide what might appear to be a well-established 'unifying framework' for encouraging domestic legislative reform, modelling youth justice statutes, formulating policy and developing practice in all nation states to which they apply (Goldson and Hughes, 2010; Hamilton, 2011). There are, however, important caveats. Crucially, as Fortin (2008: 60) has observed, the UNCRC – in the UK and in many other countries where it has been ratified – has 'not been made part of domestic law' and, as such, it ultimately remains 'unincorporated'. What this means is that although – following ratification – such nation states might be morally obliged to implement the provisions of the UNCRC, they are not legally compelled to do so. In short, the UNCRC is not legally binding and, in this sense, it might be thought to 'lack teeth' (Fortin, 2008: 60). Alternatively, the incorporation of the Convention's core principles by the Council of Europe offers – theoretically at least – the prospect of European countries being taken to task through the legal apparatus of the European Convention on Human Rights (ECHR) (incorporated into UK law through the provisions of the Human Rights Act 1998). Notwithstanding the legal technicalities, it might legitimately be argued that international standards, treaties, rules, guidelines and conventions – if they are applied in good faith – provide the basis for a 'globalised' human rights-compliant and 'child friendly' youth justice.

# MONITORING COMPLIANCE WITH THE UNCRC: THE UNITED NATIONS COMMITTEE ON THE RIGHTS OF THE CHILD

In order to monitor the translation of the UNCRC into the realm of law, policy and practice within the national borders of respective 'States Parties', an international monitoring body has been established. The United Nations Committee on the Rights of the Child comprises 18 democratically elected members drawn from the 193 States Parties. The Committee normally meets three times a year in Geneva, Switzerland, and each of its members is required to act in an independent capacity as distinct from being a 'representative' of their specific country. The Committee has two principal functions. First, to issue 'General Comments' in order to elaborate the means by which the provisions and requirements of the UNCRC should be applied within specific subject-domains.[2] Second, to periodically investigate the degree to which each State party is implementing the Convention – and retaining compliance with it – within the corpora of law, policy and practice. Two years after a State party ratifies the UNCRC it is obliged to submit an initial report to the United Nations Committee on the Rights of the Child, outlining how it is applying the UNCRC. Following the submission of the initial report, each State party is required subsequently to provide periodic reports at five-yearly intervals. The Committee also considers written evidence submitted by discrete government departments, non-governmental organisations (NGOs), national independent human rights institutions (such as Children's Commissioners and Ombudspersons) and children and young people themselves. The principal purpose of such inquiry is to ascertain the extent to which law, policy and practice within individual nation states is UNCRC-compliant and the degree to which children are treated in accordance with the spirit, if not the word, of the Convention (Goldson and Kilkelly, 2013; Goldson and Muncie, 2012; Kilkelly, 2008).

# CHILDREN'S HUMAN RIGHTS AND YOUTH JUSTICE: INTERNATIONAL EVIDENCE

Whilst many of the United Nations Committee on the Rights of the Child 'General Comments' have a direct bearing on children and young people in conflict with the law, 'General Comment No. 10: Children's Rights in Juvenile Justice' is clearly the most salient (United Nations Committee on the Rights of the Child, 2007). It particularly emphasises two key principles: first, jurisdictional systems must seek to safeguard the child's dignity at every point of the justice process; and second, recourse to judicial proceedings (and especially

---

[2] Between 2001–13 the United Nations Committee on the Rights of the Child issued 17 'General Comments': 'The Aims of Education'; 'The Role of Independent Human Rights Institutions'; 'HIV/AIDS and the Rights of the Child'; 'Adolescent Health'; 'General Measures of Implementation for the Convention on the Rights of the Child'; 'Treatment of Unaccompanied and Separated Children Outside Their Country of Origin'; 'Implementing Child Rights in Early Childhood'; 'The Right of the Child to Protection from Corporal Punishment and Other Cruel or Degrading Forms of Punishment'; 'The Rights of Children with Disabilities'; 'Children's Rights in Juvenile Justice'; 'Indigenous Children and Their Rights Under the Convention'; 'The Right of the Child to be Heard'; 'The Right of the Child to Freedom from all Forms of Violence'; 'The Right of the Child to Have His/Her Best Interests Taken as a Primary Consideration'; 'The Right of the Child to the Enjoyment of the Highest Attainable Standard of Health'; 'State Obligations Regarding the Impact of the Business Sector on Children's Rights'; and 'The Right of the Child to Rest, Leisure, Play, Recreational Activities, Cultural Life and the Arts'.

custodial detention) should only ever be operationalised as measures of last resort. In short, the 'Comment' provides that the primary aims of human rights-compliant youth justice are to meet the child's needs and to promote their best interests.

Despite the breadth and depth of international law, standards, treaties, rules, guidelines and conventions, the United Nations Committee on the Rights of the Child has concluded that the UNCRC is often only partially applied within youth justice reform. Almost two decades after the United Nations General Assembly had adopted the Convention, therefore, the Committee noted:

> [M]any States parties still have a long way to go in achieving full compliance with CRC, e.g. in the areas of procedural rights, the development and implementation of measures for dealing with children in conflict with the law without resorting to judicial proceedings, and the use of deprivation of liberty only as a measure of last resort ... The Committee is equally concerned about the lack of information on the measures that States parties have taken to prevent children from coming into conflict with the law. This may be the result of a lack of a comprehensive policy for the field of juvenile justice. This may also explain why many States parties are providing only very limited statistical data on the treatment of children in conflict with the law. (United Nations Committee on the Rights of the Child, 2007: para.1)

More recently, and even more significantly, the Committee detected regressive movement in the form of

> a growing tendency in both developed and developing regions of the world to consider – or even reform earlier progressive legislation on juvenile criminal justice – by lowering the age of criminal responsibility and increasing penalties for children found guilty, in a misguided effort to reduce increasing public insecurity and, as a result, weakening the realization of children's rights. (United Nations General Assembly, 2012: para. 38)

Concerns regarding piecemeal application or, worse still, regression in the implementation of international human rights standards, stem – at least in part – from the 'unincorporated' status of the UNCRC within the body of domestic law in many nation states: the Convention is ultimately permissive (as distinct from legally binding) and, as such, breach attracts no formal sanction. In this sense, the UNCRC might be the most ratified of all international human rights instruments but it also appears to be the most violated, particularly with regard to youth justice and, moreover, such violations occur within a context of relative impunity. Abramson (2006), for example, whilst presenting an otherwise positive assessment of the practical impact of the UNCRC in 'transforming the world of children and adolescents', argues that youth justice is essentially peripheralised and/or unduly disregarded, even to the point of being 'unwanted'. It follows that the United Nations Committee on the Rights of the Child has repeatedly reported, and continues to report, violations of children's human rights with regard to the 'administration of juvenile justice'. Recurring concerns raised by the Committee particularly relate to Articles 37 and 40 of the UNCRC (see above), and recent examples – from each of the world's continents – include:

in the Americas (Canada):

[T]he Committee is deeply concerned at the fact that the 2003 Youth Criminal Justice Act, which was generally in conformity with the Convention, was in effect amended by the adoption of Bill C-10 and that the latter is excessively punitive for children and not sufficiently restorative in nature. The Committee also regrets that there was no child rights assessment or mechanism to ensure that Bill C-10 complied with the provisions of the Convention. In particular, the Committee expresses concern that:

(a) No action has been undertaken by the State party to increase the minimum age of criminal responsibility ...;

(b) Children under 18 are tried as adults, in relation to the circumstances or the gravity of their offence;

(c) The increased use of detention reduces protection of privacy, and leads to reduction in the use of extrajudicial measures, such as diversion;

(d) The excessive use of force, including the use of tasers, by law enforcement officers and personnel in detention centres against children during the arrest stage and in detention;

(e) Aboriginal and African Canadian children and youth are overrepresented in detention with statistics, showing for example, that Aboriginal youth are more likely to be involved in the criminal justice system than to graduate from high school;

(f) Teenage girls are placed in mixed-gender youth prisons with cross-gender monitoring by guards, increasing the risk of exposing girls to incidents of sexual harassment and sexual assault. (United Nations Committee on the Rights of the Child, 2012a: para. 85)

in Australasia and Oceania (Australia):

The Committee regrets that despite its earlier recommendations, the juvenile justice system of the State party still requires substantial reforms for it to conform to international standards, in particular the Committee is concerned that:

(a) No action has been undertaken by the State party to increase the minimum age of criminal responsibility ...;

(b) No measures have been taken to ensure that children with mental illnesses and/or intellectual deficiencies who are in conflict with the law are dealt with using appropriate alternative measures without resorting to judicial proceedings ...;

(c) Mandatory sentencing legislation (so-called 'three strikes laws') still exists in the Criminal Code of Western Australia for persons under 18 ...;

(d) All 17-year-old child offenders continue to be tried under the Criminal Justice system in the State party's territory of Queensland ....

Furthermore, the Committee is concerned that:

(a) Although the majority of 17 year olds are held separately from the wider prison population, there are still cases of children being held within adult correctional centres;

(b) There have been instances of abuse of child detainees reported in the State party's Quamby Youth Detention Centre and Bimberi Youth Detention Centre. (United Nations Committee on the Rights of the Child, 2012b: paras 82–83)

in Europe (Germany):

In line with its previous concluding observations ... the Committee recommends that deprivation of liberty be used as a measure of last resort in all cases, and for the shortest possible time. In that regard, the Committee recommends that the State party take all necessary steps to expand the possibilities for alternative sentences, such as probation or community service. (United Nations Committee on the Rights of the Child, 2014a: para. 75)

in Africa (Congo):

[T]he Committee reiterates its concern that children's judges are not always available and that children are placed in detention with adults ... often in very difficult conditions. It is also concerned that children face difficulties in gaining access to legal aid ... the Committee expresses concern that:

(a) There is no minimum age of criminal responsibility, and that judges decide on a case-by-case basis whether a child incurs a criminal penalty or not;

(b) The detention of children in conflict with the law, even of young children, is preferred over the development of alternative measures;

(c) Statistical data on the number and characteristics of children currently in prison are not available. (United Nations Committee on the Rights of the Child, 2014b: para. 80)

and in Asia (The Russian Federation):

The Committee ... is concerned about ... frequent unlawful detention of children by law enforcement agencies in circumstances where there is no apparent illicit behaviour on the children's part. (United Nations Committee on the Rights of the Child, 2014c: para. 69)

As can be seen from the examples above, recurring concerns globally include: failure to increase the minimum age of criminal responsibility (or in extreme cases even to institute a statutory minimum age of criminal responsibility); neglecting to use custody as a 'last resort'; the widespread nature of racialised (in)justice (particularly the excessive and undue criminalisation of minoritised children and young people); and the prevalence of violence and abuse (particularly in penal institutions). Each of these concerns merits further attention.

## Minimum age of criminal responsibility

Although there is no categorical international standard regarding the age at which criminal responsibility can reasonably be imputed on a child, the provisions of a number of international human rights instruments are pertinent. For example, Article 4(1) of the Beijing Rules provides: 'in those legal systems recognising the concept of the age of criminal responsibility for juveniles, the beginning of that age shall not be fixed at too low an age level' (United Nations General Assembly, 1985). Furthermore, the official commentary on this provision states: 'in general there is a close relationship between the notion of responsibility for delinquent or criminal behaviour and other social rights and responsibilities (such as marital status, civil majority, etc)' (ibid.). In this way, the Beijing Rules advocate consistency and integrity within and across the wider corpora of criminal and civil law providing for 'social rights and responsibilities' within a given jurisdiction. Similarly, the 'General Comment' on 'Juvenile

Justice' states that a minimum age of criminal responsibility set at below 12 years is not 'internationally acceptable' (United Nations Committee on the Rights of the Child, 2007) (for a fuller discussion, see Goldson, 2013).

Notwithstanding the provisions of international human rights standards, the minimum age of criminal responsibility differs widely around the world. In the USA the minimum age is set at just 6 years (in North Carolina) but most states have set no minimum age at all. In some Islamic societies, such as Iran, the minimum age of criminal responsibility is linked to the age of maturity or puberty that, according to Sharia law, is ascribed at 9 years for girls and 15 years for boys. Across the UK the minimum ages of criminal responsibility – amongst the lowest in the European Union – vary from 8 years in Scotland (although from 2010 children under the age of 12 cannot be prosecuted in a criminal court), to 10 years in England and Wales and Northern Ireland. Even greater variance is evident across Europe where the minimum age of criminal responsibility is 14 years in Germany, Italy and Spain; 15 years in Denmark, Sweden, Norway and Finland; and 18 years in Belgium and Luxembourg (Goldson, 2013; Muncie, 2015). Such differences reveal both the extent to which compliance with international human rights standards – regarding the criminalisation of children – fluctuates between nation states and, more problematically, the manner in which some jurisdictions flagrantly flout their human rights obligations. Indeed, between the time of its establishment and February 2009, the United Nations Committee on the Rights of the Child has had to recommend, on no less than 65 occasions, that a State party either increase the minimum age of criminal responsibility or to institute a minimum age of criminal responsibility in jurisdictions that had failed to establish one in law (Hamilton, 2011).

## Penal custody as a 'last resort'? Excessive penal detention, life imprisonment and execution

As noted, the UNCRC provides, at Article 37(c), that the penal detention of children should only ever be applied as 'a measure of last resort and for the shortest appropriate period of time' and that 'every child deprived of liberty shall be treated with humanity and respect for the inherent dignity of the human person and in a manner which takes into account the needs of persons of his or her age' (United Nations General Assembly, 1989). Despite this, Goldson and Kilkelly (2013) trace the manner in which the human rights 'potentialities' of international law, standards, treaties, rules, guidelines and conventions are frequently compromised by 'limitations' of implementation at best, and the wholesale violation of such instruments at worst.

Indeed, authoritative sources estimate that, at any given time, approximately one million children are imprisoned worldwide (Pinheiro, 2006: 191) and the 'recurrent and banalised use of institutionalization' is commonplace (Pinheiro, 2005: 18). Furthermore, sentences of life imprisonment are imposed on children in many countries. For example, in 'reviewing the laws of the Commonwealth

States with regards to life imprisonment of children' – including 'life imprisonment without parole', 'life imprisonment with the possibility of parole', 'detention at the pleasure of the executive or the courts' and/or 'indefinite detention sentences' – Ratledge (2012, n.p.) reports that: '45 out of 54 Commonwealth States provide for one or more of the types of life imprisonment.' Moreover, in at least 40 countries of the world children can still be sentenced to whipping, flogging, caning or amputation and, in at least seven countries, child offenders can lawfully be sentenced to death by lethal injection, hanging, shooting or stoning (Child Rights International Network, 2012). At the most extreme end of the continuum of human rights violations, between 1990 and 2011 Amnesty International documented 87 executions of child offenders in nine countries, observing that:

> The use of the death penalty for crimes committed by people younger than 18 is prohibited under international human rights law, yet some countries still execute child offenders. Such executions are few compared to the total number of executions in the world. Their significance goes beyond their number and calls into question the commitment of the executing states to respect international law. (2012, n.p.)

## Racialised (in)justice

The persistent recurrence of human rights violations, over time and across space, is frequently compounded by the manifest racialisation of youth justice practice (Webster, this volume). Muncie (2008) found that of 18 Western European jurisdictions studied, 15 were explicitly exposed to critique by the United Nations Committee for negatively discriminating against children from minority ethnic communities and migrant children seeking asylum. The over-representation of such children is particularly conspicuous at the polar ends of the system: arrest and penal detention. This especially appears to be the case, for example, for the Roma and traveller communities in England and Wales, Finland, France, Germany, Greece, Ireland, Italy, Northern Ireland, Portugal, Scotland, Spain and Switzerland, for Moroccan and Surinamese children in the Netherlands and for other North African children in Belgium and Denmark.

Trends across Europe – and elsewhere – appear to indicate that the regulation and governance of 'urban marginality' is being increasingly removed from the social welfare apparatus and redefined as a 'crime problem' within burgeoning 'penal states' (Wacquant, 2009). Moreover, within such shifts minority ethnic communities and immigrant groups are bearing the brunt of a 'punitive upsurge' (ibid.). By way of illustration, 8 million Roma – the largest minority ethnic group in the European Union – endure systematic discrimination, harassment, ghettoisation, forced eviction, expulsion and detention. By collating data drawn from 22 country-specific reports, Gauci notes that 'most ... reports identify the Roma ... as being particularly vulnerable to racism and discrimination ... in virtually all areas of life' (2009: 6). Increased ghettoisation of 'foreigner' and Roma communities in various European countries – whether as a result of institutional decisions or practical realities such as chronic unemployment – is serving to consolidate structural exclusion and systematic marginalisation: 'the creation of spatial segregation and socially excluded localities where communities are effectively denied access to basic services such as water and electricity' (ibid.: 10). Welfare safety nets have all but dissolved whilst, at the same time, the 'justice' apparatus offers no relief. On the one hand, criminal justice agencies appear impotent to offer any meaningful protection for minoritised communities enduring a pan-European upsurge of hate crime and racist violence:

> Developments within the criminal justice sector were limited over the course of 2008 as the recommendations of European and international bodies, including the European Commission Against Racism and Intolerance, were not taken on by the relevant national authorities. Whilst a number of countries noted an increase in racist violence ... the legal and policy framework remained largely unchanged. (ibid.: 28–9)

On the other hand, the very same agencies are themselves purveyors of violence:

> Ethnic minorities are also disproportionately subject to excessive use of force and violence by the police ... A dramatic and emblematic episode took place in Bussolengo, near Verona, Italy where three Roma Italian families were taken away from a parking lot where they were temporarily stopped, and forced to go to the police station, and were subjected to violence for over six hours. In addition to beating and offending the adults, the Carabinieri (Italian Police) also used force with the children. A child was beaten losing three teeth whilst another was kept with his head under the water for a long time. (ibid.: 17)

In fact, an insidious process of double-victimisation is apparent whereby the very people most vulnerable to structural exclusion, systematic discrimination, hate crime and racist violence are also most likely to be criminalised and punished. In identifiable jurisdictions including Austria, Belgium, Italy and Switzerland, over one-third of their total prison populations comprises foreign nationals. Meanwhile, 100,000 prisoners in European Union nation states have no claim to citizenship within the countries in which they are incarcerated (Muncie, 2008).

Of course such phenomena are not restricted to Europe. Cunneen and White (2006) note similar processes of racialised (in)justice in Australia including the persistent, and gross, over-representation of indigenous children and young people in penal detention, alongside an apparent favouring of diversion and community based sentences for their white counterparts. If anything, such phenomena are becoming more rather than less problematic. Research conducted for the Australian Institute of Health and Welfare (2013), for example, found that 'on an average night in the June quarter 2012, indigenous young people aged 10–17 were 31 times as likely as non-indigenous young people to be in detention, up from 27 times in the June quarter 2008.'

Similarly, in the USA, African-American and Hispanic populations are markedly over-penalised. For example, whereas African-Americans comprise 16 per cent of the total population aged 10–17 years in the USA, they account for 29 per cent of all cases referred to juvenile courts, 35 per cent of the cases waived for criminal court processing, and 36 per cent of children and young people held in penal detention (Kempf-Leonard, 2007). Guerino et al. reported:

> At year end 2010, black non-Hispanic males had an imprisonment rate (3,074 per 100,000 U.S. black male residents) that was nearly 7 times higher than white non-Hispanic males (459 per 100,000) ... Black non-Hispanic females (133 per 100,000 U.S. black female residents) had an imprisonment rate nearly 3 times that of white non-Hispanic females (47 per 100,000). (2011: 7)

Indeed, wherever we might care to look, some of the most punitive elements of youth justice appear to be reserved for, and applied to, children from minority ethnic and/or immigrant populations.

## Violence and abuse

In February 2003, Paulo Sergio Pinheiro was appointed, at Assistant Secretary-General level, to direct the 'United Nations Secretary-General's Study on Violence Against Children' (the Study). The Study was undertaken in collaboration with the Office of the High Commissioner for Human Rights, the United Nations Children's Fund and the World Health Organisation. It comprises the most wide-ranging and detailed analysis of its type in history. The final report, published and presented to the United Nations General Assembly in November 2006 (Pinheiro, 2006), makes for depressing, even if salutary, reading:

> Millions of children, particularly boys, spend substantial periods of their lives under the control and supervision of care authorities or justice systems, and in institutions such as orphanages, children's homes, care homes, police lock-ups, prisons, juvenile detention facilities and reform schools. These children are at risk of violence from staff and officials responsible for their well-being. Corporal punishment in institutions is not explicitly prohibited in a majority of countries. Overcrowding and squalid conditions, societal stigmatization and discrimination, and poorly trained staff heighten the risk of violence. Effective complaints, monitoring and inspection mechanisms, and adequate government regulation and oversight are frequently absent. Not all perpetrators are held accountable, creating a culture of impunity and tolerance of violence against children. (Pinheiro, 2006: 16)

More specifically, throughout the course of the Study, a series of 'thematic consultations' – involving leading international experts – convened in order to provide periodic subject-specific reports. In the *Violence Against Children in Conflict with the Law* report, the Director of the Study observed that 'children in conflict with the law ... are one of the most vulnerable groups to the worst forms of violence' (Pinheiro, 2005: 17–18). The juxtaposition of international human rights standards on the one hand, and the pervasive and institutionalised violation of children on the other hand, is, to say the least, anomalous.

Here too, future prospects do not look good. The United Nations General Assembly notes:

[F]orms of violence, including State violence, against children … are on the rise in all regions of the world … There are approximately 70 countries that allow corporal punishment and other violent punishments as legal disciplinary measures in penal institutions. Around 30 countries permit corporal punishment in sentencing children for crimes, which in some countries includes flogging, stoning or amputation. (2012: para. 37)

# CHILDREN'S HUMAN RIGHTS AND YOUTH JUSTICE: UK EVIDENCE

In 1995, the United Nations Committee on the Rights of the Child issued its first comprehensive report on the UK's implementation of the UNCRC in the UK. The Committee expressed general concern about the impoverishment of many children:

> The Committee notes with concern the increasing number of children living in poverty. The Committee is aware that the phenomenon of children begging and sleeping on the streets has become more visible. (United Nations Committee on the Rights of the Child, 1995: para. 15)

With specific regard to youth justice it was particularly critical of the low minimum age of criminal responsibility:

> The administration of the juvenile justice system in the State party is a matter of general concern to the Committee. The low age of criminal responsibility and the national legislation relating to the administration of juvenile justice seem not to be compatible with the provisions of the Convention, namely articles 37 and 40. (ibid.: para. 17)

The Committee also condemned the introduction of secure training centres in England and Wales (private jails for 12–14 year old children) of which there are no equivalents in Europe:

> The Committee remains concerned about certain of the provisions of the Criminal Justice and Public Order Act 1994. The Committee notes that its provisions provide, inter alia, for the possibility of applying 'secure training orders' on children aged 12 to 14 in England and Wales. The Committee is concerned about the compatibility of the application of such secure training orders on young children with the principles and provisions of the Convention in relation to the administration of juvenile justice, particularly its articles 3, 37, 39 and 40. In particular, the Committee is concerned that the ethos of the guidelines for the administration and establishment of Secure Training Centres in England and Wales … appears to lay emphasis on imprisonment and punishment. (ibid.: para. 18)

The United Nations Committee produced its second periodic report on the UK seven years later, in which it expressed a general concern 'that the principle of primary consideration for the best interests of the child is not consistently reflected in legislation and policies affecting children throughout the State party, notably in the juvenile justice system' (United Nations Committee on the Rights of the Child, 2002: para. 25). Moreover, the Committee reiterated the primary concerns that it had expressed earlier, this time employing notably forceful language:

> The Committee is *particularly concerned* that the age at which children enter the criminal justice system is low with the age of criminal responsibility still set at 8 years in Scotland and at 10 years in the rest of the State party and the abolition of the principle of *doli incapax* ... The Committee is *particularly concerned* that since the State party's initial report, children between 12 and 14 years of age are now being deprived of their liberty. More generally, the Committee is *deeply concerned* at the increasing number of children who are being detained in custody at earlier ages for lesser offences and for longer sentences imposed as a result of the recently increased court powers to issue detention and restraining orders. The Committee is therefore concerned that deprivation of liberty is not being used only as a measure of last resort and for the shortest appropriate period of time, in violation of article 37 (b) of the Convention. The Committee is also *extremely concerned* at the conditions that children experience in detention and that children do not receive adequate protection or help in young offenders' institutions (for 15- to 17-year-olds), noting the very poor staff–child ratio, high levels of violence, bullying, self-harm and suicide, the inadequate rehabilitation opportunities, the solitary confinement in inappropriate conditions for a long time ... and the fact that girls and some boys in prisons are still not separated from adults. (ibid.: para. 59, emphases added)

Furthermore, under a sub-heading in the report entitled 'torture or other cruel, inhuman or degrading treatment', the Committee drew attention to 'recent figures according to which between April 2000 and February 2002, 296 children sustained injuries as a result of restraints and measures of control applied in prison' and to the 'frequent use of physical restraint ... in custody' (ibid.: para. 33).

Following the publication of the initial report of the United Nations Committee on the Rights of the Child in 1995, the *Guardian* newspaper observed that

> policy after policy has broken the terms of the UN Convention ... [the] report of the UN monitoring committee adds up to a devastating indictment of ministers' failure to meet the human rights of Britain's children ... the report is not all bad ... however, the 'positive aspects' cover only four paragraphs, and the remaining 39 are either critical or are recommendations for action. (cited in Goldson, 1997: 142–3)

Seven years later, and following the publication of the Committee's second report, the Children's Rights Alliance for England (2005) stated bluntly that the UK government had effectively 'torn up' the UNCRC. Other commentators pointed to ways in which core elements of youth justice policy also appeared to violate the Human Rights Act 1998 (an Act that gives effect to rights and freedoms guaranteed under the European Convention on Human Rights). The Act provides for the right to a fair trial with legal representation and a right to appeal, but the introduction – via the Youth Justice and Criminal Evidence Act 1999 – of what were initially almost mandatory referral orders, with lay 'youth offender panels' deliberating on 'programmes of behaviour' with no legal representation available for the child, implies the denial of such rights (Goldson, 2000). Many of the principles of restorative justice that rely on informality, flexibility and discretion sit uneasily against legal requirements for due process and a fair and just trial (Ashworth, 2003; Cunneen and Goldson, this volume). Article 8 of the European Convention on Human Rights confers the right to respect for private and family life and protects families from arbitrary interference. Parenting orders, child curfews and anti-social behaviour orders, in particular, appear to contravene such provisions (Freeman, 2002). Furthermore, curfews not only override parental discretion/authority but also seem to be incompatible with Articles 11 and 14 that serve to affirm the right to freedom of peaceful assembly to all, irrespective of age (Walsh, 2002).

The United Nations Committee on the Rights of the Child's third (and, at the time of writing, most recent) report on the UK was published in 2008. In an unprecedented move, the four Children's Commissioners for England, Northern Ireland, Scotland and Wales submitted a joint report to the United Nations prior to the publication of the Committee's own report. The Commissioners stated:

[U]nfortunately, we have to report that, not only do some of the Committee's Concluding Observations of 2002 still lack any effective implementation, but some things have actually got worse. We would cite developments in juvenile justice and public attitudes towards children and young people as examples of this. (UK Children's Commissioners, 2008: 4)

The Commissioners added:

This is the first time that the Committee will be able to make its Concluding Observations in the knowledge that there are independent institutions in the UK committed to promoting and monitoring implementation. It will assist us in our task if the Committee can hold the Government accountable through clear recommendations about specific actions and the mechanisms needed to monitor implementation. (ibid.: 4)

When the United Nations Committee itself reported, it again expressed its 'concern' that:

The age of criminal responsibility is set at 8 years of age in Scotland and at 10 years for England, Wales and Northern Ireland ... There are still cases where children, notably those aged between 16 and 18, can be tried in an adult court ... The number of children deprived of liberty is high, which indicates that detention is not always applied as a measure of last resort ... The number of children on remand is high ... [and] children in custody do not have a statutory right to education. (United Nations Committee on the Rights of the Child, 2008: para. 77)

The Committee also recommended that:

the State party fully implement international standards of juvenile justice, in particular articles 37, 39 and 40 of the Convention, as well as general comment No. 10 on 'Children's rights in juvenile justice' the United Nations Standard Minimum Rules for the Administration of Juvenile Justice ('the Beijing Rules'), the United Nations Guidelines for the Prevention of Juvenile Delinquency ('the Riyadh Guidelines') and the United Nations Rules for the Protection of Juveniles Deprived of Their Liberty ('the Havana Rules'). It also recommends that the State party ... raise the minimum age of criminal responsibility ... develop a broad range of alternative measures to detention for children in conflict with the law; and establish the principle that detention should be used as a measure of last resort and for the shortest period of time as a statutory principle ... [ensure that] children in conflict with the law are always dealt with within the juvenile justice system and never tried as adults in ordinary courts, irrespective of the gravity of the crime they are charged with ... ensure that, unless in his or her best interests, every child deprived of liberty is separated from adults in all places of deprivation of liberty. (ibid.: para. 78)

The Committee further recommended that 'the State party conduct an independent review of Anti-Social Behaviour Orders, with a view to abolishing their application to children' (ibid.: para. 80). Indeed, in reporting in this way, the Committee responded positively to the request for 'clear recommendations' that the UK Children's Commissioners had made. What is less clear is the extent to which the United Nations Committee can 'can hold the Government accountable' in the way that the Commissioners might hope. This seems unlikely, however, when account is taken of the recurring concerns and recommendations that the Committee has persistently reported and offered since its first report to the UK government in 1995.

## The criminalisation and demonisation of children

Successive UK governments have not only effectively ignored the repeated recommendations made by the United Nations Committee on the Rights of the Child to raise the minimum age of criminal responsibility – and in so doing decriminalise children's transgressions – they have also introduced a range of civil powers and statutory orders (including curfews, child safety orders and anti-social behaviour orders, or ASBOs) that have either at worst explicitly targeted or at best inadvertently been used disproportionately against children and young people, including some below the age of 10 years. As such interventions are purportedly 'preventive', they can be imposed without either the commission or the prosecution of an actual criminal offence. Equally, the same modes of pre-emptive intervention might also be accompanied by deliberate public humiliation (e.g. through open media reporting and 'naming and shaming' rituals) practises that have exercised the Council of Europe's Commissioner for Human Rights:

> It seems to me, however, to be entirely disproportionate to aggressively inform members of the community who have no knowledge of the offending behaviour, and who are not affected by it, of the application of ASBOs. It seems to me that they have no business and no need to know ... The aggressive publication of ASBOs, through, for instance the doorstep distribution of leaflets containing photos and addresses of children subject to ASBOs risks transforming the pesky into pariahs. The impact on the family as a whole must also be considered. Such indiscriminate naming and shaming would, in my view, not only be counter-productive, but also a violation of Article 8 of the ECHR. (Gil-Robles, 2005: para. 120)

At the opposite end of the continuum, children charged with, or convicted of, 'grave offences' may bypass the youth justice system altogether and instead be tried and/or sentenced in 'adult' courts (as in the case of the two 10 year old boys convicted of the murder of 2 year old James Bulger; see Davis and Bourhill, 1997; Goldson, 2001). Again, this represents a practice that has been routinely condemned by both the United Nations Committee on the Rights of the Child and the Commissioner for Human Rights at the Council of Europe (Muncie, 2015).

It is of little surprise, therefore, that the European Court of Human Rights has ruled against the UK on at least three occasions in respect of: trying children in adult courts; challenging the legality of dispersal zones; and objecting to the indefinite retention of DNA samples and fingerprints (nevertheless, over 50,000 DNA samples were taken from children and young people in 2012 alone; see Muncie, 2014). Organs of the UK Parliament itself have also expressed critique. In 2010, for example, the House of Commons Justice Committee reported that a cluster of factors drives a punitive mentality including:

> a toxic cocktail of sensationalised or inaccurate reporting of difficult cases by the media; relatively punitive overall public opinion (compared to much of the EU); a self-defeating over-politicisation of criminal justice policy since the late 1980s and the responsiveness to all these factors of the sentencing framework and sentencers. (House of Commons Justice Committee, 2010: 5)

To express the same point differently, when taken together the interconnected strands of the 'project' to criminalise and demonise represent a 'general climate of intolerance and negative public attitudes towards children especially adolescents, which appears to exist in the State party, including in the media, and may often be the cause of further infringements of their rights' (United Nations Committee on the Rights of the Child, 2008: para. 24).

## Restricting freedom of association

In addition to the civil powers and statutory orders considered above, the Anti-Social Behaviour Act 2003 gave the police new powers to disperse children and young people from specified public areas by creating 'dispersal zones' for renewable periods of up to six months. Home Office estimates show that between January 2004 and April 2006, over 1,000 areas were designated dispersal zones in England and Wales. The human rights agency Liberty (n.d.: n.p.) noted:

> This law sweeps up the innocent with the guilty, treating all young people as potential criminals ... Children have the right to freedom of movement and assembly just as adults do. Young people may have legitimate reasons to be out at night without adults, such as an after school job, club or activity.

In 2005, Liberty lawyers acted for 'W', a 15 year old boy from Richmond (in the south of England) who successfully challenged the legality of curfews for under-16s. In court 'W', described as a 'model student', explained that his social life had been curtailed by the creation of the dispersal area and he was afraid he would be 'pounced on' by police and returned to his home. He used to take a bus once a week back from band practice at a local church but became dependent on his parents for a lift so he did not break the curfew. 'I resent having to be taken home because I feel I am old enough to be independent,' he said in a written statement read out in court. 'I'm worried about being [picked up and] taken home by the police when I've done nothing wrong. I'm also worried that if I am taken home by the police other people will see me and think I have done something wrong.' He described how he would no longer meet friends out on the street, walk his dog, or visit the local Tesco to buy milk for his mother after 9pm because he was afraid of being stopped and marched home by police. (Barkham, 2005: n.p.)

In addition to 'dispersal' powers, the use of ultrasonic devices ('Mosquitoes') that transmit an unpleasant high-pitched 'buzz', the frequency of which is only audible to children and young people, is designed to prevent them from 'loitering' in public places. Such devices degrade and discriminate against children and young people and violate the 'best interest' and related principles enshrined in the UNCRC (United Nations Committee on the Rights of the Child, 2007, 2008; Walsh, 2008).

## Failures to use custody as a 'last resort' and to safeguard child prisoners

The excessive use of penal custody for children has long-placed UK jurisdictions – especially England and Wales – at odds with the human rights provisions of international law, standards, treaties, rules, guidelines and conventions. Despite a significant reduction in the number of child prisoners since 2008, the locked institution remains the ultimate backstop of the youth justice system (see Goldson, this volume). Penal institutions invoke fear in children and routinely expose them to risks and dangers. Having surveyed 942 boys and young men in prisons Her Majesty's Inspectorate of Prisons and the Youth Justice Board reported that '30 per cent ... said they had felt unsafe at their establishment ... 22 per cent said they had been victimised by other young men and 22 per cent said that they had been victimised by staff' (2013: 11). Physical assault – or physical abuse – is commonplace, under-reported and inadequately investigated in prisons and other forms of penal custody holding children. Moreover, random violence is framed within a context in which physical force is formally institutionalised:

The Office of the Children's Commissioner found evidence ... of a tendency in youth custody to focus on physical controls ... rather than on relationships. Restraint is supposed to be a 'last resort', to prevent individuals from causing harm to themselves or others. However, there were 8,419 incidents of restrictive physical intervention used in the youth secure estate in 2011/12, up 6 per cent from 2008/09 and 17 per cent from 2010/11. 254 of these restraints involved injury to young people. (House of Commons Justice Committee, 2013: 42)

For some child prisoners, the treatment and conditions that they experience in penal custody are literally too much to bear: 33 children died in penal custody in England and Wales between 1990 and October 2012; all but two of the deaths were apparently self-inflicted (Goldson and Coles, 2005; the Prison Reform Trust and INQUEST, 2012).

# DEVOLUTION, DIFFERENTIAL JUSTICE AND COMPARATIVE ANALYSIS: TOWARDS HUMAN RIGHTS COMPLIANCE?

There is an overriding and persistent tendency in much academic and popular discourse – and, in certain cases, in United Nations Committee on the Rights of the Child reports – to conflate the 'four nations' of the UK into a geographical and political monolith. In this way, the distinctive policy and practice features of Wales, Scotland and Northern Ireland are at best marginalised or, at worst, subsumed within those of England. Such English hegemony has, however, begun to unravel through processes of political devolution, particularly since 1998. Indeed, this has been taken by all devolved administrations to offer opportunities to 'rethink' their youth justice laws, policies and practices (Muncie, 2011).

Scotland has long legislated independently but has, more recently, secured greater independence through its own Parliament. Despite some evidence of 'detartanisation' and closer alignment with English youth justice (McAra, 2008), Scotland remains unique in supporting a children's hearings system largely based on child welfare principles for under 17 year olds, where tribunals are preferred – in most cases – to youth courts. Whilst the independence of the Welsh Assembly Government is more limited it has been claimed that, within Wales, there is significant impetus towards developing more progressive human-rights oriented youth justice policy and practice, underpinned by the principle of 'extending entitlement' and driven by a 'children first' logic (Drakeford, 2009; Haines, 2010). Similarly, although the legislative capacity of the Northern Ireland Assembly was compromised by its suspension between 2002 and 2007, it too appears to have made progress in crafting a youth justice system characterised by significantly different priorities to that of England, principally expressed through a discursive emphasis on conflict resolution and restorative justice rather than adversarial and retributive justice (Jacobsen and Gibbs, 2009; but for a critical assessment see Cunneen and Goldson, this volume).

Whilst it may simply not be possible to directly transfer particular modes of intervention from one jurisdiction to another, there are arguably positive lessons that can be drawn from diverse and divergent policies and practices, particularly in observing approaches that accord more closely with the human rights provisions of international law, standards, treaties, rules, guidelines and conventions. In general terms, comparative research (e.g. Goldson and Hughes, 2010; Goldson and Muncie, 2006; Hazel, 2008; Muncie and Goldson, 2006; Tonry and Doob, 2004) has revealed that the more progressive and human rights complaint youth justice systems appear to be found in jurisdictions/countries where there is a political willingness to sustain welfare protectionism or to subsume the governance of youth crime within alternative forms of conflict resolution. Significant correlations have also been found between countries with low rates of imprisonment, higher rates of welfare spending (Downes and Hansen, 2006) and lower rates of income inequality (Wilkinson and Pickett, 2007).

The Scandinavian countries, for example, have long seemed to stand out as exemplars of social democratic youth/criminal justice where systems are sustained with only minimal recourse to imprisonment. Spending on social services, levels of taxation, expressions of governmental legitimacy and trust are all high, whilst imprisonment rates and income inequality are low. Criminal justice discourses are also significantly less politicised than in other countries, particularly the USA and England (Green, 2008; Tonry and Lappi-Seppälä, 2011). Pratt and Erikson's (2013) analysis of Nordic (Norway, Sweden, Finland) penality reveals a persistent social democratic emphasis underpinned by principles of universal welfare provision, in contrast to Anglophone (England, New Zealand, Australia) jurisdictions characterised by punitive neo-liberalism, and either the withdrawal or the selective and conditional targeting of welfare support. Rehabilitative and inclusionary interventions are promoted in the Nordic countries, whereas exclusionary and retributive penality tends to prevail in the Anglophone states.

More broadly, comparative analysis implies that a cultural and political sensibility and awareness of the fact that imprisoning children and young people is not only harmful, but also self-defeating, is also crucial for maintaining more human rights compliant approaches to the delivery of youth justice. Some of the key drivers of the more diversionary, decriminalising and decarcerative youth justice systems appear to derive from restatements of a 'children first' philosophy; a commitment to pardon and to protect but, above all, a preparedness to depoliticise youth crime and justice (Goldson and Muncie, 2006; Muncie and Goldson, 2006). Privileging both the spirit and the content of the international human rights framework is pivotal (Kilkelly, 2008).

It would be unwise to idealise any international or devolved youth justice systems and/or to assume that they are completely free of the corrosive political imperatives and historically embedded cultural constraints that prevail elsewhere (particularly, it would appear, in England). That said, comparative analyses clearly suggest possibilities for progressive reform. In this sense, the construction of a more coherent and human rights compliant set of approaches that can deliver a – long absent – youth justice system with integrity is not completely 'unimaginable' (Goldson, 2015).

# YOUTH JUSTICE WITH INTEGRITY

Our ultimate aim is to mobilise knowledge and evidence in ways that offer the greatest potential for youth justice systems to truly act in children's 'best interests' and to genuinely reflect and respect their human rights. We have formulated such an approach around six core principles (Goldson and Muncie, 2006). Each necessitates a conceptual and organisational reframing of youth crime and youth justice and, paradoxically, a substantially reduced role for the conventional youth justice apparatus.

## Addressing poverty and inequality

Policy must comprehensively address the social and economic conditions that are known to give rise to conflict, harm, social distress, crime and criminalisation, particularly poverty and inequality. The practical translation of human rights standards and principles cannot be divorced from social and economic materiality. A persistent problem is how human rights might be equally distributed within a world that is profoundly divided and polarised by social and economic inequalities. Unicef (2010) has revealed that even in rich nations identifiable groups of children are unnecessarily 'left behind', subjected to poverty, denied access to 'well-being' and exposed to inequality. Worldwide, more than 1 billion children lack proper nutrition, safe drinking water, decent sanitation, health-care services, shelter and/or education, and every day 28,000 children die from poverty-related causes (Goldson and Muncie, 2006). In the UK alone, an otherwise rich nation, 23 per cent of the population live in poverty, including 3.5 million children and, under current government policies, child poverty is projected to rise to 4.7 million by 2020 (Child Poverty Action Group, 2014).

It is no coincidence that youth justice systems characteristically serve to process (and punish) the children of the poor. The children who are most heavily exposed to criminalisation, correctional intervention, surveillance, regulation and punishment are routinely drawn from the most damaged, disadvantaged and distressed families, neighbourhoods and communities. The corrosive impact of poverty and structural inequality is profound and is key to understanding and responding to the problems both experienced by, and perpetuated by, identifiable sections of the young.

## Universal welfare

The forging of the principles of universality, comprehensiveness and re-engaging the 'social' requires dispensing with forms of conditionality that bolster the 'deserving-undeserving schism', and instead providing holistic services that meet the needs and safeguard and promote the well-being of *all* children and young people. 'Normal' social institutions – including families (however they are configured), 'communities', youth services, leisure and recreational services, health provision, schools, training and employment initiatives – need to be adequately resourced and supported. Resources should be redirected from harmful 'criminogenic' youth justice interventions (McAra and McVie, this volume) towards constructive generic 'children first' services that are not only intrinsi-cally preferable but are also known to be 'effective'. One of the most ambitious and comprehensive research analyses of youth crime prevention programmes in the world, for example, demonstrated that, even for 'serious, violent and chronic juvenile offenders', some of the most effective responses emanate from initiatives that are located *outside* of the formal criminal justice system (decrim-inalisation), build upon children's and young people's strengths as distinct from emphasizing their 'deficits' (normalisation) and adopt a social-structural approach rather than drawing on individualised, responsibilising and/or med-ico-psychological perspectives (contextualisation) (Howell et al., 1995).

## Diversion

Children and young people should be routinely diverted away from formal youth justice interventions (McAra and McVie, this volume). Of course, the most effective diversionary strategy is literally to remove children and young people from the reach of the youth justice system altogether, by significantly raising the minimum age of criminal responsibility. There are strong grounds to support this proposition, not least evidence from jurisdictions where the mini-mum age of criminal responsibility is set above the European mean, for example, and where there are no negative consequences in terms of inflated crime rates (Goldson, 2013).

## Child-appropriate justice

In the minority of cases where formal youth justice intervention is deemed unavoidable, it should be provided within a child-appropriate context. The intensity and duration of intervention should be proportionate to the severity of the offence and limited to the minimum that is absolutely necessary, its rationale should be explicit, evidence-based and likely to provide positive out-comes for the 'young offender' and, where relevant, to any injured party. International human rights agencies are consistent in their critique of adulter-ised youth justice systems. It is imperative that such critique is constructively applied to inform a more child-appropriate youth justice system.

## Abolishing harm

Interventions that are ineffective or, more problematically, that violate interna-tional human rights obligations, are known to be damaging, harmful and/or aggravate the very issues that they seek to resolve should be abolished. This applies, in varying degrees to: over-zealous and criminalising modes of early intervention (Case and Haines, this volume; McAra and McVie, this volume); the net-widening effect of 'anti-social behaviour' initiatives (Edwards, Hughes and

Swann, this volume); and, in particular, the practices of child imprisonment (Goldson, this volume). This is not to imply that nothing should be done with regard to addressing youth crime, or that troubled and troublesome children and young people should simply be left to fend for themselves without the care, guidance, support and supervision that they may well need. The central argument, however, is that the youth justice apparatus is, in itself, singularly unfit for such purposes. Rather, a critical rethinking of the conceptual origins, significances and meanings attributed to terms such as 'youth disorder', 'anti-social behaviour', 'youth crime' and 'young offender' is required (Goldson, 2015). This offers an invitation to 'start from a different place'; to focus upon offending as a social harm to be resolved rather than simply punished (Hillyard and Tombs, 2007).

## Depoliticising youth justice

The politicisation of youth crime and justice can only serve to demonise identifiable constituencies of the young and to 'institutionalize intolerance' (Muncie, 1999). Politicians repeatedly refer to an increasingly anxious, risk-averse and fearful public, and selective constructions of 'public opinion' are mobilised and presented as primary legitimising rationales for tough-on-crime agendas. Such reactive politicisation not only negates evidence and distorts policy formation, however, it is also underpinned by a skewed reading of public opinion itself (Goldson, 2010). A genuinely evidence-based approach to youth crime and justice requires politicians and policy-makers to remain cognizant of the complexities of public opinion. Moreover, senior politicians have a responsibility to *inform* public opinion as distinct from simply *reacting* to over-simplified and fundamentally erroneous interpretations of it.

# CONCLUSION

Youth justice systems are temporally and spatially contingent. At face value, the human rights provisions of international law, standards, treaties, rules, guidelines and conventions appear to provide a globally unifying framework but, as we have discussed, such instruments are implemented, operationalised and ultimately realised (or not) in profoundly varied and differentiated forms. Within this context, we have attempted to present both a comparative analysis of such differentiation together with a restated formulation of a youth justice with integrity – an approach that blends the application of knowledge and evidence with human rights imperatives. Beyond this, the chapter in particular, and the volume more generally, has aimed to advance interventionist and critically engaged research and scholarship. We offer the book, therefore, to all who are committed to forging, developing and applying rational and human rights based approaches to complex and contested social phenomena.

# REFERENCES

Abramson, B. (2006) 'Juvenile justice: the unwanted child', in Jensen, E. and Jepsen, J. (eds), *Juvenile Law Violators, Human Rights and the Development of New Juvenile Justice Systems*. Oxford: Hart.

Amnesty International (2012) *Executions of Juveniles Since 1990*. Available at: www.amnesty.org/en/death-penalty/executions-of-child-offenders-since-1990 (accessed 29.9.14).

Ashworth, A. (2003) 'Is restorative justice the way forward for criminal justice?', in McLaughlin, E., Fergusson, R., Hughes, G. and Westmarland, L. (eds), *Restorative Justice: Critical Issues*. London: Sage.

Australian Institute of Health and Welfare (2013) *Juvenile Detention Population in Australia 2012*, Juvenile justice series number 11. Canberra: Australian Institute of Health and Welfare.

Barkham, P. (2005) 'Liberty challenges child curfew and dispersal orders in land-mark case', *Guardian*, 27 May. Available at: www.theguardian.com/uk/2005/may/27/humanrights.society (accessed 29.9.14).

Child Poverty Action Group (2014) *Poverty*, Issue 148. London: Child Poverty Action Group.

Child Rights International Network (2012) *Ending Inhuman Sentencing of Children*. Available at: www.crin.org/violence/campaigns/sentencing/ (accessed 29.9.14).

Children's Rights Alliance for England (2005) *State of Children's Rights in England*. London: CRAE.

Council of Europe (2009) *European Rules for Juvenile Offenders Subject to Sanctions or Measures*. Strasbourg: Council of Europe Publishing.

Council of Europe (2010) *Guidelines of the Committee of Ministers of the Council of Europe on Child Friendly Justice* (adopted by the Committee of Ministers on 17 November 2010 at the 1098th meeting of the Ministers' Deputies). Strasbourg: Council of Europe Publishing.

Cunneen, C. and White, R. (2006) 'Australia: containment or empowerment?', in Muncie, J. and Goldson, B. (eds), *Comparative Youth Justice*. London: Sage.

Davis, H. and Bourhill, M. (1997) '"Crisis": the demonization of children and young people', in Scraton, P. (ed.), *'Childhood' in 'Crisis'?* London: UCL Press.

Downes, D. and Hansen, K. (2006) *Welfare and Punishment: The Relationship Between Welfare Spending and Imprisonment*, Briefing No. 2. London: Crime and Society Foundation.

Drakeford, M. (2009) 'Children first, offenders second: youth justice in a devolved Wales', *Criminal Justice Matters*, 78: 8–9.

Fortin, J. (2008) 'Children as rights holders: awareness and scepticism', in Invernizzi, A. and Williams, J. (eds), *Children and Citizenship*. London: Sage.

Freeman, M. (2002) 'Children's rights ten years after ratification', in Franklin, B. (ed.), *The New Handbook of Children's Rights*. Abingdon: Routledge.

Gauci, J.-P. (2009) *Racism in Europe*. Brussels: European Network Against Racism (ENAR).

Gil-Robles, A. (2005) *Report by Mr Alvaro Gil-Robles, Commissioner for Human Rights, on his Visit to the United Kingdom 4th–12th November 2004: For the Attention of the Committee of Ministers and the Parliamentary Assembly*. Strasbourg: Council of Europe Office of the Commissioner for Human Rights.

Goldson, B. (1997) 'Children in trouble: state responses to juvenile crime', in Scraton, P. (ed.), *'Childhood' in 'Crisis'?* London: UCL Press.

Goldson, B. (2000) 'Wither diversion? Interventionism and the new youth justice', in Goldson, B. (ed.), *The New Youth Justice*. Lyme Regis: Russell House.

Goldson, B. (2001) 'The demonisation of children: from the symbolic to the institutional', in Foley, P., Roche, J. and Tucker, S. (eds), *Children in Society: Contemporary Theory, Policy and Practice*. Basingstoke: Palgrave.

Goldson, B. (2010) 'The sleep of (criminological) reason: knowledge-policy rupture and New Labour's youth justice legacy', *Criminology and Criminal Justice*, 10 (2): 155–78.

Goldson, B. (2013) '"Unsafe, unjust and harmful to wider society": grounds for raising the minimum age of criminal responsibility in England and Wales', *Youth Justice: An International Journal*, 13 (2): 111–30.

Goldson, B. (2015 in press) *Re-imagining Juvenile Justice*. Abingdon: Routledge.

Goldson, B. and Coles, D. (2005) *In the Care of the State? Child Deaths in Penal Custody in England and Wales*. London: INQUEST.

Goldson, B. and Hughes, G. (2010) 'Sociological criminology and youth justice: comparative policy analysis and academic intervention', *Criminology and Criminal Justice*, 10 (2): 211–30.

Goldson, B. and Kilkelly, U. (2013) 'International human rights standards and child imprisonment: potentialities and limitations', *International Journal of Children's Rights*, 21 (2): 345–71.

Goldson, B. and Muncie, J. (2006) 'Rethinking youth justice: comparative analysis, international human rights and research evidence', *Youth Justice: An international Journal*, 6 (2): 91–106.

Goldson, B. and Muncie, J. (2012) 'Towards a global "child friendly" juvenile justice?', *International Journal of Law, Crime and Justice*, 40 (1): 47–64.

Green, D.A. (2008) *When Children Kill Children: Penal Populism and Political Culture*. Oxford: Oxford University Press.

Guerino, P., Harrison, P. and Sabol, W. (2011) *Prisoners in 2010*. Washington, DC: US Department of Justice.

Haines, K. (2010) 'The dragonisation of youth justice', in Taylor, W., Earle, R. and Hester, R. (eds), *Youth Justice Handbook*. Cullompton: Willan.

Hamilton, C. (2011) *Guidance for Legislative Reform on Juvenile Justice*. New York: Children's Legal Centre and UNICEF.

Hazel, N. (2008) *Cross-national Comparison of Youth Justice*. London: Youth Justice Board.

Her Majesty's Inspectorate of Prisons and the Youth Justice Board (2013) *Children and Young People in Custody 2012–13*. London: The Stationery Office.

Hillyard, P. and Tombs, S. (2007) 'From "crime" to social harm?', *Crime, Law and Social Change*, 48 (1–2): 9–25.

House of Commons Justice Committee (2010) *Cutting Crime: The Case for Justice Reinvestment, First Report of Session 2009–10*. London: The Stationary Office.

House of Commons Justice Committee (2013) *Youth Justice: Seventh Report of Session 2012–13*. London: The Stationery Office.

Howell, J.C., Krisberg, B., Hawkins, J.D. and Wilson, J.J. (eds) (1995) *Serious, Violent and Chronic Juvenile Offenders: A Sourcebook*. London: Sage.

Jacobsen, J. and Gibbs, P. (2009) *Making Amends: Restorative Youth Justice in Northern Ireland*. London: Prison Reform Trust.

Kempf-Leonard, K. (2007) 'Minority youths and juvenile justice: disproportionate minority contact after nearly 20 years of reform efforts', *Youth Violence and Juvenile Justice*, 5 (1): 71–87.

Kilkelly, U. (2008) 'Youth justice and children's rights: measuring compliance with international standards', *Youth Justice: An International Journal*, 8 (3): 187–92.

Liberty (n.d.) 'Curfews'. Available at: www.liberty-human-rights.org.uk/human-rights/fighting-discrimination/young-people/curfews (accessed 29.9.14).

McAra, L. (2008) 'Crime, criminology and criminal justice in Scotland', *European Journal of Criminology*, 5 (4): 481–504.

Muncie, J. (1999) 'Institutionalized intolerance: youth justice and the 1998 Crime and Disorder Act', *Critical Social Policy*, 19 (2): 147–75.

Muncie, J. (2008) 'The punitive turn in juvenile justice: cultures of control and rights compliance in western Europe and the USA', *Youth Justice: An International Journal*, 8 (2): 107–21.

Muncie, J. (2011) 'Illusions of difference: comparative youth justice in the devolved United Kingdom', *British Journal of Criminology*, 51 (1): 40–57.

Muncie, J. (2013) 'International juvenile (in)justice: penal severity and rights compliance', *International Journal for Crime, Justice and Social Democracy*, 2 (2): 43–62.

Muncie, J. (2015) *Youth and Crime*, 4th edn. London: Sage.

Muncie, J. and Goldson, B. (eds) (2006) *Comparative Youth Justice*. London: Sage.

Pinheiro, P.S. (2005) 'Opening remarks from Paulo Sergio Pinheiro', in NGO Advisory Panel for the United Nations Secretary-General's Study on Violence Against Children, *Violence Against Children in Conflict with the Law: A Thematic Consultation*. Geneva: United Nations.

Pinheiro, P.S. (2006) *World Report on Violence Against Children*. Geneva: United Nations.

Pratt, J. and Eriksson, A. (2013) *Contrasts in Punishment: An Explanation of Anglophone Excess and Nordic Exceptionalism*. Abingdon: Routledge.

Prison Reform Trust and INQUEST (2012) *Fatally Flawed: Has the State Learned Lessons from the Deaths of Children and Young People in Prison?* London: Prison Reform Trust.

Ratledge, L. (2012) *Inhuman Sentencing: Life Imprisonment of Children in the Commonwealth*. London: Child Rights International Network. Available at: www.crin.org/en/library/publications/inhuman-sentencing-life-imprisonment-children-commonwealth (accessed 13.10.14).

Tonry, M. and Doob, A.N. (eds) (2004) *Youth Crime and Youth Justice: Comparative and Cross-national Perspectives*, Crime and Justice, Vol. 31. Chicago: Chicago University Press.

Tonry, M. and Lappi-Seppälä, T. (2011) 'Crime, criminal justice, and criminology in Scandinavia', in Tonry, M. and Lappi-Seppälä, T. (eds), *Crime and Justice in Scandinavia*. Chicago: Chicago University Press.

UK Children's Commissioners (2008) *Report to the UN Committee on the Rights of the Child*. London: 11 Million, NICCY, SCCYP, Children's Commissioner for Wales.

Unicef (2010) *The Children Left Behind: A League Table of Inequality in Child Well-being in the World's Rich Countries*, Innocenti Report Card 9. Florence: Unicef Innocenti Research Centre.

United Nations Committee on the Rights of the Child (1995) *Concluding Observations of the Committee on the Rights of the Child: United Kingdom of Great Britain and Northern Ireland*. Geneva: United Nations Office of the High Commissioner for Human Rights.

United Nations Committee on the Rights of the Child (2002) *Consideration of Reports Submitted by States Parties Under Article 44 of the Convention – Concluding Observations: United Kingdom of Great Britain and Northern Ireland*. Geneva: United Nations Office of the High Commissioner for Human Rights.

United Nations Committee on the Rights of the Child (2007) *General Comment No. 10: Children's Rights in Juvenile Justice*, 44th session, 15 January–2 February. Geneva: United Nations Office of the High Commissioner for Human Rights.

United Nations Committee on the Rights of the Child (2008) *Consideration of Reports Submitted by States Parties Under Article 44 of the Convention: United Kingdom of Great Britain and Northern Ireland*. Geneva: United Nations Office of the High Commissioner for Human Rights.

United Nations Committee on the Rights of the Child (2012a) *Concluding Observations on the Combined Third and Fourth Periodic Report of Canada, Adopted by the Committee at its 61st Session*. Geneva: United Nations Office of the High Commissioner for Human Rights.

United Nations Committee on the Rights of the Child (2012b) *Consideration of Reports Submitted by States Parties Under Article 44 of the Convention: Concluding Observations: Australia*. Geneva: United Nations Office of the High Commissioner for Human Rights.

United Nations Committee on the Rights of the Child (2014a) *Concluding Observations on the Combined Third and Fourth Periodic Reports of Germany*. Geneva: United Nations Office of the High Commissioner for Human Rights.

United Nations Committee on the Rights of the Child (2014b) *Concluding Observations on the Combined Second to Fourth Periodic Report of the Congo*. Geneva: United Nations Office of the High Commissioner for Human Rights.

United Nations Committee on the Rights of the Child (2014c) *Concluding Observations on the Combined Fourth and Fifth Periodic Reports of the Russian Federation*. Geneva: United Nations Office of the High Commissioner for Human Rights.

United Nations General Assembly (1985) *United Nations Standard Minimum Rules for the Administration of Juvenile Justice*. New York: United Nations.

United Nations General Assembly (1989) *United Nations Convention on the Rights of the Child*. New York: United Nations.

United Nations General Assembly (1990a) *United Nations Guidelines for the Prevention of Juvenile Delinquency*. New York: United Nations.

United Nations General Assembly (1990b) *United Nations Rules for the Protection of Juveniles Deprived of their Liberty*. New York: United Nations.

United Nations General Assembly (2012) *Report of the Committee on the Rights of the Child*. New York: United Nations.

Wacquant, L. (2009) *Punishing the Poor: The Neo-Liberal Government of Social Insecurity.* Durham, NC: Duke University Press.

Walsh, C. (2002) 'Curfews: no more hanging around', *Youth Justice*, 2 (2): 70–81.

Walsh, C. (2008) 'The mosquito: a repellent response', *Youth Justice: An International Journal*, 8 (2): 122–33.

Wilkinson, R.G. and Pickett, K.E. (2007) 'The problems of relative deprivation: why some societies do better than others', *Social Science and Medicine*, 65 (9): 1965–78.

# INDEX

Children and Young Persons Act (1969), 10, 11
Children, Young Persons and their Families
    Act (1989), 141
Children's Hearing (Scotland) Act (2011), 123
children's human rights
    comparative analysis of, 248–249
    integrity and, 249–252
    overview, 227–229
    United Nations Committee on the Rights of
        the Child and, 233–234
    youth justice and, 229–233, 234–248
    *See also* United Nations Convention on the
        Rights of the Child (UNCRC)
Children's Rights Alliance for England,
    180–181
Chitty, C., 89
Clarke, R., 89–90
Clinton, B., 175
Coalition government (2010–)
    anti-social behaviour and, 41
    community safety and, 194, 195–198
    on effective practice, 67–68
    Secure Colleges and, x–xi
    support for young people and, 35
    Youth Justice Board and, 84
Coles, B., 216
community safety
    in Europe, 201–205
    policing of young people and, 198–201
    power and, 205–206
    rise and (possible) demise of, 191–197
community safety partnerships (CSPs), 193,
    194–195, 202
Conservative governments (1979–1997),
    12–13, 84, 123, 172–176, 193
Conservative Party, 172, 173–174, 178
Convention Against Torture and Other Cruel,
    Inhuman or Degrading Treatment or
    Punishment, 228
Convention on the Elimination of All Forms
    of Discrimination against Women, 228
Cook, K., 144, 148
Cormack, Lord, xi
Cornish, D.B., 89
Corrigan, P., 213
Council of Europe
    children's human rights and, 228, 230,
        231–233, 245–246
    restorative justice and, 140, 149–150
Craine, S., 218
Crime and Disorder Act (1998)
    anti-social behaviour and, 41
    community safety and, 196
    crime and disorder reduction partnerships
        and, 193–194
    on penal custody, 170

Crime and Disorder Act *cont.*
    principal aims of youth justice system in,
        72, 179
    on reprimands and final warnings, 74–75
    Youth Justice Board and, 84
crime and disorder reduction partnerships
    (CDRPs), 193–194
Crime Reduction Programme (CRP), 88
Crime Survey for England and Wales (CSEW),
    68, 73, 76
criminal careers, 211–220
Criminal Justice Act (1948), 170
Criminal Justice Act (1982), 170, 173n1
Criminal Justice Act (1988), 170, 173n1
Criminal Justice Act (1991), 72–73, 173n1
Criminal Justice and Public Order Act
    (1994), 170
Crisp, R., 36
Croft, I.J., 89
Cunneen, C., 141, 240

Daly, K., 138, 152
Davis, M., 25
decarceration, 137
decentralisation, 137
decriminalisation, 137
Defence for Children International, x
delegalisation, 137
Denmark, 238
deprofessionalisation, 137
desistance from crime
    age and, 157–160
    definition of, 160–162
    internal factors and, 163–165
    policy and, 165–166
    social factors and, 162–163
Detention Centres, 170, 172
developmental theories, 101
devolution, 248
*Disconnected Youth?* (MacDonald and
    Marsh), 210–211
discrimination, 232
diversion and diversionary paradigm
    integrity and, 251
    need for, 119–120, 133, 137
    New Labour governments and, 74–76,
        83–85, 123
    overview, **121**, 122–123
*doli incapax*, 70–71, 227
Drew, J., 90–91
drug-using careers, 211–215, 218
Dumortier, E., ix–x

early intervention, 100, 106–114
Economic and Social Research Council
    (ESRC), 210

House of Commons Justice Committee, 179,
181–182, 246, 247
housing careers, 211–212, 215
Howard, M., 174, 175–176
Hughes, G., 194, 198
human rights. *See* children's human rights
Human Rights Act (1998), 233, 243

Independent Commission on Youth Crime and
Antisocial Behaviour, 148–149
indigenous peoples, 139
Industrial Schools Act (1857), 6
inequality, 250
informal social control, 162
informalism, 137
Ingleby Report, 10–11
institutionalised racism, 19
integrity, 249–252
International Convention on the Elimination
of All Forms of Racial Discrimination,
228
International Covenant on Civil and Political
Rights, 228
International Covenant on Economic, Social
and Cultural Rights, 228
interventionism, 108
Irwin, J., 162

Jacobson, J., 151
Johnson, B., 199–200
Johnston, L., 210–211
Jones, D.W., 73, 83–84
Jordan, B., 23
Joseph Rowntree Foundation, 210
just deserts paradigm, **121**, 122
Juvenile Detention Alternatives Initiative
(JDAI), x

Key Elements of Effective Practice (KEEPs),
91–92, 93
Kilkelly, U., 238
Kruttschnitt, C., 163

labelling theory, 85–86, 120–122, 131–133
Labour Party, 174. *See also* New Labour
governments (1997–2010)
Lancaster Group, 123
Larsen, J.J., 138–139, 151
Laub, J.H., 160, 162, 163
Legal Aid, Sentencing and Punishment of
Offenders Act (2012), 78
leisure careers, 211–213
Lemert, E.M., 120, 161
Liberal Reform Programme (1906–11), 7–8
life course theories, 101
Little, M., 106

Livingstone, R., 200–201
Loeber, R., 106–107
Loftus, B., 41–42
Luxembourg, 238

MacDonald, R., 36, 210–211
MacIntyre, A., 86
Macpherson of Cluny, W., 38
Maguire, M., 88, 95, 196
Mair, G., 87–88
Major, J., 173–174
managerialism, 123
Marsh, J., 210–211
Marshall, T., 138
Maruna, S., 151–152, 160, 161, 163, 164
Mason, P., 92–93
Massoglia, M., 160, 164
May, T., 42–43
Mayor's Office for Policing and Crime
(MOPAC), 199–201
McAra, L., 40–41, 43, 75, 122
McCord, J., 163
McKnight, J., 159
McLaughlin, E., 137
McNeill, F., 165
McVie, S., 40–41, 43, 217
mental health, 55, 56
migrant girls and young women, 52
Miller, J., 182
Mills, C. W., 209, 219
Ministry of Justice, 180, 183, 185
*Misspent Youth* (Audit Commission), 72–73
Mods, 10
Moffitt, T.E., 159
Monbiot, G., 41
moral category, 22
moral panics, 27, 50
Morgan, J., 193
Mosquitoes (ultrasonic devices), 247
Muir, R., 151
multi-agency diversion, 123
Mulvey, E.P., 159
Munby, Mr Justice, 181
Muncie, J., 54n6, 141, 239
murder rates, 39–40
Murray, C., 210
Murray, R., 180
Myers, R., 59

Nacro, 69, 176
National Audit Office (NAO), 90–91, 92
net-widening, 5, 70, 78–79
New Labour governments (1997–2010)
community safety and, 193–195, 198
diversion and, 74–76, 83–85, 123
early intervention and, 106–108

risk-based early intervention, 100, 106–114
risk factor prevention paradigm (RFPP), 100–101
Riyadh Guidelines (*United Nations Guidelines on the Prevention of Delinquency*), 229–230
Roma and traveller communities, 239–240
Rose, N., 12
Rousseau, J.-J., 4
rule of law, 232
Rutherford, A., 172

Salz, A., 142, 146, 153
Sampson, R.J., 160, 162, 163
Sayer, A., 205
Scaled Approach, 54, 109–111
'Scared straight' programmes, 86–87
school to work careers, 34–36, 211–213
Scotland, 123–124, *125*, 248. *See also* Edinburgh Study of Youth Transitions and Crime
secondary deviance, 161
secondary labelling, 132
Secure Children's Homes, 180
Secure Colleges, x–xi
Secure Training Centres, 170, 180, 183, 242
self-harm, 55n8, 56
self-identity, 120, 163
self-report studies, 51, 158
Shapland, J., 94–95
Sharpe, G., 58–59
Shaw, M., 89
Sherman, L., 152
Sherman, L.W., 94, 95
Shildrick, T., 211
Shore, H., 4
Shover, N., 158
Shur, E., 122
Smith, D.J., 75, 86, 217
Smith, N., 153
Smith, R., 67–68
Snacken, S., ix–x
social class
    criminalisation and, 17–23
    police and, 42
    social control and, 24–28
    social exclusion and, 23–24, 209–212, 220
    *See also* poverty; unemployment
social control, 24–28
social exclusion, 23–24, 209–212, 220
Social Exclusion Unit, 183–184
social identity, 23–24
social justice, 203
Social Research Unit at Dartington, 94
Solomon, E., 109
Stephen Lawrence Inquiry, 32

Stern, V, 184–185
stop and search, 41
Strang, H., 152
substance misuse, 56
systems management, 123

Teesside studies, 210–220
Thatcher, M., 173
Thompson, S., 33
Thorpe, D., 11
trafficked girls and young women, 52
Trasler, G.B., 162
treatment, 8

Uggen, C., 160, 163, 164
ultrasonic devices (Mosquitoes), 247
underclass, 22
unemployment, 18, 20–22, 24–25, 36–37
Unicef, 250
United Nations
    human rights and, 228, 232–233, 241–242
    penal custody and, x
    restorative justice and, 140–141
United Nations Committee on the Rights of the Child, 233–234, 235–237, 242–246
United Nations Convention on the Rights of the Child (UNCRC), 108, 122, 227–229, 230–231, 233, 235–237
United Nation's Economic and Social Council (ECOSOC), 140–141
*United Nations Guidelines on the Prevention of Delinquency* (Riyadh Guidelines), 229–230
*United Nations Rules for the Protection of Juveniles Deprived of their Liberty* (Havana Rules), 230
*United Nations Standard Minimum Rules for the Administration of Juvenile Justice* (Beijing Rules), 229, 237
Universal Declaration of Human Rights, 228, 229
universal welfare, 250–251
urban security, 191, 201–205. *See also* community safety
USA
    age of criminal responsibility in, 238
    children's human rights in, 249
    drop in murder and violent crime rates in, 157
    gender-specific programming in, 57
    penal custody in, x, 56
    race and racialised justice in, 26, 240–241
    United Nations Convention on the Rights of the Child and, 227–228

Printed in Great Britain
by Amazon

86393769R00160